Best Of The

DOLL READER
Collector's Guide To Dolls

P9-EFJ-037

TABLE OF CONTENTS

ABOVE: Patsyette dressed as Little Red Riding Hood. The shoes and stockings are replacements but the dress and cape are original to the doll. This outfit also came on Patsyettes with mohair wigs glued over the painted red hair. *Photograph by John Axe.*

TITLE PAGE: 16-½in (41.9cm) French bébé marked. "H" with bisque socket head. She has fixed eyes, closed mouth and pierced ears. Her wig is mohair. She has a composition ball-jointed body. Manufacturer unknown. *Photograph by Magda Byfield.*

FRONT COVER: From left to right. Composition Black Doll 10in (25.4cm), ca. 1940, *Saucy Walker* 31in (78.7cm), Ideal, ca. 1960, *Peter Playpal* 38in (96.4cm), Ideal, ca. 1960, *Patti Playpal* 36in (91.4cm), Ideal, ca. 1960. Front row from left to right. *Kathe Krause* 12in (30.5cm), ca. 1950, Teddy Bear 14in (10.2cm), 1981-1982, *Pinocchio* 10in (25.4cm), Ideal, ca. 1940, *Bubbles* 16in (40.6cm), ca. 1925. *Photograph by John Axe.*

BACK COVER: Two early twentieth century German dolls, *Eva* and *Alba*. Bisque heads on composition bodies. Height, 16in (40.64cm). Doll in original white chemises marked: HEINRICH HANDWERCK//SIMON & HALBIG//Germany//0 ½. Doll in checked pinafore is marked: B½ made in 6½//Germany//167. *Photograph by Elspeth and Frank D'Aquila.*

The Best Of The
DOLL READER

edited by Virginia Ann Heyerdahl

Article Reprints 1975 - 1981

Published by HOBBY HOUSE PRESS, INC.
Cumberland, Maryland 21502

Additional Copies of this book may be purchased at $9.95
from
HOBBY HOUSE PRESS, INC.
900 Frederick Street
Cumberland, Maryland 21502
or from your favorite bookstore or dealer.
Please add $1.25 per copy postage.

ISBN: 0-87588-187-4

Introduction

It has been our pleasure to publish research oriented articles for doll collectors. From our newsprint paper beginnings in December of 1972 many asked to have the articles appear in a format that was more permanent. Thus with December 1978/January 1979 was born the present **DOLL READER** magazine format with its high quality paper. Then because our circulation has grown from its modest beginnings of 1500 to over 30,000 the newer subscribers asked for repeats of those previous magazine articles.

You will find this book divided into three areas of interest - collectible/modern dolls, antique dolls and doll artist dolls. The collectible era is defined by the age of the doll being less than 75 years old but greater than 25 years old. The modern doll would therefore be 25 years or less in age, and the antique doll would be 75 years or older. Doll artist dolls are dolls usually made with a limited number (much smaller than a manufacturers run) whereby the artist does the original design, execution and finishing work.

Now with the publication of the *Best of the Doll Reader* as a compendium of articles, a collector will have in a handy volume a wealth of research material. This is the first of several volumes of the *Best of the Doll Reader* with the goal of making the rich resource material available once again. There remain many articles that were not included, because of space, from the first six years in the newsprint format.

The **DOLL READER** delights in its role of funding research. Because of the ability to focus on very specific areas of interest collectors are treated to knowledge that might conceivably never be printed or expanded into book form. Also, timely reports such as American Toy Fair highlights provide not only a window to what is currently of interest to collectors, but also relevant resource material for doll historians.

It is our belief that collectors who study and learn more about their dolls derive more pleasure from their hobby, because with knowledge comes appreciation!

Virginia Ann Heyerdahl
Editor - May 1982
Gary R. Ruddell
Publisher - May 1982

COLLECTIBLE/MODERN

MADAME ALEXANDER'S COMPOSITION DOLLS

by John Axe

The composition dolls from the Alexander Doll Company seem to have developed an uncanny mystique. They are more popular than ever. They are now entering collections that formerly consisted of only antique dolls. Prices are soaring. Collectors talk about Madame Alexander making dolls as if she sat in front of each one as it was being assembled and painted the eyebrows on it herself. Most of Madame Alexander's dolls are "someone." They have names of famous personalities from the movies, from royal families, from fiction and from the pages of the newspapers. Even though there have been countless series of dolls dressed in foreign or regional costumes, the ones from the Alexander Company are always "better." An ordinary bride doll is "special" if she is an Alexander. The Alexander dolls have always had more detailing in the costumes than many others and the dolls themselves show more attention to design and execution than dolls from the less prominent companies do. The all-composition Alexander dolls shown here are all-original. And most of them are indeed "special."

For color photograph of a beautiful Madame Alexander doll see page 140.

Princess Elizabeth. Ca. 1939. This 17in. (43.2cm) version is marked on the head: PRINCESS ELIZABETH // ALEXANDER DOLL CO. On the back there is incised the number 17, which also appears in reverse at the tops of each arm where they are joined. The wig is blonde human hair. She has green sleep eyes and an open mouth with teeth. Her costume is one of the more rare ones. It is a one-piece white cotton blouse with a pink necktie with attached pale yellow serge jodhpurs that have a strap that fits under each foot. The fitted riding jacket, tagged "Princess Elizabeth," is black velvet and the hat is black felt. The high black leatherette boots have a snap in the front. *Pat Slabe Collection.*

Princess Elizabeth. From about 1937. She is 13in. (33cm) tall and has a blonde human hair wig and blue tin sleep eyes. This head, with dimples in the cheeks, was also used for *Betty* and the *Little Colonel.* She is wearing a crown set with "jewels" and her dress is a pale lavender taffeta with rosebuds applied to the front. The doll is not marked. Her dress is tagged "Princess Elizabeth."

Left:
Sleeping Beauty. From ca. early 1940s. She is 14-1/4 in. (36.9cm) tall and has the "Wendy Ann" head with blonde human hair and blue sleep eyes. The head is marked: MME. ALEXANDER. Her long red velvet gown is tagged. She has long stockings and gold sandals.

Dionne Quintuplet. About 1935. She is 10in. (25.4cm) tall with brown painted hair and brown sleep eyes. This is a baby version with chubby curved legs. Her original dress is white organdy with matching undergarments. The sweater, cap and booties may be original also, but none of the clothing has retained its tags. The head is marked: "DIONNE" // ALEXANDER. The back is marked: MADAME // ALEXANDER.

7

Snow White. From about 1939. She is 13in.(33cm) tall and her complexion is very pale. She has a black mohair wig and brown sleep eyes with eyeshadow. The head is marked: PR. ELIZABETH//ALEXANDER. The dress is labeled "Snow White" and is cream colored taffeta with an overskirt of net. The cape is a pale lavender and the hairbow is a pale blue. Her slippers have wooden heels and pink bows in front.

Upper Right:
Flora McFlimsey of Madison Square. Early 1940s. She is 15in. (38.1cm) tall and the head is marked: PRINCESS ELIZABETH // ALEXANDER DOLL CO. She has a light red human hair wig, blue sleep eyes with eye shadow and an open mouth with teeth. There are freckles across the bridge of her nose. The dress is tagged "Flora McFlimsey of Madison Square" and is a bright yellow cotton with navy blue flowers and has attached bloomers. The high-button shoes are navy blue.

Left:
McGuffey Ana. Early 1940s. She is 16in. (40.6 cm) tall with a blonde human hair wig in pigtails, brown sleep eyes with eye shadow and an open mouth with teeth and a metal tongue. The dress, with matching bonnet, is tagged "McGuffey Ana" and is white dotted swiss trimmed in dark blue.

Right:
Peasant. Late 1930s. 9in. (22.9cm) Tall with a black mohair wig and blue painted eyes. The back is incised WENDY-ANN // MME ALEXANDER // NEW YORK. The outfit is complete and is tagged "Peasant." The side-snap shoes are white.

Right:
Bride. Ca. early 1940s. She is 14in. (35.6cm) tall and is the "Wendy Ann" with a dark red mohair wig and blue sleep eyes. The head is marked: MME. ALEXANDER. She has lost her veil and the tag has been snipped off the dress.

Spanish. Late 1930s. The doll is 9 in.(22.9cm) tall and has a black mohair wig with brown painted eyes. The doll's back is marked: MME. ALEXANDER // NEW YORK. The original dress is tagged "Spanish" and has attached bloomers. The mantilla is black lace.

Betty. Ca. 1935. She is 13 in.(33cm) tall and has the "bent" right arm of Patsy from EffanBee. Under the blonde mohair wig there is molded hair in the Patsy style. The blue tin sleep eyes have real lashes and painted upper lashes. The doll is not marked; the dress is tagged "Betty." The shoes are old but they may not be original to the doll.

Carmen. In the 1942-1943 Alexander Catalog this 9 in.(22.9cm) doll was described as "dressed in a Pan-American or Bahaan [sic] costume." The doll, as buyers would know, tied in to the popularity of Brazilian movie star Carmen Miranda. The black mohair wig is in a chignon at the neck; the painted eyes are brown. The back is marked: MME. ALEXANDER // NEW YORK. The original outfit is not tagged and it has lost the headdress, earrings, jewelry and hose. The sidesnap shoes are red.

The (nearly!) Impossible Alexander Dream

by RHODA SHOEMAKER
Photographs by ROBERT L. BECK
© 1978 Hobby House Press, Inc.

Illustration 1.

One of the favorite fantasies of a doll collector is the finding of a doll that no one else owns - well, perhaps rather that very few other people own. With Alexander dolls, it is sometimes possible to achieve that dream. There are several reasons for this phenomenon, the most common being the "special order" dolls that were manufactured to be sold as an "exclusive" item by some of the more fashionable outlets, notably F.A.O. Schwarz, one of the most interesting chain of toy stores in the United States. When this happened, the dolls were not included in the yearly catalogs sent to stores to aid them in their ordering, so of course they did not show up on the shelves of your friendly neighborhood toy store. A fairly late example of this is the 8in (20.3cm) Alexander doll in a special sewing kit (Illustration 1) offered by the Schwarz Company. I have heard that this item was pictured in the Schwarz Christmas Catalog in the late 1960s. The particular kit shown here was purchased in the

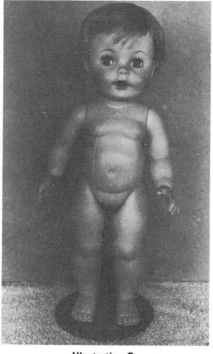

Illustration 3.

Schwarz San Francisco store in the early 1970s. The sewing box is made of a braided plastic stripping, and is lined with a rayon silk print. The cover lining is tufted, to hold needles, pins, etc. The doll itself is the regular 8in (20.3cm) *Alexander-kins,* marked "ALEX" on her back, a non-walker with bending knees. She is blonde and wears her original little cotton playsuit. Also included were sewing directions, materials and "findings" for a blouse and skirt set, a robe and a nightgown. It is interesting to note that the materials were of the same types and patterns used for Alexander factory-made clothes. Included when I acquired this item was a riding habit for an *Alexander-kins,* but the

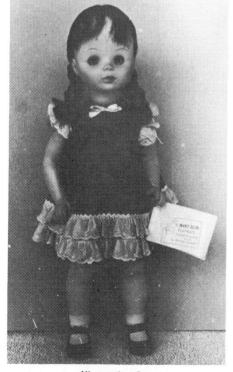

Illustration 4.

young lady for whom this was originally a Christmas gift does not remember whether it was actually included in the kit or whether it was purchased separately. The box itself measures 9in (22.9cm) by 6in (15.2cm) by 4½in (11.5cm), rests on four little feet, is handled and has a hasp closure.

Another special issue is "A *Mary Ellen* Playmate," shown in Illustration 2. Now *Mary Ellen* was a 31in (78.7cm) hard plastic doll of the mid 1950s, while this little Playmate is the basic 14in (35.6cm) hard plastic/vinyl *Mary Ann* mold first issued in 1965, a whole ten years later. So the question arises - and remains unanswered to date - was she issued as a follow-up to the earlier *Mary Ellen* or as a special "companion" to some little girl and/or her doll?

A different route to owning one of the limited issue dolls is finding

Illustration 2.

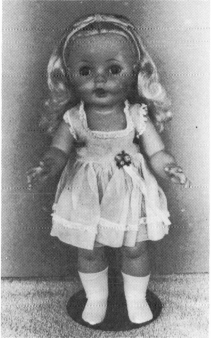

Illustration 5.

Illustration 7.

Illustration 6.

the bottom of the music box is a paper label which says simply "Ballerina."

Not a "mystery," as such, is the doll in Illustration 8, since she is definitely of the 10in (25.4cm) *Cissette* mold, but with the painting of the later *Portrettes, Jacquelines* and *Margots* - blue eyelids, darker and emphasized lashes and pink lips with matching fingernail polish. Her body construction is identical to that of the *Portrettes,* rather than *Jacqueline* and *Margot* whose bodies are made like that of *Cissette.* However, her hairdo, while similar to that of *Jacqueline* and *Margot* is different enough to be very noticeable. She has no original clothing, so who is she? A friend recalls seeing, in the early 1970s, such a doll displayed in an F.A.O. Schwarz store as an "exclusive" with them, in this size and with an extensive and elegant wardrobe, at the then astronomical figure of $150.00. She cannot recall the exact name but thinks it was either Miss Millionaire or Miss Debutante. Perhaps this is she.

There are also the Alexander dolls that were issued and catalogued for one year only. Among them is the little 12in (30.5cm) hard plastic *Ring Bearer* (Illustration 9) who came to me in his original box. He is pre-1952 and from a mold used for other hard plastic toddlers. Now I am looking for the Flower Girl to go with him, as surely there must have been one!

From the first set of the larger size Sound of Music dolls is 11in (27.9cm) *Kurt* (Illustration 10) who is dressed in the blue school outfit used

one that started out as a specific issue and then became a projected doll of another name, but for some reason or other never made it as an issued doll. Such a doll is the boy shown in Illustration 3, who was originally issued as *Caroline* (Kennedy), 1961-62, and shown here in Illustration 4. I owe this interesting boy doll to Pat Gardner who tells me that the Alexander Doll Company says he was meant to be one of the Trapp Family boys in the larger Sound of Music set. Her own pet theory is that perhaps he was destined to have been John-John Kennedy, to be a companion for *Caroline.* Wishful thinking, maybe, but fun to speculate! If you are lucky, you may find a third variant of this particular mold, as shown in Illustration 5. Now this mold was also used for *Little Mary Sunshine* in 1961, but *her* hair was silvery blonde in a very distinctive bangs-and-ponytail hairdo, while this particular little girl appears to be another *Caroline* with hair that is a shade more blonde and in a longer and looser hair style. Her dress is not tagged but is definitely

Alexander and closely resembles some of the clothing used for *Caroline.* Illustration 6 is a close-up of all three dolls to show the identical faces with their entirely individualistic rooted hair.

Then there is the "mystery" doll - the one that you are *sure* is an Alexander but you cannot actually prove it. The musical girl in Illustration 7 is one of these. She is hard plastic, 14in (35.6cm) tall with the small "Margaret-type" face and a body from the mold that Alexander shared with the American Character Doll Company at the time of the early hard plastic doll - the late 1940s. Her pink satin and lace dress is trimmed with silk braid and certainly looks like an Alexander outfit. Her blonde wig is mohair, her lashes and lips are painted more emphatically than the general run of Margaret-faced dolls, and her paint finish is lovely. One foot is attached to the top piece of a two-part music box which, when wound, plays as the doll slowly revolves. Her other foot is positioned upward and outward. On

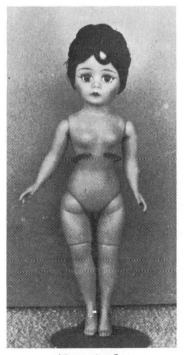

Illustration 8.

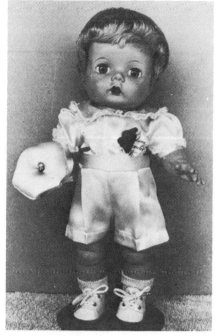

Illustration 9.

Illustration 10.

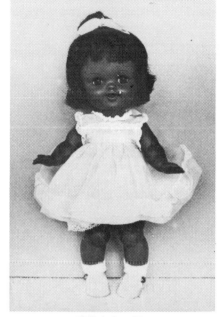

Illustration 11.

for all of the children in the first issue of this set. He has the same toddler body as the later *Frederich* (catalog spelling) but his face is that of *Smarty* (1962 to 1963), rather than the face of *Janie,* which was used for the two younger girls, *Gretl* and *Marta,* from the beginning, and then for *Frederich.*

Also with *Smarty*'s face is black *Katie* (Illustration 11) who is described, but not pictured, in the 1965 Alexander catalog, in the same section as *Janie.* Because of this, many collectors expect her to be a black version of *Janie,* rather than the *Smarty* she really is.

There are quite a few such one-year-issue Alexander dolls: *Sitting Pretty, Mary Ann, Gidget, Shari Lewis, Nancy Drew, Marlo Thomas* and so on. They are not really impossible to find, just difficult, being very desirable, they are also expensive, and therefore they are the Alexander dolls that you dream about.

Madame Alexander
by ELEANOR WATSON

Recently, I viewed an original of the folder regarding Madame Alexander's *Doll of the Month Club.* This folder was reprinted in the Fall 1973, Madame Alexander Fan Club News (MAFC).

The question that arose, in my mind, at that time was: were all these dolls of the 7½in (19.1cm) composition size?

I have now encountered several of these dolls' photographs and can place one in each of the categories shown. It would now appear that they were all 7½in (19.1cm) compos. I will still hold a bit of reserve until additional conclusive facts are in.

In the *1942-1943 Album of Dolls* of Madame Alexander creations, we find a 7in (17.8cm) *Bride* - number 1050 and a 7in (17.8cm) *Carmen* - number 7A. Add this to our evidence in dating these dolls. It is quite possible we can place these little dolls in the 1935 to 1943 era.

Two, found recently, were in their original boxes and in mint condition. The boxes are approximately 9in (22.9cm) square cardboard with a floral design of yellow, pink and blue flowers on a white background. The box, which is labeled, reads: "RED

RIDING HOOD 072." The doll's dress tag reads: "Fiction Doll//Riding Hood//Madame Alexander//New York." The other box, which is unlabeled, contains a doll whose dress is tagged: " 'Wendy Ann'// Gardening on Tuesday//Madame Alexander//New York."

The previously mentioned folder also launched our next quest. Is this where the name "Wendy Ann" began? Is this the evolution of the name - to begin with 7½in (19.1cm) dolls and end with 8in (20.3cm) hard plastics? OR, did the 13in (33.0cm) composition *Wendy Ann* with the molded hair begin the name. Again we will have to wait until we can find dated evidence such as catalogs to finally prove this note. *Wendy Ann* has been very much in evidence throughout the Madame Alexander creations.

For the collection revolving around names only, I thought we would depart from the usual discussions of one doll type and talk about names. It is not enough to say you would like to have a *Wendy Ann* doll. Which one do you want? There are many sizes and types as you will note by the following descriptions.

Wendy Ann in the 7½in (19.1cm)

size composition belonged to the "Dolls of the Week," according to this brochure. ". . . A fascinating set of seven dolls - all 'Wendy Ann,' each dressed for a different occasion! Each day of the week brings a new duty, a new delight! Washing on Monday; Gardening on Tuesday; Ironing on Wednesday; Cleaning on Thursday; Marketing on Friday; Baking on Saturday and Party on Sunday . . ."

Wendy Ann is also found in the 9in (22.9cm) composition size doll. This is another painted eye doll of the same period. This *size* is also listed in the *1942-1943 Album of Dolls.*

Wendy Ann, circa 1938, is a 13in (33.0cm) composition with a swivel waist. She can be found with painted eyes and molded hair or with sleep eyes and a wig.

In the 1940s *Wendy Ann* appears as a hard plastic miss with long tosca hair. My 14in (35.6cm) doll has a blue nylon dress with pink yoke and trim. A large bow is in her hair.

The name "Wendy" is then applied to the bride dolls - *Wendy-Bride* - in the 1950s catalogs. In 1953 *Wendy Ann* becomes part of the *Alexander-Kins,* the 7½in (19.1cm) quality hard plastic dolls we all love and which have become a focal point in many a collection. As some of the other dolls of the 1950s she had a lovely woven wig of finest hair which could be washed and curled.

Madame Alexander

by ELLA WATSON

Forty years have passed since the issuance in January 1935 of the "Quints" trademark. The dolls' continuing appeal to collectors is seen by their scarcity and sharp rise in value, as noted in recently published price guides.

Most commonly found are those of all-composition construction with swivel heads and jointed arms and legs.

Less common are those noted on the *Montgomery Ward Christmas Catalog* pages for 1935 (Courtesy of Marge Meisinger). These have the composition head, arms and legs, but softly stuffed cloth bodies.

They were 23in (58.4cm) long, had teeth, sleep eyes and cry voices. Dressed in organdy dress, bonnet, slip, rubber panties, socks and shoes, they retailed at $4.39.

Illustration 1. 7½in (19.1cm) *Dionne* baby, 1936; all-composition; fully-jointed; painted eyes; brown mohair wig. The molded hair shows under the wig, but is not painted. She is a bent-leg baby marked "Dionne// Alexander" on the neck and "Alexander" on the body. She is dressed in a diaper, dress and attached slip of organdy, trimmed at the arm openings, fastened with a tiny pin at the back. Bonnet is organdy and ruffled around the face. This outfit is simply marked "Madame//Alexander//New York." The bib is white organdy and embroidered with the name "Yvonne."

The 7½in (19.1cm) to 8in (20.3cm) dolls are either bent-leg babies or straight-leg toddlers. They have painted, molded hair or they can be found with a brown mohair baby wig. They have brown painted eyes and lashes.

The Christmas catalog (above) noted the following:

7½in (19.1cm) all-jointed composition in organdy dresses, hats, slips, diapers, cotton booties and bibs with their names embroidered.

10½in (26.7cm) same as above, but no bonnet.

17½in (44.5cm) same as above, but sleep eyes and cry voices.

Another styling added pink corduroy coats and bonnets trimmed with lace and marabou.

Also listed was a set of five babies - 7½in (19.1cm) dressed in diaper, shirt and name bib in a white enameled 20in (50.8cm) wooden bed. This included two pink blankets, pillow and the mattress. The complete set retailed for $4.39.

The trademark listings for *Quints, The Five Babies, Quints and Quinties* are to be found in *Spinning Wheel's Complete Book of Dolls,* under the 1936, January 30, listing.

To show a comparative price interest, the *1973 Price Guide for Composition Dolls* by Rhoda Shoemaker notes the 8in (20.3cm) toddler with molded hair and painted eyes at $175.00 for the set. In the *1975 Price Guide for Madame Alexander Dolls* by Rhoda Shoemaker, we find the same set listed at $250.00. We must note that these are guidelines only and belong to those dolls found in excellent top quality condition and dressed in original clothing.

Most of these dolls are marked on the doll's head and body with Dionne//Alexander. The word *Dionne,* may be dropped on many. Their clothing may be tagged simply "Madame//Alexander//New York" or the more elaborate "Genuine//Dionne Quintuplet Dolls//All Rights Reserved //Madame Alexander, N.Y."

I have seen these dolls in a variance of heights and dresses: pique rompers and bonnets; organdy dresses, a different color for each baby; snowsuits and buntings. These are only a few, I realize. A little wooden swan rocker has their names painted on; a wicker basket has the five babies with two complete sets of clothing plus rattles.

The completing touch to these dolls is finding them with the gold metal name tags. These pins are a small horizontal bar with a circle drop having each doll's name engraved. It appears these pins were on the dolls not having the bibs with embroidered names.

Alexander Dolls

SOME THAT ARE NOT IN THE CATALOGS
by JEANNE NISWONGER
©1977 Hobby House Press, Inc.

Alexander dolls are cherished by collectors and children alike. Catalogs showing Alexander dolls have been reprinted. It may come as a surprise to know that there are still more Alexander dolls not in catalogs. We will discuss a few in this article.

Most collectors are familiar with the *Cissette* doll of all hard plastic, 9½in (24.2cm) with high heel feet and glued-on attractive wigs. She is marked "Madame Alexander" on the back. She came with many changes of clothing and was used in the *Portrette* series. There were still others that have never been shown in a catalog or booklet that may have been especially produced back in 1962 and possibly handled only by the F.A.O. Schwarz Co. At least, that company's name has appeared on the original box of some of the dolls we are showing here, including *Klondike, Gibson Girl, Iceland, Gold Rush, Denmark, Sleeping Beauty,* Doll in Ballgown, and a mystery doll.

Illustration 2. *GIBSON GIRL* is a study in purple and lavender shades. Her skirt, slightly trailing, is purple velvet fastened at the waist with a black buckled belt (attached). The blouse is lavender and white striped cotton with white collar and cuffs on the long sleeves and a purple bow at the neckline. An orchid straw hat tops her dark brown hair and it is adorned with feather organza strips of varied pink and white shades and a black veil that covers her head. Her jewelry consists of rhinestone earrings and a ring on her finger and she also has eye make-up including blue eye shadow and red nail polish.

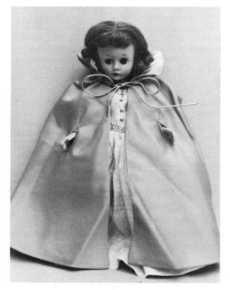

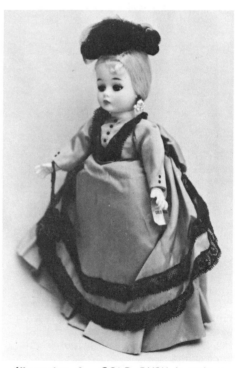

Illustration 1. *KLONDIKE* wears a red velvet floor length sheath with red braid trim down the front and red net ruffles at the bottom and on the sleeves. The gown is cut low both in the front and back. She has red high heeled shoes, a "diamond" bracelet and ring with a double row of pearls around her neck. Rhinestone earrings are fan shaped and there are several red feathers adorning her brunette hair which is fashioned in an upswept style fastened with a gold and "diamond" hair ornament. She also has blue eye shadow and special eye make-up.

Illustration 3. DOLL IN BALLGOWN is most typical of the basic *Cissette* in coloring, facial features and hair arrangement. However, I have never seen her outfit in any catalog or booklets that were published by the Alexander Company. She wears a full length satin brocade dress gathered at the waist with gold buttons down the front. There is a V shaped neckline edged in a dainty gold braid which also trims the long sleeves and forms the waistline. The rose pink taffeta coat is lined with the same material and is tied with a gold metalic tie.

Illustration 4. *GOLD RUSH* is truly a beautiful creature. She has blue eye shadow and dark lashes painted on in addition to the plastic eyelashes. Her long blonde hair is styled in a French twist with a spit curl on the left. Rhinestone earrings adorn her ear lobes and a black tulle hat and feather grace her head. Her long bustled gown is an unusual shade of orange taffeta trimmed in black lace and it has leg-of-mutton sleeves. She carries a black velvet reticule. The doll has matching nail polish and a "diamond" ring on her left hand.

Illustration 5. *Miss ICELAND's* costume is a fully gathered red taffeta skirt with white organdy blouse all in one piece. There is a wide gold trim at the waist and sleeves with rows of green and black braid giving the costume a very provincial look. Narrow gathered cotton lace trims the neck and sleeves also and she wears a flowered headpiece with red and green satin ribbon streamers. Her blonde hair is worn in a flip and she has two rings and a "diamond" bracelet.

Illustration 7. *SLEEPING BEAUTY* differs from the *Denmark* doll only in that she has straight legs which do not bend at the knees and flat soled feet. Her garment is aqua blue taffeta with gold across the bottom of the skirt, a gold netting over the waist and long sleeves. A cape of matching gold netting is tied with gold ties and a pearl tiara adorns her blonde hair worn loose.

Illustration 8. *MYSTERY DOLL* is similar to the basic *Cissette* doll yet is distinctly different in the type of plastic used. It has a shiny appearance in contrast to the porcelain look of the other dolls' finish. Otherwise it seems to be from the same mold, however, it is not marked. Her hairdo is quite elaborate and styled in tight curls across the back and bangs worn in a fashion reminiscent of Farrah Fawcett-Majors! A doll before her time! One wonders if this was perhaps an early prototype of the *Cissette* doll or an experimental model? Her dress is a fine cotton pink and white checked with rose print, lace and braid trim. All the little garments have cloth tags saying "Madame Alexander" only.

Illustration 6. *DENMARK* is again more like the basic *Cissette* in facial color in that there is no eye shadow or painted-on eyelashes. Her hair is long, blonde and curled on the end. Her provincial dress is a gathered pink taffeta skirt attached to a white organdy blouse with puffed sleeves that are lace-trimmed. There is a black velvet weskit and black bow at the neckline which is also lace trimmed. A separate apron of orchid taffeta with gold and black trim is tied over the dress and it is adorned with embroidered flowers. The hat is unusual and looks like hand-crocheted work, gathered at the top and trimmed with flowers.

Illustration 9. The three dolls discussed, from left: basic *Cissette* doll, the mystery doll and the body of *Sleeping Beauty.*

The Wonderful Hard Plastics Of Madame Alexander

by RHODA SHOEMAKER
Photographs by ROBERT KOCH

Illustration 1. 14in (35.6cm) *Godey Lady.*

Illustration 2. 20in (50.8cm) *Lady Churchill.*

In the doll world, one of the phenomena of the post-World War II era is the hard plastic doll. Immediately after the end of the war, while most of the doll manufacturers were still producing composition dolls, much experimentation was going on with plastics. Some of the earlier plastic dolls of this time were composition-based, with one or more layers of a plastic material over the composition and one or more layers of paint over that. Some of the dolls were of a completely hard plastic mixture and those can be found with a paint finish and, alternately, with a "buffed" finish. Many of the dolls of the very late 1940s and early 1950s have a finish that glows softly and resembles early bisque. By the year 1953 all of the major doll factories had converted to the use of plastic in one form or another.

Among the very best of the hard plastic dolls are, of course, those produced by Madame Alexander.

Some of them were obviously made in the same, or similar, molds that had been used in the later of the composition dolls. Whether shiny or matte, the finish on all of them is exceptionally fine and, with the release of the wartime restrictions on materials, their costumes are very elaborate and beautifully done. One of the prettiest examples I have ever seen is a 14in (35.6cm) *Godey Lady* (Illustration 1) with a delicate little face and small hands, dating from 1947. Her hair is parted in the center and pulled to the sides, then coiled over her ears. Her full-length gown is apricot satin with self-material pleated trim, and the wide sleeves have a fancy under-sleeve that ends in a ruffle to fit snugly at the wrist. Underclothes and leather slippers are original; her dress tag reads "Godey Lady," as does the clover leaf wrist tag she wears. It is interesting to note that another 14in (35.6cm) *Godey Lady,* all original and tagged, is dressed in a differently-styled, rose-colored out-fit.

Another prime example of the dolls of this hard-plastic period is *Lady Churchill,* circa 1949 to 1950 as shown in Illustration 2. She is 20in (50.8cm) tall, pre-dating the current *Portrait* series, with the aforementioned beautiful, bisque-like finish. Her hair is elaborately arranged and topped by a "diamond" tiara; her "diamond"-trimmed full-length evening coat is of pale pink patterned satin and is worn over a full-length pale pink satin dress. Underclothing and shoes are original. She is tagged only "Madame Alexander, New York, U.S.A.," however, advertisements of the period do identify her as *Lady Churchill.*

Illustration 3 shows an interesting pair of the ever-popular 14in (35.6cm) *Alice in Wonderland,* in hard plastic. The doll on the right is probably a year or two earlier, since she appears to have been made in one of the composition molds. The doll on the left, circa 1949 to 1950, has the face

Illustration 3. A pair of 14in (35.6cm) *Alice in Wonderland* dolls.

Illustration 4. 14in (35.6cm) *Beth* from the *Little Women* series.

Illustration 6. 8in (20.3cm) *Parlor Maid*.

Illustration 5. 11½in (29.2cm) *Lissy*.

we all call a "Kathy and/or Annabelle" face, with large round eyes. Her skin tone is slightly darker and her hair is pulled back in a different arrangement. There is very little difference in their costumes; the dress on the doll at the left is lavender silk, on the doll at the right blue cotton, both wear white organdy pinafores and white ruffled cotton underclothes, and both outfits are tagged "Alice in Wonderland." The doll on the right wears replaced Alexander slippers.

One of the prettiest dolls from the many *Little Women* sets is the

14in (35.6cm) hard plastic *Beth* shown in Illustration 4. She is from the early 1950s and has much the same face as the big-eyed *Alice*, although her complexion tone is slightly different and her cheeks are rosier. Her plaid dress is tagged, eyelet-trimmed pantalettes are be-ribboned, her black leather shoes with bows are original, and there is a Fashion Award gold tag on her wrist. Some of the *Little Women* sets in this size were divided as to mold, with *Jo* being the same mold as *Beth* while *Meg* and *Amy* were of the mold with

smaller eyes and more pointed chin. When *Marme* was included she also was of the longer-faced mold.

The 11½in (29.2cm) *Lissy* (Illustration 5) was a product of 1956, while the *Lissy* line issued in 1957 and 1958 was 12in (30.5cm), as were the later *Lissy*-faced *Little Women*, Classics Group and others. They were all extremely popular and still are. The *Lissy* shown here has red hair, more uncommon than other shades used, and a creamy complexion. She wears a red polished cotton dress with label, white organdy feather-stitched pinafore, strap sandals, and a wrist tag message "To Little Girls Everywhere."

By 1956, when the little 8in (20.3cm) *Parlor Maid* shown in Illustration 6 was issued, the majority of dolls were no longer exclusively hard plastic. A combination of hard plastic and vinyl was in use, as well as dolls made completely of vinyl. The 8in (20.3cm) size (which incidently is strictly a catalog size since generally the doll actually measures closer to 7½in [19.1cm]) has always been an exception to this and through the years continues to be called hard plastic although a more accurate term would be "rigid" or "firm" vinyl as opposed to the soft vinyl now in use. The first of these small

dolls had a shiny, almost waxy finish - now they are softer and not quite as clearly defined. The *Parlor Maid* wears a black cotton dress, white organdy apron and lace cap, and carries a little "duster" with a wooden handle. Her dress is tagged "Parlor Maid" while wrist tag states "A Doll, created by Madame Alexander."

The time span covering the production of hard plastic dolls is relatively short - from approximately 1947 to the early 1950s. For this reason, it is my personal opinion that as time goes along and these dolls become more difficult to find, they are destined to be among the most sought after of all of the modern collectible dolls, especially those beauties created and produced by Madame Alexander.

EFFANBEE'S 1979 LIMITED EDITION DOLL

The Effanbee Limited Edition Doll Club responded to the numerous requests that one of their limited editions be Skippy. The 1979 limited edition doll is this 14in. (35.6cm) doll with the same impish charm of the cartoon character by Percy Crosby. Skippy-79 is all-vinyl with unruly blonde-sprayed, molded hair. The trademark of this character is provided with a slouch houndstooth hat worn in the devil-may-care manner. A matching double-breasted coat with a reproduction of the original Skippy button plus a big blue white-polka dotted tie complete the "look." Underneath his coat, he is wearing a white shirt and burgundy short pants. The doll is marked on both the back of head and body:

EFFANBEE
LTD. EDITION
SKIPPY
© 1979
SKIPPY INC.
© 1979

At the time of this writing, over 75% of the maximum limited edition of somewhat over 3400 possible dolls has been subscribed to.

Illustration 1. Top row: *Martha Washington*. Middle row, left to right: *Abigail Adams, Elizabeth Monroe*. Botton row, left to right: *Louisa Adams, Martha Randolph, Dolley Madison*.

Madame Alexander's
"*First Ladies*"
by SANDY WILLIAMS

"**To commemorate the two hundredth birthday of our country, Madame Alexander proudly presents her interpretation of six of the 'First Ladies' who graced the White House. This year's limited edition of these beautifully gowned 'First Ladies' highlight our 1976 collection . . .**" (Editor's note - This is an excerpt from Madame Alexander's 1976 catalog.)

This group of dolls was so much in demand that supply was soon depleted. The dolls retailed at $240.00 per set of six dolls. Single dolls could also be bought at $40.00. Many stores had long waiting lists for each set they received; so many Alexander collectors were unable to acquire a set. There were even reports of an advertisement in an antique publication for a set of dolls for $500.00!

These 14in (35.6cm) dolls are made of plastic and vinyl. They are jointed at the neck, shoulders and hips so they can stand and sit gracefully. They all have sleep eyes and rooted hair. Their underwear consists of pantalets and half slip, white stockings and slippers in colors to compliment each outfit. Each doll comes with two tags: a paper booklet tied to the left arm bearing a brief historical sketch of each of these six "First Ladies;" and a cloth label sewn onto the dress, such as "FIRST LADIES//"Dolley Madison"//By Madame Alexander, N.Y.U.S.A.//ALL RIGHTS RESERVED."

Martha Washington, No. 1501, was the wife of George Washington (1789-1797). She is marked at the nape of the neck "ALEXANDER// 19 © 76." *Martha* is dressed almost entirely in ivory. Her ivory and gold brocade full-skirted dress has a wide ivory lace ruffle around the hem to the waistline which gives the effect of an overskirt. Wide ivory lace ruffles also edge her three-quarter sleeves and

square neckline. *Martha* wears a very long ivory lace shawl around her shoulders. Her ivory lace and ribbon mob cap covers her blonde hair. *Martha*'s hair is center-parted and pulled into a mass of curls atop her head. She has white cotton pantalets and half slip trimmed with white lace beading with pink ribbon run through, white stockings, and beige satin slippers. She carries a brown velvet handbag. A seed pearl necklace completes her costume. She is blue-eyed.

Abigail Adams, No. 1502, was the wife of John Adams (1797-1801). She was the first to act as a hostess in the White House. She is marked at the nape of the neck "ALEXANDER//? © 6? The first two and last numbers are illegible. Abigail has full rosy cheeks and dark brown eyes. Her honey blonde hair is arranged in two long side curls with her back hair in a pageboy. Her top hair is pulled back with a deep blue velvet ribbon to match her gown. *Abigail* is gowned in a sapphire blue brocade silk with a white lace fichu tied at her neckline. A sapphire and "diamond" pin holds the fichu in place. Her white cotton pantalets are trimmed with white lace ruffles and her half slip is trimmed with white lace beading with blue ribbon run through. She has white stockings, black velveteen slippers and a seed pearl necklace.

Martha Randolph, No. 1503, served as hostess to her father Thomas Jefferson (1801-1809). She is marked at the nape of the neck "ALEXANDER//19 © 73." *Martha* is exquisite in her gown of pink taffeta. A center ivory lace panel extends from her round neckline to her hemline. Ivory lace ruffles border neckline, center panel and hemline. A pink tulle ruffle edges her hemline. A full-length black crepe cape is tied under her arms to her back waistline. The cape is trimmed in narrow rose and moss green ribbons. Both front edges of the cape are trimmed with a wide ribbon embroidered in turquoise, rose, green and gold threads. Her light-weight pink pantalets and half slip are trimmed with white lace beading and a pink ribbon run through. Pink satin slippers and a seed pearl necklace complete her outfit.

Dolley Madison, No. 1504, was the wife of James Madison (1809-1817). She is marked at the nape of the neck "ALEXANDER//19©76." *Dolley* wears a floor-length sleeveless ivory satin gown with printed silver flowers. Ivory lace ruffles trim her armholes and an ivory satin ruffle trims her neckline. An ivory and silver glitter braid is sewn onto her bodice to give a square neckline effect. Over her gown *Dolley* wears a full-length, lined matching coat. The coat is also edged in the braid. She has large black eyes. Her beautiful dark brown hair is piled into curls atop of her head, with a fringe of curls around her face. A draped ivory chiffon headband offsets her dark hair and eyes. *Dolley's* underwear consists of white cotton pantalets and a half slip trimmed with white lace beading with pink ribbon run through, white stockings and ivory satin slippers.

Elizabeth Monroe, No. 1505, was the wife of James Monroe (1817-1825). She is marked at the nape of the neck " © ALEXANDER 1965." Her large black eyes are delicately lashed. Elizabeth's round rosy cheeks complement her beautiful auburn hair. Her hair is center-parted with three curls on each side of her ears and the front and back hair are pulled up and held by a "diamond" tiara. *Elizabeth* is wearing a rose and gold brocade full-skirted gown. A floor-length train of the brocade falls from her shoulders. Ivory ribbon and lace ruffles adorn the three quarter sleeves. Her ivory lace fichu is pinned to her waistline with a gold metal ribbon pin. She wears white cotton pantalets and half slip with white lace and ribbon, white stockings, and ivory satin slippers. She wears a gold chain necklace with a "diamond" pendant.

Louisa Adams, No. 1506, was the wife of John Quincy Adams (1825-1829). She is marked at the nape of the neck "ALEXANDER 19 © 78." This blonde, blue-eyed beauty is dressed in a high-waisted white satin gown. The gown is trimmed with white tulle ruffles and silver glitter braid around the neckline, on the short puff sleeves, on the waist and on the hem. *Louisa's* blonde hair is center-parted and pulled up into a cluster of curls atop her head; a neckline braid is pulled up into the curls, and a spray of pink flowers is set into the curls. White cotton pantalets and half slip are trimmed with white lace beading and white ribbon pulled through. White satin slippers and a seed pearl necklace complete her outfit.

Anili, Madam Lenci's Daughter

BY CAROL & BILL BOYD

"Anili" is the inheritor of one of the most famous names in the current doll world, but is yet not widely well-known. How did we "discover" her, in the wake of many hundreds of European collectors of contemporary dolls who prize her highly? Because Carol both makes and collects fine dolls and when we first arrived in Italy in 1976, even before we had settled into living in Rome, our early stops were the toy stores. (We had soon learned that there were no shops in Rome specializing in contemporary dolls as such—and only one or two catering to the antique doll trade.) Rome has many toy stores, but the two best and most well-known are De Sanctis, on the Via Veneto (of "La Dolce Vita" fame), and Berte, set in a corner of the lovely Piazza Navona. In these two beautiful stores, but nowhere else in Rome, we found some extraordinarily beautiful dolls which silently shouted to us: L-E-N-C-I! But the tags read ANILI. "Who," we asked the clerks, "is Anili"? "She is the daughter of 'Madam Lenci' and is making dolls from the old masks," we were told. In fact, when we first asked to see one of the dolls, which stood out like a diamond among the zircon-quality dolls surrounding it, the clerk said, "Oh. The Lenci."

Two tantalizing years later, we were finally able to travel to Turin, home of both the Lenci and Anili dolls, and to meet personally with Anili in order to talk with her about the beautiful dolls which bear her name. She is indeed the daughter of Elena Scavini, the original "Madam Lenci and, just as Lenci was the reported baptismal name of Elena Scavini (made into the acronym for the Latin phrase Lundus Est Nobis Constanter Industria by the Italian poet Hugo Jetti*), so is Anili the baptismal name of her daughter. The mother and daughter began a doll-making business together shortly after World War II, under the Anili label, continuing the type of artistic dolls which Elena had begun originally under the Lenci trade name. (The Lenci trademark and dolls with perhaps some exceptions had been sold before World War II to another family —the Garellas.

Anili, who is married and also has a daughter, told us that she and her mother had been making artistic dolls of felt since 1946. She and her mother were collaborators in making the "Anili" items (which later expanded into a number of other types of dolls, felt decorative pieces and a lovely line of children's clothing and accessories) until Elena Scavini suffered a stroke in her 80th year and could no longer work on the products she knew and loved so well. Since then, Anili has been carrying on in her mother's tradition, making and selling beautiful dolls and related items from an unassuming, aqua-painted shop in the heart of Turin—a shop with a simple brass scroll-worked name "ANILI" and a small card showing the hours of business (the card carefully covered with hand-painted flowers and hearts, obviously the work of Anili herself). Although she has never exported her dolls to the United States, Anili does a lively business in France, Germany and Switzerland, as well as with discerning Italian lovers of fine-quality contemporary dolls.

When the Anili firm began after the ravages of World War II, their "equity" was four faces, originally sculpted by Elena Scavini. These four faces, in numerous costumes and body sizes, are still the backbone of the artistic doll production of the Anili firm. Most of the line can be seen by visiting the retail shop tucked away in a gallery on the Piazza Castello in Turin although, even there, some of the items can be "out-of-stock" because of the very, very personal way in which "la signorina Anili" treats her business. For example, we saw in Turin a bed doll we had never seen at her two outlets in Rome. We also mentioned that we owned an "antique" pouty-type Lenci and showed her the photograph from Dorothy Coleman's fine book, Lenci Dolls Fabulous Figures of Felt. Anili immediately said that she still made these "pouty" faces, and that she was surprised to find that none were available in her shop at the time.

Thank heaven Anili still has that kind of business. She is totally involved in making the dolls and other items. She is the sole artistic director and designer. (Although her livelihood depends on sales, her interest is in the production of a fine product, not on its acceptance in the marketplace—a trait she evidently inherited from her mother.) The dolls are, of course, all hand-done, as are the other articles for sale in the Anili shop. The work on the individual dolls is sent out to artisans, some of whom worked for Lenci before World War II and who still work in their own homes. Anili presides over a cottage industry on a commercial basis—as usually the case with fine dolls such as those of Peggy Nisbet and Ann Parker.

We asked Anili a doll-collector's question: some dolls look to the left, some to the right, some up, some down—why? The answer was: simple whim. Each artisan paints as the fancy strikes him or her. If the artisan wants eyes to the right, eyes to the right is is!

Anili told us that since her mother's death in 1976 (as well as the loss to the Anili firm after her embolism in 1972), the struggle to maintain the high quality of the Anili doll has become ever more difficult. Elena, disparing at the lack of interest in what she considered her truly artistic skills and distaining the increasing general interest in what she thought of as only commercial efforts, chose to destroy most of what she had made in the the post-war years. Despite the pleading of her daughter, Madam Lenci destroyed molds for porcelain pieces, original sculptures in wood, molds and masks for felt dolls—everything she had made in her later years. The world can only weep at the loss of so many pieces sprung from the creative mind of "Madam Lenci"—Elena Scavini.

Yet, despite all the industrial problems of modern Italy, her daughter carries on—a vibrant, wonderful woman, making beautiful, charming dolls under the trademark of Anili. We are proud to own three of them. After talking to Anili and seeing her work as displayed in her shop on Piazza Castello, we would love to own them all. All doll collectors visiting Europe— or anyone who loves dolls—must find a means to visit Turin, Italy, and the modest shop at Piazza Castello 33, to see the range of the Anili creations and to choose something to take home as a modern "collectible." The clerks do not speak English, but the universality of their love for their dolls will break down every barrier...they are tireless in their happiness to show clients the dolls of Anili.

Although it is true that the dolls in the shop do not bear a tag that says "Lenci," to any knowledgeable collector they certainly shout it loud and clear!

*Editor's Note: Ugo Ojetti is another reported spelling.

"BABY SANDY"

by JOHN AXE

Illustration 2. Close-up of the original pin that came on *Baby Sandy* dolls. *Marge Meisinger Collection.*

Illustration 1. 7½in (19.1cm) *Baby Sandy* in an original pink dress. She has yellow painted and deeply molded hair and blue painted eyes. She is all-composition and fully-jointed. On the back of her head she is marked "BABY SANDY." *Marge Meisinger Collection.*

Baby Sandy has already celebrated her 40th birthday. The little movie star was born on January 14, 1938, in Los Angeles, California. Her screen career was finished by 1941. She cannot even recall that time in her life. Now she is a legal secretary and her husband is a carpet installer. Like many other film personalities of the past, her chief fame today rests in the dolls that were made to represent her during the time of her popularity.

Movie stars used to be the "royalty" of America. Everyone had their own favorites whom they followed and admired. The most telling status of their popularity was their drawing power in movie theaters. The number of tickets that were purchased to see them on the screen gave them a ranking in a Popularity Poll tabulated by film exhibitors. An interesting comment on the American perspective towards entertainment is that many of the most popular actors and actresses have been children who were under school age. Many of these child actors were also very talented. Jackie Cooper received

an Academy Award nomination when he was only nine years old. Shirley Temple, Margaret O'Brien, Judy Garland, Deanna Durbin, Mickey Rooney and others were honored with special miniature Oscars for their childhood performances. As box office champions, Shirley Temple was Number One in 1936, 1937 and 1938; Jane Withers was sixth in 1937 and eighth in 1938; Margaret O'Brien was ninth in 1945. Such luminaries of the screen as Joan Crawford, Norma Sheerer and Greta Garbo were far behind the tots in popularity.

Baby Sandy only appeared in "B" productions for Universal Pictures. The "B" picture was a low-budget presentation that was intended to be part of a double bill or as a support for a more important feature. The running time was from about 60 to 90 minutes.

Sandra Lee Henville got her start in motion pictures when her mother read in the papers that director David Butler was looking for a baby to play a role in his film *East Side of Heaven.* The director had already tested from 300 to 400 aspiring hopefuls for the part and none had proven satisfactory. Director Butler was a customer on Sandy's father's milk route. Prodded by the mother, he left photographs of Baby Sandy with the milk order one morning and when the maid brought in the milk and the photographs the director had found his star. The future star was only nine months old at the time. Her curly blonde hair and large expressive brown eyes and her winning smile entitled her to a larger salary than her father had ever earned.

In her second film, *Unexpected Father,* the unconcerned coo of the baby star succeeded in upstaging Bing Crosby and Mischa Auer. Sandy's chief acting function was to be placed between two principal players and look back and forth from one to the

Illustration 3. Baby Sandy on the New Year's cover of *Movie-Radio Guide,* 1940.

other while they spoke and to be cute at it. For her third 1939 film, *Little Accident,* Sandy was top-billed. This was her first role as a girl. In her first two films she played boy's parts. She became so popular that her two 1940 releases had her name in the title - *Sandy Gets Her Man* and *Sandy is a Lady.* The *American Magazine* in October of 1940 called her the "heir apparent to the Hollywood throne of Shirley Temple, who abdicated recently to struggle through the 'awkard age' in queenly seclusion."

Shirley Temple was not shaking in her dancing slippers. Sandy's 1941 release, *Bachelor Daddy,* still found her top-billed under her own name but with the December release of *Melody Lane* the same year, she was at the bottom of the credits as "with Baby Sandy." She was only a minor part of the supporting cast in her last film, *Johnny Doughboy,* released in 1942, which starred a fading Jane Withers (age 15) in a minor production from Republic, one of the "poverty row" studios.

Sandy, unfortunately, was not a gifted actress. Her films presented her as a baby and she got by with being cute. For dialogue all Sandy did was coo and chortle and for histronics she made funny faces. Most critics were unfavorable to her. The *New York Times* review of *Sandy is a Lady* on June 28, 1940, suggested that she be deposited in a kindergarten. Because of lack of offers, she retired from her film career at age three.

Baby Sandy also advertised the product of her father's milk company, for which he was promoted to an executive position. (*Hygeia* magazine reported in December of 1939 that she consumed a quart of milk every day.) There was a Baby Sandy drinking mug, a pull toy, a storybook, a coloring book and paper doll books. And of course, the *Baby Sandy* doll. The doll rendition caused Shirley Ross, the leading lady in *Unexpected Father,* to tell her, "Now that you have a doll named for you, Sandy, you're as important as the Quints!" Bing Crosby overheard this and said, "At least one fifth as important."

The *Baby Sandy* doll was introduced to the market in 1939. The doll, like Sandy's movies, was not a first-class product. It was manufactured by Ralph A. Freundlich, Inc. in Clinton, Massachusetts. Original boxes state that this company was "the largest doll factory in the world." Unlike the well-finished and packaged dolls from Madame Alexander, EffanBee and Ideal, among others, the *Baby Sandy* doll was manufactured to retail at a modest cost. All the *Baby Sandy*

dolls that the author has examined are made of a grainy composition that is lighter in volume than the "better" composition dolls. This causes a rougher surface finish. The seam marks from the metal molds in which the composition was formed are not sanded smoothly and are not joined neatly. The ears, for example, appear crude because of improper finishing before the doll was painted. The fingers and the toes of the doll are suggested rather than being clearly delineated. The paint finish itself is a very thin layer and does not have an accurate flesh tone. None of the dolls can be called truly "pretty."

On the other hand, thinner layers of paint on a composition doll have less tendency towards flaking and peeling because of age. The author has never seen any *Baby Sandy* dolls that appeared to have had wigs, although a *Playthings* ad in April of 1940 shows a wigged *Baby Sandy.* Molded, painted hair on dolls also holds up better over the years than

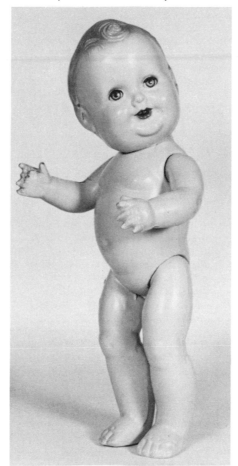

Illustration 5. 11-1/8in (28.2cm) all-composition, fully-jointed *Baby Sandy* with molded and painted yellow hair. The sleep eyes are blue and are tin with hair lashes. There is also light eye shadow above the eyes. Like this version, the larger size dolls have an open mouth with two upper teeth and a felt tongue. The back of the head is marked "BABY SANDY."

Illustration 4. 7in (17.8cm) *Baby Sandy* in a different original outfit with her original box. This is the same basic doll as the one shown in Illustration 1. *Rodolfos Collection. Photograph by Fay Rodolfos.*

wigs do. Some of the dolls have painted eyes and others have tin sleep eyes. Tin eyes, unlike eyes of glass or glassene, never discolor or crackle. It seems that the more economically produced dolls are less impervious to the passage of time than are the more carefully finished ones.

Original clothing on the *Baby Sandy* doll is of a quite simple design and the cloth itself is not a durable fabric. The dolls originally wore a pin with a picture of Sandra Lee Henville.

The *Baby Sandy* doll came in sizes of 7in (17.8cm), 12in (30.5cm) and 16in (40.6cm). (These are approximate sizes because of differences in measuring and in the mold variations.) The smallest size doll has painted eyes or blue tin sleep eyes. (Sandy herself had brown eyes.) All of the dolls are of the "toddler" type, with chubby straight legs.

Sandra Lee Henville is now a California housewife. She has never sought celebrity attention as an adult. The films of her babyhood will never be considered classics nor motion picture art. They were of the type whose only purpose was to provide entertainment. The tradition of the "B" film continues today with situation comedies on television. However, *Baby Sandy* dolls will continue to be collected and prized and represent a more enduring artifact of that era.

23

AMERICAN TOY FAIR 1978

The 75th Annual AMERICAN TOY FAIR was held in late February 1978 in New York City. Presented were the complete new toy lines that you wlll be seeing in toy stores later this year. Of prime interest to doll collectors is the increased awareness of your doll collections by the manufacturers. Some of the notable items we saw were Effanbee's new *Currier and Ives Collection* (six 11in [27.9cm] dolls), two new 15in (38.1cm) *Passing Parade* dolls, *Innocence Collection* of different dolls and a sneak look at Effanbee's Limited Edition doll - *Crowning Glory*.

CROWNING GLORY is the 1978 presentation of the Effanbee Limited Edition Doll Club. This doll will no doubt be the most popular offer yet! Since this club's inception in 1975 we have seen *Precious Baby* (826 models sold), *Patsy - 76* (2199 models sold), and *Dewees Cochran Self-Portrait Doll* (all 3166 models sold). It is our understanding that hundreds of checks were returned on the sellout

of the Dewees Cochran edition. Now comes Effanbee Limited Edition Doll Club's *CROWNING GLORY* . Only 3485 of these 16in (40.6cm) all-vinyl dolls will be made. Naturally, those who bought the 1977 model will be given first rights to buy this new addition.

Eugenia Dukas, Effanbee's chief doll designer for the last 31 years, designed *Crowning Glory* exclusively for the Effanbee Limited Edition Doll Club. The doll itself is 16in (40.6cm). Made of all vinyl with moving blue eyes. Her hair is exquisitely curled and coiffed auburn in a pompadour style. Her ball gown is a touch of regal elegance with lavish fabrics. Made of luxurious brocade lame, with a pleated underskirt and a bouffant overskirt edged in delicate gold braid. The bodice suggests soft femininity and is gracefully enhanced by a stand-up collar of starched, ecru-colored lace edged in matching gold braid. Her jewels include an imitation diamond necklace as well as a matching

tiara. This magnificent costume is completed with the taffeta ruffled crinoline petticoat with matching pantaloons, silk stockings and gold brocade lame pumps. *CROWNING GLORY* sells for $55.00.

One charming new collection of 11in (27.9cm) dolls brings to life the world famous lithographs of CURRIER and IVES. The six new dolls are costumed nicely. A pair can be made of the boy and girl skaters. The *Boy Skater* (no. 1251) has velveteen trousers and braid-trimmed jacket, velveteen cap with muffler, buckle shoes and carrying ice skates. His companion *Girl Skater* (no. 1252) wears a pleated taffeta skirt, velveteen jacket with capelet and matching velveteen-trimmed bonnet. To complete her outfit is slip, pantaloons, pumps and ice skates! *Life in the Country* (no. 1253) is outfitted in a print dress with lace and velveteen trim and velveteen hat. There is also a cameo on the neckband, slip, pantaloons and pumps. Another delightful doll, *Wayside Inn* (no. 1254) has a ruffled taffeta skirt with velveteen bodice and overskirt with a taffeta ruffle. The *Wayside Inn* also has a velveteen bonnet with flowers and marabou, matching slip and pantaloons, and pumps. Another part of this collection is the *Central Park* doll (no. 1255) who is outfitted in a lace-trimmed taffeta walking dress with matching flowered bonnet. A matching slip and pantaloons and pumps complete this doll. The doll that completes this collection is the doll named *A Night on the Hudson* (no. 1256). She is costumed in a multi-ruffled taffeta dress with fringe-trimmed taffeta overskirt caught at the sides with flowers, matching marabou-trimmed bonnet. Completing her costume is a matching slip and pantaloons with pumps.

The *Passing Parade Collection* also returns once more this year but, with a larger parade! New dolls include the *Gay Nineties* (no. 1504) and *The Hourglass Look* (no. 1505). The 15in (38.1cm) *Gay Nineties* is elegantly outfitted in a fringe-trimmed velveteen skirt with bustle, lace-trimmed velveteen jacket, lace jabot with matching bonnet with fringe and marabou. Completing her costume are slip, pantaloons, pumps and pocketbook. *The Hourglass Look* is also 15in (38.1cm) in size with velveteen walking coat with fur trim and cape. A matching fur-trimmed bonnet as well as slip, pantaloons, pumps and fur muff complete this gorgeous outfit. *The 70's Woman* (no. 1508) has been completely recostumed from last year with a lace-trimmed wide yoke chiffon blouse caught at the neck with a jewel. A velveteen skirt, slip with wide band of lace trim, nylons and pumps completes her outfit. Collectors will be able to tell the 1977 editions from the 1978 models in that the doll heads have all been changed. The costumes for the *Colonial Lady, Frontier Woman, Civil War Lady, Gibson Girl* and *Flapper* remain essentially the same.

Another new collection that caught our eye was Effanbee's *INNOCENCE COLLECTION*. There are nine young ladies in their breathtaking white embroidered outfits. Included are an 11in (27.9cm) *Caroline* (no. 1221 - also available as black doll), 15in (38.1cm) *Chipper* (no. 1521), 16in (40.6cm) *L'il Suzie Sunshine* (no. 1621), 18in (45.7cm) *Miss Chips* (no. 1721), 19in (48.3cm) *Suzie Sunshine* (no. 1821 - also available as black doll), 17in (43.2cm) *Twinkie* (no. 2521), a cute 11in (27.9cm) *Half Pint* (no. 6221), a 15in (38.1cm) *Little Lovums* (no. 8321) and an 18in (45.7cm) *Sweetie Pie* (no. 9421 - also available as black doll). Every little "innocent" will want a beauty from the INNOCENCE collection.

MADAME ALEXANDER also introduced her new 1978 line at the American Toy Fair in New York City in February 1978. There are new dolls of course! The portraits are all-new with dolls named *Gainsborough, Cornelia* and *Scarlett*. The *Gainsborough* portrait has a pink gown with beige lace. *Cornelia* portrait has a turquoise gown with cloak. *Scarlett O'Hara* has a rose patterned dress with green parasol and straw hat (completely different from the last several years' offering). Other new Madame Alexander dolls included a *Baby Sister* dressed in pink gingham which accompanies *Baby Brother*. Another new addition is *Goldilocks*. This storybook doll is dressed in blue taffeta with a black vest trimmed with white lace at the neck. A pair sure to capture the hearts of Madame Alexander collectors is *Romeo* and *Juliet*. *Romeo* has red tights and a purple jacket with boots and cap. *Juliet* is graceful in her flowing white gown outlined in gold brocade.

We were priviledged to hear portions of a new 1978 product from Madame Alexander Productions, Inc. This new product is a stereo record album - MADAME ALEXANDER COLLECTOR'S ALBUM 1978. This album "presents, in words and music, the story of the magic of dolls. Children and all doll lovers will welcome

this invitation to join Madame Alexander on a journey through her very special world." This recording is narrated by Madame Alexander with music and lyrics by John Braden. Original songs and dramatic vignettes include "Imagination," "The Doll In The Taffeta Gown," "The Magic's All In You," and "Waltz Of The Dolls." The album is full stereophonic sound.

Ideal Toy Company is celebrating its 75th year with a release of a reproduction of the original teddy bear which started that company. This teddy bear will be packaged quite distinctively.

VOGUE DOLLS, which last year under its new owner, Lesney Products Corporation, upgraded the quality of their dolls, is re-releasing *GINNY*. Yes, *Ginny* has been updated for the now look and comes dressed in fashions that every little girl dreams of having today. Fully posable with knees that bend, this 8in (20.3cm)

doll has sleep eyes and long beautiful hair. *Ginny* has at least 18 different outfits. In addition there is a black companion doll - *Ginnette*.

PEGGY NISBET has a wealth of new dolls for 1978 including a limited edition self-portrait doll of *Peggy Nisbet*. The year 1978 Is Peggy's Silver Jubilee and the self-portrait was designed especially to commemorate her 25th anniversary of making dolls. This self-portrait of *Peggy Nisbet* is limited to 500 pieces. Another collector series is the *Charles III & three mistresses* which will only have 500 sets made. One thing that is different with this year's Peggy Nisbet models is that they have a rather matte look to them this year (non-glossy). Of course there are other new models offered this year.

Tower Treasures, the limited edition collectors club of Peggy Nisbet has announced *Lady Jane Grey* as the next limited edition.

American Toy Fair - 1979

CONTRIBUTED BY GARY RUDDELL

From left to right: *Scarlet* (#2240); *Melanie* (#2220); and *Agatha* (#2230).

The American Toy Fair of 1979 was only partially covered in the April/May 1979 issue of DOLL READER (pages 32-33). It seems that doll companies are responding to the increased interest in doll collecting by offering collectors a greater choice of models from which to choose.

ALEXANDER DOLLS

For 1979 Madame Alexander has released three new portrait dolls shown above (left to right): Scarlet (#2240), Melanie (#2220) and Agatha (#2230).

Scarlet is 21in. (53.3cm) with green eyes and elegant shoulder-length brunette curls. She is dressed in a plush green velvet gown with lace cap sleeves and braid trim. A matching bustle-length jacket is trimmed with braid and ecru lace ruffles on her cuffs. She wears high-heeled sandals and nylon stockings under her wide petticoat and green ribbon and lace-trimmed pantaloons. Jewelry includes emerald green stone on gold-colored chain around her neck and a diamond-like ring on her finger.

Melanie, also 21in. (53.3cm), is dressed in white-dotted nylon with three tiers of ruffles accented with pink ribbon. A wide pink sash is around her waist. Her neckline is high-lighted with flowers. Melanie has long curls of blonde hair that are partially covered by a wide-brimmed straw hat trimmed with tulle, flowers and rib-bons. She wears high-heeled sandals and nylon stockings under her wide petticoat and pantaloons. Her jewelry

includes a heart pendant worn around her neck accompanied by diamond-like ring on her finger.

The last of the new portrait dolls is *Agatha*, who is 21in. (53.3cm). This lovely doll's face is accented by her lovely auburn hair and the lavender and lace gown made of taffeta. The taffeta overskirt is scalloped and caught up daintily with rosebuds and is draped over an accordian-pleated taffeta underskirt. The waist is graced with wide purple velvet sash and rhinestone buckle. A flowered straw bonnet is tied with ribbons to go under her chin. High-heeled sandals with nylon stockings under her wide petticoat and pantaloons complete her outfit. A diamond-like ring adorns her finger.

Elise Ballerina (#1640) is 17in. (43.2cm) and is newly dressed in a sparkling silver tulle ballet outfit. Silver sequins and tiny braid-like trim grace the bodice. Pantyhose tights with silver ballet slippers complete the outfit. Elise wears a silver coronet tiara around her hair which falls into long curls at the nape of her neck.

LENCI

There is some additional news from Lenci "re-creations" for 1979. *Clo Clo Green* of 1978 is available again this year but with a change to her costume. *Clo Clo Green* is named "Matelda Green" (20in. or 50.8cm) in the 1979 line and her perky outfit is brown felt dress trimmed with green felt border. She wears a coat of green felt accented with brown felt trim.

Matelda Green's hat is green felt accented with brown felt trim and brown felt bow.

Not seen by this reviewer at the New York American Toy Fair was *Colette* (20in. or 50.8cm). Long blonde curly hair sets this beauty off. Several shades of blue felt are used for the mid-calf-length dress which is set off by a two-tiered ruffle at the bottom of the dress. A blue felt hat has green felt flower. Blue felt shoes are tied over ankle-length white socks. Colette holds a small bouquet of felt flowers.

Samantha is the new large-size (27in. or 68.6cm) Lenci re-creation. Is she a Lenci beauty! Her long dress is made of blue felt which has three over-lapping tiers each trimmed with three thin strips of yellow-gold felt trim. This yellow-gold felt trim also en-hances the long sleeves and neckline. The dress partially covers a blouse with ruffled lace trim around neck highlighted with a small "box" of rib-bon at neck. Her wide-brimmed felt hat has blue felt lining with yellow-gold top. The ever-popular Lenci felt flowers trim the hat. The new 1979 editions are not expected to arrive un-til sometime this summer. Although some of the 1978 dolls might still be found, it is our understanding that supplies are dwindling, as they were limited editions.

Discontinued Effanbee dolls from 1978

Betsy Ross (#1152), Davy Crockett (#1154), Florence Nightingale (#1155), Pocahontas (#1157), Robin Hood (#1181), Maid Marian (#1182), Tinkerbell (#1183), Central Park (#1255), Night on the Hudson (#1256), Madame DuBarry (#1535), Lady Grey (#1540), Champagne Lady (#1735), Coquette (#1538), Fleurette (#1736), Blue Danube (#1738), The Queen Mother (#1846). The Blue Heaven Collection has been redressed into Rainbow Parfait.

EFFANBEE

The Effanbee Doll Corporation is proud to announce several new pro-ducts to accompany their dolls, ex-pressly made for collectors! First, three sets of paper dolls to accompany "collections" of 1979 Effanbee dolls. Each paper doll booklet is in complete color with paper doll; each and every costume is offered from the "collec-tion" of 1979. Also included are several costumes in black and white for you to color or adorn with fabric to make your own designer originals! Series of paper dolls includes: **Through the Years with Gigi 1830-1900** (with six costumes), **Currier & Ives** (with six costumes) and **Storybook** (with ten costumes). Now along with your collection you can enjoy a paper doll replica!

Now Effanbee collectors can have their own personal **1980 EFFANBEE CALENDAR**. An exciting selection of both the best of Effanbee's past dolls (historical, Patsy, Dy-Dee, American Children, Tommy Tucker & Majorette) as well as today's current collectibles (Currier & Ives, Gigi,Innocence, Bridal, Crocheted Classics)are presented in Full Color! After the month is over use as postcards or for scrapbooks. Who wants to grow older but, with a selection like this, one longs to see what 1981 will bring for collectors(photos by Elspeth).

Faith Wick, a NIADA artist, who works in porcelain, has given Effanbee the exclusive rights to reproduce in vinyl, her famous caricatures. Four very collectible first-year in vinyl editions are two pairs. **Party Time** has both a 16in. (40.6cm) boy and girl. The **Boy** (#7001) is dressed in a royal blue "Little Lord Fauntleroy" velvet suit and hat. The shirt has a Peter Pan collar accented with oversized bow; he has white shoes and blonde hair. The **Girl** (#7002) has a ruby-red velvet coat dress with Peter Pan collar, accented with pink bow. She has a matching beret. Bloomers, stockings and high-laced shoes complete her outfit. A sailor set is the other Faith Wick first-year vinyl edition . The brunette hair is accented against the white sailor suits of these 16in. (40.6cm) dolls. The **Boy** (#7003) fittingly referred to as "Anchors Aweigh" has a "crew" cloth sailor suit trimmed with blue stripes and red bow and traditional hat with red pompon. The **Girl** (#7004) has a "crew" cloth sailor dress with pleated skirt and matching hat. She has bloomers, stockings and high-laced shoes.

The **"Soft 'n Sweet Collection"** is a redressed "Memories Collection" of 1978 with the addition of brunette hair and a 15in. (38.1cm) "Buttercup" (missing from "Memories Collection"), 11in. (27.9cm) boy and 15in. (38.1 cm) "Little Lovums."

The **"Grandes Dames Collection"** has only two repeats of 1978 ("Downing Square," #1539, and "Nicole," #1737. There are also new dolls. **Blue Bayou"** (#1531) is 15in. (38.1cm) and has a blue taffeta dress with lace-trimmed hem and velveteen jacket. There is a matching chapeau with marabou. Ensemble is complete with slip,

pantaloons, pumps and black purse. **"Magnolia"** (#1532) is 15in. (38.1cm) and the picture of femininity in her two-tiered pink taffeta gown. Lace amply adorns her dress and slip pantaloons, pumps and purse complete her outfit. Matching bonnet and fan are her lovely accessories. **"Emerald Isle"** (#1533) is 15in. (38.1cm) and a green vision in her taffeta dress with lace and pleated underskirt. She comes fashioned with matching hat accented by flowers, slip, pantaloons, pumps and handkerchief. **"Lady Snow"** (#1731) is 18in. (45.7cm) and smartly dressed in an attractive walking coat, made of woven floral taffeta and trimmed in fringe and braid. Slip, pantaloons, pumps and purse complete her outfit. **"Cherries Jubilee"**(#1732) is 18in. (45.7cm) and richly attired in ruffled print dress over which she wears a velveteen bodice and overskirt. She comes with slip, pantaloons, pumps and purse and wears a cameo at neck. 18in. (45.7cm) **"Crystal"** (#1733) is fashionably dressed in lace-trimmed taffeta coat dress highlighted with embroidered oval medallion on bodice. Matching taffeta hat, slip, pantaloons, pumps, and handkerchief complete her outfit.

The **"Innocence Collection"** welcomes 15in. (38.1cm) **"Buttercup"** (#9321) who wears a charming white dress, accented with eyelet trim and design with pink ribbon insert. To complete her outfit, she wears pink bows in her hair and little booties on her feet.

The **"Keepsake Collection"** adds 11in. (27.9cm) **"Old Fashioned Boy"** (#6241) and 11in. (27.9cm) **"Old Fashioned Girl"** (#6242). The adorable **Boy** wears a blue velveteen knicker suit with braid and matching cap. Lace-trimmed shirt in addition to socks and side-button shoes complete his outfit. The **Girl** is graced with a lace-trimmed embroidered dress with velveteen accent. To complete her darling outfit she comes with a bonnet with flower, tights and side-button shoes.

As always, 1979's additions are sure to please collectors of discriminating taste. Their exquisite costuming and charming faces will win them all a place in collectors' hearts this year.

French Mechanical Toys in 1919

SUBMITTED BY DOROTHY S. COLEMAN

After World War I, France returned to the manufacture of mechanical toys. The American Trade Magazine, *Toys & Novelties* in 1919 described this industry:

"Most of the Mechanical Toys now sold in France are made by small manufacturers, and, to a lesser extent, by individuals..."

"In the good old days of Vaucasan and the Droz Brothers, mechanical toys were something rather unique, and their prices were way beyond the reach of the average individual. But today, mechanical toys belong to the regular toy industry in France and can be obtained by everybody at a small figure.

"In fact, once the model has been made, it is an easy matter to apply the same inside mechanism to the various types and different models. However, the making of these mechnical toys, needs preliminary study, as they are reproductions of scenes or human persons. In fact, they are imitations of living and existing things. The model is made from wax. From the soft wax, the artist models his figures from life, the same way as does the sculptor with his clay.

"The painting of the heads, the coiffures and the various minute details, require particular attention, and the costumes are selected with taste. The mechanism of each mechanical toy is the same in general, but varies in detail. It is composed of a sort of watch movement—a spring—and has to be wound up. The music of these toys starts when the watch moves. The most important factory in Paris is Triboulet's."

The pictures accompanying this article show dolls performing various activities. It is not clear whether the wax model is used for making molds from which many heads could be produced. Certainly the clay models made by sculptors were used thusly for making molds used for the manufacture of bisque or composition heads.

American Toy Fair - 1979

CONTRIBUTED BY GARY & MARY RUDDELL

From left to right: Six additions to the First Ladies series— Jane Findlay, Sara Polk, Angelica Van Buren, Julia Tyler and center front, Betty Taylor Bliss.

The American Toy Fair was held in New York City February 18-21 in the midst of a big snowstorm. The snowstorm did little to diminish the enthusiasm of toy manufacturers who were intent on showing the new line of dolls and toys for the coming year. Dolls in general seem to be more plentiful and there is exciting news for the collectors of all varieties of dolls.

MADAME ALEXANDER DOLLS

The distinctive showcases in the Madame Alexander Doll showroom had much in store for collectors to take note of in the way of changes. The first six First Ladies (released 1976) have been discontinued. The following are descriptions of six additional First Ladies in this 14in. (35.6 cm) size which are to be available later this year. **Sarah Jackson**, the wife of the President's adopted son, has peach cotton dress with beige lace overlay with lace neck trim. Her brunette hair has long curls with tortoise-shell hair comb and opal necklace. Another wife of a President's son who acted as the First Lady is **Angelica Van Buren**. She has a sleeveless blue velvet dress with white lace shawl around the neck and pinned at waist. Her brunette hair has a gold headband with white feather (not shown in above photo) and her face is accented with beguiling blue eyes. The untimely death of President William Harrison only a month after taking office presented little time for **Jane Findlay** to perform her duties as First Lady (while Mrs. Harrison prepared to come to Washington, D.C.). A beautiful brown velvet dress with squared neck and long sleeves graces this charming blond-haired doll (hair styled in buns at both sides of head). The dress is tastefully enhanced by simple white trim at neck and wrist. A green pendant on a gold-colored necklace adorns her neck. The White House gained a very lively and supportive First Lady in **Julia Tyler**. Julia's dress is made of white-tiered organdy with pink flowered trim on the tiers, neck and short sleeves. Her brunette hair is complimented with gold tiara (not shown in above photo). **Sarah Polk** is attired in a blue brocade dress with vee-neckline and short sleeves. The front has lace in tiers with lace trim on sleeves highlighted with blue accent bows. A pendant on a blue satin ribbon hangs from this blue-eyed, auburn-haired doll's neck. The last doll to complete this second series of First Ladies dolls is **Betty Taylor Bliss**. Her blonde hair is braided and worn atop her head. Her dress is of burgundy taffeta with tiered, plaid-trimmed ornamentation. The neckline is trimmed in black velvet ribbon and white lace attached at waist. A cameo necklace accents this graceful doll.

The Portraits are all new. **Scarlett** is dressed in the perennial green velvet, heavy-green-trim outfit, imitating the dress Scarlett wore made from curtains in *Gone With The Wind.* She also has beige lace trim at wrist, green pendant and green velvet hat, completing the outfit. Her eyes are green; she appears to be a brunette. **Agatha**, another portrait-size, has auburn hair with blue eyes. Her dress is of purple satin with light purple pleated underskirt. **Melanie**, the last portrait-size, has a white dress with pink ribbon trim and white floppy hat, trimmed in pink. Her blue eyes will certainly attract those not-already as they come under the trance of this Southern Belle's charm.

Other new items from Madame Alexander include a new ballerina silver costume with large tiara. The Baby Brother and Sister of last year are joined by identical smaller versions this year. Victoria has a new christening dress. Puddin has new outfits of pink, blue and yellow gingham.

PEGGY NISBET DOLLS

Peggy Nisbet, known for her English-related costume dolls (also celebrities) and limited edition bisque dolls (Tower Treasures) was represented at the American Toy Fair by Jack Wilson and his wife, Alison (daughter of Peggy Nisbet). We were treated to a personal viewing of the many new 1979 dolls. Alison is creating a line of children's clothes that utilize Beatrix Potter scenes in the fabric.

There is a *Peggy Nisbet Supplement Catalogue* for the *1978 Collector's Reference Book* for $3.00 that shows all of the new 1979 additions in color as well as former models still available.

One group of new dolls has royalty themes. **The Royal Family** includes Princess Margaret, Edward VIII and Mrs. Wallis Simpson. "Crowned Descendants of Queen Victoria" include Victoria, Empress of Germany/ Kaiser Frederick III, Tsaritsa Alexandra, Empress of Russia/Tsar Nicholas II and Queen Ena of Spain/King Alfonso XIII. Also new is King Edward VI with **The Edwardians** (Lillie Langtry, Countess of Warwick and Hon. Alice Keppel). A limited edition of 500 sets of dolls derived from famous paintings—Ruben's "The Straw Hat," Gainsborough's "The Hon. Mrs. Graham" and Renoir's "The Box." English figures include The Lord Mayor of London, The Life Guards and the Blues and Royals.

The new inch-to-foot miniatures historical series is King Henry VIII and his six wives. The American Presidents series is joined by a doll of Dwight D. Eisenhower. Great Leaders include Joan of Arc, Sir Winston Churchill (from Karsh portrait) and an addition is Pope John XXIII. Danny Kaye was chosen as "Film Stars in their Celebrated Roles" for his work with children (International Year of the Child, United Nations). Captain James Cook is the new addition to the "Explorers Series." A number of new International Ladies include Germany, Russia, Spain, Greece, Romania, Yugoslavia, Norway, Sweden and Denmark. "Scottish Historical Characters" rounds out the new Nisbet 1979 line with Rob Roy, St. Margaret and Robbie Burns.

Collectors certainly have a number of lovely dolls to update previously started series as well as new series from which to start collecting. The Nisbet Company opened their new company facilities last autumn and it appears by the number of new items they are testing storage capacity already. Incidentally the child's photograph attached to the Teddy Bears is William Wilson, the one-year-old son of Jack and Alison (and Peggy's grandson).

MISCELLANEOUS

Finally **Lenci Doll Company** of Turin, Italy has introduced two new dolls for 1979. Both are the smaller-sized 20in. (50.8cm) doll. **Matilda** is dressed in a yellow short-sleeve A-line dress with red trim. She wears a red yoke coat with yellow trim and red felt shoes with white anklet socks. Her reddish-brown hair is topped with a cloche red hat with yellow trim. **Corinne** has a brown box-pleated dress with orange-yellow windowpane trim. The brown jacket with a yellow-orange windowpaine trim does not hide the dress and brown shoes with white anklet socks. The brown-haired doll is topped with a brown hat with accents of windowpane trim. Both of these new additions noted by this viewer appeared to have better eye-painting treatments, towards the Lenci varieties of a bygone era. Some of the varieties from last year can still be obtained.

Other news from American Toy Fair includes: The famous Gerber baby which is being made into doll form this year by Atlanta Novelty. The doll is sculptured with the features of the 50-year-old baby advertising company symbol. Following the reintroduction in 1978 of the Ginny Doll, Vogue dolls has added a Ginny Carry Case, more new outfits and a Ginny Sweet Shop set. Mattel introduces a kissing Barbie doll. The doll tilts her head, puckers her lips, makes a real kissing sound and leaves a tiny lipstick print. In addition Barbie has a Dream House and Dream Furniture.

From left to right: Gigi Through The Years 1830-1900—Papa's Pet, Grand-mére, Schoolgirl, MaMa, Ingenue and Femme Fetale.

EFFANBEE DOLLS

Effanbee has released a new set of costume dolls that will beguile collectors. **Gigi Through The Years 1830-1900** are all 11in. (27.9cm) in height. This series shows the progression of a doll at six different times in her life. **Papa's Pet** (1838) (#1161) has a white mid-length dress tiered at bottom. The puff sleeves are accented by pink bows as well as the brunette, pulled-back hair. **Schoolgirl** (1842) (#1162) has a navy blue sailor suit and spat-type shoes over white tights; white straw hat with blue ribbon covers brunette hair. **Ingenue** (1846) (#1163) wears a blue long dress with puffed sleeves trimmed with white lace and a white straw hat with pink ribbon. **Femme Fetale** (1851) (#1264) is dressed in stunning pink wth tiers of beige lace at bottom and around neck. Rose-colored bows and belt set dress off; pink flowers highlight dark-brunette pinned-up hair. **MaMa** (1865) (#1164) is quite the proper lady with cameo broach in long-sleeved dress heavily accented with beige lace. Her hat has beige veil over dark brunette hair. **Grand-mére** (1895) (#1266) represents the oldest version of Gigi, featuring frosted hair. She is graced with rust-colored, long velvet dress with lace sleeves accompanied by peaked hat with bow.

The very popular **Currier & Ives Collection** is back. Two repeats are **Boy And Girl Skaters**. **Life In The Country** (#1253) is slightly altered with different print for dress, redder ribbon trim and blonde hair.

Castle Garden (#1257), a newly-designed miss, wears colorful purple velvet overskirt and bodice, blue satin sleeves and pleated underskirt. She also comes with white straw hat with purple and blue ribbon accents perched atop blonde hair. **Plymouth Landing** (#1258) features a full red satin long dress with red velvet trim. There is also beige lace bib and red velvet hat with beige lace veil.

Wayside Inn (#1254) has green velvet long dress with beige satin, featuring trim at wrist, neck and bonnet. Her green hat is tied with beige bow.

Exciting news is the design of collector-oriented paper dolls and outfits to match doll sets made by Effanbee including **Gigi Paper Doll, Currier & Ives Paper Doll** and **Storybook Paper Doll**. Full-color paper doll with all outfits to match those of dolls of series comes with extra Historical Costume and fantastic storage container. More information to follow. Also available will be a 1980 **Effanbee Calendar**—all color photographs with dates—the photos can later be used as postcards. Features six collectible Effanbee doll favorites from many years past plus six current Effanbee vinyl doll favorites. Toy stores as well as Paul A. Ruddell Books will carry these fine Effanbee products.

Other Effanbee doll changes to note: **Passing Parade Frontier Woman** is now outfitted in brown gingham with brown shawl; **Gibson Girl** is bedecked in white leg-of-mutton sleeves with long black skirt and straw hat; **Hourglass** wears mustard-colored velvet with white bib and black trim; **Flapper** has blonde hair; **Seventies Woman** has black net dress with sheer sleeves. International Series has added **Matador** (#1117) to be paired with **Miss Spain**. Storybook Collection has added **Goldilocks** and a cute pair of **Jack 'N Jill**.

New York Toy Fair February 11-22, 1980 held in New York City was the gathering place of nearly all the Toy Manufacturing Companies. Collectors in the coming months will find to their delight that their desires are being increasingly noted in many manufacturer's lines. Limited production or limited edition dolls and toys abound. This article could be a guide of items to look for in the coming months of 1980. Perhaps you had better start saving now!

The House of Nisbet from England should be congratulated on putting it all together for collectors! They are releasing 14 different "Victorian Birthday Dolls" this year. Perhaps you will recall the popular Nursery Rhyme for the days of the week:

Monday's Child is Fair of Face,
Tuesday's Child is Full of Grace,
Wednesday's Child is Full of Woe,
Thursday's Child Has Far to Go,
Friday's Child is Loving and Giving,
Saturday's Child Works Hard for a
    Living,
Sunday's Child - A Child that is Born
    on the Sabbath Day is Bonny and
    Blithe, and Good and Gay.

Each day of the week is portrayed as a couple -- a 12" (30.5cm) boy doll and a 12" (30.5cm) girl doll. There are seven different sculpted heads -- the boy with molded hair and the girl with a wig. Each is made of genuine Staffordshire fine bone china. Each doll's expression is brought out through the sculpting. Dolls will have a date incised as well

as a foil marking on the back of the four time fired head. Hands and feet as well as the body are made of cloth. Each costume vividly recreates a Victorian styled garment (sewn-in label). Each doll is attractively priced considering the china head and quality of finish work. The new styrene doll models released by the House of Nisbet include 8" (20.3cm) historical portraits and costume dolls depicting Princesses' Elizabeth and Margaret Rose, H.R.H. Prince Charles, Prime Minister Margaret Thatcher, Bob Hope (dressed in Road to Morocco), Queen Nefertiti, Charlotte Bronte, Anne of Green Gables, and special collectors set #17 (limited edition of 500 sets including Cardinal Wolsley, King Henry VIII, and Catherine of Aragon).

The Effanbee Doll Company has dramatically altered their collection. Included are the following highlights: a limited production (only during 1980) of a remarkable likeness to W.C. Fields in vinyl. The doll has a pinkish-red large nose and molded hair. Atop his head is a top hat of grey felt with a wide black ribbon accent. This comedian is decked out in a black top coat with fur cuffs over a purple ascot tie and a white shirt. He wears houndstooth trousers and carries a cane. Faith Wick has repeated both Anchors Aweigh and Party Time series from 1979. New vinyl dolls by this doll artist are a boy clown (7005) with oversized blue shirt and red and white striped overalls. The straw hat, red stockings and black puffy shoes complete the clown's makeup. The other clown girl (7006) has puffy white pants and shirt with wide white collar and red pom-pons down the front which is accented in red trim. Astry

Campbell, a noted doll artist, has her bisque babies made in vinyl. The newborn (1011) is a reproduction in vinyl of the bisque doll on display at the Smithsonian Institute. The christening gown is tied in the middle by a pink ribbon. Another baby (1012) has a christening dress with long sleeves accented with pink ribbon. The bonnet is white with rows of lacy trim. The third baby (1013) has a pink gown plus a pink diaper (both white lace trimmed). A wicker traveling case includes two extra outfits -- crocheted gowns, pants and white gowns.

Effanbee also introduces a grouping of French fashion Damselles-- the Petite Filles. The smaller sizes include Madaline (6232), Mimi (6233), and Brigitte (6234). The tall dolls include Gabriel (1632), Lili (1631), Monique (1633) and Giselle (1634). Each doll is exquisitely dressed. The Grandes Dames include Jezebelle (1571) who was formerly "the Civil War Lady" of the now discontinued Passing Parade collection. New additions to the Grandes Dames are La Vie en Rose (1773) wearing a two tiered beige dress with rose print design. Night at the Opera (1774) is attired in a black full length dress with white lace accents plus a feather collar with a black bow. Ruby (1572) is dressed in a long printed red dress with a low neck line under a black short jacket. Carnegie Hall (1772) wears a long white satin-type dress with a green sash under a long green cape. Coco (1771) is attired in a long off-white dress with lace-type overlay plus a dark brown cape with feather hat.

Another new collection from Effanbee is called Day by Day. Effanbee's version has seven girls in their interpretation of this Nursery Rhyme. Monday's girl doll (1401) is "fair of face" in a pink dress with white apron overskirt (holding a hand mirror). Tuesday's girl doll (1402) "full of grace)) with a ballerina's outfit of pastel blue. Wednesday's girl doll (1403) who is "full of woe" has a red and white long sleeved gingham dress with white apron. She is holding a jump rope and wears a straw hat. Thursday's girl (1404) "has far to go" and is dressed in a green dress with matching green hat plus a white muffler. Friday's girl (1405) is "loving and giving" and is dressed in a long sleeve white dress with a blue belt of ribbon. Of course she is holding a wrapped present. Saturday's girl (1406) "works hard for a living" is dressed for working in a quilt looking fabric, white apron and yellow kerchief. Finally, Sunday's girl (1407) who was "born on Sabbath day is bonny, blithe, good and gay". She is dressed for church with a long white robe underneath a red overlay. Other new dolls from Effanbee include a series called Ships Ahoy, Rhapsody in Blue, Cotton Candy, Heart to Heart (special fabric with "Effanbee" spelled out), Cream Puff, International dolls (Miss Israel, Greek Boy and Miss Brazil) takeoff on a Carmen Miranda outfit, Storybook Series (Mother Hubbard, Sleeping Beauty, Prince Charming and Heidi).

The Alexander Doll Company always has news for anxious collectors. There are four new dolls for 1980 -- Josephine and Napoleon and Cleopatra and Mark Anthony (under the Portraits of History). The 11" (27.9 cm) Josephine has a floor length empire waisted dress with pink trim. Her jewelry includes a gold arch with silver trim worn in her brunette hair plus pearls and gold necklace. The 11" (27.9cm) Emperor Napoleon is dressed in a dark blue uniform with white breech pants and black shoes (also medals-of course!). The 11" (27.9cm) Cleopatra wears a white pleated dress accented by a gold waistband and a blue, red and black striped shoulder decoration. This Queen has royal jewelry including a gold hairband around her brunette hair. She wears gold sandals. Her male escort is the 11" (27.9cm) Mark Anthony. This doll has a red cape over his white uniform trimmed in blue. The chest armour is gold colored. The sandals are knee-high. Discontinued Alexander dolls are 25" (63.5cm) Big Huggins (6820), 14" (35.6cm) Sweet Tears (3624), and the both large sized 20" (50.8cm) Baby Sister (6555) and Baby Brother (6550). The Alexander costume changes are: Goldilocks dressed in blue polished cotton, Poor Cinderella in grey dress with orange apron, Puddin dressed in yellow gingham, Pussy Cat in both blue floral print for the white doll and pink floral print for the black doll. The second set of six First Ladies as well as the portrait dolls remain the same as 1979.

Teddy Bear collectors would have oohed and ahed at the great wealth of bears in attendance at Toy Fair. A special note is a line called "Colonel Teddy" with the Teddy Bear

dressed in a blue colonel uniform, kakhi rough rider uniform and black Presidential tuxedo. Each of these bears has wire rim glasses. The most spectacular news is that the Steiff Company commemorates their 100th Anniversary in 1980 and is bringing out a limited edition re-creation of their 1903 Bear. The European edition (with certificate in German) will number 5,000. The United States edition (with certificate in English signed by Hans Otto Steiff) will number not less than 3,000 nor more than 5,000. The assigned number will appear both on the certificate as well as on the back of the distinctive Steiff ear tag.

Other doll and related news of note will be a new character to be introduced on T.V. in late March 1980, Strawberry Shortcake. Strawberry Shortcake will be available with strawberry scented hair. She will have other friends from her own land that include Blueberry Muffin, Huckleberry Pie, Apple Dumplin' as well as two plush toys (that smell like their namesakes). A strawberry-shaped carrying case will be available that opens into a bake shop.

Ideal Toy Company reintroduces Shirley Temple in a newly-designed doll dressed in a replica of the curly-topped child star's outfit in the original Little Miss Marker movie. This is Ideal's fourth Shirley Temple doll, a Sara Stimson doll modeled after the new upcoming 1980 version

of the "Little Miss Marker" movie. Ideal also introduces Chew Suzie Chew that chews on her food with realistic mouth action and a Newborn Snuggles line of soft dolls who "snuggle" when the strings in their backs are pulled.

Mattel introduces the new Beauty Secrets Barbie with poseable wrists, bendable elbows and hip length hair and is mechanically actived. Also new is Skating Barbie, Skating Ken, the Barbie Super 'vette and boyfriend for Superteen Skipper.

Sasha Dolls made in England have several new models available in 1980. The big news to look for will be the late 1980 Sasha limited edition doll. It has been reported that 5,000 are to be produced worldwide with the United States to receive 2,500. Dean's Rag Dolls of England have announced that they will be reprinting selected cloth doll gems from their past. Available this spring will be a reprint of their 1912 Peggy and Teddy (Dolly Dingle lookalikes). These are to be available in both uncut and completed form. The new Marjorie Spangler doll collection is most beguiling. Dolls by Pauline who introduced the Ling Ling 18" (45.7cm) Chinese doll last year has several new dolls. Stolle, a West German doll manufacturer showed their new line of four Bisque dolls. In addition this company released several molded felt dolls with fluffy hair that are available in finished or kit form.

Collectible Alice In Wonderland

BY SHIRLEY BUCHHOLZ

Illustration 1. Sold by Disney Productions. Left: 15 in. (38.1cm) vinyl head, hard plastic legs and body made by Effanbee. Right: 7½ in. (19.1cm) hard plastic. Apron labeled "Alice"; body marked Alexander.

Probably the most coveted of the Alice in Wonderland dolls is the cloth set made by Martha Jenks Chase. According to her family, they were designed in 1905. They were advertised in *Playthings* magazine in 1921. Photographs may be seen in *The Collector's Encyclopedia of Dolls* by the Colemans.

A few other "Alice" dolls are mentioned in the early years of the 20th century, but information is sketchy during the years of World War I. Perhaps our child of fantasy had no place in that world. But in 1930 she again appears, springing from the mind of Beatrice Behrman, known to us as Madame Alexander.

One of Madame's first dolls was "Alice" made of cloth, and during the past 50 years she has appeared steadily in the Alexander line of dolls. She has

Alice in Wonderland was a real little girl, but not the one we were accustomed to seeing with flowing long blond hair held back by the band of ribbon that is named for her. The real Alice may have worn the familiar outfit of the blue frock and white pinafore, but she had short dark hair with straight bangs.

Her name was Alice Pleasance Liddell and she was the second daughter of Henry Liddell, Dean of Christ Church at Oxford. In the introduction of the book *Alice in Wonderland* she is referred to as "Secunda."

On July 4, 1862, Charles Dodgson, better known to us as Lewis Carroll, and his friend the Reverend Robinson Duckworth (later to become the Canon of Westminster) took the three little Liddell girls for a boat ride on the Thames. The girls were aged 13, 10 and 8. As usual, they begged Dodgson for a story, so he spun them the tale of a little girl called "Alice" and her adventures underground.

Upon their return to the deanery Alice Liddell asked if he would write the story for her. Promising he would, Dodgson went back to his quarters and sat up most of the night writing his recollections of Alice's adventures. He illustrated it and later presented it to his little friend.

When the book was to be published, he sent the noted illustrator, John Tenniel, a picture of another child, Mary Hilton Badcock, to be used as a model. (Dodgson himself photographed many children.) Whether Tenniel used the photographs is debatable, but at any rate, Dodgson was not terribly pleased with the results.

Irregardless, Alice, fashioned after Tenniel's drawings, is one of the most familiar figures in English literature. Even if they have not read the book, most people will recognize her or be able to describe her. We have Walt Disney films to thank for that!

For the doll collector as well as the bibliophile, Alice is fun. There have been many interpretations through the years, and in most cases she is blond and wears a blue dress with white pinafore and stockings.

Commercial doll makers have given us many delightful "Alice" dolls since the book made its appearance in 1865. It is only reasonable that if they made dolls depicting children they would make dolls depicting characters in children's books. Shortly after the book was published, dolls appeared on the market wearing the circular bands on their heads of china, parian, wax and composition.

Illustration 2. Marionettes. Left: 15 in. (38.1cm), marked under hair: PPP (Peter Puppet Playthings). Right: 12 in. (30.5cm) marked on back: Tony Sarg//Alexander. Both are composition.

worn most of the faces familiar to the Alexander collectors and her clothes have progressed from cotton through rayon and into today's wash and wear synthetics. She has worn a few dots and checks, but for the most part, she was dressed in the familiar blue dress and white pinafore (right, *Ill. 1*).

Effanbee has produced their own more mature-looking "Alice", and one for Walt Disney Productions that was designed by the Disney artists from the cartoon character. She bears a credible likeness to the Alice of the film, but is not, to many children, as appealing as she might be. Collectors would consider her a character (left, *Ill. 1*).

Horsman, Vogue, Mego, Mattel, Shackman and no doubt many others have given us Alice. An intriguing version is one made in Greece by Kehagias. She is a "dead ringer" for the Alexander "Alice" I purchased in 1976, but the hair is coiled around her ears and the arms are straighter.

Commercially, Alice and her friends appeared on the market as marionettes (*Ill. 2*), 19th century lead toys, wooden games and cloth dolls. In addition to the "made-up" rag dolls, many patterns have been published for sewing at home. Recently a set of Alice in Wonderland cloth dolls manufactured by the Chase Bag Company was given by a firm for the use of their product. Unhappily, they were not advertised in my area and I missed them.

Illustration 4. 8½ in. (21.6cm) by Ann Parker. Wrist tag reads: English//Costume Dolls// ☉ //Ann Parker//Hand Made in Great Britain. There is a brief description on reverse side.

England, Alice's homeland, no doubt has had many versions of her. Chelsea Art Dolls offered some in 1954 and Mrs. Fleishmann, maker of Old Cottage Dolls, says she did Dum and Dee and the Duchess.

My favorites are those made by doll artists—the hand produced, individually designed and costumed dolls. Here we find a depth of character not possible in the assembly line creations. Each artist tries to capture in the model her conception of the spirit of Alice in Wonderland.

They are marvelously different. Helen Bullard's hand-carved wooden "Alice" stands submissively before the intimidating Red Queen (*Ill.3*). Astry Campbell saw her as a sweet little girl in her all-porcelain doll with wig (not pictured), while Ann Parker's is modeled after the Tenniel illustrations and carries a plump pink felt pig. This particular doll has light brown hair, which I find an enchanting departure, but some are blond (*Ill. 4.*)

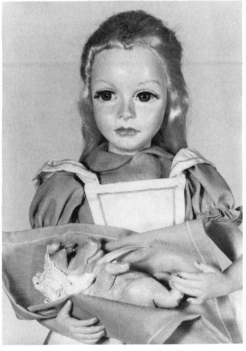

Illustration 5. 16 in. (40.6cm) papier-mâché and cloth. Head marked: J.C. Kintner 1978 Alice #1A.

Pittsburgh artist Joyce Kintner's first attempt to doll making was a molded papier-mâché "Alice" holding a laughing pig. The head was first sculpted in clay but the limbs are done freehand. The body is cloth. She looks a bit bewildered by the pig she carries (*Ill. 5*).

Cathy Redmond sculpts directly in the porcelain. She is best known for her colorful figures of English royalty, but she did make just one "Alice" marked with her insignia,

Illustration 3. Helen Bullard, NIADA. Carved wood, Alice: 7¼ in. (18.4cm); Queen: 8½ in. (21.6cm).

Illustration 6. Wonderland Fantasy by Betsey Baker, ODACA, IDMA. Alice: 10¼ in. (26cm); size of base: 28 in. (71.1cm). All dolls are marked on feet: Betsey Baker 1977.

Illustration 7. A tiny teaparty by Hemy Emmich. The rabbit is of porcelain.

Illustration 8. Cornhusk by June Kilgore. Alice: 5 in. (12.7cm). Marked on base: JK 79.

a cat. She has a wig instead of the usual carved hair. This Alice almost looks like an older person playing at being Alice because of the severity of the sculpture (not pictured).

Betsey Baker's specialty is character. Her Wonderland Fantasy is a joy. All the figures are sculpted directly in papier-mâché, a difficult medium to handle this way. Their outfits are vibrant with color and the whole array is filled with humor. The bodies are padded wire armature covered with cloth. They have their own special base (*Ill. 6*).

Alice is present in the miniature world, too. Hemy Emmich of Los Angeles does the "Mad Teaparty". The little bead heads on felt bodies with handsewn clothes and shoes are a tribute to nimble fingers (*Ill. 7*).

Unusual Wonderland scenes of beautifully-colored cornhusk are done by June Kilgore. "Alice" and the "White Rabbit" stand on a driftwood base with natural straw flowers (*Ill. 8*). She also does the "Mad Tea Party", "Alice" and the "Caterpiller". All accessories are handmade by her husband.

Specializing in a single type doll such as Alice could be the basis of a collection or, as with me, another facet of a most interesting and rewarding hobby.

THE NEW BABY

BY ALMA WOLFE

There's a new baby in town. Her arrival brings joy to children and collectors alike. Several years have elapsed since the last member of her "family," the Gerber baby doll family, delighted doll lovers of all ages.

During these years, many collectors had regularly checked Gerber Product labels, hoping to "see" that another Gerber baby doll was being offered. And now, "the biggest and the best" replica of the adorable trademark baby is available, not as a premium offer, but sold in the toy departments of leading stores, and also in many doll shops.

The new Gerber doll is "a remarkable likeness" of the "world's most famous baby face."[1] This dear face was "discovered" in 1928 when Gerber sponsored a contest to find a captivating illustration for their advertising.

"A small, unfinished charcoal sketch"[1] taken from a snapshot of Ann Turner, six months old, was submitted by artist, Dorothy Hope Smith. The judges were enchanted. It was the ideal portrait — "fresh and appealing."[2] The contest was won.

The lil' cherub's portrait became Gerber's symbol and was officially registered as their trademark in 1931. Through the years, this trademark has represented the company's commitment to provide babies with a well-balanced nutritional program. Today, Gerber offers babies not only a diversified line of 150 foods, but also accessories, toys and clothes.

In 1979, 51 years after the contest, the "real" baby is now Ann Turner Cook, a grandmother and chairman of the English Department at a Florida high school. And for the little people and the collectors, a new Gerber baby doll, unique and dear, is again available.

The renowned sculptor, Neil Estern, was commissioned to reproduce the winsome expression of the Gerber baby. He has truly "captured" the precious baby — the sweet smile, the open rosebud mouth, the expressive blue eyes, the wisps of hair.

Mr. Estern is well-known for his portraits of famous personages. He has "sculpted portraits for *Time* magazine and sculpted the portrait of J. Edgar Hoover that appeared on the cover of a 1971 *Life* magazine." One of his most famous works is "the portrait of John F. Kennedy for the Kennedy Memorial in the Grand Army Plaza, Brooklyn, New York."[1]

"Estern has been a doll sculptor for many American toy companies. With his wife, Anne, who designs fashions, hair pieces, make-up and frequently the overall finished look of her husband's dolls, Estern creates dolls from the initial concept stages to the prototype ready for production."[1]

The Atlanta Novelty Company of New York, a division of Gerber Products Company, is the manufacturer of the doll and introduced her at the American Toy Fair in February, 1979.

The new, soft-bodied doll is a cuddly 17 in. (43.2 cm) tall. Her arms, legs and head are vinyl. Her molded hair is sandy-brown. The Gerber Company had devoted considerable time to deciding whether to produce a boy or a girl doll. The final decision produced an innovative, charming doll. The author will "imply" the "girl" pronouns, for the doll is packaged wearing a white eyelet skirt — a lil' girl. Remove the skirt and you have a little boy in a checked romper.

The checked rompers, red or blue, are an integral part of the doll — the body. The white bib collar, with eyelet trim, enhances the costume and is removable.

She is barefoot. "Why?" collectors have asked. A Gerber spokesman says, "The doll is a baby doll and is designed for a young child."

Her flirty eyes intrigued a little girl at a recent doll show. "Real eyes," she said, as she watched the infant doll "look" from right to left, and then "cross" her eyes.

The sales slogan of the new doll is "Shouldn't your baby's first doll be the Gerber baby?" A slogan paraphrase for collectors could be, "Shouldn't your next baby doll be the Gerber baby?"

---

[1]Press releases regarding the Gerber trademark and new doll from the desk of Lisa Glenn, Burson-Marsteller, New York.

[2]Gerber baby doll box. Thanks to Mr. Adrian Borsetti, Manager, Toy Department, Woodward and Lothrop; Mrs. Cork Chaffee, Archivist, Gerber Products Company; Mr. John Whitlock, Director, Public Relations, Gerber Products Company. Photographs courtesy Burson-Marsteller.

The Gerber Company tradmark since 1931.

The "biggest and the best" replica of the famous Gerber baby.

A little girl and her new doll — the Gerber baby.

Dolling In And Around London

BY JAN FOULKE

It was a dream come true! Ever since high school days when I spent a whole year contemplating Big Ben and the Houses of Parliament pictured on the cover of my English literature book, I had a longing in the back of my mind to travel to London and see the sights with my own eyes. London, mother of the English-speaking world; center of the once so-powerful British Empire; home of Westminster Abbey, St. Paul's Cathedral, The Tower of London and Buckingham Palace; the place where Shakespeare, Dickens and other literary greats worked. And now I was really there, with my daughter as companion. And it was every bit as wonderful as I had always expected it to be!

The DOLL READER asked me to write about some of my experiences there relating to dolls. In this first article, I will discuss three museums. In a later article, I will write about the doll shops. Hopefully these will be of some help to you when you make your own "dream" trip to London.

Bethnal Green

Consider this museum a *must* on your London tour, and allow at least a half day to see it properly. Although Bethnal Green Museum is a branch of the world famous Victoria and Albert Museum, many London guide books have overlooked listing it. Easy to reach, Bethnal Green is just a short ride from downtown London via the underground (subway). The Bethnal Green station is only a half block from the museum's front door. A sign points

(From the 2nd Blue Book, Page 295) A Pierotti-type poured wax doll in original clothing with blown glass eyes and inset hair and eyebrows. *Emily Manning Collection. Photograph by Howard Foulke.*

the way, and it is impossible to get lost. The museum is devoted primarily to antiques of childhood—dolls, dolls' houses and toys—although there is also a small section displaying costumes.

Dolls are carefully displayed so that you can actually study them. Many are presented undressed so their bodies can easily be studied. Dressed dolls appear to be attired in original clothes. In most cases a tracing of the mark from the back of the doll's head is shown. Information about each doll in the exhibit is posted on small cards beside the doll, but for a few pence you can purchase a catalog which gives a little more information.

Dolls shown include examples from the factories of Bru (one of the very early ones with circle dot and crescent mark), Jumeau and Steiner, as well as other French makers. German dolls included a rare Kämmer & Reinhardt 109 girl, a beautiful Simon & Halbig 1469 lady character, a doll marked "Einco" with a very expressive character face (I saw quite a few of

(From the 2nd Blue Book, page 297, bottom right) An English wax doll with a slit in the top of her head for insertion of a wig. The glass eyes on this type of doll sometimes are made to open and close by means of a wire. *Emily Manning Collection. Photograph by Howard Foulke.*

these in England, but they seem to be more rare here in the United States) and a doll with adult body stamped H. Handwerck with an Armand Marseille 390 head, an interesting combination showing the relationship between these two companies.

The Bethnal Green's collection of wax dolls was outstanding as would be expected in London, which was, after all, the home of many of the finest wax doll makers. In addition to many lovely unmarked dolls were signed examples of the lovely life-like baby and child dolls from the latter half of the 19th century, by Meech, Marsh and Peck, as well as the more commonly found Montanari and Pierotti dolls. These were the luxury dolls of their time, with lovely blown glass eyes and real inset hair and eyebrows. Their clothes also were of the very finest fabric elaborately trimmed with many tucks, real lace insertion, ruffles and fancy satin ribbons. Also represented in the museum were many of the lady fashion dolls of the early 19th century, having heads of wax or wax over composition, and all wearing original attire. Other dolls of wax over composition, were of German and English manufacture and represent children in original attire. Some of these have eyes which

An early fully jointed Teddy Bear with long arms, big feet, long snout, hump and shoe-button eyes. One with personality plus! The tiny teddy has a child's face of celluloid. *H&J Foulke. Photograph by Howard Foulke.*

open and shut manually by means of a wire, and one of these wire-eyed dolls had an open mouth, quite an unusual feature.

England is also a great place to study wooden dolls whose history there dates back to the 17th century. Bethnal Green has a good selection

Pollock's Toy Museum, Scala Street, London , England. *Photograph by Beth Foulke.*

of wooden dolls from the 18th and 19th centuries. These are in a remarkable state of preservation, again displayed in original clothes. It is a real treat to see so many of these dolls, as they are relatively few and far between in the United States (unless you attended the last sale of the Winthrop Collection).

Many of the Bethnal Green dolls not only had original clothes, but also had complete wardrobes. The most spectacular was that of "Princess Daisy" an English wax doll of 1895, a presentation doll for the Princess herself. She had a cradle and

A French clown doll with bisque head by J. Verlingue, pressed cardboard torso and wooden limbs. Costume is all original. From *Pollock's Toy Museum. Photograph by Beth Foulke.*

a complete layette with a christening gown, a cap, a robe, three dresses, pillows, blankets, undergarments, jewelry, grooming items, bottles and feeding instruments. She was every doll collector's dream!

For people interested in miniaturia, the museum has a fine collection of dolls' houses, the earliest being a Nuremberg house of 1673, still retaining its stars on the roof. About 1700 Nuremberg law required that the stars be removed from the roofs of the houses as they had a tendency to blow off and presented a hazard to anyone passing by on foot.

Doll house furnishings are delightful, especially the variety of small dolls which live in the houses. Many are rare types, such as tiny glass-eyed parians, the parian with long blond molded hair, the Frozen Charlotte with bent knees to sit in a chair, the lovely carved woodens with real wigs and the parian man with a molded top hat.

Also fun was the display of 13 teddy bears dating from 1908–1975, large and small, presenting an array of bears with personality plus.

I did not mean to slight the museum's toy collection, but I spent so much time with the dolls, dolls' houses and costumes that I never had a chance to view the toys, which

I understand is a noteworthy grouping.

Pollock's Toy Museum

Pollock's is a fun place to spend a few hours. It is located in London and is easily accessible via the tube (subway), being just a few minutes walk from the Goodge Street Station to the corner of Whitfield and Scala Streets. Pollock's is a tiny corner house, its gaily painted exterior indicating the delights to be found inside. Steep winding stairs lead the way to three floors of tiny rooms full to the bursting point with treasures of Victorian childhood. No possible display space is wasted including the walls of the stairwells which are inset with recessed display cases. These contained dolls in ethnic costumes, Eskimo and American Indian dolls, as well as English peg-wooden varieties, Japanese and Chinese dolls.

After the magic lanterns and other viewing toys, lithographed-on-wood castles with soldiers and toy paper theatres came the doll displays. Two displays which we loved evoked the charm of by-gone days. They featured life-size rag doll boys with molded mask faces, painted features and real hair wigs dressed in Buster Brown fashion. One boy was riding a rocking horse which had glass eyes and a real horse hair mane; the other boy was rolling a hoop.

Another intriguing room was the Victorian playroom crammed full of dolls and toys including German

A cloth doll, all original, made by Dean's Rag Book Co. From *Pollock's Toy Museum*. *Photograph by Beth Foulke.*

bisque character babies, Rockabye babies and a large black bisque character baby. (The black babies must have been very popular novelties in England as they are much more common there than in the United States). What a delight! We were like children at a toystore window with our noses pressed against the glass which blocked off the doorway to this special room.

Fortunately, most of the dolls in Pollock's were properly identified, saving one from the frustration felt in many museums which simply display, but do not identify the dolls, or worse yet, give wrong information about the dolls.

As expected in a London museum, there were quite a few lovely poured wax dolls by such makers as Lucy Peck and Montanari. Also there were some interesting examples of wax over composition dolls. I was especially drawn to a group of pumpkin heads in original gauze dresses. Also on display was a good selection of bisque heads from the English potteries. Dolls marked "Melba" and Cecily" were among those exhibited. While these are not pretty dolls, they are interesting for the part they play in the overall history of dolls, especially to Americans as we seldom see one of

An early Jumeau doll with original mohair wig. From *Pollock's Toy Museum. Photograph by Beth Foulke.*

these dolls in the United States.

One room was so full of gorgeous bisque dolls, that it was difficult to know in which case to look first. There were two Simon & Halbig 1249 girls, always a favorite of mine, one sitting in an antique carriage, and a very large one dressed in her Sunday best and sitting quietly in a chair. An unusual Simon & Halbig 1299 character was sitting at an antique sewing machine . A sweet Kammer & Reinhardt 115A boy was playing with a tin toy.

Always a rag doll fan, I enjoyed the display of fine cloth dolls, including a group of characters by Norah Wellings and a printed-on-cloth girl by Dean's Rag Book. Beth enjoyed the 11 fine old Teddy Bears including a large one named "Edmund" of 1911 with his long arms and big feet and cute little "Eric" of 1906 with no hair left at all!

Again I have slighted the toys, dolls' houses and miniatures in favor of the dolls, but there was much to be seen in that area also.

Dolls in Wonderland

We rented a car for the day and drove down to Brighton, several hours from London, to this most delightful of all doll museums I have ever visited. It is easy to find as it is right along the seafront. Although it might be difficult to arrange a trip to Dolls in Wonderland, it is well worth the extra effort. The train runs to there, if you don't have access to a

car. (Driving in London is an experience unto itself. Beth drove; I navigated.)

In the first section of the museum, the dolls are shown in small lighted tableaux illustrating nursery rhymes and childhood stories. These are fun and very well done including accessories, and for the person who really wants to study dolls, this is an excellent place. Each doll is numbered and fully identified in a very detailed catalog. The emphasis of this museum is on bisque dolls; many of the rare German characters and desirable French dolls are included. This museum has just about everything including an A. Marque, Brus, all types of Jumeaus, Schmitt, Steiners, Kämmer & Reinhardt characters, Fany, A.T., Bébé Mothereau, A.M. characters, Kestner characters, Simon & Halbig characters, Heubachs and SFBJ characters, including a Poulbot.

In the second part of the museum, the dolls are in larger floor-to-ceiling displays, just crammed with dolls. The time we had to spend here went by too fast. There was so much to see with over 500 dolls that it was almost overwhelming.

There are quite a few other doll museums near London, which I did not get to visit. If your are planning a trip to England and want to visit doll museums, there is a very good guide *Discovering Toys and Toy Museums* by Pauline Flick available at Pollock's Toy Museum.

Dolling in & Around London
(Part II) - Markets & Shops

BY JAN FOULKE

Photographs by Beth Foulke

Illustration 1. A figurine collector's dream--a whole booth crammed full. This is just a tiny portion of those on display.

It is everyone's dream on a trip to find a sensational doll tucked away in the dusty corner of some tiny shop, or better yet to stumble onto a group of dolls for which the owner is asking a very low price. Most of us know that with today's awareness of dolls, this probably is not going to happen, but it might! So we go on looking. In this part of my article, I will tell you some places to search out dolls in London.

Portobello Road

This Saturday market has a world-famous name as far as antiques are concerned. We arrived by taxi, but the underground station is only several blocks away. Nearly all of the shops here are divided into tiny stalls, most only four feet wide and about as deep, to accommodate hundreds of dealers. The sidewalks in front of the stores and the street curbs are also lined with tables, leaving only a narrow space for walking along the sidewalk and down the middle of the street. Most arcades (inside areas) do not open until 9 o'clock, but the outside dealers are setting up by 8 o'clock which is a good time to arrive. By 10 o'clock the

streets are jammed, and you just get pushed along in a giant wave. Hang on to your companion or you are sure to lose each other. The taxi driver warned us to beware of the famous London pickpockets plying their ancient trade, who thrive in crowded places, especially street markets, but fortunately, we did not run into any. (At the Petticoat Lane market, there is a police van at the beginning of the street warning about pickpockets. Petticoat Lane is a fun street market for clothes, household goods and other items, but there are no antiques there.)

We noticed one creative feature here lacking in American outdoor markets: each outside table had round holes at the corners for insertion of a metal framework over which to throw a canvas to form a canopy in case of rain, which is almost sure to come everyday in London.

Since anyone on Portobello Road is likely to have a doll, we just started at the top of the road and worked down the hill. Here is a listing of some of the dolls we found: (Sizes

are approximate as I did not have a tape measure in my purse this time. I have converted all prices to the exchange rate of $2.25 to one pound.)

12in. (30.5cm) china heads with common hairdos, old cloth bodies, $45 each;

12in. (30.5cm) Heubach pouty with closed mouth, intaglio eyes, common face, but very nice body, $562.50;

16in. (40.6cm) Kestner character baby with painted eyes, $675;

7in. (17.8cm) A.M. 323 Googly, $562.50;

22in (55.9cm) S&H 1294 baby, $371.25;

22in. (55.9cm) SFBJ 301 child, $483.75;

18in. (45.7cm) Simon & Halbig 939, open mouth, composition body, $1125;

24in. (61cm) Jumeau, open mouth, $1125;

12in. (30.5cm) American Schoolboy with flocked hair, cloth body, $517.50;

15in. (38.1cm) Simon & Halbig 1079 girl, $315;

22in. (55.9cm) Black A.M. 351 baby with flirty eyes, composition body, $348.75;

26in. (66cm) Handwerck girl, composition body, $348.75;

16-17in (40.6-43.2cm) Heubach character child #8192, $337.50.

Out of all of these, the only dolls which were good buys were the black baby, the S&H 1294 baby and perhaps the Heubach #8192 character. The other dolls could be purchased for the same price or less at a doll show here in the United States. English collectors seem to favor the bisque, china, papier-mâché and wax dolls. We found no composition or hard plastic dolls in the shops or the market; bisque was predominent.

There are several dealers on Portobello Road who specialize in dolls, but the two with the best selection are Carol Ann Stanton at 109 Portobello Road (front left of arcade) and Grannie's Goodies (owned by Brenda Clark), 290 Westbourne Grove, just a few steps off Portobello Road, all the way in the rear of the arcade. Across from Brenda's stand is a dealer who has what must be the world's largest selection of bisque figurines, Heubach and others, at prices comparable to those in the United States. What a super display!

In shops of doll dealers, we found the following dolls:

24in. (61cm) A.M. 351 baby, composition body, $198;

24in. (61cm) Jutta character baby with flirty eyes, $641.25;

22in. (55.9cm) Simon & Halbig 121 character baby, large cheek rub, $337.50;

18in. (45.7cm) A.M. 351, black baby, composition body, $438.75;

26in. (66cm) Handwerck child, composition body, $675;

18in. (45.7cm) Simon & Halbig 1299 character child, $393.75;

6in. (15.2cm) Heubach pouty baby, intaglio eyes, $146.25;

24in. (61cm) SFBJ 301 child, $618.75;

20in. (50.8om) Tommy Tucker, composition body, $832.50;

20in. (50.8cm) Tete Jumeau, closed mouth, all original, $2700;

15in. (38.1cm) Bahr and Proschild toddler, $832.50;

small bathing beauties, common, $45-55;

pincushion dolls, common, $30;

20in. (50.8cm) Dream baby-type infant, $337.50;

16in. (40.6cm) Franz Schmidt character baby, $393.50;

18in. (45.7cm) shoulder head, kid body, closed mouth, $1001.25;

15in. (38.1cm) A.M. 351 Rockabye baby, composition body, $216.

A fairly good variety of dolls was available. Again, although a few of these would be nice buys for collectors, most could be bought here for the same price or less. I guess the days are gone when one could go to London or anywhere else and find dozens of dolls at bargain prices.

Allow plenty of time to spend at Portobello Road because the antique part of the market gives way to a fantastic fruit and vegetable market with bakeries, poultry and meat stalls; then to a clothes market, then to a junk market. We had tons of fun here Fruits and pastries were delicious.

Bermondsey Market

This Friday antiques market is across the Thames from London. Most of it is outdoors, but there is one large indoor section. This is not as large as Portobello Road and you should finish by noon. Go by taxi and get there early as things are in full swing by 7 o'clock.

There were quite a few dolls here. Some dealers specialize in dolls; some dealers have one or only a few. You have to look carefully. Take your own bags and wrapping. Nobody here has any. We bought a sweet 20in. (50.8cm) A.M. character baby for $112.50, but we had to stuff it in my purse as we forgot a bag! German open

Illustration 2.   25in. (63.5cm) Vinyl dolls at Hamley's, priced $90-100.

mouth girl dolls here ran from $395 to $450 for one about 22in. (55.9cm) with a composition body. Shoulderheads on leather bodies are very desirable in London and were all over $450 for medium sized ones with open mouths. Jumeaus with open mouths in 22-24in (55.9-61cm) sizes were $1350. Small German character babies with common marks were $225-285; medium ones were $285-335. This seemed to be a good place to look for small items, as it was not nearly so crowded as Portobello Road. We found some small pincushion dolls for about $9 each, not rare, but nice.

Individual Shops for Antique Dolls

There are at least half a dozen doll shops in London. Call before you go; the pay telephone is only two pence, the biggest bargain in town. Because of time problems---we did want to see Buckingham Palace, Westminster Abbey, Houses of Parliament, St. Paul's and the Tower of London also---we did not get to all of the shops. One not to miss is Kay Desmond's shop at 17 Kensington Church Walk. This is a charming little shop with a good selection of dolls and miniatures. Do not be discouraged if you cannot find it right away. It is off Kensington High Street and Kensington Church Street, and is a tiny walkway, just as the name says, behind Kensington Church! It is easy to reach

by underground, but you do need a map to find it. Kensington Church Street is lined with antique shops on both sides. In one where we stopped to look at Royal Doulton items, we found three tiny early peg-wooden dolls for about $10 each. We hoped to find cloth dolls by Norah Wellings and Chad Valley especially as they are English, but they are in short supply in London, apparently not highly esteemed at all. We found quite a few Lenci types, but only one real Lenci, faded and worn at $337.50. Lenci dolls are popular here and in great demand.

For small dolls and miniatures, do not miss Pat Walker's stall in the Antiquarius arcade. She has hundreds of tiny things. It is at 139 King's Road. Go in the entrance to your right, and she is just inside the door on your left. There are lots of general line dealers in this arcade with interesting small items, so plan to spend several hours here. Victoriana Dolls, a tiny shop at 112 Brompton Road, across from the large Harrod's Department Store, had the best selection of French dolls.

Here are some of the dolls we found in various shops:

24in. (61cm) Heubach Koppelsdorf character baby, $220.50;

18in. (45.7cm) Einco character baby, painted eyes, interesting face, $562.50;

14in. (35.6cm) Heubach pouty, common face, $596.25;

14in. (35.6cm) wood or composition head SFBJ character boy, $213.75;

tiny A.M. girl, 5-piece composition body, $184.50;

small Unis girl, 5-piece composition body, $78.75;

24in. (61cm) long-face Jumeau, $10,125;

7-8in. (17.8-20.3cm) open mouth German girl with jointed body, 4 original dresses in cardboard box, $787.50;

7in. (17.8cm) Simon & Halbig all bisque, with high black stockings, $472.50;

tiny all bisque pair with glass eyes, $175.50;

5½in. (14cm) all bisque with swivel neck, $191.25;

cloth Lupino Lane by Chad Valley, $78.75;

A.M. lady doll, flapper body, small size, $551.25;

wigged bathing beauty, $85.50;

all bisque Heubach character child with egg, $101.25;

pincushion doll, arms not extended, $56.25;

5½in. (14cm) all bisque with swivel neck, long blue stockings, $202.50;

7in. (17.8cm) all bisque Kestner girl with swivel neck, $281.25.

Modern Dolls

We were anxious to visit Hamley's Toy Store at 200 Regent Street, as it is an old one and their label is sometimes seen on antique English wax dolls. The guide book teased us by saying there were over 300 different dolls, but the store did not have nearly that many. That was a disappointment. Hamley's did have a few of the Old Cottage Dolls which are charming. The Welsh girl was $43, and the Pearly boy was $32. Their biggest rage the day we were there was a walking and talking doll from Gotz, West Germany. Ranging from 20-22in. (50.8-55.9cm) these vinyl dolls sold for $45-85, depending upon their outfits. People were lining up to buy them! Hamley's also carried a large selection of the Amanda Jane dolls in both black and white, baby and little girl versions. These cute dolls have large wardrobes available. The doll was about $5, and clothes ran from $3-5 per packaged outfit. Featured in one display cabinet were 25in. (63.5cm) vinyl lady dolls in lovely fancy costumes ranging in price from $90-100. Stuffed toys by Chad Valley were in abundance in the $20-36 price range. Most interesting for doll collectors were 6in. (15.2cm) copies of English peg-wooden dolls in nice costumes for $3.95.

Harrod's Department Store had a very small doll section, but surprisingly carried the Vogue Black Ginny for $7.80. Harrod's were also featuring 10-12in. (25.4-30.5cm) teddies by Chad Valley for $23.85. Old Cottage dolls were $38-40, but their supply was small.

Part of the fun of doll collecting is in the hunt. We enjoyed our doll roamings in London, and brought home a few goodies. I am sure your trip there will be great also!

NOTE: After this article was completed, information was received that Carol Ann Stanton closed her stand in Portobello Road and has opened a new shop, Pleasures & Treasures, at Hauley Road, Dartmouth Devon.

Illustration 3. *Amanda Jane* in a variety of outfits. In this country Neiman Marcus and The Enchanted Doll House carry these dolls.

Illustration 4. *Amanda Jane* baby.

The EFFanBEE Doll Company is one of America's oldest doll producers. Bernard E. Fleischaker ("F") and Hugh Baum ("B") formed the company in 1910. EFFanBEE is still producing high quality dolls. All EFFanBEE dolls are collectible but the most loved of all are the ones made in composition. EFFanBEE perfected the "satin smooth" finish for its composition dolls and this look still enchants doll lovers and makes the dolls from the company's "Golden Years" highly sought-after today. The dolls presented here are only a sample of the many outstanding composition dolls from EFFanBEE. Each doll shown is all-original.

by John Axe

Above: *Baby Dainty,* circa 1924. She is 14½ in. (36.9cm) with a cloth body that has a mama cryer. Her blond mohair wig is over molded hair and she has blue tin sleep eyes with lashes. She wears a yellow organdy dress over matching undergarments and has a matching bonnet. She is incised on the back of the shoulder plate:

EFFANBEE
BABY DAINTY

Right: *Bubbles,* circa 1925. Bubbles was the first big seller for EFFanBEE and she came in many sizes. This one is 16 in. (40.6cm) and has a cloth body with a cryer inside. She has yellow sprayed hair, blue tin sleep eyes, an open mouth with two upper teeth and a tongue. The white organdy dress is labeled: EFFanBEE// BUBBLES // REG. U.S. PAT. OFF. The back of the shoulder plate is embossed:

EFFANBEE
DOLLS
WALK - TALK - SLEEP
MADE IN U.S.A.

Patsyette Texas Ranger, 1936. Like all Patsyettes, the doll is 9½ in. (24.2cm) tall. She has painted red hair and the unusual painted blue eyes. Her outfit is red and white checked cotton. The felt hat has a round label reading: TEXAS // 1936 // CENTENNIAL. She is marked on the shoulders:
EFFANBEE
PATSYETTE
DOLL

Charlie McCarthy, circa 1938. He is 15¼ in. (38.7cm) tall with painted brown hair and eyes. A pull string through the back of the head makes him "talk." He is on a cloth body and wears a navy blue felt blazer with white felt pants. The shoes are composition. He is marked on the back of the shoulder plate:
EDGAR BERGEN
CHARLIE McCARTHY
AN
EFFANBEE PRODUCT

Patsy Tinyette Toddlers in Tyrolean costumes, circa late 1930s. They are 7¾ in. (19.8cm) tall. The boy's painted eyes are brown; the girl's are blue. The round buttons are from White Horse Inn, a gift shop, where they were purchased. The shoulders are marked:
EFFANBEE
BABY TINYETTE

Snow White, circa 1939. This variation of the Anne Shirley doll is 14½ in. (36.9cm) tall with an open mouth and four teeth, a blond human hair wig and green sleep eyes. The dress is pink taffeta trimmed in maroon. Her paper tag cites that she is "Snow White from Grimm's Fairy Tales." Her head is embossed EFFANBEE and the back is embossed:
EFFANBEE
ANNE-SHIRLEY

Patsy Ann, circa 1930. Patsy Ann is 19 in. (48.3cm) tall. This version has brown glass sleep eyes and a brown human hair wig. Her pleated organdy dress is labeled and she wears her EFFanBEE heart bracelet. She is marked across the shoulders:
EFFANBEE
"PATSY-ANN"
©
PAT. #1283558

Martha and George Washington Patsyettes. They have white mohair wigs and brown painted eyes. The clothing is organdy and felt. These dolls were sold as souvenirs at Mount Vernon in the 1930s and the 1940s.

Little Lady from the World War II years. She is 17½ in. (44.5cm) tall with brown sleep eyes. Due to scarcities of essential materials her wig is yellow yarn. The original box says that she is style #8500. She wears a long taffeta gown. The head and back are marked: EFFANBEE U.S.A.

Left:

Little Lady Gibson Girl from the 1940s. At 27 in. (68.6cm) she is the largest Anne Shirley/Little Lady doll. She has brown sleep eyes and a dark brown human hair wig. The blouse is white organdy and the skirt and matching umbrella are taffeta. Only the head is marked: EFFANBEE.

Right:

Anne Shirley, circa early 1940s. This 15 in. (38.1 cm) Flower Girl from a wedding party series wears a pink net dress over pink taffeta with matching pantaloons. She has a blond human hair wig and blue sleep eyes. The head is unmarked; the back is marked:

EFFANBEE
ANNE-SHIRLEY

44

Left: *Suzanne*
from the early 1940s.
She is 13½ in. (34.3cm)
tall with brown sleep eyes
and a dark blond mohair wig.
The sheer white gown is trimmed
in black lace. The back is marked:
SUZANNE
EFFANBEE
MADE IN
USA
Right: *Kewpie,* 1948. The 13 in. (33cm)
fully-jointed Kewpie is No. 9713 in the 1948
EFFanBEE catalog wearing this sunsuit. The doll is
described as "The original Rose O'Neill 'Kewpie'
Doll/a Cameo Doll Product." This doll is not marked.
Middle: *Candy Kid Champ,* 1948. He is 13 in.
(33cm) tall with painted brown hair and blue sleep
eyes. The boxing gloves are real leather. This is one
of the very last composition dolls from EFFanBEE.
Both the head and back are embossed: EFFANBEE.

This Is "Bubbles" By Effanbee Part I

BY PATRICIA N. SCHOONMAKER

Santa has one for every little girl

Illustration 1. Illustration from advertisement in *Ladies Home Journal* of December, 1926. Paper label reads: "This is Bubbles//Just Bubbling over with//life and laughter//An Effanbee Doll". This early version has the bent cloth legs with long stockings and lace-trimmed combination suit.

"Bubbles" was a new doll in 1925 although some of the earliest models are actually marked "1924" on back of the shoulder-yoke composition head. Other examples are marked "1924" as well as "Bubbles," making these dolls especially desirable as collector's items. "Betty Bubbles," "Charlotte Bubbles" and "Dolly Bubbles" were included in early advertising. Oftentimes such identities are merely a matter of being dressed in a specific costume, illustrating a catalog. Regrettably, many of the early Effanbee catalogs have been lost but we are ever hopeful that some copies will yet be discovered.

Bubbles was one of its makers first big commercial successes. It was designed by Bernard Lipfert who also created Patsy, Dy-dee, Shirley Temple and the Dionne Quints. We have felt that Bubbles was not fully appreciated by collectors, at least in former years. This may be due to the fact that this doll is not too difficult to locate, at least in one form or another. Yet in-depth study will reveal some versions of the doll that are extremely hard to locate. A challenge for museums (or private collectors) around the country, would be to assemble famous dolls by *groups*, especially those in original

costume, to make a record of the great variety of American production. It is the never-ending versatility that keeps doll collecting so fascinating.

The earliest catalog Doll Research Projects has acquired containing Bubbles advertising is Montgomery Ward, 1926. Just below the Bye-lo Baby is "Bubbles—Our Ray of Sunshine! One year old." This advertisement has never been reproduced before in any book and will give a clear picture of how to dress the doll for those not being fortunate enough to find her in original garments.

By-lo Baby and Bubbles were approximately the same age and to a degree, in competition. Although it was the rage to own a Bye-lo at this time, Bubbles might have been more appealing to many a child. She was not breakable (with reasonable care), she had composition arms completely to the shoulder and some versions had completely hard composition legs of a rosy hue. The expression was merry with dimples in the cheeks. Montgomery Ward offered sizes 25-1/2in. (64.77cm) at $11.48; 20-1/4in. (51.44 cm) at $9.25; 18in. (45.72cm) with cotton legs at $6.25; and 15-1/2in. (39.37cm) with cotton legs at $4.29. As well, there was a separately listed Effanbee Walking Bubbles which was 20in. (50.80cm) tall for $8.98. This is

the less common *Toddler* version. (The emphasis was on the babyhood of the doll.) Yet manufacturers usually managed to have more than one type to suit all tastes.

By 1927 Bubbles was featured as "Nationally Advertised." A sketch shows a young girl removing the bonnet to show the head. The sizes offered at this time have changed to 16in. (40.64cm), 18in. (45.72cm), 22in. (55.88cm) and 24in. (60.96cm). The two smallest were said to have cotton stuffed legs and bended knees like those of a real baby. We have never seen Bubbles in the version of dress shown in 1927 which is dotted swiss with a plain yoke and lace trim. The plain, soft organdy material is much more usual.

In 1928 Montgomery Ward proudly headlined, "This is Bubbles Effanbee" (see *Illustration 5*) and boasted that they were the exclusive mail order distributors for Bubbles dolls. This, no doubt, referred to retail catalogs since a very informative advertisement depicting different types of Bubbles dolls ran in the Butler Brother's Wholesale catalog of 1928 (see page 588 in Coleman's *The Collector's Book of Doll Clothes*). More elaborate clothing could add considerably to the price of the doll. Montgomery Ward offered five sizes this year: 16in. (40.64cm) at

"Bubbles"—Our Ray of Sunshine! One Year Old

She Goes to Sleep

You know some real Baby just like her—some year old baby with twinkling roguish eyes and one wet little finger that must always be pulled out of her rosy mouth before you can give her a kiss.

The forefinger on Bubbles' left hand just fits into her slightly opened mouth. Composition arms jointed at shoulders. Sleeping eyes. Sheer white organdy lace trimmed dress. Full length petticoat; bonnet with blue ribbon strings.

The two larger size "Bubbles" have composition legs, and they wear little combination suits, petticoats and soft pliable white leather bootees and half socks.

Six Photographs of Bubbles:
With each Bubbles Baby we send six of her photographs. Grandma and Aunty will certainly want one.

449 E 2545—
25½ inches tall... **$11.48**
449 E 2544—
20¼ inches tall..... **9.25**
Postage: 22¢ and 20¢ extra
• Two smaller sizes have cotton stuffed perfectly shaped legs. Diapers, long white stockings and shoes. Petticoats. Crying voices.
449 E 2543—
18 inches tall...... **$6.25**
449 E 2542—
15½ inches tall...... **4.29**
Postage: 18¢ and 16¢ extra

Illustration 2. From Montgomery Ward, 1926. Complete with her own "Carte de Visite." Somewhat enlarged from original for greater clarity.

$3.98; 17-1/2in. (44.45cm) at $4.79; 20in. (50.80cm) at $6.29; 22in. (55.88 cm) at $7.98 and 24in. (60.96cm) at $9.98. The two large sizes had voices which actually said "mama" and real leather booties, and the smaller sizes had cry voices and imitation leather booties.

Our 1929 Montgomery Ward catalog (St. Paul, Minnesota Edition) still carried a similar illustration with the headline, "I AM BUBBLES" and the same sizes as offered in 1928. We have not yet obtained a 1930 copy of Montgomery Ward's catalog, but Effanbee's "Lovums" with head that could be tilted from side to side or backward and forward, would soon supersede Bubbles.

Good Housekeeping of November, 1931 (as illustrated in our book *Effanbee Patsy Family and Related Delights*), offered the 13in. (33.02cm) Bubbles which cries and shuts her eyes in white organdy dress and cap with blue or pink jacket. As well, Pattern N-24 for a long dress, two long slips, bunting and sunbonnet was offered for 30 cents! (We have never been able to locate any of these patterns including those for the Patsy family.)

Effanbee advertised in the *Ladies Home Journal*, November, 1926,

The Adorable Baby from Toyland

Illustration 3. "The Adorable Baby from Toyland"; *Junior Home*, October, 1929. Here we see heart necklace and paper tag, frilly clothes, as well as the composition legs with short socks and shoes.

"Here they are, Children//The dolls with the golden heart//Santa has one for every little girl. Take your choice of these two adorable dolls. (Lovey Mary or Bubbles.) There is Bubbles, the wonder doll of her generation, just bubbling over with life and laughter. No little girl can cry or look cross with this darling doll in her arms. Bubbles' happy smile keeps you smiling too.

"Bubbles was modeled after an adorable real baby. She has rosy cheeks, the sweetest laughing face, beautiful big blue eyes that will go fast asleep, and precious little white teeth. And you ought to hear her cry for you!"

Illustration 4. Actual rotogravure newspaper advertising from December, 1927, showing heart necklace and paper tag on arm.

Illustration 5. Montgomery Ward's catalog (Oakland, Ca. Edition), 1928. Illustration slightly enlarged for greater clarity. The sketch of child shown with doll so greatly resembles "Bubbles" that one wonders if this could have been done from a photograph of the actual child who inspired the doll.

Also included is a description of "Lovey Mary" which appears to be a version of doll marked "Rosemary." No such marked doll, ie. "Lovey Mary," has ever surfaced. (Does anyone own a version with paper tags?) The company publicity continues, "The nice thing about these dolls is that they won't wear out. That is because they are Effanbee Dolls. You can play and play with them, and they will last until you grow up. Ask Santa please to bring you Bubbles or Lovey Mary, whichever one you prefer. Bubbles and Lovey Mary come in all sizes. Shown here they are 19" tall and cost $5.00. At all better-class department and toy stores.

"You can tell them, in your favorite department or toy store, by their dear little golden heart necklaces. Every Effanbee doll wears a golden heart."

Incredibly enough, any child could obtain a metal "gold" necklace marked Effanbee by clipping the magazine coupon and enclosing a six-cent stamp.

By December 1926 the headline was changed to, "Here Santa, is the Doll I want! The Doll with the golden heart." The advertising must have been quite successful as by April 1927 (with headline, "Oh Mother, how I'd love that doll for Easter or my birthday!"), the copy reads, "If your little girl was one of the many disappointed children because there weren't enough 'Bubbles' dolls for Christmas, you can now make her happy. There are thousands of new 'Bubbles' just sent out to foremost department and toy stores." The company again emphasizes that the dolls won't wear out and that every genuine Bubbles wears the golden heart necklace. The $3.00 size of 14in. (35.56cm) is newly-mentioned.

Our files do not include any magazine advertising for 1928 but by October, 1929, Bubbles is shown in *Junior Home* magazine. Most of the publicity is similar except for an over-enthusiastic boast, "See her smile, see her pout." Clothing mentioned were "lace trimmed baby clothes with a gay bonnet to match and dear little white booties—and the cutest rubber panties! You will be so proud of her and she is so happy that she makes you happy too." The "playmate" doll at this time is "Jan Carol"- none of which have shown up, so marked. Has anyone this doll with original paper tags? She appears to be a version of Rosemary, the special designation due to her costume of the period. Bubbles now offers children a golden heart necklace but the price has jumped to ten cents!

By April of 1931 Bubbles was of-

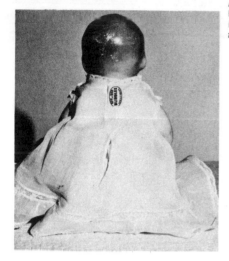

Above:
Illustration 6. Back view showing Effanbee label, so desired by collectors but not mentioned in their advertising. Red, white and blue.

fered under the headline, "Oh Mother, How I'd love that Doll" (along with choice of Patsy) as a Premium doll, sent free for three subscriptions of Junior Home magazine for $7.50 collected.

The advertising copy now reads, "Modeled after a real live baby who laughed and cooed all day. No little girl can be cross or unhappy with this doll in her arms. Rosy dimpled cheeks, beautiful big blue eyes that open wide or go fast asleep. She can put her little finger in her mouth—a rosebud mouth with tiny pearly teeth.

"Bubbles is 14" high, has a sweet little voice and eyes that open and close. Movable arms and legs. Attractively dressed with shoes and socks." In November, 1931, a choice of three "Gift Dollies" was given, Baby Lamkin, Bubbles or Patsy." Little teeth in her tiny mouth" are mentioned as one of Bubbles' fine points.

Tiny Town Alice and Marie

by THELMA BATEMAN

© 1976 Hobby House Press, Inc.

Illustration 1. Lenna Lee's Tiny Town Dolls, 4½in (11.5cm).

If Mommie is listening, she will soon be checking up on these two little sisters. No sound is coming from the cello but jumping noises from the music room accompanied by a piano? How could this be? Want to bet *Marie* will lose her jump rope, at least for a time?

These darling little dolls were made in San Francisco, California, from 1949 on through at least 1955 by Alma Le Blanc, doing business as "Lenna Lee's Tiny Town Dolls."

The trademark was registered January 11, 1949, number 529394.

Both dolls are alike except for color of hair and type of clothing. *Alice* has a small silver tag once fastened to her wrist with "Tiny Town Dolls" printed in black on one side and "Alice" on the other. *Marie* probably had a similar tag.

The nicest thing about these little dolls is the fact that they are made on a wire armature of some sort and their feet are molded metal,

painted as white shoes or black slippers and properly weighted to stand alone. Their arms and legs are wound with cord and the hands are felt, mitten type. The molded face is also of felt with delicately painted features. Nostrils are indicated; eyes on both dolls are painted blue with black lashes, *Alice*'s mohair wig is blonde with a black ribbon; *Marie*'s wig is a lovely auburn tied with a narrow yellow ribbon. Both have cupids' bow mouths.

Marie wears a white lacy short-sleeved thin cotton blouse and a corduroy jumper with the tiniest ribbing and flowers painted on the waistband, front and straps. This simulates embroidery and is charming. Both girls have simple white undies. *Alice*'s medium blue dress with plain upper and gathered skirt has tiny lace around bottom of full skirt and a narrow black ribbon band around the skirt about 1in (2.5cm) above the lace; simple but attractive and very "Wonderlandish."

Girls, here comes Mother!

This Is "Bubbles" By Effanbee Part II

  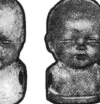   

Eight phases in the life of a perfect doll. **BUBBLES**

by Patricia N. Schoonmaker

To tell the full story of "Bubbles" we must introduce you to Effanbee's "Honeybunch." She was a new doll in 1923, following the first copyright for the "Bye-Lo Baby" in 1922. Although the company created "Baby Effanbee," its own composition version of a Bye-Lo, they also issued a flange-neck Bubbles, identical as far as basic sculpture, eyes, mouth, etc. Yet the original identity was Honeybunch, *not* Bubbles! The hands are composition, wired onto muslin cloth arms, the legs are cloth with a seam up the front and the back and there is a mama voice. The marking is: EFFANBEE//HONEYBUNCH//Made in USA.

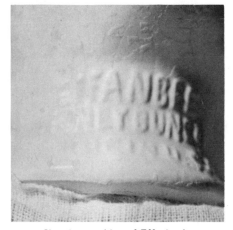

Showing marking of Effanbee's "Honeybunch," 1923.

The doll wears a long cotton slip with sleeves and christening gown. The height of the one pictured is 12-1/2in. (31.8cm) with head circumference of 9-3/8in. (23.8cm). There is a molded tongue with open mouth, and two glued-in teeth with red felt behind them. We have not found this doll pictured in any doll book to date. Surely there are others? It appears the model was discontinued in favor of the more deluxe Bubbles who could wear short sleeves and pose her arms in various positions.

The following is from a publicity

Early Effanbee publicity photograph for new doll "Bubbles," 1924. (Eight phases in the life of a perfect doll.) From left to right: Showing front and back half; two halves glued together; head sanded and cement on seam; eyes punched out and enamel dipped; rosy cheeks and hair sprayed on; complexion coat added, brows, lips: complete with eyes, brows, teeth.

story originating with Effanbee describing Bubbles (see photo above):

"It seems almost incredible that our loveliest, most childlike American dolls are made of such unromantic substances as wood flour, flake glue, rosin, starch, and other similar ingredients. But out of a doughlike mixture made of these ingredients manufacturers produce almost unbreakable composition heads. The mixture is put into heated steel presses to make the front and back of the head and shoulders, and then the two halves are glued together, the seam is ground smooth and, in the better quality of dolls, is covered with cement. The heads that are molded with the neck and shoulders, including the armpits, are less likely to break than those with the short neck and shoulders."

One drawback from the collector's viewpoint was that the steel-sprung arms sometimes unfastened causing the arms to be lost. A number of the dolls are found with replacement arms. The mechanism for inserting the eyes

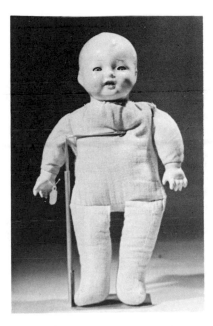

Full-length view of Honeybunch, 12-1/2in. (31.8cm) high; undressed to show body type.

Four sizes of Bubbles in original clothing. From left to right: 13in. (33cm), 16in. (40.6cm), 16-1/2in. (41.9cm) and 17-1/4in. (43.8cm) tall.

All-original clothing on Bubbles, 17-1/4in. (43.8cm) tall.

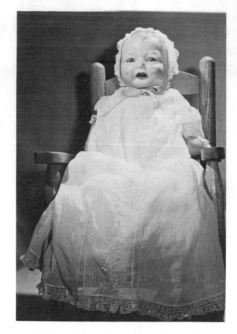

25-1/2in. (64.8cm)—Largest baby made. White doll modeling antique christening clothes.

with two shorter strokes just above it to denote a laughing expression. This costume is quite different with stitched ribbon frill at neck and on matching bonnet. Sleeves are a straight band with a row of pink embroidery trim. The skirt has no ruffle and the dress front is trimmed with two rows of pink machine-embroidered rosebuds and leaves. The original Bubbles woven label was sewn into the left-back yoke seam. We have clipped it out carefully and resewn it to the front yoke so that it may be seen when the doll is on exhibit. (We hope this is a forgivable change of authenticity.) This doll once wore rubber pants.

The next largest baby doll, courtesy of Virginia Tomlinson, is 17-1/4 in. (43.8cm) tall. Marking is EFFANBEE//BUBBLES//Copr. .924//Made in USA (with no oval). The teeth are glued in the open mouth. The forefinger goes into the mouth but the thumb is straight out on the hand. The legs are all-composition. This size's markings: EFFANBEE//BUBBLES// CORP. L924//Made in USA. The straight yoke of this dress is very plain making one suspect this model originally had the fancy knit bonnet and sweater or pink or blue silk jacket seen in Butler Brothers catalog. There is no yoke in the back of the dress and original label is attached at neckline. The ruffle material is a dainty ribbed organdy, lace-edged.

Another version of medium-sized baby is 16-1/2in. (41.9cm) long, head circumference 12in. (30.5cm), but

was unique, with a steel spring device making it nearly impossible to poke them out. Publicity pointed out that this often happened to imported dolls.

The smallest Bubbles (as opposed to the toddler) is difficult to locate yet it was the least expensive. Our own example is only 13in. (33cm) with legs extended, head circumference 9-3/8in. (23.8cm). The teeth and tongue are molded in the composition and the mouth is open. (One small toddler version was issued with open-closed mouth, no opening.) The legs on this tiny baby are curved cloth. With this size only, it is the thumb rather than the forefinger which fits into the mouth, with all fingers extended out. Marking is a surprising EFFANBBE (two B's instead of E)//Bubbles// Copr. 1924//Made in USA. Her original white organdy dress compares to *Illustration 2*, shown in Part I

Next in our size comparison is a baby approximately 16in. (40.6cm) tall, head circumference 10-5/8in. (27 cm). The forefinger points up to the mouth and the thumb is modeled inward towards the palm. What seem to be celluloid teeth are applied behind mouth opening. This marking is the familiar EFFANBEE//DOLLS// WALK TALK SLEEP// within an oval design with Made in USA below. The original dress is similar to *Illustration 2* shown in Part I with cross-bar dimity yoke and a bit more of a sleeve and ruffle similar to *Illustration 3*, Part I, with lace insertion on the ruffle.

Our second medium-sized baby has the same markings and characteristics of the preceeding doll. She is in nearly mint condition except for the brows being worn away. The original painting of these was not the typical arched brow, but an inverted stroke

with stuffed cloth legs, marked with doll name and 1924 year. The blue romper may not have been original. Loaned by Frankie James.

Last of all in the Baby Bubbles are the 25-1/2in. (64.8cm) "superstars," both white and black, from the Frankie James Collection. This largest size does not have composition legs to hip; legs are wired-onto a fitted muslin top beginning just above the knee. The black Bubbles were made to special

All-original Bubbles with tag and heart necklace (no longer on metal chain).

25-1/2in. (64.8cm) Black Baby Bubbles, a rare model. The doll models antique christening clothes.

order. The tin eyes are brown and the composition parts are painted a rich chocolate shade. The hair is black. It would be hard to describe the tremendous appeal of this rare doll, larger than a newborn baby. The head circumference is 17-1/4in. (43.8cm); teeth are celluloid. The right arm is bent, and the thumb of the right hand is bent into the palm. It has the inverted brows of three strokes still somewhat in evidence. There is a seam up the body front; the back is one-piece heavy muslin. These two dolls sit in matching child chairs, modeling christening clothes of real babies. The owner, Mrs. James, often hosts Brownies and other groups of young girls to view her collection. The largest Bubbles pair are the center of attention, with youngsters always begging to pick them up.

Contrasting the smallest—13in. (33cm), and the largest—25-1/2in. (64.8cm) Baby.

CISSETTE

10in (25.4cm) doll by Madame Alexander

by THELMA BATEMAN

Illustration 1. 10in (25.4cm) *Cissette* by Madame Alexander; in all-original clothes. 1957.

Candles and soft music, flowers, jewels and frothy lace surround lovely *Cissette*'s wedding day.

This dewey-eyed debutante with shining auburn hair is made of the finest hard plastic bisque-like in color and texture. She is jointed at the neck, shoulders, hips and above the knees and can walk, with a bit of help. Her tiny feet are designed to wear very high heels and with her bridal gown she has silver slippers, nylon hose and ONE blue garter.

Cissette's beautiful bouffant dress with its scalloped edge and all-over leaf circle design is of luscious lace. The tight sleeveless bodice has a veiling scarf and a circle of tiny flowers fastens the long sheer veil to her head.

Cissette's blue eyes have long lashes and sleep. Her tiny closed rosebud mouth is adorable. The modeling and tinting of her whole person is exquisite; fingers separated, toes defined, ears pierced, Saran wig of tosca shade.

Would that every young bride could have such beauty of face and figure; the perfection of *Cissette*'s attire.

This lovely doll, in all-original clothes, first came out in 1957.

This Is "Bubbles" By Effanbee Part III

BY PATRICIA N. SCHOONMAKER

THE TODDLERS

The much desired toddlers were actually advertised as "Walking Bubbles." Collectors usually favor dolls who can stand since they are easier to pose in action and display very attractively. A 20in. (50.8cm) size was advertised in Montgomery Ward's 1926 catalog. The copy reads: "Bubbles is looking for a mother. She's standing with her finger in her mouth and feet wide apart, uncertain of her balance and very anxious to come to your arms. Perfectly proportioned, she looks like an adorable baby. Her unbreakable composition head has dimpled cheeks, painted hair and eyes that go to sleep. Her mouth is slightly open so that one of her fingers will just slip into it. She has full composition arms jointed at the shoulders, dimpled composition legs, a cotton stuffed body and finest quality voice that says "Ma-Ma." She's just right in size, not too large or too small to be a real playmate.

"You'll love her exquisite little blue silk crepe dress trimmed with white lace. She wears a hood to match with dainty lace ruching and pink silk ribbon ties; petticoat and bloomers to match; shoes and mercerized blue stockings. We never sold a more

beautiful or lifelike doll at this price. Height, over all 20in. ... $8.98." (The price of a 16½in. (41.9cm) bisque Bye-Lo Baby was $8.25.)

Illustration 2 shows an earlier version 13in. (33.0cm) with the open-closed mouth and two painted teeth. (This would have been a cost saving procedure at the time.) A painted-eye Bubbles was made as well.

Illustration 3 shows a 16½in. (41.9cm) tall toddler with set-in teeth rather than molded composition ones and tannish blond hair rather than the usual golden blond. She does not say Bubbles in her marking but has simply "EFFANBEE // DOLLS //WALK-TALK-SLEEP" within an oval and "Made in USA" beneath. The toddler legs are not as heavily dimpled and curved as a larger size but very appropriate.

Illustration 2. Rare open-closed mouth toddler, no opening; two painted teeth; 13in. (33cm) tall: *Celina Carroll Collection.*

Illustration 3. 16½in. (41.9cm) toddler in original pink sheer china silk dress and bonnet trimmed with fine Valenciennes lace; 2in. (5.1cm) hem is hemstitched; hand embroidery on yoke and bonnet band.

EFFANBEE Walking "Bubbles"

Bubbles is looking for a mother. She's standing with her finger in her mouth and feet wide apart, uncertain of her balance and very anxious to come to your arms. Perfectly proportioned, she looks like an adorable baby. Her unbreakable composition head has dimpled cheeks, painted hair and eyes that go to sleep. Her mouth is slightly open so that one of her fingers will just slip into it. She has full composition arms jointed at the shoulders, dimpled composition legs, a cotton stuffed body, and finest quality voice that says "Ma-Ma". She's just right in size, not too large or too small to be a real playmate.

You'll love her exquisite little blue silk crepe dress trimmed with white lace. She wears a hood to match with dainty lace ruching and pink silk ribbon ties; petticoat and bloomers to match; shoes and mercerized blue stockings. We never sold a more beautiful or lifelike doll at this price. Height, over all 20 inches.

49 E 2568 . . . .$8.98

Postage, 22¢ extra

Illustration 1. From Montgomery Ward's 1926 catalog. (The prices given are **not** the prices of today.) This was an expensive, quality item. Several dolls on the same catalog pages ranged in price from less than one dollar to of two and three dollars. Trade language for the doll was "Walking Bubbles", rather than the collector's term "Toddler."

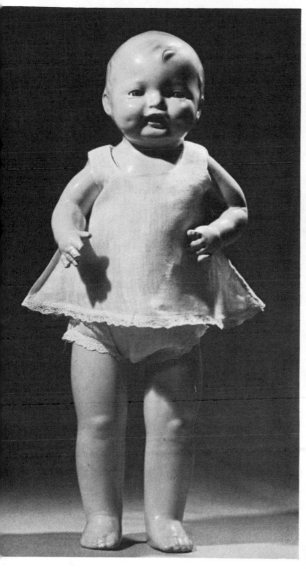

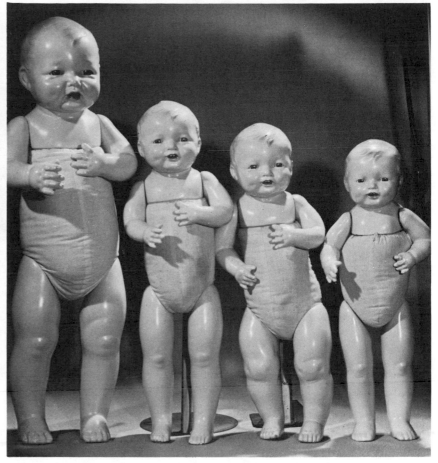

Illustration 5. Comparative view of toddlers 24in. (61cm), 19in. (48.3cm), 17-5/8in. (44.8cm) and 16½in. (41.9cm) tall. Doll on left: *Virginia Tomlinson Collection*. Doll, second from left: *Judy Johnson Collection*.

Illustration 4. 16½in. (41.9cm) toddler modeling original pink mercerized one-piece combination suit and very brief slip. This the length intended under a short, full dress.

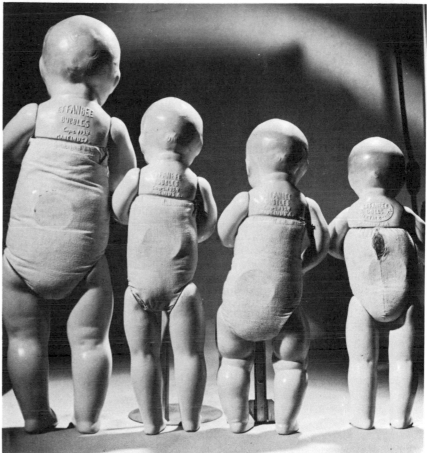

Illustration 6. Rear view showing differences in leg shapes, yet all original. Doll on left: *Virginia Tomlinson Collection*. Doll, second from left: *Judy Johnson Collection*.

Illustration 7. Close-up to show markings. First three are alike except for spacing and the fourth shows often-used oval with no Bubbles name. See accompanying story. Doll on left: *Virginia Tomlinson Collection.* Doll, second from left: *Judy Johnson Collection.*

Illustration 8. Rare form of Bubbles doll as a swing-leg MaMa doll; has 19 (C) 24 above the Effanbee within an oval mark; 20in. (50.8cm) tall. This is a different marking combination than all others. *Judy Johnson Collection.*

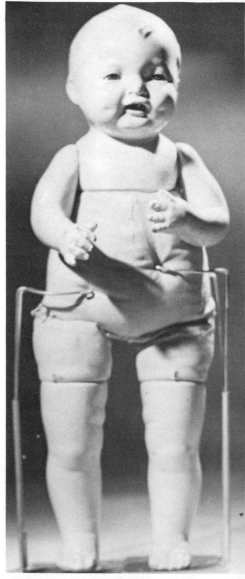

The original costume of pink sheer china silk is now very fragile but still intact. The length is much shorter than that of the 1926 version. Fine Valenciennes lace was used to trim the dress yoke and bonnet and net ruching was used about the face. The bonnet and dress yoke were embellished with a hand embroidered daisy flowerlet and leaf design. Mercerized pink loop braid was utilized on the dress yoke and bonnet ruffle. From the center neck to the bottom of the hem is a bit more than 6in. (15.2cm). The crown of the bonnet is gathered white lace. The very brief pink one-piece combination suit and slip is of mercerized cotton and trimmed in white lace.

The next largest toddler measures 17-5/8in. (44.8cm) with a head circumference of 12in. (30.5cm). Two teeth are molded in, yet the mouth is open in back of the molded tongue. The forefinger goes into the mouth when the arm is raised; the thumb is molded out straight. The marking is "EFFANBEE // BUBBLES // Copr. 1924//Made in USA" with no oval enclosure. The legs on this model must have been specially designed as for a plump baby just barely walking. There are two dimples in each knee. The soft voile dress has raglan sleeves, net ruching at the neck and on the sleeves. There is a pink hemstitched front panel and hem; and there are bits of blue hand embroidery on the panel.

The 19in. (48.3cm) doll has the same 12in. (30.5cm) head circumference, the difference in size due to the leg mold. The legs are actually "girl" legs, slender of ankle and more elongated, an off-beat version. (They have not been changed around.) This leg mold was used on one edition of "Rosemary" which was not the more usual swing-leg model. This *maybe* the advertised "Joan Carol" but unless one is found with the original paper tag it cannot be proven.

The arms on the 19in (48.3cm) toddler have the thumbs molded out and forefinger tilted up for mouth. The left hand has curved fingers with the middle two together. The teeth are molded in the upper lip and there is an open mouth with felt behind it. The marking is "EFFANBEE//BUBBLES// COPR. 1924//Made in USA" with no oval enclosure.

The largest doll in the size grouping is a beautiful BIG 24in. (61.0cm) in superior condition. She is marked the same as the previous doll with both the Bubbles name and the year 1924. This one has glued-in separate celluloid teeth, with felt behind the opening. The thumb on the right hand is molded under into the palm. There are still red marks on the nails and knuckles in the style of the German bisque dolls.

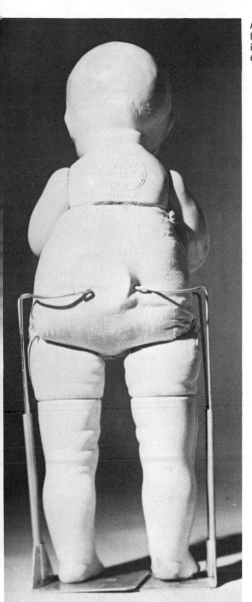

Illustration 9. Rear view of the swing-leg Bubbles MaMa doll showing baby wrinkles in legs and body detail. *Judy Johnson Collection.*

A variation of the chubby leg toddler is a swing-leg MaMa doll approximately 20in. (50.8cm) tall, with a head circumference of 13¼in. (33.7cm). The legs have two baby wrinkles above each knee, exactly suitable for this version. (This leg mold is also used on one "Rosemary" edition which had been a puzzler since that doll is an older version of child.) This doll has a third variation of marking with 1924 and a C within a circle (copyright) between 19 and 24. Below this is the familiar "WALK-TALK-SLEEP" within the oval (under "EFFANBEE//DOLLS" also within the oval) with "Made in USA" beneath. (Does anyone have this in other sizes and in original clothes?) A similar doll in a very large size, possibly 30in. (76.2cm), was seen at one time. The leg shape was like the solid fat ones of large Effanbee mama dolls. The doll was in mint condition except for the loss of its garments and had not been changed around in any way. No advertising has been found on these special models, yet they were issued.

By September, 1932, Effanbee was introducing the NEW "Bubbles," of real live rubber. *Playthings* magazine had two full pages from Effanbee which advised retailers to "Cash in on the popularity of the *New Bubbles* Baby." Made of the finest quality real live rubber. Our new ingenious publicity campaign will bring thousands of Mothers and Children to your store. Be sure and display Bubbles as prominently as the Patsy Family. DON'T FORGET PATSY and her famous family, including Babykin (Patsy Baby). The "staple" line of the doll field, PATSYETTE, PATSYKIN, PATSY, PATSY JOAN, PATSY ANN, PATSY LOU, PATSY BABYKIN, PATSY FLUFF, AND SKIPPY. FLEISCHAKER & BAUM, Creators of DOLLS THAT ARE DIFFERENT, 45 E. 17 Street, New York."

The head of this doll was composition, with glassene eyes and two upper and lower teeth. The original and most famous "Bubbles" was no more. The "new" edition appears to have been the beautiful LOVUMS with painted hair, with only the rubber body causing her identity to be "new Bubbles." Still later the company would issue a vinyl Bubbles, circa 1960, with still another different face.

Illustration 11. From *Playthings* magazine, September, 1932.

Illustration 10. Close-up to show different marking from all others. 19-(C) 24 above the oft used oval insignia. Courtesy of Judy Johnson.

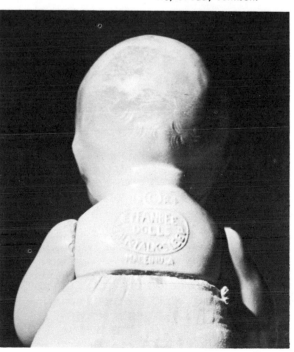

55

The Evolution of Baby Grumpy

by PATRICIA SCHOONMAKER

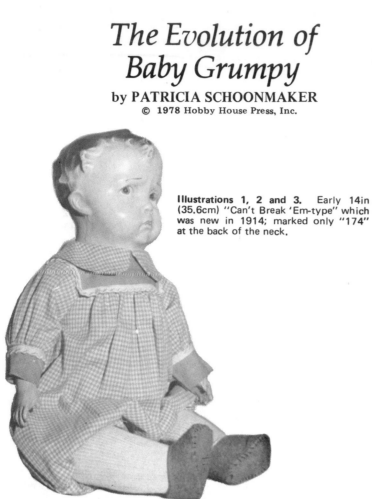

Illustrations 1, 2 and 3. Early 14in (35.6cm) "Can't Break 'Em-type" which was new in 1914; marked only "174" at the back of the neck.

Illustration 1.

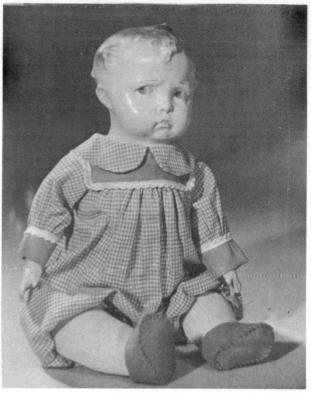

Illustration 2.

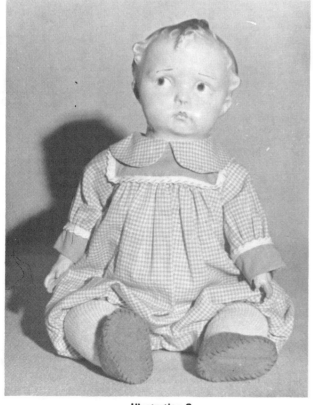

Illustration 3.

There is no area left in the doll collecting world still needing in depth research study as does the American composition doll. It is a fascinating field, although still clouded with much confusion for the average collector. We have studied these dolls since the 1950s and find many questions still to be answered. Fortunately, there is now considerable interest in bringing about the solution to many of the mysteries. Comparison of many similar dolls tells us much. (In time, a "put-together" doll becomes evident. Rare is the factory doll of which only one or even one dozen were made; the truth is likely one hundred dozen or more.)

According to the Colemans who have access to much source material, *Baby Grumpy* was new in 1914. The earliest advertising in "Doll Research Files" is 1915, which states that Effanbee Character Dolls are the sensation of the toy world - true products of the largest American doll factory. "Baby Grumpy is only one illustration of the many sweet-faced dolls with life-like childish character faces," they claim. Another advertisement of the same year explains that other models have smiling, happy faces and the buyer would find them in all baby moods. This emphasis on character faces followed Germany's lead in 1908 with competition among outstanding artists for realistic dolls. (American manufacturers made extravagant claims for dolls, many of which were

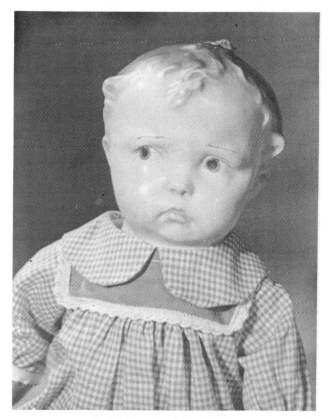

LEFT: Illustration 4. Close-up of the early "Can't Break 'Em-type."

RIGHT: Illustration 5. Advertisement from *The American Woman,* November 1916.

Made in America

BABY GRUMPY is the doll sensation of the year. Her face is a wonderful reproduction of a charming baby in a passing moment of petulancy. Every mother will see her child in Baby Grumpy. The complexion is truly wonderful, but the best part of it is that it is absolutely waterproof and unbreakable. You may drop her on a hardwood floor without doing any damage. Baby Grumpy stands 14 inches high and is fully jointed, so that she will sit down and place her hands in any position desired. She comes fully dressed just as shown in the picture; her clothes may be taken off and put on and additional dresses may be made as desired. Her dress is fancy white pique, lace-trimmed around neck, and with hem, sleeves, and yoke edged with pink - and - white trimming. She wears white stockings and white pique hat with pink cord and balls, held in place by an elastic under chin. Baby's cheeks are pink, her mouth red, eyes blue, and hair light.

SPECIAL BARGAIN OFFER. If you will send us a club of **four** new subscriptions to The American Woman at our regular subscription-price of **25 cents** each, we will send each subscriber this paper one year, and we will send you Baby Grumpy (Premium No. B 1600).

Illustration 6. Advertisement from *Ladies' Home Journal,* December 1916.

not characters, such as naming a sober, expressionless doll "Jolly Jack"); but *Baby Grumpy* actually was a character doll of touching expression. Many of the first American dolls were at least inspired, if not actually copied right off the German originals. There is a Grumpy-type bisque model of superb creation by Heubach, figurine or doll, as well as a rare S.F.B.J. doll. In turn, some excellent bisque models of *Baby Grumpy* have been made in later years by our current doll artists, making him more preservable than the composition model.

Some of the earliest specimens of *Baby Grumpy* are marked "DECO." Dorothy Coleman states that this is a marking of Otto Ernst Denivelle, an early pioneer of a secret formula for composition dolls. Effanbee, Amberg and Gund were to use his formula in time. Whether he could have owned the mold or sculpture of the "Can't Break 'Em" type doll is unknown at present, but the early models are not marked Effanbee, although some other dolls, early enough to be stuffed with ground cork, are marked. One 1915 ad states, "If a doll hasn't our tag it isn't an Effanbee." This was a circular paper tag which has been reproduced in early advertising. It read: "Guarantee - This toy is made under sanitary conditions of the most durable and expensive materials and by the most modern machinery. It is guaranteed to give satisfactory wear. Signed, Fleischaker and Baum, New York, EFFANBEE."

Our own earliest *Grumpy*, stuffed with ground cork, is marked only "174" at the back of the neck, and measures 14½in (36.9cm). The finish is hard and smooth with the mold seam running just behind the ear and over the top of the head. A knife had been used to smooth rough edges but no further sanding had been done. The counterpart in gingham romper and bonnet, sketched on a *Good Housekeeping* toy page of 1916, is similar to one shown in an advertisement of that year. The price given was $1.25, although ads of 1915 say from 50 cents and later, from 65 cents. This same type was shown in 1919 premiums and was also made in 1920. The verse by Claudia Cranston was as follows:
"Though Baby Grumpy wears a frown,
She's sweet and pink and soft as down,
And what she needs more than
   another
Is just a little patient mother.

Grumpy

Given for Eight Subscriptions

No. 6173. It is that winsome little frown that gives Grumpy her charming personality.

Baby Grumpy stands 14 inches high and is fully jointed; she will sit down and place her hands in any position. She comes fully dressed as shown in the picture; her clothes may be taken off and put on, and additional dresses may be made as desired. Her dress is white pique, lace-trimmed around neck, and with hem, sleeves, and yoke edged with pink-and-white trimming. White stockings, white pique hat with pink cord and balls, held in place by an elastic under chin. Pink cheeks, mouth red, eyes blue, and light hair.

Grumpy's head is made of unbreakable bisque; her features are permanently stamped.

Illustration 7. Advertisement from *The American Woman,* October 1919.

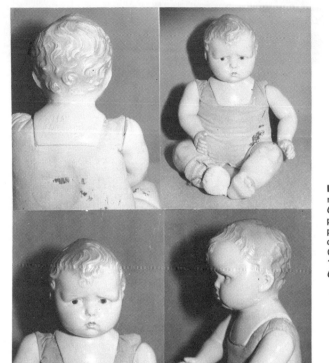

Illustration 9. Second rare version of *Baby Grumpy* with full composition arms and composition legs; marked in oval "EFFANBEE//Baby Grumpy//1923;" new in 1924. *Madeline Selfridge Collection.*

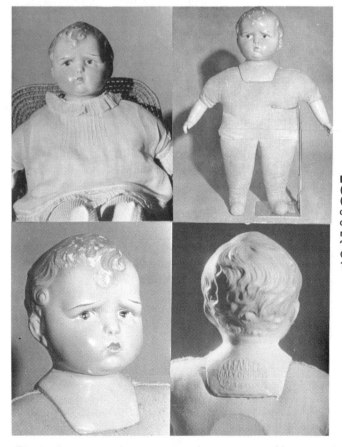

Illustration 8. 17½in (44.5cm) composition (wood pulp) *Baby Grumpy* designed by E. Peruggi; original little girl clothes; marked within oval "EFFANBEE//Baby Grumpy//1923;" new in 1923.

Remember you are just as grumpy
When your sense of humor's humpy,
So pet her up on Christmas day
And let her have her own sweet way."

Next evoked the first wood-composition *Grumpy,* which was designed by E. Peruggi, bore the Effanbee name on the shoulder head and

stood about 17½in (44.5 cm). Within an oval frame, the "EFFANBEE// BABY GRUMPY//Copyr 1923" was boldly marked in three lines. Our own example has the original clothes which are as wide as she is. There are lacy, little girl clothes which identify her as either *Grumpy Joan* or *Grumpy Gladys,* as opposed to *Peter* or *Billie.* (See Coleman's *Collector's Encyclopedia of Dolls*). This is not the same doll as the 1914 original, but the basic facial expression is the same. The first doll had deeply incised eyes.

By 1923 the *Grumpy* mama-doll was cotton-stuffed with a shoulder head, wire-on arms about to the elbow, a muslin torso, with flesh-colored material for the legs only. The seam was down the front and back of the leg with a squared-off toe. There was wonderful detail in the curly hair over the entire back of the head. The eyes were much more deep-set on this doll though not incised, with brows pulled down in discontent. By 1924 full composition arms (of heroic proportions) had been added, as well as composition legs to above the dimpled knees. These may have been the only two years these particular models were issued as they are very difficult to locate. We have seen only three in 25 years.

Next came a smaller 14in (35.6cm) shoulder head mama-doll with swing legs that was known to be selling in 1926 and possibly earlier.

The marking within the oval has changed to "EFFANBEE//DOLLS// WALK TALK SLEEP" without the actual Grumpy name. This seems so regrettable to the collector who yearns to identify each doll, but may have been done in the name of versatility. Effanbee sold a *Grumpy Aunt Dinah* in 1926, advertised in Montgomery Ward's as "a real colored mammy with a heart of gold back of her frown." The costume was a red checked dress with white apron and a red bandana around the head. Her head and hands were of unbreakable composition. At this time the legs were cotton-stuffed. We once owned a similar *Aunt Jemima* doll by a rival company which was 14in (35.6cm) and sold for 98 cents.

By 1924 Effanbee was manufacturing the doll *Bubbles* with continuous yoke or breast-plate which was wired onto cloth torso. By 1925 they were using this style head for *Grumpy*, with arms strung on springs through the yoke. Considerable modeling was used on these little arms with dimples at the elbows and backs of the hands. This model then evolved from a cloth-legged infant to a toddler with very solid, short legs (the type most easily found), and later a bit taller black version with three yarn pigtails. The legs had been remodeled with slim ankles and curved thighs, super smooth and polished. Arm shape is now similar to that of the *Shirley Temple* only the inside top is smooth to fit the yoke.

Effanbee is known to have sold dolls to various other sources for their

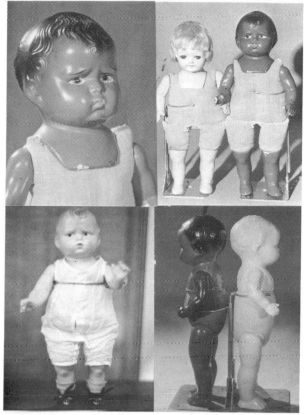

Illustration 10. 14in (35.6cm) black shoulder head mama doll with swing legs. The marking within the oval has eliminated the *Grumpy* name and now reads "EFFANBEE// DOLLS//WALK TALK SLEEP." Full-length view of earlier *Baby Dainty* type with the black doll, both with unpainted molded shoes and socks. *Grumpy* wearing original old shoes over molded shoes and socks. *Rhoda Gage Collection.*

own dressing or costuming. One example of this (which is the researcher's dream) are Amish dolls which were sold with a paper document as to which sect the doll represented, the 1936 copyrighted date, as well as a blue and white sticker of E. G. Hoover, Jeweler, Harrisburg, Pa. The set consisted of Father, Mother, Son and Daughter. The parents were Grumpy-variants, the pouty expression apparently considered suitable to portray sternness of attitude toward life. The lady models had the improved shape leg as in the black child doll, and the men had cloth bodies with molded shoes and no socks. There is still another variant with molded shoes and black socks that was once dressed as a Catholic sister.

Collectible Patsy Dolls and Patsy-Types

by JOHN AXE

©1978 Hobby House Press, Inc.

The *Patsy* doll holds a unique position in the chronology of American dolls.

The Fleischaker & Baum Doll Company, or *EffanBee,* introduced the first doll named *Patsy* in 1924. However, the most successful version of *Patsy* was the one that was patented in 1928, 50 years ago. This *Patsy* was the first really popular all composition American doll personality to be joined by a "family" of dolls, ranging from the 5¾in (14.7cm) *Wee Patsy* to the 30in (76.2cm) *Patsy Mae.* She is also credited with being the first American doll to have available an extensive ready-made wardrobe and accessories.

Patsy reflects the American view of society from her era. Until the Depression of 1929, the "midas touch" was in evidence everywhere in America. The 1920s were a time of extraordinary prosperity. Unemployment was negligible. Wages were constantly rising. Installment-buying permitted the average worker to own an electric vacuum sweeper, a refrigerator, a Ford automobile. Advertising, an old invention that reached new heights of perfections, instructed the public how to be glamorous, sexy and happy by using the right toothpaste,

applying the best hair lotion and dressing in the newest styles like the movie stars.

Publicity and the art of sham were the most effective when it came to creating a new image for the American woman. The ideal of beauty was the flapper. Flappers bobbed their hair, painted their lips to resemble a "Cupid's bow," wore short skirts and had an enormous enthusiasm for life. The most popular flappers of all were those who demonstrated their new freedom in the American films of the period. The "It Girl," Clara Bow, was totally representative of the 1920s in her beads and bangles and other enthusiastic flappers of the movies, such as Nancy Carroll and Colleen Moore, competed for equal acclaim.

Illustration 1. *PATSY RUTH.* Except for *Patsy Mae,* this is the largest of the *Patsy* dolls. She can measure 25in (63.5cm) if she has a cloth body and a composition head set on a shoulder plate that was also used for the EffanBee *Lovums Baby.* The all-composition *Patsy Ruth* is 27in (68.6cm) tall. Unlike most members of the *Patsy* family, the two largest sizes have a plain head covered with a wig, usually human hair, of various shades. The doll shown has perfect green sleep eyes and a long blonde human hair wig and is in the 25in (63.5cm) size on the cloth body. The head is incised "EFFANBEE//PATSY RUTH." *Rosemary Hanline Collection.*

Illustration 2. *PATSYETTE.* The *Patsyette* dolls, which appeared in 1931, are smaller editions of *Patsy* and measure 9½in (24.2cm). Like *Patsy* they also came in a dark-skinned version with black painted hair and others wore wigs over the molded hair. Another rare *Patsyette* has blue painted eyes, rather than the usual brown. The doll shown here wears an all-original cotton print dress with a matching hat. *Patsyettes* are marked across the shoulders "EFFAN-BEE//PATSYETTE//DOLL."

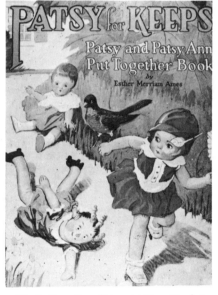

Illustration 3. *Patsy* book with full-color cover published by Samuel Gabriel Sons & Company, 1932, 95 pages. The book measures 10-1/8in (25.7cm) by 8in (20.3cm).

Illustration 4. *PATSY.* This is the version from the 1928 mold, the first in all composition. The hair is molded and painted red with a molded headband. The painted eyes are brown. The all-composition *Patsys* are 13½in (34.3cm) tall. A version from circa 1933 does not have the headband and is marked on both the head and shoulders. The version from 1946 is not marked and does not have the molded headband. The *Patsy* pictured is shown wearing an original outfit that was purchased as an accessory for her at the time. It is a red wool, two-piece snowsuit with a matching hat. The rubber galoshes also have working zippers. The doll is marked on the shoulders "EFFANBEE//PATSY//PAT. PEND.//DOLL." *Rosemary Hanline Collection.*

Illustration 5. *WEE PATSY*. The smallest member of the *Patsy* family, introduced in 1934, measures 5¾in (14.7cm) and has moveable arms and legs only. Her hair is molded and painted red like *Patsy's* with the molded headband. The painted eyes are blue. *Wee Patsy* was a doll house doll and was also used as an advertising promotion for the Colleen Moore doll house that was placed on exhibition around the country during 1935. The construction of the doll house cost Miss Moore $100,000. It is a castle measuring 9 feet by 14 feet and is scaled 1 inch to the foot. The proceeds from the exhibition were given to charities caring for crippled children in each city in which it was shown under Colleen Moore's supervision. The *Wee Patsy* shown is all original, wearing a red and white cotton dress and a Colleen Moore pin in yellow with a red background. *Wee Patsy* is marked across the shoulders "EFFANBEE//WEE PATSY." *Patricia Gardner Collection.*

The *Patsy* doll that became available to the public in the election year of 1928 was the child of emancipated women like the flappers of the movies. She was the first composition doll to resemble a real child and she was properly proportioned. She too was a "modern girl" with bobbed hair, a tiny Cupid's bow mouth and short skirts. *Patsy* was designed by America's foremost doll designer, Bernard Lipfert, who also created *Shirley Temple,* the *Dionne Quintuplets, Sonja Henie, Toni* and many other popular doll personalities. *Patsy* had dresses, beach pajamas, coats, swimsuits, roller skates, toys and everything else required to make her happy. Her little mothers could be proud of her.

Patsy was a mass produced doll who was presented to the public at the time that Americans were rapidly entering a new phase of development - mass culture, created by an increasingly industrialized society. Just as *Patsy* had more personal property than did any doll before her time, so did Americans in general. In 1928 it seemed that life could only get better and better and that the American people would have more and more of the material goods that should keep them happy forever.

In the 1920s those who elected to make the most of the present listened to a new kind of music - Jazz. Jazz expressed their emotions because it was the music of the new times and it was a music that expressed protest against tradition. Some Americans were repelled by the materialistic values and the conservative politics of the Jazz Age, although the general public, seeing the futility of the past and remembering the first total war that touched lives world-wide, preferred the pleasures of the present. Most intellectuals were alienated by by American society and the most writers of the 1920s chose to remove themselves from the materialism that Americans loved. F. Scott Fitzgerald and Ernest Hemingway went to Paris; others of lesser incomes went to Greenwich Village, the Bohemian section of New York City. They all attacked the culture that they hated.

By contrast, most American intellectuals during the Depression years of the 1930s, instead of scorning the American present, portrayed American culture with enthusiasm. Malcom Crowley, in *Exiles Return,* 1934, said that the "Lost Generation" of the 1920s was lost "because its training had prepared it for another world than existed after the war. The generation belonged to a period of transition from values already fixed to values that had to be erected." In the 1930s, admist the despair of unemployment and faith in President Roosevelt, an affirmative view of American tradition arose again. Flappers were gone from the movie screen and a child of three took their place and became better known and more loved: Shirley Temple was the American tradition personified. In her films she bravely marched through cemeteries at midnight; she seldom cried; she was never frightened. She provided Americans with the escapism that they needed from the grim realities of the Depression.

Patsy survived the transition period and became even more popular than ever. She is one of the great phenomena of the period. Even with her bobbed hair and short skirts that belonged to the Jazz Age, her real

Illustration 6. *Patsyette* dressed as Little Red Riding Hood. The shoes and stockings are replacements but the dress and cape are original to the doll. This outfit also came on *Patsyettes* with mohair wigs glued over the painted red hair.

Illustration 7. Colleen Moore and Gary Cooper in the silent film *Lilac Time,* 1928. Colleen Moore, born in 1900, was on-screen from 1917 until 1934, first as a flapper and later as a dramatic actress. Studio publicity for Colleen Moore always called attention to the fact that she had one blue eye and one brown eye. In the past decade she published three books: *Silent Star,* her autobiography; *Colleen Moore's Doll House;* and *How Women Can Make Money in the Stock Market.*

"heyday" was the 1930s. EffanBee continued to promote *Patsy* and all her companions with "*Patsy* Doll Clubs," newsletters and an "Aunt Patsy" who traveled around the

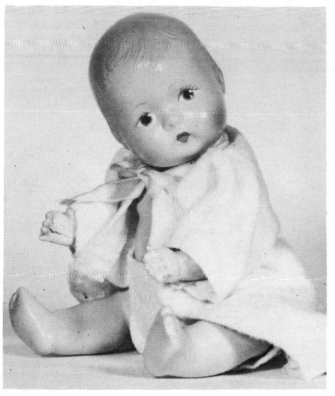

LEFT: Illustration 8. BABY TINYETTE. These baby versions of *Patsy* were advertised as *Patsy Tinyette* and are 6½in (16.5cm) tall with curved baby legs. Painted red or brown hair is more common for a *Tinyette* but this one has yellow hair and blue eyes. There is a toddler edition of *Tinyette* with straight legs which measures 7¾in (19.8cm). *Tinyette* was placed on the market by EffanBee in 1933 and was called *Patsy Tinyette*. The doll pictured wears her original diaper and bathrobe. *Tinyette* is marked "EFFANBEE" on the head and is also embossed across the shoulders "EFFANBEE//BABY TINYETTE."

RIGHT: Illustration 10. *Shirley Temple* paper doll dressed in pajamas and holding a *Patsy* doll. This is Saalfield #2112 from 1934. The actual paper doll is 8in (20.3cm) tall.

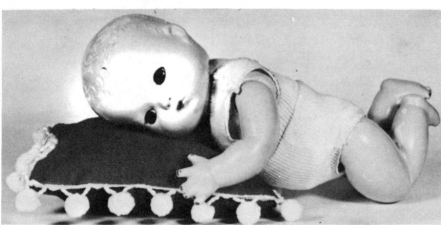

Illustration 9. *PATSY BABY*. Dating first from 1932, the largest baby version of *Patsy* was advertised as *Patsy Babykin*. In the white rendition she has painted yellow, light brown or dark brown hair and also comes with wigs. All have sleep eyes of blue, brown or green, like this yellow haired baby. The black version has painted hair with yarn pigtails and has either sleep or painted eyes. *Patsy Baby* also had a cloth body during the World War II years because of supply shortages. *Patsy Babies* are marked on the head and also on the body "EFFANBEE//PATSY BABY."

Illustration 11. Two EffanBee dolls that incorporate features of the *Patsy* dolls. At the left is a 9in (22.9cm) all-composition and fully-jointed girl. She has blue side-glancing eyes and molded and painted brown hair. She dates from the late 1920s and the body construction is similar to *Patsyette*, although the torso is slimmer. The doll pictured is not dressed in original clothing. She is marked on the back "EFFANBEE//MADE IN U.S.A." On the right is an 8in (20.3cm) toddler that is similar to the *Patsy Tinyette* toddler. She is *Button Nose* from the late 1930s and she has brown hair and blue, raised side-glancing eyes. Her print cotton with matching underpants may be original. She is marked on the back "EFFANBEE."

country to introduce new members of the EffanBee family of dolls. *Patsy* could count among her close friends and relatives *Wee Patsy, Patsy Tinyette, Patsyette, Patsy Babyette, Patsy Baby, Patsy Jr., Patsy Joan, Patricia, Patsy Ann, Patsy Lou, Patsy Ruth, Patsy Mae* and *Skippy*.

Patsy dolls were the protagonists of two books for children - *Patsy For Keeps* by Esther Merriam Ames in 1932 and *Patsy Ann Her Happy Times* by Mona Reed King in 1935. *Patsy* dolls even appeared in the movies. Shirley Temple had a *Patsy Mae* in the 1936 film *Captain January*.

Today in the United States there are many women who were born during the era of the *Patsy* dolls (the late 1920s until the late 1940s) who are called Patricia, Patsy, Patty or Pat. These names for baby girls were not so common before that time and have not had the same degree of popularity since.

Patsy herself certainly was successful. During her time all the leading American doll manufacturers, EffanBee included, produced popular play dolls that incorporated the features and the styling of the *Patsy* dolls. There were also countless unmarked and unknown dolls of this type advertised during the period. Most of the unmarked dolls were sold through catalog distribution sources

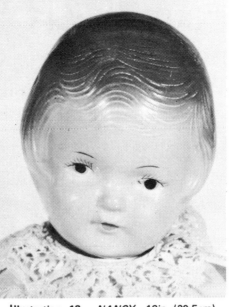

Illustration 13. *NANCY.* 12in (30.5cm) *Nancy* is Arranbee's version of *Patsy,* circa 1930s. *Nancy* also came in other sizes and styles. The doll shown is all-composition and fully-jointed with painted and molded reddish hair and blue painted eyes. This *Nancy* has the "bent" right arm like *Patsy* and most of her family members that are girl-types. She is marked on the back "NANCY."

Illustration 15. 17in (43.2cm) unknown girl of the *Patsy* style. She is of superior construction and finishing and is fully-jointed. She also has the "bent" right arm that is typical of the *Patsy* dolls. She has deeply molded brown painted hair and blue tin sleep eyes with lashes. The upper right arm is incised at the joint " J d ." The upper left arm is incised at the joint " Γ4 ."

Illustration 12. 15in (38.1cm) all-composition girl that is fully-jointed. She seems to be the identical doll from Sears, Roebuck & Co. Christmas catalog in 1943 that sold for $1.17. She has very deeply molded brown painted hair and blue painted eyes with heavy eyelashes and eye shadow. She is an economically produced product and her torso is identical to that of the *Patsy* mold, although the arms and legs are thinner. She is all original in a matching print dress and bonnet. The white shoes are oilcloth.

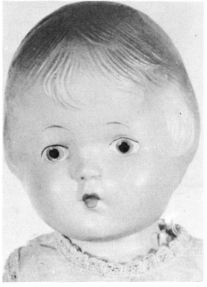

Illustration 14. This is a 16in (40.6cm) unmarked *Patsy*-type doll. She is fully-jointed and has painted red hair and blue eyes. She is wearing her original pink slip.

like Ward's and Sears' or by five and ten cent stores like Woolworth's and G. C. Murphy. Almost all composition doll parts were molded and cast by companies who specialized in this process and then distributed them to the respective doll company or dealer who finished and dressed the dolls. The "marked" dolls from the leading companies (who controlled their own molds) were usually quality products. The unmarked and unknown dolls were of varying degrees of quality with regard to finishing and costuming.

The other dolls had names like *Betty* (Madame Alexander), *Sally* (American Character), *Nancy* (Arranbee) and some were even called *Patsy Ann* with a "naturally shaped composition body, moveable arms and legs" (John Plain Catalog, 1938). The *Patsy* imitations and copies range from cheaply finished dolls that sold for about 25 cents to others that were as well produced and designed as

Patsy herself. These dolls all reflected the style of the 1920s more than they did that of the 1930s, although there was an abundance of contemporary dolls that were characteristic of their own period.

Today, half a century after the inception of the all composition *Patsy,* she is one of the most collectible of the "collectible dolls" (i.e., dolls that are not old enough to be considered "antiques"). She did not

represent a famous person, but became one in doll form. *Patsy,* because of her hairdo and her clothing, is from the late 1920s. Yet she enjoyed her highest popularity during the 1930s, the era that at the present time, holds the most nostalgia for Americans and whose artifacts seem to be the most collectible. *Patsy* is the *epitome* of that great period of nostalgia!

A Few BEAR Facts, Figures and Pictures

by THEODORE B. BEAR
(As told to Beverly Port)

© 1976 Hobby House Press, Inc.

Illustration 1. A pair of old and well-loved Teddies on either side of *Gladdie.* Both have Steiff buttons in their ears and shoe-button eyes. The one on the left is 18in (45.7cm) tall while the one on the right is 12in (30.5cm) tall.

Many bear-related items are seen in collections, such as pins, charms, plates, bowls, spoons, cups and buttons with pictures or embossed bear designs on them. There are many paper items - postcards, several series of them; books, including the Roosevelt Bear books; and paper dolls. The Teddy Bear comes in all sizes, all

Illustration 2. That's me! - Theodore Bear, in the middle holding the big book - big to me, since I am only 5in (12.7cm) tall. The book is an old Linenette by Gabriel Co. Many people collect bear-related items and we are now called Animal Dolls by many doll collectors. The Steiff bear on the other side of the book moves his head 'round and 'round when you wind his tail. My friend on the right is completely covered with hand-stitching in long over-stitch to preserve his life and limb, as his skin is all worn out.

Illustration 4. This sassy-looking bear has an extra large hump in his body and a rare musical mechanism in his body. There is no key to wind, nothing on the outside of his body; just push and squeeze his body to make the music play! He is gold colored, fully-jointed, has shoe-button eyes and dates from the early 1900s.

Illustration 5. A group of miniature Teddies of various colors and sizes from 5in (12.7cm) down to a tiny 1in (2.5cm) baby and even he is jointed. See postage stamp for size comparison. Miniature bears are used in doll houses and some have their own "bear houses."

Illustration 3. A pair of unusual bear muffs. The top one has a Steiff button in his ear, shoe-button eyes and is from the early 1900s. The lower one is from the 1930s and has glass eyes. The original "squeakers" in the front white paws still work. The muffs are both flannel lined and made of tan plush.

Illustration 6. The bear on the left is a musical mechanical Teddy who turns his head back and forth to the tune "Teddy Bear's Picnic," emanating from a Swiss music box in his tummy. The other one is old and mechanical. Press his tummy and his jaws of wood open and close. Both have glass eyes. The one on the left is 14in (35.6cm) tall and the one on the right is 17in (43.2cm) tall.

Illustration 7. A rare bear - a two-faced fellow - split personality - actually a doll! "Bear-Baby" was patented in June 1914. The bear-doll on original patent papers looks almost exactly like this one. One based on the same patent is shown in *More Twentieth Century Dolls* by Anderton on page 974 with the description on page 975. This one has shoe-button eyes on the teddy bear side and blue glass eyes in the baby face. He is golden mohair plush, excelsior stuffed, completely jointed and has an old knit blue hat that covers the baby face.

ages and all colors. He has been popular with all ages since the early 1900s. During the time of his greatest popularity Teddy was sold by the millions. He is still great today!

Teddy Bears have been giving love, loyalty and tenderness to millions of children for more than 70 years; they are always there "when the world goes wrong," to dry the tears and listen quietly to problems, then sitting up all night to watch over the tired child when he falls asleep. They wait patiently for morning when the sun will shine again to share in childhood's happiness. Yes, Teddy Bears are certainly like that!

Illustration 8. *Smokey the Bear* is much-loved by children and has helped teach important fire prevention lessons. He appears in all sizes and styles, from plush stuffed models to this all-jointed fellow with cloth trousers, removable vinyl hat and shovel in hand.

Illustration 9. This rare bear blinks his electric "eye-bulbs" when his porcelain "tummy-button" is pressed. Wires from his eyes go through a tube in his neck and down to a power pack and control in his body. He is 20in (50.8cm) tall and from the early 1900s.

Illustration 10. The three bears: Panda, Koala and Pooh!

Illustration 11. "Grumpy" is his name and honey is his game! This 24in (61.0cm) Steiff bear dating from the early 1900s has an extra large "hump" on his back.

Preview of Collector's History of Teddy Bear

BY PATRICIA SCHOONMAKER

Soft Cuddly Animals

Being a collector of Teddy Bears, along with antique dolls, I first wrote about them for the Souvenir Book of the United Federation of Doll Clubs, for 1963. Later my husband John (whose hobby is photography) and I were to do a slide program, "The Great Teddy Bear Saga" for a Regional Conference in California which was eventually repeated by request at a National Conference.

We had longed to know for ourselves, more in-depth information surrounding the Teddy Bear than we had acquired at this point. We had kept Teddy Bear files and scrapbooks for some years prior to the first article and in the following years.

But we needed not only the material that had been written before, but the source material such as the trade magazine *Playthings* and early catalogs in the era of the Teddy Bear craze. Many reporters had made trips to Europe to settle the origins of the Teddy Bear and still did not decide the debate between the strongest American claimant, Ideal Toy Company, and the German firm of Steiff. We decided the journey to take was to amass as much source material as possible and let you, the reader, come

Our Leader Teddy Bear Value

This is a teddy the baby will go wild over. He will sleep with it and play with it all day. The two will be inseparable. Nice quality, 14-inch bear with lifelike glass eyes, movable head, arms and legs. He is made of good quality brown plush and has a squeaker voice. A dandy value for our price. Every kiddie should have one. Shpg. wt., 1⅛ lbs.

49D4314 . . . . **98c** along back through the years to 1902.

There is no better way to understanding an era, or event than that of reading the actual language of the period. The name of the game in *Playthings* was salesmanship. Everyone spoke in superlatives, hoping to create the highest opinion for his product. Yet by a thorough reading of all of the material the basic truths are apparent. The success of the Teddy Bear was overwhelming. The original popularity was not so much due to President Roosevelt, but to the uniqueness of the toy. The soft and silky mohair plush had not been used to any extent before, and earlier animals were not fully jointed. Some specimens had been made with soft outer coverings but the inner core was hard and unyielding until Margarete Steiff began using scraps of felt from her family's factory for stuffing.

The combination of the flexible stuffing, the basic appeal of the bear animal, and the concealed joints was an unbeatable combination. He was originally conceived as a bear-doll by the Steiff Company intended for a boy child, and named "Friend Petz." This apparently was picked up by American advertisers. No one had any idea of the immense popularity and demand that would follow. Things moved slower in the days of no radio or television, so it was not until 1905-1906 that the demand began to build in America. The first advertisement of jointed bears in *Playthings* appeared in May 1906 entitled "This is Bruin's Day." By December 1906 the first mention of the name "TEDDY" appears in an advertisement by Horsman.

Three Jolly Fellows
Our Medium Grade Teddy Bears With Voices

See these perky little faces, fat roly-poly bodies. Heads, arms and legs move. Have lifelike glass eyes. Bodies are covered with soft, long pile, brown color plush, and all have voices which squeak every time baby hugs them on the back. The bodies are better shaped than our lower priced bears and the arms are longer and more shapely.

| 10-Inch Bear. 49D4308 Shpg. wt., 1⅛ lbs.... **98c** | 12-Inch Bear 49D4309 Shpg. wt., 1¼ lbs... **$1.39** | 14-Inch Bear 49D4310 Shpg. wt., 1¾ lbs.... **$1.79** |

Preview of Collector's History of Teddy Bears

PART II

BY PATRICIA SCHOONMAKER

Big Teddy Bear Free for You

NEARLY 12 INCHES TALL

They are all the Rage

Teddy Bear is a fine specimen of his kind, made of **Shaggy Cinnamon Plush**, and most 12 inches tall. His **head**, his **arms** and his **legs** are **jointed** on to the body so that they can all be turned in any direction. And you should see him shake his head and hear him **grunt** when you hit him in the stomach! **Teddy** is all the rage in the cities. The children carry him to school and even the grown-up ladies carry him with them when they go out for a walk or ride, or to the theatre. The more costly Teddys sell as high as $25.00 each. We have picked out this one for you on account of his good **size**, his **jointed head, arms** and **legs**, his **cute grunt** and his **fine cinnamon color**. We will send him to you **free by mail**, together with one of these fine latest hand-tinted novelty

"WHOLE-BEAR-FAMILY"

Pillow-tops, if you will get **six** of your friends each to give you **25 cents** to pay for their subscription to our popular WOMAN'S HOME JOURNAL for **two whole years**. This is surely the easiest way you will find of owning one of these fine Teddys yourself or of getting one to give to some friend. We make our plan very clear and simple because we want every one to understand it thoroughly and to be pleased when they get the Bear, the Pillow-top and the magazine. Remember, if they do not all reach you just as we describe them we want you to let us know. **We guarantee satisfaction.**

WOMAN'S HOME JOURNAL, Dept. 6,
291 Congress St., Boston, Mass.

THE WHOLE BEAR FAMILY

Pillow-Top is 21 inches square.

THE MAGAZINE: THE WOMAN'S HOME JOURNAL is one of the best of the popular priced magazines. It gives you every month 32 pages or less of interesting stories, household departments, fancy work, etc. The regular price is 15 cents a year, two years for 25 cents. For that small sum you get an amount of good stories and reading matter that would cost you five or ten times as much if bought in book form.

TEDDY IS FREE. Remember we send you this fine Teddy Bear and a beautiful tinted "WHOLE-BEAR-FAMILY" pillow-top **Free of charge. The bear and pillow-top are for yourself.** Just take this advertisement along with you to show to your friends, and tell them about it and you can easily get the **six subscribers** and we will send the Teddy Bear and Pillow-top just as soon as we receive the money for the six subscriptions, **$1.50 in all.** We hope you will go right out and get them at once so that we can send you the Teddy Bear. We know you will like him as he is very good company and we guarantee that you and your friends will like the magazine and the beautifully tinted pillow-top. We will be glad to send you sample copies of the magazine if you need them to show your friends, but we think you **can** easily get them to subscribe without waiting so long. We send the Teddy Bear and pillow-top to you **at once and guarantee them** to be as here described. Write your letter to

WOMAN'S HOME JOURNAL, Dept. 6
291 Congress Street, - - - - **Boston, Mass.**

The Americans would begin their struggle to compete with the superior imported product. If they used imported bearskin, or as much as used imported voices in domestic bears, this was a point to feature in their advertising. They hired German workers to come to America and divulge any secrets they could. The Steiffs have often mentioned that it was a simple matter for anyone to rip apart one of their specimens for a pattern, but this did not bother them. They felt the finished product would not be the same.

Stabel and Wilken advertised in 1907 "We have secured control of a new line of Teddy Bears manufactured here by experts formerly connected with a well-known foreign maker. The goods turned out by this American factory are fully equal to, and in fact cannot be distinguished from the best imported article."

Hahn and Amberg advertised in 1907: "We also manufacture very largely a line of golden, cinnamon and white Teddy Bears, made of imported plush and perfectly formed. This article is today virtually taking the place of the doll, and never since it was first introduced has the sale been so large as at the present time. It is practical, durable, and (unlike the doll) unbreakable. Every child wants one. Follow the advice of Oliver Cromwell and 'strike while the iron is hot.' Buy them now."

We will present to you in the forthcoming *The Collector's History of Teddy Bears*, many illustrations from *Playthings*, 1906 through 1908 and will develop the history of the famous toy, in pre-teddy days — delineating what brought about this phenomenon of popularity. The Teddy Bear was said to be the fad which simply would not fade away.

Included will be catalog pages from 1907 through the 1950s, as well as the fascinating premium offers over several decades. The language of the day gives great understanding of the history of the bear. Sears, Roebuck and Co. in 1907 advertised that the bear was not just a campaign article, thereby hoping to gain sales from either political party.

The market for clothing for bears was equally as great as the bear itself, as well as patterns to make at home, which we have researched in our chapter, "Needle and Thread."

Included will be old portraits of children with their bears, as well as sec-

Pettijohn's Breakfast Food
ALL THE WHEAT BUT THE OVERCOAT

1899

tions on collecting Teddy Bear books, the bear paper dolls, Post Cards, Memorabilia, Related Items. If you haven't been bitten by this particular collecting bug, you have a world of excitement and pure enjoyment ahead of you. Teddy Bear collecting is now at a high peak. Today, they need not be antique to be appealing or need not necessarily be imported. There are a whole battalion of charmers out there to be located and treasured.

69

The First Gerber Dolls

by ALMA WOLFE
©1978 Hobby House Press, Inc.

ABOVE: Illustration 1. The Gerber baby girl with her original mailing carton and advertising folder. *Courtesy Gerber Products Company.*

LEFT: Illustration 2. Original advertisement for the first Gerber baby doll. *Courtesy Gerber Products Company.*

Gerber Products Company advertised the first offer of their fabric trademark dolls in 1936. The "last appearance" of these babies was in 1939.

The baby girl and the baby boy dolls were made of sateen - *pink* for "her," *blue* for "him" - and silk-screened with the Gerber Baby face. Mrs. Sylvia Fogg of Gerber Products Company gives a graphic sketch of the dimensions of the babies - "8 inches long; 2¾ inches at the top; 5¾ inches at the bottom, and 1/2 inches in depth." They were "filled" with cotton-soft stuffing. Close, heavy, overcast outside stitches seamed each doll together.

The little girl wears a long dress, bootles, bonnet and a sweater with collar, "tied" with a sewn-on pink satin ribbon; a sweetheart in pink! She holds a blue stuffed dog in her right hand. In her left hand, she holds a blue and white labeled can of strained Gerber baby food.

The little boy was dressed in a blue pram suit. He carried his toy, a stuffed duck and also held a jar of Gerber baby food.

Gerber Company customers could obtain the winsome cherubs by sending in ten cents and three Gerber labels for each baby. Coupons were found in the leading magazines.

The Fremont Times-Indicator of March 11, 1936, reported in a column entitled "Storm of Doll Coupons Arrives With Blizzard:" "At just about the time that we were all snowed in here at Fremont, we [Gerber] also received a regular blizzard from the new magazine advertising which mentioned the new Gerber Doll . . . Over 100 coupons came in from one magazine in a single day . . . With the arrival of the dolls from New York, however, we quickly set to work and now have these little Gerber Dolls in the hands of babies all over the country."

The "babies" were shipped in color-coordinated boxes - the girl in a pink box, the boy "traveled" in a blue box. Each doll was "accompanied" by an ad insert entitled "A New Flavor Treat for This Year's Gerber Babies." This folder extolled the advantage of the "latest thing in baby food processing-shaker cooking."

When the dolls were first offered, "nine fine Gerber products" were marketed - "Strained Vegetable Soup, Carrots, Spinach, Beets, Green Beans, Prunes, Peas, Tomatoes, and Cereal." "Apricot," "Apple Sauce" and "Liver Soup" had been added to the list when the dolls were last offered in 1939. Today, in their "fifieth year of caring," Gerber tempts baby appetites with 150 foods.

Illustration 3. Front of the Gerber baby doll.

Illustration 4. Back of the Gerber baby doll.

Approximately 26,690 dolls were shipped during the years offered. Early in 1978, as Gerber began its Golden Anniversary Year, one of the dimpled darlings, a baby girl "returned home."

The September-October 1977 issue of *The Gerber News* carried an article captioned "First Gerber Doll Sought for Archives." The search for the first "Gerber Doll" was mentioned in Bob Talbert's column in the *Detroit Free Press.* One of the column's readers wrote to Gerber to say in effect that her "baby" has become a family heirloom. She had received the doll when she was a baby in 1937, gave it to her little son in 1960 and he is keeping the doll to give to his children. *Gerber News* quotes the doll's owner as stating "It's too bad that there aren't more toys nowadays that wear as well for 10¢ and 3 labels."

Mrs. Ida Evans of Fremont, Michigan, called the Gerber Company just before the holidays of 1977 with the happy news that she had the baby girl complete with original mailing carton and advertising folder, and would donate the doll to the company archives.

The fabric baby girl joined the other Gerber dolls in the collection, those dolls "offered in 1955, 1965, and 1972" in January 1978. The Gerber Company hopes that her "brother" will join the group during their Golden Anniversary Year at the Gerber Products Company, 445 State Street, Fremont, Michigan, 49412.

Bibliography
(correspondence): Mrs. Sylvia T. Fogg, Editor, Company Publications and Company Historian (now retired)

The Gerber News, Vol. 42, No. 1, January 1978, page 2.

Copy of clipping from *The Fremont Times-Indicator,* March 11, 1936, from the Gerber Company file.

Ads from the company file.

"Dearest Dolls"
Tiny Tears

by THELMA BATEMAN

© 1976 Hobby House Press, Inc.

Whenever I see or hear of a *Tiny Tears* doll, I always remember the day I took my two small granddaughters, Janet and Gail Corwin, to a large department store toy section to buy them each a new baby doll. Janet had already worn out one *Tiny Tears* and I showed her all the other baby dolls hoping she would choose another kind.

After seeing all the other available babies, however, they both chose another *Tiny Tears*. So the sales lady gave each one a box with *Tiny Tears* and all her accessories inside. I had other toy items to purchase so took the girls and boxes into a quiet corner of the toy section and gave permission to open their boxes while I shopped.

Presently, a very disturbed floor-walker came over to the sales lady and said: "Mrs. Larsen, there are two little girls sitting on the floor over there. Each one has a *Tiny Tears* doll in a box with her clothes and other things and they are taking everything all apart!"

Mrs. Larsen calmed him down by telling him the truth about the dolls and all had a good laugh.

Tiny Tears, patented December 19, 1950, has embossed markings on back of her head down low where the head fits on to the neck piece "Pat. No. 2, 675644" and underneath that "American Character." There is no mark on the body but it does have five deep dimples on the chubby shoulders and back. Both dolls are identical except for size and color and the black doll has brown eyes and no red paint on her lips. The white doll has blue eyes. Both dolls have squeakers inside; both cry tears, blow bubbles, drink and wet. *Tiny Tears* was first introduced by having a full page in the June 2, 1950, issue of *Life* magazine.

Both dolls originally came with layettes composed of the following: a diaper and pins; bubble pipe; tiny cake of Ivory soap; washcloth; bottle and nipple; a pacifier; a small package of Kleenex; pink and white machine-made booties, tied with pink ribbons; a white cotton sunsuit, piped in pink with "Tiny Tears" embroidered in red on the front; and a simple pink and white cotton dress, lace trimmed bonnet and panties to match.

The heads are made of vinyl with molded hair. The eyes have long, thick lashes and sleep. The bent-limb bodies are made of latex, jointed at neck, shoulders and hips.

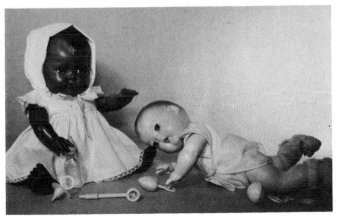

Illustration 1. 8¾in (22.3cm) black *Tiny Tears* and 7¾in (19.8cm) white *Tiny Tears* by American Character. *Frances W. Dobkins Collection.*

71

Gerber Baby Doll
The Family Tree

BY ALMA WOLFE

Six doll replicas of the world's most famous baby portrait have been issued in the 49 years (adopted in 1931) that this dear face has "looked out" from the labels and boxes of Gerber Products Company's baby food and baby accessories.

The "family tree" began in 1936 with the first premium offer of the 8in. (20.3cm) sateen baby dolls, "silk-screened with the Gerber baby face." The lil' girl was dressed in pink—long dress, booties, a bonnet and a sweater sacque. The lil' boy wore a blue pram suit. Both carried a toy and a jar of Gerber baby food. The purchase price of each winsome cherub was ten cents and three Gerber baby food labels. "Approximately 26,690 were shipped during the years offered" (1936/39). ("The First Gerber Dolls," **DOLL READER** (June/July 1978)

Sixteen years elapsed before the Gerber Products Company offered the second premium doll. In 1955 the darling company logo was superbly translated into doll form by the Sun Rubber Company. This lovable, 12in. (30.5cm) drink-and-wet, dimpled baby "cried," had a soft vinyl swivel head, inset plastic eyes, a rubber body and jointed arms and legs. It came dressed in a diaper and a bib with "Gerber Baby" printed in blue.

The doll was marked on the neck:

GERBER BABY
© GERBER PRODUCTS COMPANY
and on the body, above the "crier"
THE SUN RUBBER COMPANY
BARBERTON, O. U.S.A.
Pat. 2118682
Pat. 2160739

The baby "brought along" a glass bottle with a rubber nipple and a black collar (just like the real baby bottle of that era); a blue-on-the-inside, white-on-the-outside metal baby bowl, a blue plastic spoon and four miniature non-filled Gerber cereal boxes.

The Sun Rubber Company's doll, advertised as a "$3.75 value" was obtained for 12 Gerber baby food labels or cereal box tops and two dollars. At the end of the promotion, the tally showed that 367,718 were ordered.

The third facsimile of the world-famous Gerber baby was the first of the line to have sleep eyes and also, the first doll not to "show" the dimples.

This doll was manufactured by the Arrow Toy Company and was marketed from 1966 to 1968. The 14in. (35.6cm) "happy" baby was all vinyl with the same body structure and nursing feature of the 1955 premium offer; it also "wore" a diaper and the "name" bib, and came with a plastic nursing bottle.

It was incised on the neck:
GERBER
© GERBER PRODUCTS COMPANY

The lil' one was advertised as a "$3.98 value," and was the same price as the 1955 doll--two dollars and 12 labels. The Arrow doll "checked out" 36,013 sales.

The fourth and fifth versions of the Company trademark "arrived" in the next decade. Amsco Industries produced a 10in. (25.4cm) Caucasian baby in 1971; and in 1972 introduced the first ethnic Gerber baby doll, also 10in. (25.4cm) tall. These all vinyl babies had painted eyes and a "skin-soft" fully-articulated body. They had the open/closed nursing mouth, but did not come with a bottle. The babies were clothed in a cotton rosebud-printed sleeper, tagged "GERBER, made in the British Crown Colony of Hong Kong."

The neck mark was:
THE GERBER BABY
GERBER PROD. CO.
1971 or 1972

The adoption fee was $2.50 each, plus four labels from any Gerber Toddler Meal, Strained or Junior High Meat Dinner, or two box tops from Gerber fruit cereal. Sixty thousand Amsco babies found homes.

The newest Gerber baby doll, created to commemorate Gerber's 50th anniversary, was exhibited at the 1979 Toy Fair by the Atlanta Novelty Company, "a division of Gerber Products since 1973." The story of the largest and most innovative Gerber doll appeared in the **Doll Reader,** February/March 1980. This is the only Gerber baby doll that has not been offered as a Gerber premium.

Looking at *The Gerber Baby Doll Family Tree,* you will see six issues of the charming cherub. Each doll prototype produced of the adorable trademark of the Gerber Products Company has been a different concept. All were dear and all were eagerly purchased.

Where are the Gerber baby dolls of 1936 to 1972? Were they "played to pieces" or have they become treasured family heirlooms? Collectors are most lucky if they can add to their collection any of the first five premium doll offers of Gerber Products Company.

Ad copies courtesy of Gerber Products Company.
A bouquet of thanks to Mrs. Cork Chaffee, Archivist, Gerber Products Company.

Illustration 1:
The first "real" Gerber baby doll offered in 1955. Sun Rubber Company doll.

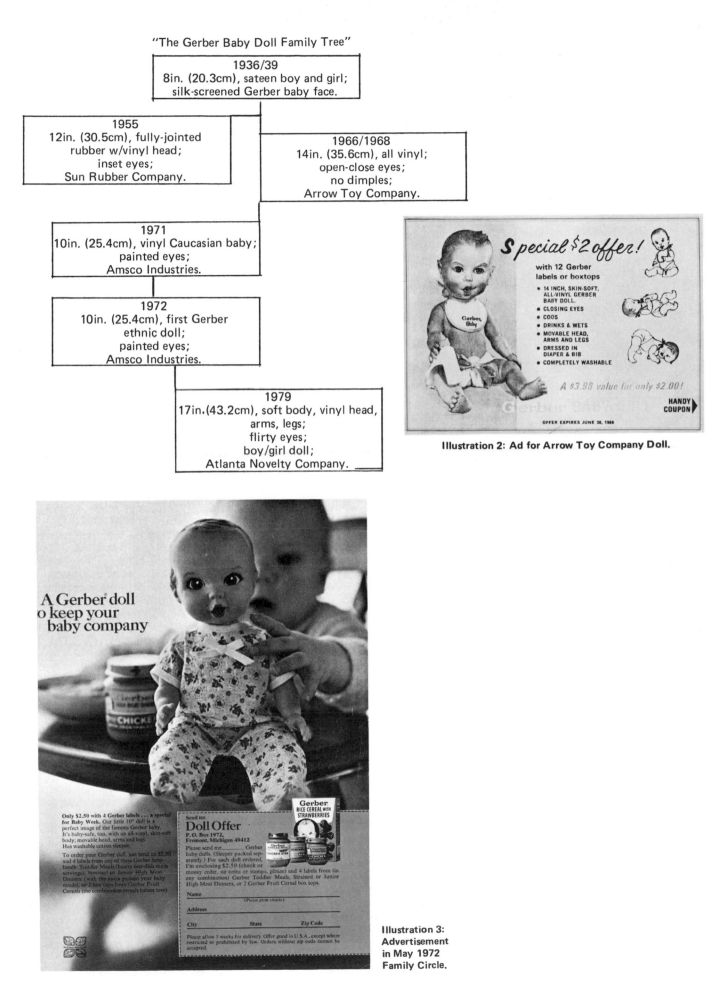

"The Gerber Baby Doll Family Tree"

1936/39
8in. (20.3cm), sateen boy and girl;
silk-screened Gerber baby face.

1955
12in. (30.5cm), fully-jointed
rubber w/vinyl head;
inset eyes;
Sun Rubber Company.

1966/1968
14in. (35.6cm), all vinyl;
open-close eyes;
no dimples;
Arrow Toy Company.

1971
10in. (25.4cm), vinyl Caucasian baby;
painted eyes;
Amsco Industries.

1972
10in. (25.4cm), first Gerber
ethnic doll;
painted eyes;
Amsco Industries.

1979
17in.(43.2cm), soft body, vinyl head,
arms, legs;
flirty eyes;
boy/girl doll;
Atlanta Novelty Company.

$pecial $2 offer!

with 12 Gerber
labels or boxtops

- 14 INCH, SKIN-SOFT,
  ALL-VINYL GERBER
  BABY DOLL.
- CLOSING EYES
- COOS
- DRINKS & WETS
- MOVABLE HEAD,
  ARMS AND LEGS
- DRESSED IN
  DIAPER & BIB
- COMPLETELY WASHABLE

A $3.98 value for only $2.00!

HANDY COUPON

OFFER EXPIRES JUNE 30, 1966

Illustration 2: Ad for Arrow Toy Company Doll.

**Illustration 3:
Advertisement
in May 1972
Family Circle.**

73

Ideal's Toni Dolls

by JOHN AXE

LEFT: Illustration 1. 14in (35.6cm) *Toni* waiting for her permanent to "take." Dark brown hair; blue eyes. Head marked "P-90//Ideal Doll// Made in U.S.A." and back marked "Ideal Doll//P-90." Original box and Toni supplies. *Wanda Lodwick of Wanda's Doll House.*

RIGHT: Illustration 3. 14in (35.6cm) *Toni,* marked "P-90," with vinyl arms and red painted finger-nails. (These arms are also found on the *Harriet Hubbard Ayer* doll.)

Illustration 2. 15in (38.1cm) brunette and blonde *Tonis*; marked "Ideal Doll//P-91." The shoes on the blonde doll are made of vinyl and marked "Ideal." They are rather awkward looking but these shoes are original and are found on many *Toni* dolls. Other *Tonis* wear a more dainty leatherette shoe that snaps in the center at the ankle.

Back in the late 1940's the manufacture of composition dolls came to an end after almost a half century of production. This was because of the improvements in synthetic plastics. The almost indestructable "hard plastic" doll was only manufactured by the leading doll companies for about 15 years but during this time some of the most detailed and beautiful dolls ever made in the United States were produced for the mass market.

Synthetic plastics were a perfect material for rendering play dolls. Dolls made from hard plastic had a greater variety of facial expressions and other minute details such as realistic fingers than any commercially manufactured dolls made up to that time. The first universally popular hard plastic dolls were Ideal Novelty and Toy Company's *Toni,* which were first nationally distributed on an extensive basis for Christmas of 1949. The *Toni* doll was sold by the thousands in stores until about 1955.

Toni who is now 27 years old was new to the market during beginning of the Korean War, a time of peak sales and production records. Distributors were alarmed over the possibility of shortages occurring because of the availability of materials and bought and ordered more dolls and toys than could be sold.

In June of 1950, when the United States entered the Korean Conflict, there were approximately 42,000,000 children in the country under 15 years of age, a record number. The merchants knew that the "war babies" would need Christmas toys and bought "over their head," fearing Government restrictions on strategic materials. Orders of the Ideal Novelty and Toy Company in July of 1950 were 167 per cent above what they were in July of 1949. At that time 2,600 workers were busy on Christmas orders; by August more than 3,000 were running extra shifts on the assembly lines. The total volume of orders in 1950 for Ideal reached more than $15,000,000, $4 million above 1949. This is a reason why there are so many *Toni* dolls in doll collections today.

But Toni was a home permanent before it became a doll.

In January of 1948 the Gillette Safety Razor Company bought the Toni Company for $20 million. Toni had earned a staggering $5 million profit the preceeding year so this seemed like a good investment. A college football player, Richard Neison Wishbone Harris, began the Toni Company in 1936 by buying the "broken-down" Noma Company, which made hair waving equipment for beauty shops, for $5,000. By shrewd advertising Mr. Harris had cornered more than 50 per cent of the home-permanent business. The Toni Home Permanent kit sold for $1.25 and $2.00 for the deluxe model at a time when curls at the beauty shop cost from $10 to $50. The name for the permanent was originally planned as *Tony,* which in the slang of the time meant "classy; high-class; top-rate." *Toni* sounded more appealing.

A cold wave, which curled hair chemically for $1.25 was very appealing to millions of women who were used to paying 10 times as much for heat-waved hair in beauty salons. Clever advertising, costing $5 million a year, instructed every woman in the country that she needed a Toni.

The slogan "Which Twin Has the Toni?" is still a part of the American colloquial jargon. In a comparative-advertising scheme magazines carried pictures of identical twins, one of whom had a Toni Home Permanent and the other a beauty parlor job. A twin searching and testing staff was set up under Miss Coralie Shaefer, who interviewed identical females between 14 and 25 who could be pictured in magazines and testify over the radio.

By the end of 1948 Toni's share of the home-wave market was 86 per cent. And beauty shop profits were

Illustration 4. 14in (35.6cm) *Tonis* with red, brunette and blonde hair; marked "P-90."

Illustration 5. 14in (35.6cm) and 16in (40.6cm) *Toni* walkers. Both have blonde wigs and eye shadow. The smaller doll is marked "P-90" on her head and "90-W" on the back. The larger doll is marked "P-91" on her head and "16" on her back.

cut by more than 20 per cent. In New York, Mississippi, Virginia, South Carolina, California and Wisconsin beauty shop forces appealed to state legislators to pass a variety of laws to hamstring the use of home waves. Florida beauticians tried to have Toni Home Permanents banned because the waving lotion was considered dangerous; Kentucky operators tried to make the practice of curling hair at home declared illegal because those who gave the permanent were not licensed; in Louisiana the beauty shops hired lobbyists to put in a bill to drive home permanents out of business through the state legislature, promising a payment of $30,000 after Toni's were banned. The professional hair wavers were unsuccessful in their bid to monopolize the market and retaliated only by running specials for "home-ruined hair." The beauticians admitted their defeat when they advertised "Toni Wave Given Professionally" in local newspapers and shop windows.

By 1948 Toni sponsored the popular radio programs *Give and Take*,

Ladies Be Seated, and *Don McNeil's Breakfast Club* which were audience-participation shows slanted heavily at women listeners and the soap opera *This is Nora Drake,* making Toni and the Toni slogan a household word.

When *Toni* became a doll by Ideal her name already had an international reputation. (Toni Home Permanents were also sold in Western Europe.)

So with a doll shortage anticipated and the doll industry expected to suffer a lack of allocations because of the war in Korea, Ideal produced an abundance of *Toni* dolls and pushed sales "like crazy." Their skill in plastics helped to put Ideal out in front. A staff of 150 technicians working in the plastic division translated doll ideas into new materials as they became available. Synthetic nylon for example made a good material for *Toni's* hair when shortages were occurring in other types of wig fibers.

Ideal became a leader in American doll production in 1902 when Morris Michtom, the founder of the company, gave the Teddy Bear to the world. This began a new trend towards

dolls that could be played with instead of merely looked at, as was the case with dolls that had bisque and china heads. And it came about because in 1902 President Theodore Roosevelt went hunting in Mississippi. One day a cute little bear cub wandered into the camp. T.R. was too "soft-hearted" to shoot it and adopted it as a pet. A cartoonist made a drawing of the incident and called it "Teddy's Bear."

Mr. Michtom, who operated a toy shop in New York, quickly designed a plush bear and rushed a sample off to the White House along with a letter asking permission to call it

Illustration 6. 20½in (52.1cm) *Toni;* platinum hair; eye shadow. Marked "Ideal Doll//P-93." The label on her dress says "Genuine Toni Doll with Nylon Wig."

Illustration 7. 18½in (47.0cm) *Toni,* light red hair; eye shadow. Marked "Ideal Doll// P-19."

"Teddy Bear." "Dear Mr. Michtom," came the prompt reply, "I don't think my name is likely to be worth much in the bear business, but you are welcome to use it."

Ideal Novelty and Toy Company was founded to produce the bears. And in 1933 Mr. Michtom hit the biggest doll jackpot ever with another famous name, Shirley Temple. When the first shipment of *Shirley Temple* dolls arrived in Hollywood by air express, it was met at the airport by an escort of motorcycle police and conducted with screaming sirens to the store where it went on sale. Other cities reacted with similar, if not such elaborate, enthusiasm. By the time Mr. Michtom, "the Teddy Bear man," died in 1938, sales of the *Shirley Temple* doll had totaled more than 6 million dollars. This was back in the Depression when a family could be fed for a week for the same price as a *Shirley Temple* doll cost.

Enormous outputs are maintained by fresh new ideas. Ideas, and Ideal was always an innovater, not a copier. A doll that could be given a home permanent was another of Ideal's major successes.

The chemists of the DuPont Company were enlisted to create a fiber for this doll's hair. Even a new type of glue was developed to hold the hair firmly to the doll's head during her frequent shampoo sessions.

In 1949 the 14-inch size *Toni* doll sold for $9.95. (This equals $23 in December of 1975.) *Toni* came in a box with the same magenta and gray stripes as the famous Toni Home Permanent kits. She had her own lanolin "creme shampoo," a Toni "play wave" consisting of a sugar and water solution, 12 plastic "Midget Spin Curlers," papers for wrapping the hair in the curlers and her own personal comb. And of course the "Directions for Toni Play Wave."

As a caution to Toni's beautician's "Mother" a notice was included stating that the "play wave" was absolutely safe in the hands of children" but they should "NEVER . . . play with real home permanent waving lotion." A recipe was given to make more Play Wave Lotion: "Mix 1 teaspoon of sugar with 1/8 cup water."

In 11 easy steps with pictures the little owner was instructed how to give *Toni* her permanent and then style her hair.

Following these instructions, the procedure requires considerable concentration, dexterity and patience. And even with great care *Toni* lost more hair each time she needed a new permanent because the glue holding the wig to her head was not completely nonwater-soluble. The Play Wave Instructions had informed the young beauty operator that "The Magic Nylon Wig on your *Toni* dolls is very expensive to make. It's the only kind of doll hair that you can shampoo and wave over and over again and still keep it looking like new. Naturally, the more gently you treat her hair . . . the prettier it will stay . . . so treat it carefully as you would your prettiest party dress."

Toni was so popular that she came in several sizes ranging from the easy-to-find 14 inch to 20½ inch.

In October of 1950 *McCall's Magazine* offered the first pattern for additional outfits for *Toni.* Pattern No. 1561 enabled *Toni* to be a Cowgirl, complete with boots, fringed skirt, shirt, bolero and hat; a Drum Majorette; and Fluffy Ruffles in a calico dress and picture hat.

By 1951 the very popular *Toni* doll with variations of heads and bodies was also *Mary Hartline, Harriet Hubbard Ayer, Miss Curity* and *Betsy McCall.*

Ideal's Toni Dolls

Part II
Featuring Mary Hartline, Betsy McCall, Miss Curity and Harriet Hubbard Ayer

by JOHN AXE
©1976 Hobby House Press, Inc.

The *Toni* doll of 1949 from Ideal Novelty and Toy Company was a creation of Bernard Lipfert, the doll sculptor who rendered the most popular play dolls of the 1930s, such as EFFanBEE's *Patsy* series, Madame Alexander's *Dionne Quintuplets* and Ideal's *Shirley Temple* dolls. A successful and widely sold doll has always been imitated and copied. Johanna Gast Anderton's *More Twentieth Century Dolls* shows a doll manufactured by Pedigree, one of England's leading doll producers, (pg. 1000) which looks exactly like *Toni.* She is called the *Pin-up Doll* with "magic nylon hair" that can "be shampooed and play-waved with the Pin-up Play Perm outfit."

Pin-up is so identical to *Toni* that it is likely that this doll and similar Canadian dolls were authorized by Ideal, unlike the hard plastic dolls of other leading American manufacturers who copied the shampoo-able hair concept for their dolls. Ideal itself released two other dolls in 1952, utilizing the *Toni* doll mold.

The first of these dolls, which is basically the same as *Toni,* was *Mary Hartline.* I have only seen the *Mary Hartline* doll in the 15in (38.1cm) size with the head and body marked (P-91) (not considering a 7¾in (19.8cm) *Mary Hartline* also made by Ideal). *Mary Hartline* has long, golden side-parted hair and heavy eye shadow above and below the eyes. She is

76

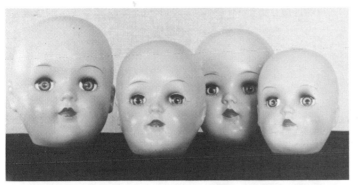

Illustration 1. The four sizes of marked Ideal heads for the *Toni* doll. From left to right: P-93 for the 20½in (52.1cm) doll; P-91 for the 15in (38.1cm); P-92 for the 18½in (47.0cm); P-90 for the 14in (35.6cm). These heads were available from a doll supply company in the 1950s and were used as replacements for damaged *Toni* dolls and are still "like brand-new."

Illustration 2. Two 15in (38.1cm) all-original P-91 *Mary Hartlines*. The baton seems much too large to be considered as belonging to the doll but it is original. The white hearts and the music notes on the red dresses are painted on and are washable.

dressed in a bright red majorette costume with matching underpants, wears gold-trimmed boots and came with a small baton in the original package. A metal barette holds her hair back.

Mary Hartline was an early television personality. From 1949, when she was 23 years old, until 1956 she was the band leader on a popular children's show *Super Circus*, which originated live from Chicago and was presented by ABC on Sunday evenings from 5:00 p.m. to 6:00 p.m. The show featured guest acrobats, animal acts and other circus specialities, announced by ringmaster Claude Kirchner. Providing the comedy were the clown Cliffy the Tramp, Scampy the Boy Clown and Nick Francis "the Fat Clown."

Now Mary Hartline is the widow of Woolworth Donahue and she lives in elegant Palm Beach, Florida, although she still maintains her membership in the American Federation of Musicians.

Ideal's other new doll for 1952 was *Betsy McCall,* which used the P-90 14in (35.6cm) *Toni* body with a different head.

Betsy McCall originated as a paper doll in the May 1951 issue of *McCall's Magazine* and was drawn by Kay Morrissey. At that time *Betsy* was described as "five, going on six." The *Betsy McCall* paper dolls appeared in the magazine monthly for several years and featured about four new outfits in each issue. In subsequent editions of the full-page series *Betsy* was joined by her cousins *Barbara* and *Linda* and her friend and neighbor, *Jimmy Weeks,* among others.

In September of 1952 *Betsy's* mother took her shopping for a new dress and also promised her a doll. *Betsy,* of course, selected a doll that "looked just like" herself. And the *Betsy McCall* page featured paper doll outfits for the new doll that were identical to *Betsy's* own. The same issue of *McCall's* introduced "*Betsy McCall's* new doll," not crediting her

to Ideal. This first *Betsy McCall* doll had a vinyl, stuffed head with a glued-on dark brown wig and round, brown sleep eyes. This material is an early vinyl called "soft plastic" then. It has not deteriorated with age or become sticky to the touch as have some forms of vinyl from that era. Her hair could be washed and curled with the accompanying curlers. Also

Illustration 3. Original box for the *Mary Hartline* doll showing the star of *Super Circus* with the doll that represents her.

included was a tiny McCall's pattern for a simple apron whose most creative feature was a pocket. McCall's regular patterns 1728 and 1729 were more outfits for the doll.

Within a few years *Betsy McCall* dolls had been issued by several of the American doll companies in sizes ranging from 8in (20.3cm) to 35in (88.9cm) and some closely resembled the picture of the paper doll while others bore little similarity to her features.

In time for Christmas of 1953 Ideal marketed two more dolls that are variation of *Toni*. *Miss Curity* is the 14in (35.6cm) P-90 mold and is identical to the same size *Toni* except that her hair was a yellow-blonde and she, like *Mary Hartline,* had a liberal application of eye shadow above and below her blue eyes. "The First Lady of First Aid" could also have her hair

shampooed and curled with "Ideal's doll curlers."

A "Play Nurse Kit" came with *Miss Curity*. The instructions told how to use the packages of Curity bandages, sterile pads, gauze and absorbent cotton, all products of Bauer and Black, a division of the Kendall Company. Other nursing equipment came in the cardboard suitcase: a tongue depressor, scissors, candy pills, thermometer, hypodermic syringe, eye chart and a fever and temperature chart. These items were so *Miss Curity* could "keep your doll Family healthy." The booklet in the kit told the owner of the doll how "to play nurse" and informed her that for herself a play nurse's uniform from Ideal was "available now in most department stores."

Ideal's other newcomer in 1953 was *Harriet Hubbard Ayer* who was

Illustration 4. 14in (35.6cm) *Betsy McCall* by Ideal; marked ''P-90'' on her shoulders and ''McCall Corp.'' on the vinyl head. Her blouse is white and the jumper is bright red rayon. The apron pattern was included with the doll. Pictured on the tag hanging from the doll's left arm is the first *Betsy McCall* paper doll drawn by Kay Morrissey.

Illustration 5. 14in (35.6cm) all hard plastic *Miss Curity;* marked ''P-90'' on her head and shoulders. She stands between her original box and the kit containing her nurse supplies. Her uniform is white and her cape is navy blue lined in red.

Illustration 6. 14in (35.6cm) and 15in (38.1cm) *Harriet Hubbard Ayer* dolls. Both dresses are gray. The aprons are white with green stripes on the smaller doll and red stripes on the larger one. The vinyl heads are marked ''MK 14//Ideal Doll'' and ''MK 16//Ideal doll,'' although the larger *Harriet Hubbard Ayer,* like other dolls using the P-91 *Toni* body is 15in (38.1cm) tall. The shoes and sox are not original.

even more versatile than the other doll characters in the *Toni* line. This doll endorsed a brand of cosmetics named after the founder of the company, a beautiful and stylish New York businesswoman of the Gilded Age.

Harriet Hubbard Ayer began her professional career as an interior decorator for the newly wealthy of New York City in the 1880s. Previously she had been a fashionable Chicago society woman but her husband had lost his money in bad business investments and then had gone through her money and afterwards had become

separated from her, leaving two daughters in her care. Her decorating business became more successful after she accepted a commission to redecorate the yacht of James Seymour, an oil baron, whom she assumed had become her friend. Mrs. Ayer felt compelled to earn a great deal of money to regain her former security and so that her daughters would never have to suffer her setbacks.

The older of Harriet Hubbard Ayer's daughters married the son of Mr. Seymour. By this time Mrs. Ayer had entered the cosmetics business, her first successful item having been cold cream, and in a few short years was earning a fortune from this enterprise. In early 1893 Mrs. Ayer was forcibly taken to a private mental institution and declared insane. Her now divorced husband and her daughter Mrs. Seymour claimed when they had her confined that she had become addicted to drugs and was incapable of controlling her own affairs. The ex-husband and the daughter both advanced a claim in the courts saying that they were entitled to manage Mrs. Ayer's property, including her lucrative cosmetics empire. Harriet Hubbard Ayer spent 14 months in confinement but the courts saved her company by permitting business associates to manage her affairs. Mrs. Ayer had appeared in court herself in 1889 to accuse her former client, Mr. Seymour, of attempting to drive her insane. She said that the oil baron was turning robber and that he foresaw great profits in her company, which he planned to control.

The colorful Mrs. Ayer was rescued from this dilemma and later went on speaking tours to vindicate her character by relating her experience in the ''madhouse'' to sympathetic audiences.

By the 1950s the ownership and management of Harriet Hubbard Ayer,

Incorporated, had no connection with Mrs. Ayer or the persons she accused of trying to steal her business. It was the successor company that collaborated with Ideal to produce a doll who used Harriet Hubbard Ayer cosmetics.

The Harriet Hubbard Ayer doll came in the four *Toni* sizes - 14in (35.6cm), 15in (38.1cm), 18½in (47.0cm), and 20½in (52.1cm) - and used the standard *Toni* body. Her head, like the one on the *Betsy McCall* doll, is vinyl and stuffed with cotton batting and she also has round sleep eyes that open and close independently and a glued-on wig. The color of the hair on different dolls is various shades. Another feature of the *Harriet Hubbard Ayer* doll is vinyl arms with long red fingernails. Her clothing is a gray dress, over which she wears a green or red striped apron.

The face on this doll is rather pale, with no coloring on the cheeks or lips. She arrived with a generous assortment of cosmetics packed in a kit, so that the proud owner could practice the art of cosmetology in ''making-up'' her face. The beauty aids were nonpermanent so that different effects could be achieved to accommodate her moods and occasions. This concept was as innovative in its time as was the first *Toni* with hair that could be washed and curled.

Simply designed and durable, yet attractive and appealing, dolls like *Toni* and Ideal's other girl dolls of the 1950s are not produced today. Ideal Novelty and Toy Company is still partly under the auspices of the Michtom family, heirs of the founder of the company, and this concern still manufactures many creative and original dolls for the popular market. The girl dolls are more mature and sophisticated in appearance and are also typical of the tastes of the times. And they too will one day be highly sought after by collectors.

Illustration 1. Left to right: Susan B. Anthony, Babe Ruth, Annie Oakley, Amelia Earhart, George Washington Carver and Chief Joseph.

Very Special Doll People

BY ALMA WOLFE
Photographs Courtesy of Hallmark Cards

The characteristic of heroism is its persistency...
...when you have chosen your part, abide by it, and do not weakly try to reconcile yourself with the world...
...Adhere to your own act, and congratulate yourself if you have done something strange and extravagant and broken the monotony of a decorous age...
Ralph Waldo Emerson*

How well the men and women, who are now portrayed, and who will be portrayed, in the historic doll series by Hallmark Cards exemplified this sage counsel.

The "Famous Americans" Series of Collectible Dolls was inspired by the success of the innovative Bicentennial Commemorative Dolls. Hallmark Cards desired to create a line of dolls, not only for dollologists, but dolls that would "be a history lesson to youngsters and adults alike."

Hallmark product manager, Tom Nocita stated, " . . . we wanted to do something different. . . . We're striving to be unique with our new line."

To meet this challenge, a committee was appointed to decide on the category to be represented, and to establish the criterion for choosing the historical personages who would become doll people.

Several categories were discussed--political, military, sports, entertainment, authors, etc. The committee's final decision was to produce a varied, diversified group of Americans from all fields of endeavor. Women and minority figures will be equally represented.

The individuals who will be chosen for the Series must have risen above the norm, excelled in their endeavor, and become "special" people. Their costume must be

Illustration 2. "FAMOUS FEMINIST Susan B. Anthony, who led 19th century women's rights campaign...one of a collectible doll series from Hallmark Cards..."

readily identifiable with them—"either by trade or time period."

And it is imperative that each character have a familiar environment, for each doll facsimile will be uniquely packaged in an easily recognizable "house." Inside the "house" lid will be a mini biography of the figure.

The personages chosen for Series I are Susan B. Anthony (to be honored by issuance of a dollar in 1979), George Washington Carver, Amelia Earhart, Babe Ruth, Chief Joseph of the Nez Perce Indians and Annie Oakley.

A year-and-a-half of painstaking research was done on various periods of each individual's life. Countless

pictures were closely examined. The dolls, the costumes and the "houses" would be authentic in every detail.

An example of the striving for authenticity is the George Washington Carver doll, who "resides" in a facsimile of the Tuskeegee Institute. A Hallmark designer contacted the Institute and obtained a photograph of it as it appeared in Carver's time. The package was then designed from this photograph.

These dolls, that make history come uniquely alive, appeared in the marketplace on February 1, 1979. "The beautifully handcrafted cloth dolls in classic silk-screen designs" are 6½ in. (16.5cm) tall. Each doll rates a descriptive paragraph, but space does not permit.

They sell for $4.00 each—indeed a bargain. The figures can be procured only where Hallmark Cards are sold. They cannot be ordered from Hallmark Cards. If you do not live near a store selling this Series, perhaps you can enlist the aid of a friend in another locality.

The Summer 1979 issue of *Hallmark Expressions* (free at Hallmark stores) gives directions for constructing a display hutch for the Series.

A Market Research Questionnaire, plus a SASE, is enclosed with each doll. You will have the opportunity to evaluate the Series, and also to let Hallmark know how the doll "will be used," etc.

Illustration 3. Advertising.

And conjure up visions of Series II which will include P.T. Barnum, Juliette Gordon Low, Davy Crockett, Clara Barton, Mark Twain and Molly Pitcher. They will be available in August 1980. Future Series will include John J. Audubon and Harriet Tubman.

Mr. Nocita said, "Our dolls are meant . . . to begin a tradition, and we believe people will find it's a tradition worth starting."

Yes, these dolls can be treasured today and passed on to future generations as prized possessions.

* *Poems and Essays* by Ralph Waldo Emerson Quotes from ad and press release from the desk of Jane Hodges-Reiminger, Mgr.,Public Information, Hallmark Cards.

REAL DOLLS
THE DIONNE QUINTUPLETS

by JOHN AXE

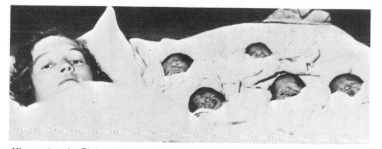

Illustration 1. Elzire Dionne and the Quintuplets when they were two days old. This picture, taken by *The North Bay Nugget,* is one of the most published photographs in newspaper history.

Illustration 2. The Dionne Quintuplets, summer 1939.

At four o'clock in the morning on the 28th of May 1934, Oliva Dionne of Corbeil, Ontario, excitedly called at the home of Dr. Allan Roy Dafoe of nearby Callander to beg him to come to his house. Mrs. Dionne had entered a complicated labor two months early and it appeared that her life was in danger. When Dr. Dafoe arrived at the humble Dionne home Elzire had already given birth to two babies and a third was being delivered by a pair of local midwives. Two more baby girls were aided into the world by Dr. Dafoe. The five tiny girls weighed a total of 10 pounds, 1¼ ounces when they were first weighed a day and a half later. No one thought that these babies would live. But they miraculously survived and became the most celebrated babies the world ever knew. The Dionne Quintuplets held the attention of everyone who had ever heard of them after their first

Illustration 3. One of the last portraits of the four surviving Dionne Quintuplets, December 1965. Left to right: Cécile Langlois, Annette Allard, Marie Houle and Miss Yvonne Dionne.

picture, posed in bed with their mother, was published in newspapers throughout the world.

Today news of a quintuplet birth would not command much notice. There are more than 30 sets of quintuplets throughout the world today. But the Dionne Quints were a genuine miracle because they were the first to survive. People everywhere were interested in them and followed their development throughout their childhood. Photographs appeared in the newspapers daily for several years. It was a big news item when they gained weight; when the first Quint, Annette, cut a tooth it was reported on the front page of the paper as were the first baby steps taken by Emilie; bold headlines cited the fact that Marie and Cécile kissed the Queen of England in 1939; and it was a major "scoop" that Yvonne shook hands with the King in a very dignified way during the Royal Couple's visit to Canada. The Quints themselves were real live princesses and they were revered almost as religious figures.

During the Depression of the 1930s people did not have the money to indulge in expensive vacations. Yet they were able to dream of visiting the Quints and seeing them for themselves - - and thousands made the trek to northern Ontario to do so. An average weekday brought 3,000 visitors and on weekends and holidays the number was about triple. During the early years an average of 100,000 visitors came to Corbeil each summer to see the Quints at play for a couple of minutes. About 70,000 tourists came from the United States each year. The annual value of the American tourist traffic to Ontario was estimated at between $100,000,000

Illustration 4. 7in (17.8cm) all-composition *Marie* with movable head, arms and legs; marked on head "Dionne//Alexander;" marked on back "Alexander." She wears her original diaper, undershirt and bib and is from a set of five who came in a white wooden bed. The brown painted eyes are glancing to the doll's right.

Illustration 5. 23in (58.4cm) *Cécile*. The construction and the markings are similar to the 16½in (41.9cm) size, the difference being an open mouth with a tongue and two upper teeth and straighter hair. The original dress carries a label reading "Dionne Quintuplets// Madame Alexander//Reg. N.Y." The name pin of a gold color metal came on Dionnes of the different sizes. *Barbara DeVault Collection.*

Illustration 6. 16½in (41.9cm) baby with a composition swivel head on a shoulder plate; composition arms and legs; brown sleep eyes with lashes. The soft cloth body has a cry voice. Marked on head "Dionne//Alexander." Some 17in (43.2cm) toddlers have this same head marked only "Alexander." *Connie Chase Collection.*

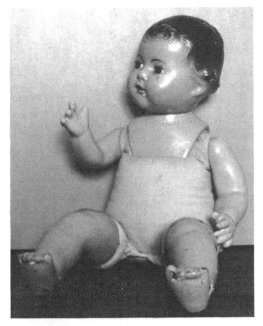

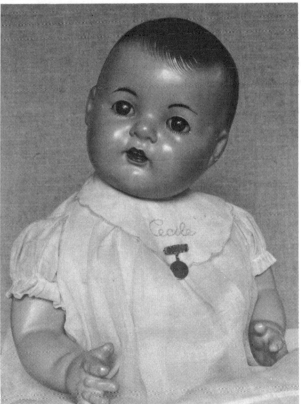

Within 24 hours of the Quint's birth their father ill-advisedly signed a contract to exhibit the babies at the Chicago World's Fair. Because of this Attorney General Arthur W. Roebuck of Canada obtained a court order to save the Quints from "certain death in some vaudeville show" and appointed the first set of "guardians" for the new daughters of Mr. and Mrs. Dionne. The girls were secluded in a specially built nursery under the care of Dr. Dafoe. The parents were entitled to visit them if they first donned sterile gowns and masks and did not

and $125,000,000. In an average year the money earned by, and because of the Quints, was nearly a billion dollars, which left them with few industrial rivals in the world. The Dionnes should have been very happy.

The Quintuplets earned a fortune for themselves and for their family with product endorsements, the sale of photographs and souvenirs and lucrative motion picture contracts. However, because of the unprecedented attention they gained, they and their parents led lives of unhappiness and misery inspite of their wealth.

interfer with the rigid schedule of the "Hospital," named in honor of the doctor.

Oliva Dionne was attempting to raise money when he signed the contract for the World's Fair and had rushed into it without thinking of the alternatives. Elzire Dionne had no other reason for existing except to be a good wife and mother and the government had denied her this right. The parents entered litigation that lasted for ten years to have the Quints restored to their care. In the meantime, Mr. and Mrs. Dionne had become

irretrievably bitter and frustrated and the girls' childhood was permanently affected by their being the center of the controversy.

The Dionne family was reunited in 1944 and went to live in an elegant mansion built on their property out of funds earned by the Quintuplets. The five millionaires were not permitted to enjoy the money they had earned but were forced to lead routine lives within the family after a lifetime of world-wide attention. They who were exuberant babies and precocious children became shy introverts who never again were able to accept intimacy nor to find the "normal" lives that eluded them.

After August of 1954 the Quints became estranged from their parents when Emilie suffocated to death in a convent during a serious epileptic attack. Emilie's affliction, which developed after she left the Nursery-Hospital, was considered a shameful secret and the family guarded it from everyone, including the doctors who could have helped her. In February of 1970 Marie was found, having been dead for three days, face-down in her bed - - the same way that Emilie had died. Officially Marie died of a blood clot of the heart, but she had lost her enthusiasm for life some months prior to her death. She, like Annette and Cécile had been married, but none of the relationships continued to be happy and the three sisters had become permanently separated from their husbands. Yvonne, who works in a library near Montreal, where the surviving Quints live today, never married.

Oliva and Elzire Dionne still live in far-away Corbeil in a small ranch house, within yards of the site where

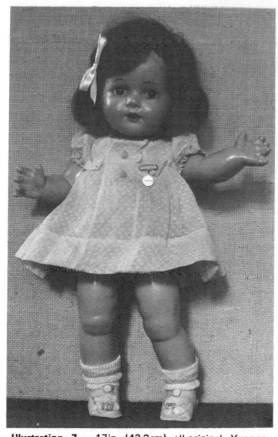

Illustration 7. 17in (43.2cm) all-original *Yvonne* toddler with labeled dotted swiss dress in pink, her color; fully jointed; open mouth with four teeth; brown sleep eyes with lashes; human hair wig. Only the body is marked "Alexander." The other colors assigned by Madame Alexander were lavender for *Emilie;* yellow for *Annette;* green for *Cécile* and blue for *Marie.* The pins for *Emilie* read "Emelie" for some unknown reason. *Lois Barrett Collection.*

Illustration 8. 17in (43.2cm) all-original *Yvonne* girl; composition swivel head on shoulder plate; full arms and legs; tightly stuffed cloth body; human hair wig; brown sleep eyes with lashes; open mouth with teeth. The legs are thinner and straighter than on the toddler dolls. This doll is not marked at all; her pin and the tag on her dress carry the Madame Alexander markings. The gold paper label on the front of the dress refers to the wig and reads "Human Hair."

the Quints were born and practically next door to their former mansion. The original homestead was moved to the main highway near Callander in 1962 as a tourist attraction. Since 1967 the house in which the Quints were born has been a museum of Dionne Quintuplet memorabilia operated by Mr. and Mrs. Stan Guignard, whose collection is authentic Dionne mementos, purchased from the family. The museum contains the original furniture of the Dionne home and most of the belongings of the Quints from their childhood years.

The generation who was born after World War II is scarcely aware of the Dionne Quintuplets. Most young people in Ontario today have never heard of them. Yet there are small "museums" all over the country that feature collectibles of the Dionne Quintuplets.

Collections that contain Dionne Quint items include booklets and paper dolls, toys and puzzles, calendars and fans, spoons and dishes, scrapbooks and pictures, postcards and sheet music, handkerchiefs and baby

Illustration 9. The original Madame Alexander box in which *Yvonne* was packaged.

bibs and all kinds of dolls that were sold as "Quintuplets." The only "genuine Dionne Quintuplets dolls" were those marketed by the Alexander Doll Company from 1935 to 1939. This was the only doll manufacturer who had exclusive rights to produce dolls bearing the Dionne name, having gained this privilege by a secret agreement with the Quints' guardians. All other American doll companies manufactured doll replicas that looked like the famous Quints and retail outlets obligingly displayed them in groups of five. Japanese manufacturers produced an immense variety of small

dolls that were called the "Five Sisters," "Quinties," and even "The Quintuplets," and sometimes included a nurse with the set to remind purchasers of whom the dolls were supposed to be.

The Madame Alexander Dionne Quintuplet dolls, made of composition, were a quality product. During the years of production, Dionne Quint dolls were made in several variations. The following lists the Dionne dolls from Alexander which the author has personally inspected, but it is conceded that there may have been other variations distributed.

BABIES   MARKINGS

7in (17.8cm)	All composition straight hair painted eyes	Head: "Dionne//Alexander' Back: "Alexander"
7in (17.8cm)	All composition curly hair painted eyes	Head and Back: "Alexander"
10in (25.4cm)	All composition straight hair closed mouth	Head: "Dionne//Alexander" Back: "Madame//Alexander"
11½in (29.2cm)	Cloth body curly hair open mouth	Head: "Alexander"
16½in (41.9cm)	Cloth body straight hair closed mouth	Head: "Dionne//Alexander"
17½in (44.5cm)	Cloth body curly hair closed mouth	Head: "Alexander"
23in (58.4cm)	Cloth body straight hair open mouth	Head: "Dionne//Alexander"

TODDLERS   MARKINGS

7½in (19.1cm)	All composition mohair wig over straight hair painted eyes	Head: "Dionne//Alexander" Back: "Alexander"
7½in (19.1cm)	All composition curly hair painted eyes	Head and Back: "Alexander"
11½in (29.2cm)	All composition mohair wig over straight hair closed mouth	Head: "Dionne//Alexander" Back: "Madame//Alexander"
11½in (29.2cm)	All composition curly hair closed mouth	Head: "Alexander"
11½in (29.2cm)	All composition curly hair open mouth	Head and Back: "Alexander"
11½in (29.2cm)	All composition curly hair open mouth	Head: "Alexander" Back: "Madame//Alexander"
11½in (29.2cm)	All composition (can be 11¼in [28.6cm]) chubby legs curly hair open mouth	Head: "Alexander" Back: "Madame//Alexander"

The Dionne Quintuplets are not photographed and written about in news articles now as they were for many years after their birth. They are nearly forgotten by the public in general but collectors are helping to insure their immortality. The Quints as children were very cute and very photogenic and all the items that were made because of their popularity and lovingly treasured since 1934 are proof of the endearment that people had for them. The Dionne Quintuplets are still the only identical set ever reported in the history of the world and although they never did anything amazing themselves they will always be remembered because there *were* Five of Them who were all alike.

Illustration 12. 3-7/8in (9.8cm) all-bisque dolls with movable arms in the original box. The dolls have brightly painted gold and silver hair; the facial features are poorly sketched. The clothing is silk floss wound around the upper torso and silk glued-on skirts. The dolls and the skirts are marked "Made in Japan." These date from the late 1930s to capitalize on the rage for the Quints.

11½in (29.2cm)	All composition human hair wig over plain head closed mouth	Head: "Dionne//Alexander" Back: "Madame//Alexander"
11½in (29.2cm)	All composition human hair wig over plain head open mouth	Head: "Dionne//Alexander" Back: "Alexander"
14½in (36.9cm)	All composition curly hair closed mouth	Head and Back: "Alexander"
14½in (36.9cm)	All composition human hair wig over plain head open mouth	Back: "Alexander"
17in (43.2cm)	All composition curly hair closed mouth	Head and Back: "Alexander"
17in (43.2cm)	All composition human hair wig over plain head closed mouth	Back: "Alexander"
17in (43.2cm)	All composition human hair wig over plain head open mouth	Back: "Alexander"
GIRLS		**MARKINGS**
17in (43.2cm)	Cloth body human hair wig over plain head open mouth	no markings on doll

The Dolls with the Contagious Smile...

A Photographic Essay

By Patricia Schoonmaker

Largest composition Scootles made for Effanbee by Joseph Kallus. 21 inches (53.3 cm) tall with green eyes. Inset illustration reveals rear view of Scootles showing detail of modeling with dimples in elbows, shoulders, buttocks and backs of knees.

Side view of green eyed Scootles, two in original rompers. 21 in. (53.3 cm), 15½ in. (39.4 cm), 12 in. (30.5 cm) versions. Note dimples and details of modeling.

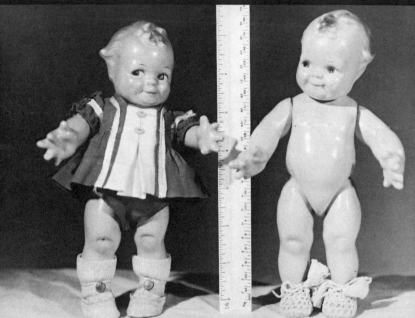

Smallest size (8 in. (20.3 cm)) Rose O'Neill Scootl. Doll on left is in original red and white dress, sh. and socks. Doll on left from the late **Sara Barrett Collectic**

Kewpie group. Left to right: composition talcum powder shaker; composition "Can't Break Em" type with ground cork stuffed body; celluloid Kewpie; 12 in. (30.5 cm) bisque rigid leg composition Kewpie. Scootles joins the group in front. **Gladys Hollander Collection.**

9½ in. (24.2 cm) Painted eye compo. tion Scootles poses with bisque Kewp. and more recent "Kewpie-types" from 196.

Rare bisque head, cloth body Kewpie from Germany. Similar dolls of composition would soon follow. Kewpie label can be seen on dress front at waist. From **Needlecraft** magazine, September, 1914.

Early advertisement for all bisque Kewpies showing original box. **Toys at Special Rates,** *Butler Brothers, Minneapolis, May, 1913.*

14½ in. (36.9 cm) Rare Kewpie issued at the same time as original Scootles. A version of the Scootles body has been utilized.

...e comparative ...otograph showing ...½ in. (29.2 cm) rigid ...g composition Kewpie ...d fully jointed 12½ in. ...1.8 cm) model from ...44-1946 with rare 14½ ...(36.9 cm) Kewpie ...m 1936.

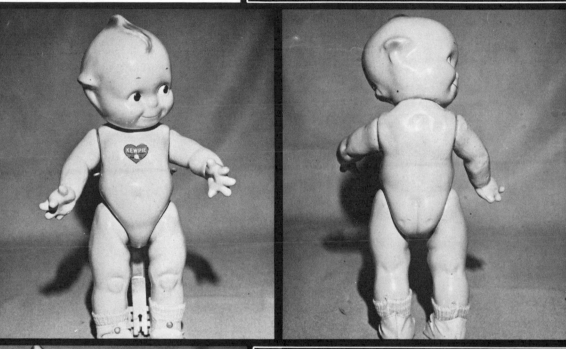

Close-up of rare composition Kewpie, 14½ in. (36.9 cm) issued with Scootles.

Cuddly Kewpies. Original advertisement for King Innovations, Inc. **Toy World** *magazine, April, 1930.*

"A hug of Scootles." The sizes range from 21 in. (53.3 cm), 15½ in. (39.4 cm), 14 in. (35.6 cm), 12 in. (30.5 cm), 9½ in. (24.2 cm) and 8 in. (20.3 cm). The earliest were green-eyed, while the 8 in. (20.3 cm) and 9½ in. (24.2 cm) came only with painted eyes.

tammy and Dolls You Love To Dress

BY JOHN AXE

Dolls, one of the minor arts or the decorative arts, in America are going through the same phase that the major arts experienced. Until the middle of the Nineteenth Century, art was not considered "good art" if it was not European. By 1850 an American school of art had developed. Modern dolls—dolls that were created in the past twenty five years—are now being elevated to the status of desirable collectibles. The modern collectible doll was usually a product of American ingenuity and imagination and was produced in this country.

Of all the modern dolls my favorite is the Tammy family of dolls from Ideal. Tammy came into being in 1962 as a response to the Barbie fashion dolls from Mattel which came out in 1959. Tammy was "all American" and so was her family of dolls. They were advertised as "the doll you love to dress." My book *Tammy and Dolls You Love To Dress* details the great variety of dolls from this series.

By 1963 Tammy was joined by Mom, Dad, brother Ted and little sister Pepper. From the beginning Tammy had ready-made fashions and there was a large selection of outfits for her family. There were also accessories, cars, boats, carrying cases, paper dolls, books and other Tammy-inspired items. Tammy, Pepper and Ted later came in "Pos'n" versions that could assume natural human positions. In 1964 Tammy gained a little brother named Pete and Pepper found friends Salty, Dodi and Patti.

Left: The original *Tammy* doll is 12in. (30.5cm) tall and has a vinyl head with rooted blond hair, vinyl arms and plastic legs and torso. This version is marked on the head:

IDEAL TOY CORP.
BS—12

The back is marked:

IDEAL TOY CORP.
BS—12
1

The outfit is part of the set called "Walking Her Pet."

Above: *Pos'n Pepper* and *Pos'n Tammy* in all-original outfits. There is wire inside the vinyl arms and legs of 12in.(30.5cm) Tammy and 9-1/4in.(23.6cm) Pepper so that they will pose in all positions. These two dolls were from Canada by Ideal Toy Co. of Canada; the dolls themselves were made in Japan.

Left: Pepper's Tree House is made of plastic with heavy cardboard for the foliage of the tree. The tree house dates from 1965 and is 32in. (81.3cm) high. The Pepper is "New Pepper" (a slimmer version) from 1965 and she wears the outfit called "After School." The two boys are different versions of Pos'n Pete and they are 7-3/4in. (19.8cm) tall. *Lee Jenkins Collection.*

By 1965 the Tammy doll was "Grown Up" with a slimmer body and black versions of the same Tammy doll were available. Tammy gained a new friend Glamour Misty who dyed her hair various shades and wore exotic make-up. She even had a boyfriend Bud, who is the most difficult to find of the series.

The Tammy line of dolls was also distributed in Canada by Ideal of Canada and Reliable of Canada made Tammy dolls under license from Ideal. Tammy was one of the first dolls advertised on national television in the United States and was the first doll ever advertised on television in Italy when she became a great success there in 1964. There were more Tammy-type dolls on the market during the 1960s than there were versions of Tammy herself. Many of these other dolls are close lifts of the Tammy mold from Ideal; others also include various family members for the basic doll. The doll that is the closest to the original Tammy is the Sindy by Pedigree of England and Sindy by Marx Toys, an American-based firm.

By 1966 Ideal was phasing out the Tammy line of dolls. "Out-of-production" dolls are always desirable collectibles. In the case of Tammy her production years were not all that long ago and many fine examples have survived. All of the variations of Tammy dolls are chronicled in *Tammy and Dolls You Love To Dress* to aid in identification and recognition. There are also charts that describe the fashion ensembles that were available for the dolls, along with photographs of the outfits in their original packages.

The Pedigree Sindy was introduced in England, Australia and New Zealand in 1963. Fortunately for collectors of these dolls they have never been out of production, and they have changed over the years, gradually becoming more articulated. The Pedigree Sindy dolls were also joined by other family members, like boy friend Paul. The American Marx Sindy seems to be one of the most popular dolls on the current market, as witnessed by the displays in retail stores along with furniture and accessories.

The all-American Tammy dolls are becoming more and more popular with collectors who appreciate modern dolls. And they are still affordable.

Above: Sindy by Pedigree from the 1960s. The costume is called "Honalulu Holiday" [sic]. The doll is 11-1/2in. (29.2cm) tall with blond rooted hair and blue painted eyes like Tammy. Pedigree is an English company and its dolls are primarily distributed by F.A.O. Schwarz. The dolls are unmarked. The original stand is incised: PEDIGREE // MADE IN HONG KONG. *Dori O'Melia Collection.*

Left: The American version of *Pos'n Tammy* sitting on her wooden bed that is all-original. Tammy's jumper is from the clothing set called "Cutie Co-Ed."

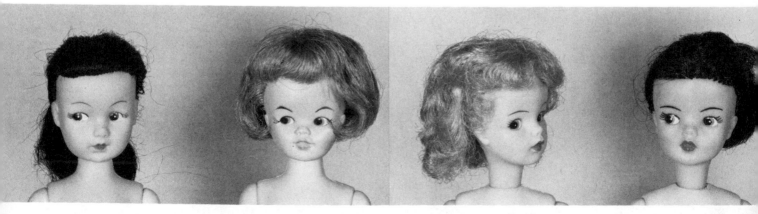

Two dolls that are Tammy-types. On the left is an 11-3/4in. (29.9cm) with black rooted hair marked on the head: 19 © 63 // GRANT PLASTICS INC. The doll on the right with rooted blond hair is 12in. (30.5cm) tall and her head is incised: AE // 18.

A blond and black haired Tammy made by Reliable of Canada. The dolls are the same as the dolls from Ideal but are marked on the backs: RELIABLE // CANADA. They have painted blue eyes like all white versions of Tammy.

Left: Susi is also similar to Tammy. She has dark blond rooted hair and stationary blue glass eyes with lashes. She is fully jointed including a swivel waist. Susi was made in Brazil and this model is No. 10.46.50 Susi Tenista (Tennis player). She is marked on the back ESTRELA S.A. The wire stand is like some of the stands that were included with Tammy from Ideal.

Right. One of the many Tammy paper doll booklets. This one is by Little Golden Press, Inc., #GF221. It is copyright 1964, 1963 by Ideal Toy Corp.

Below: The American *Sindy* is manufactured by Louis Marx & Co. She is 11in. (27.9cm) tall with rooted hair and painted eyes. She is fully jointed and poseable with extra joints at the waist and the wrists. The white doll has blond hair; the black one, called *Sindy's Friend,* has rooted black hair and brown painted eyes. The room setting is the Marx Scene-setter #1601. The furniture is dining table and chairs with dinnerware, *#1235;* the breakfront with desert service is #1236. Both dolls are marked on the head:

2 GEN 1077
033055X

The backs are marked:

MADE IN
HONG KONG

Illustration 1. Boxed # 1 Barbie doll. End papers say "Barbie T.M.". Fashion booklet says "Barbie T.M."

Will the Real #1 and #2 Barbie Come Forward?

by Sibyl DeWein

Editor's Note: Sibyl DeWein is coauthor (with Joan Ashabraner) of The Collector's Encyclopedia of Barbie Dolls, *and author of the new book,* Collectible Barbie Dolls of 1977-1979.

The recent avalanche of publicity about Barbie dolls selling for $500.00 is somewhat misleading and needs clarification. It is true that a **MINT-IN-THE-BOX** #1 or #2 Barbie doll of 1959 is worth at least $500.00, but an unboxed #1 or #2 is worth only $150.00 or less, depending on condition.

(My definition of a mint-in-the-box doll is a boxed doll in the same new condition it was in when it left the factory, one **NEVER REMOVED** from the original box!)

Except for the first two dolls and a few later rare issues, unboxed dolls in the Barbie line are worth under ten dollars. This very inexpensiveness has always been one of the reasons for the doll's popularity with collectors. Of course cost is not the only reason. Abundant supply, wide variety, excellent size, perfect proportions, and something that can only be called "the Barbie Mystique," all make the Barbie doll highly popular with a growing number of collectors of all ages.

Hopefully this article will help the seller as well as the buyer know the difference between the first two valuable dolls and the less valuable ones that followed.

A #1 Barbie doll has the following characteristics:

1. White irises - not blue as the #3 doll of early 1960.
2. Pointed (arched) eyebrows - not slightly curved as the #3 doll.
3. Now has pale (ivory or whitish) skin - not tan-toned as the #4 doll of the last half of 1960.
4. Metal tubes in the legs and feet with the openings (holes) in the balls of the feet. The first posing stand was a black plastic disc with two prongs on it; the doll's feet and legs fit down on these prongs.
5. Either blond or brunette soft, silky saran hair in a ponytail style with curly bangs.

Illustration 2. # 1 Barbie. White irises, arched eyebrows and pale skin.

Illustration 3. # 2 Barbie. Same as # 1 except it has no metal tubes in the feet and legs.

Illustration 4. # 3 Barbie. Notice the eye and eyebrow differences from the first two dolls. This doll has blue irises and slightly curved eyebrows, but it still has the pale skin.

6. Bright red lips and nails.

7. Slightly heavy torso.

8. Slightly soft silky feeling skin.

9. One-piece black and white striped swimsuit. (The same suit was used until 1962.)

10. Black high heel shoes with holes in the soles to correspond with the holes in the feet and the posing stand prongs.

11. "Barbie T.M." on the end papers of the doll's box.

12. "Barbie T.M." on the fashion booklet accompanying the doll.

13. Since at the time there was only one hair style, only the hair color (blond or brunette) was listed on the box. (The 1961 boxes were 1/3 in. (.83cm) longer and began listing hair style as well as color.)

14. Marked on hip: "Barbie T.M.// Pats. Pend.// c MCMLVIII//by//Mattel //Inc." (The dolls of 1961 and 1962 had these same markings except they had "Barbie ®" instead of "Barbie T.M..")

The #2 Barbie doll was exactly like the #1 with these exceptions:

4. The metal tubes were eliminated from the feet and legs. The prongs of the posing stand were replaced by a black "T" wire that fit up under the doll's arms; this made the "holes" in the doll's feet and legs unnecessary.

10. A few dolls still had shoes with the holes; most had shoes without holes.

11. A few came in the "Barbie T.M." box; others were in the "Barbie ®" box.

12. Most had the second fashion booklet with "Barbie ®" on the cover; a few had the first booklet.

Illustration 5. The first four Barbie dolls - two in 1959 and two in 1960. Notice that the skin of the first three has turned pale; the fourth retained the tan-toned color.

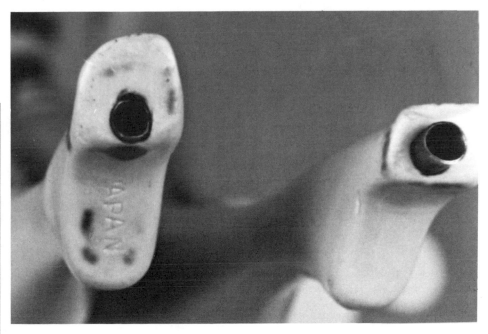

Illustration 6. ABOVE. The #1 Barbie had metal tubes in the feet and legs; these fit down on the prongs of the first posing stand.

Illustration 7. LEFT. The first three Barbie doll posing stands.

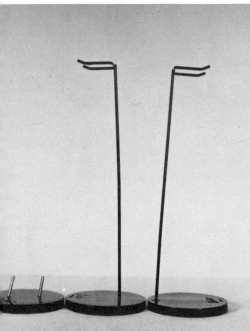

Illustration 1. This rare still shows Shirley in the pink satin and net dancing costume from the movie, *Baby Take a Bow*. In the 1930s, editors often cut off the dolls on the outside edges of the photograph to better fit the space available. *Arline Roth Collection.*

came from the song and dance the little actress had done with Jimmy Dunn in *Stand Up and Cheer*.)

The movie, *Baby Take a Bow,* had been held over in mid-July, 1934 for a third week at Manhattan's *Roxy* theatre. It broke box office records in Kansas City and Chicago and would be one of the most profitable Fox productions of the year. The production, *Now and Forever,* with Gary Cooper and Carole Lombard was the next movie completed on loan-out to Paramount.

According to *Time* magazine, a five year contract was signed in early 1934 in which Shirley was to receive $150.00 a week when adult stars of the same pictures were earning $3,000 or more a week.

Therefore, Shirley's father, a branch manager for the California Bank, informed the studio that Shirley would not begin work on her new movie, *Bright Eyes,* without a considerable raise in salary. When the new contract was negotiated, an additional benefit stipulated that a large group of dolls would be given to Shirley from the studio. While no specific evidence can be located, these were almost surely the first Lenci group. These were luxury dolls not owned by the average child in these depression days.

Shirley Temple's Lenci Dolls

by PATRICIA N. SCHOONMAKER

Imagine receiving 15 deluxe Lenci dolls all at once. Shirley Temple's official doll collection had an auspicious beginning! No doubt she had various other dolls before acquiring the 15 fabulous Italian made Lencis of felt, organdy and lace but those would have been the dolls of any fortunate little girl's early childhood.

Shirley had made a tremendous success with the debut of the movie, *Stand Up and Cheer,* in April 1934. By July 1934 *Time* magazine stated that Shirley was marked by Fox Studio as a natural overnight star who needed no press build-up. *Little Miss Marker* followed the first movie feature, breaking attendance records in New York. The studio then had a movie especially written for Shirley titled *Baby Take a Bow.* (The movie itself was not outstanding; the title

Illustration 2. (Doll marked 1 in Illustration 1). This close up of doll number 1 is a very rare type with caricature face, sculpted hair of felt and long, slender arms and legs. She is a flapper or boudoir doll.

94

Illustration 3. (Doll marked 2 in Illustration 1.) Fox photo by Gene Kornman. Publicity on the back of the photograph reads, "A very costly costumed doll is this lady with the lace fan, and one of the largest in the collection of Lenci washable felt dolls that Shirley Temple has received from admirers in foreign lands." A large Lenci label on left shows through from beneath the bottom ruffle of the gown,

Illustration 4. (Doll marked number 3 in Illustration 1.) Publicity read, "A rather elaborately gowned milkmaid is this doll with pail and wooden shoes. It is one of the largest of the many felt dolls sent by various admirers of the little Fox Film star in different parts of the world." Two shades of pink edge the organdy ruffles, the skirt is black trimmed in multicolored flowers. The blue hat is edged in chartreuse. This is one of the largest dolls made.

Illustration 6. (Doll marked number 4 in Illustration 1.) This is Pinkie, the favorite Lenci, gowned all in pink. The organdy material was stitched in a large diamond pattern with a felt circle dot sewed at the points of each diamond. Doll is shown here with Jane Withers who, in the movie, *Bright Eyes,* received this doll for Christmas. Illustration shows good detail of doll's face and hair.

Illustration 5. (Doll 5 in Illustration 1.) This very large doll is ...sed in shades of blue with white organdy cap and apron, and ...wristlets on her arms. *Lucille McClure Collection.*

Publicity writers were not severely troubled by truthful accuracy in the 1930s. Since the doll, Pinkie, (said to be so-named by Shirley as her favorite in the group) was used as a "prop" in the movie, *Bright Eyes*, Winfield Sheehan of Fox was given credit for giving the doll to Shirley at the completion of the movie. Actually, she received the entire group in the summer of 1934 before *Bright Eyes* was filmed.

Following the publication of these photographs of Shirley with her Lenci dolls, the Fox publicity department began talking about Shirley Temple's doll collection. People at the studio and fans then began giving her dolls in profusion. Many Lencis would follow including several with glass eyes and more than a dozen of the very tiniest sizes.

We do not know if these dolls were sent by the Lenci factory or purchased in Los Angeles shops, but they make a valuable contribution to collector's knowledge of dolls in 1934. The costumes are fresh and the face painting mint. Shirley worked out an arrangement with the studio in which her various dolls were rented to them for movies and publicity poses with the fees going into a milk fund for underpriviledged children.

Illustration 7. Some of the Lenci poses were done to be used for the Christmas season, 1934. This shows dolls marked 2 and 3 on left; Shirley holds doll 9, with dolls marked 5 and 4 on the right. *Carole Fogle Collection.*

Illustration 8. (Doll marked 11 in Illustration 1.) A clipping from an old scrapbook was all that was available of this doll. Unfortunately, the elaborate skirt is not shown but the pouty face with side-glancing eyes and a matching flower motif in the hair, to four on the skirt front is depicted.

Illustration 9. (Dolls numbered 8 and 9 in Illustration 1.) This precious pair may have represented Germany according to the braided buns hairdo of the little girl.

Illustration 10. (Dolls marked 13 and 14 in Illustration 1.) This marked pair representing Scotland could not be more charming. The eyes are painted to side-glance at each other. The plaid effect, even in socks, is accomplished by sewing single strips of vari-colored felt together. Lenci tag shows beneath Laddie's skirt.

ABOVE: Illustration 11. (Doll marked number 4 in Illustration 1.) Shirley hugs the favorite Pinkie who was soon to take part in the movie, *Bright Eyes,* as a doll given to Jane Withers.

RIGHT: Illustration 12. (Doll 7 in Illustration 1.) The back of this still reads, "Shirley Temple, Fox Film Star, with one of the many dolls from foreign lands. This boy doll, in Tyrolean costume, is a present from an admirer in Switzerland." The Lenci tag with "Made in Italy," is seen at jacket bottom. The boy's mate is girl number 15.

VOGUE DOLLS: Old and New
THE GINNY DOLL STORY
Part 1

by JEANNE NISWONGER
© 1977 Hobby House Press, Inc.

Also, it is interesting to report here that the Vogue Doll Company, a subsidiary of Tonka Toys, has recently been sold to the Lesney Corporation in New Jersey. The name of Vogue Dolls will be continued, according to information received, but it is not known whether the new company plans to continue the pro-

Illustration 1. *Ireland.*

Illustration 2. *Italy.*

Illustration 3. *Scotland.*

Vogue's *Ginny* doll has been one of the most enduring little dolls of all times, barring none, even *Barbie* or any other doll in modern times or foregone eras. *Shirley Temple* dolls have come and gone, being re-issued periodically as were the *Dionne Quintuplet* dolls, *Kewpies* and many others. *Ginny* has been around for more than four decades and her story is an interesting one. The next several columns will deal with the *Ginny* saga from her beginnings in the late 1930s through her heyday of the 1950s to the present time.

Although many collectors are familiar with *Ginny,* still others may not be; so, by way of introducing *Ginny,* it seems appropriate to give you information on the current *Ginny* dolls now on the market. This will be of help to collectors who may be wanting to collect *Ginnys* now while they are available and will need to know just what to be on the lookout for as some of the modern *Ginnys* have already been discontinued.

duction of *Ginnys* now being manufactured in the Far East.

First of all, here is a description of the *Ginny* dolls of the 1970s. She is constructed totally from vinyl plastic, has sleep eyes that open and close, rooted saran hair, is fully-jointed with delicately painted facial features. The doll can be posed. She is marked "GINNY" on the head (back of neck) and on the back the marking reads,

VOGUE DOLLS   1972
Made in Hong Kong
8

The number 8 indicates her size as 8in (20.3cm).

The first Hong Kong doll offered in 1972 was *Ginny* in a boxed set with three changes of outfits including a granny nightie, yellow overall crawlers and a turquoise skirt with Tyrolean design suspenders over a white blouse. This set was not on the market the next year but was replaced by the "GINNY COLLECTOR DOLL FROM FAR-AWAY LANDS." The original nine of this new line were

Illustration 4. *Dutch Girl.*

Illustration 6. *France.*

Illustration 5. *Scandinavia.*

girls from the following countries: *Holland, Scotland, Germany, Ireland, Spain, Mexico, Switzerland, France* and one labeled simply *"Tyrolean." Italy, Poland* and *Scandinavia* were added in 1974, making a dozen different dolls. In 1975 *Russia, Africa, Canada* and *North American Indian* brought the total number to 16 dolls in the series. By early 1976 only 12 of the dolls were being offer-

ed; those dropped were the *North American Indian, Germany, Italy* and *Poland.* No new ones were on the market. Apparently 1975 was the peak year for this series with the 16 different countries being produced.

These dolls all came packaged in an attractive see-through box with the doll fastened securely inside. The box is a bright pink color, a distinctive trademark of the Vogue line and the box is printed clearly as follows: "AN ORIGINAL VOGUE DOLL, A COLLECTOR SERIES: 8" GINNY FROM FAR-AWAY LANDS," all vinyl-jointed surface washable doll "IS MADE TO BE LOVED. MADE EXCLUSIVELY FOR VOGUE DOLLS INC. IN THE BRITISH CROWN COLONY OF HONG KONG." The box is also labeled according to the nationality of the doll. Unfortunately, if the box is lost, the doll does not carry a label designating the country. For this reason, we will give a brief description of the costumes of each doll in the hopes that it will help collectors in identifying dolls they may already have in their collection, or possibly are still searching for and may be able to find.

AFRICA 1802. This is a black doll and the vinyl is colored a nice shade of deep brown and the doll has a bouffant hairdo of glossy black hair. Her garment is a bright orange cotton print draped over one shoulder and there is a green blouse underneath.

She wears gold jewelry; ankle and arm bracelets and a necklace.

RUSSIAN 1814. This brown-eyed, dark-haired doll is attired in a long yellow cotton tiered double-ruffled skirt with black rickrack trim, long sleeves, and a red bolero trimmed in white braid. She wears red boots and has a red fez (hat). Her hairdo is distinctive, parted in the middle with a bun in the back.

IRELAND 1815. A green outfit is becoming on this doll who also has brown eyes. Our Irish colleen is dressed in lace-trimmed flowered print cotton skirt with a white cotton bodice and a kelly green apron and shawl with black fringe. There is a white dust cap also lace-trimmed with green bow and long white knit hose.

ITALY 1819. Sunny Italy is captured in the colorful costume of our Italian Miss. There is a flower print cotton dress over which she sports a yellow ribbon-trimmed apron. The lace trim of her sleeves matches the fancy hat. This doll is also a brown-eyed brunette.

CANADA 1820. This blue-eyed blonde doll typifies the provincial dress of our northern neighboring country. She has a one-piece white cotton dress with a full gathered skirt with rows of red, yellow and green velvet ribbon trim. There is a green velvet weskit worn on top and an elaborate lace peaked hat with red, yellow and green rayon satin ribbon streamers down each side.

99

Illustration 7. *Spain.*

Illustration 8. *Switzerland.*

Illustration 9. *Poland.*

Illustration 10. *Tyrolean.*

SCOTLAND 1826. Our Scottish Lassie is dressed in a red plaid cotton skirt and sash with white, lace-collared bodice and black velvet jacket. She also has a real bunny fur high hat and white felt spats. Her long blonde hair is worn in a ponytail style.

DUTCH GIRL 1837. The little Dutch maid is dressed in a crisp sky blue lace and velvet trimmed blue cotton skirt with flower print bodice and white sleeves and an embroidery and velvet trimmed white apron. She

also has an eyelet tulip cap, long yellow knit stockings and hand-carved real wooden shoes. To complete her Holland look she has sunny yellow braided hair and blue eyes.

NORTH AMERICAN INDIAN 1840. This dark-skinned doll has a different color to her than our African Miss. Her skin is reddish-brown, and hair is shiny black braided in two

pigtails and, of course, she has brown eyes. Her costume is fashioned of deep tan suede cloth with appropriate Indian design trims at the sleeves and edge of the tunic. Her long pants are fringed as well as sleeves and over-blouse. She wears soft moccasins.

SCANDINAVIA 1841. Another pretty blonde doll with long braids is this little miss representing the

100

Illustration 11. *Germany.*

Illustration 12. *Mexico.*

countries of Scandinavia. Her one-piece dress has a green cotton skirt with attached white blouse with lace trimming the long sleeves. Her white apron boasts a red, yellow and green diagonal flowered trim. She has a black velvet bodice and red shawl with black fringe and a lace-trimmed black velvet hat with unusual embroidery trim forming the crown.

FRANCE 1848. Our young Mademoiselle is wearing her native provincial outfit of a bright red skirt trimmed in black and yellow velvet banding and lace at the hem. She also has a black velvet bodice with applique over her white bodice. Her striking high-peaked hat boasts lace and ribbon streamers worn over her short auburn hairdo. She, too, has brown eyes.

SPAIN 1859. With all the gentility of Old Spain, our Senorita is dressed in a tiered, delicate, white ruffled lace long gown with black velvet top adorned with red roses and a black lace shawl. Roses also grace her lovely black lace mantilla, worn over her dark hair pulled back in a tight low bun. She also has brown eyes

and wears black velvet shoes tied on with satin ribbons.

SWITZERLAND 1865. Our Alpine Miss is wearing a bright red dress, embroidery banded, and a yellow lace-trimmed apron. Over her white long-sleeved blouse is a black velvet flower-decked vest and a large lace and velvet black hat.

POLAND 1876. Ready for a polka in native costume of white skirted cotton dress with embroidery-trimmed apron is our Miss Poland. She also has an applique trim on her puffed sleeves and a bright blue velvet bodice that tops her long skirt. Her black velvet cap has embroidery matching the apron. She wears high black velvet boots over long red stockings.

TYROLEAN 1887. Just as cheerful as a yodel is this gal in her gaily colored green skirt with wide trim at hemline and white cotton blouse with lace. She has a black velvet vest, green felt feather-trimmed Alpine hat and long yellow stockings. Her blonde hair is pulled back in a low bun.

GERMANY 1897. Miss Germany is so pretty in her Black Forest gown bedecked with floral and ribbon trim. The skirt is black, apron and blouse are white cotton and there is a blue velvet laced bodice. Her large black felt hat boasts 4 bright red pompons that signify she is not yet married.

MEXICO 1899. It is fiesta time in Old Mexico and our Senorita is appropriately dressed in bright clothing. There is a fiery red polished cotton skirt and flower-trimmed white apron. Her white blouse has ruffled sleeves and she wears a yellow suede weskit. Her long hair is covered with a sheer red mantilla and she is all ready to dance with her red suede shoes and ribbon ties.

All the clothes described originally carried a paper label inside reading "MADE IN HONG KONG." Some of the outfits may vary slightly as to trim, color and headdress according to the year manufactured.

The Ginny Doll Story
Part II

by JEANNE NISWONGER

Illustration 2. *Mary Had a Little Lamb* in a pink-flowered cotton dress with white ruffled sleeves and matching bonnet. This doll has separate panties and her shoes, stamped on the bottom, are side-snap pink leatherette. Her dress has the hook and eye closing and there is no tag.

More than anything else the story of *Ginny* and the Vogue Doll Company is an American success story; the personal success of one woman, a woman before her time who became the head of a million-dollar doll business out of sheer persistence, a talent for sewing and designing of clothes combined with courage, faith and imagination. The woman is Jennie Graves (now deceased) founder and president of Vogue and creator of the *Ginny* doll.

Mrs. Graves was well equipped for designing and making doll clothes for she had done this since childhood days. She made her first doll dresses at the age of nine and her family recalls that she dressed two china dolls in Red Riding Hood costumes for two small cousins. This warm act of generosity marked the earliest beginning of her creative interest in dolls at the turn of the century.

Born in West Somerville, Massachusetts, Mrs. Graves was the eldest of four children. At the age of 15, her father died. It was necessary for her

to work and help support the family. She graduated from business school and found a job in a fine lingerie shop. It was here amid new surroundings of lace curtains, plush draperies and velvet rugs that she found her first inspiration and enthusiasm for dolls. She resigned to be married when she was 21. She had three children, two of them girls, so her talent for making doll clothes was not wasted.

Her decision to enter the business of dressing dolls came about by coincidence. While shopping in a Boston Department store she came upon cases of dolls she had dressed for a woman who had said she was selling them in church bazaars. It developed that other stores too were selling her dolls as a high quality children's item. It was her drive and imagination that led her to start her own tiny enterprise in 1922. She bought three large dolls and dressed them in the same style dresses she had been making for her own daughters. A buyer bought the dolls at once and gave her an order for more. Her own kitchen was her first workshop with card tables to work on. She began importing a variety of fine bisque dolls from Germany such as the K★R. By the late 1920s through the early 1930s she also

Illustration 1. *Just Me.*

imported small bisque dolls in three sizes, 7in (17.8cm), 9in (22.9cm) and 11in (27.9cm) known as *Just Me* and marked "Armand Marseille." These were chubby child dolls with composition bodies and bisque heads with human hair wigs, some in a poodle cut. Later ones were fashioned entirely of composition. Technically falling in the classification of "googlie" dolls, the *Just Me* face features round eyes and cute little girl expressions. Vogue offered them

Illustration 3. Cinderella Group - the *Fairy Godmother* is attired in an elaborate medieval-style gown of pink dotted swiss with panniers and sleeves of flower-print pink satin. Her matching hat has ribbon streamers and she carries a wand. Shoes are pink leatherette, marked "Fairy Godmother" on the sole and she wears long pantaloons. *Prince Charming* sports pink cotton knit tights with a long blue satin jacket and a white cotton lace-trimmed shirt. His hat is also blue and is feather-trimmed. *Cinderella* wears blue organdy over a full petticoat and attached pantalettes. Her high blue hat has a long veil. All dolls have light brown mohair wigs over molded hair.

in trunks with whole wardrobes of clothing over the years. Vogue also made clothes for *Patsy* dolls.

By 1937, with World War II raging in Europe, the supply of dolls from Germany was cut off, and Vogue was forced to turn to domestic sources of doll supply. Thus began a successful alliance with Arranbee (R & B) Doll Company which was later absorbed by Vogue. They produced an all-composition 8in (20.3cm) doll that bore a striking resemblance to the *Just Me.* There is a great similarity in construction such as the chubby legs and body and especially the right arm bent at the elbow with thumb and little finger slightly separated from the other fingers. Facial features also are very similar; such as the eyes glancing to the right, full cheeks, button nose, rosebud mouth and thin eyebrows painted high on the head. Thus, we have the birth of the composition *Ginny,* a term that has been popularly used over the decades in describing this early Vogue doll. However, an obscure price list used by toy dealers reveals that this doll was named *Toddles* by the company, but apparently never widely promoted as such in the media or sales literature. So, the name of "composition *Ginny*" has endured and since it seems appropriate we have designated her as *Ginny* No. 1.

Mrs. Graves' husband died in 1939. One of her daughters was in

Illustration 4. *Hansel & Gretel.* These dolls are dressed in felt costumes with white cotton shirt/blouse. *Hansel's* lederhosen is red with yellow tiny rickrack trim and dark blue suspenders. He has a yellow felt Tyrolean-style hat. *Gretel's* outfit has attached cotton panties and her separate vest is navy blue felt with hook and eye closing in back although the blouse has a string tie. She has a yellow felt bonnet with white ruffle trim.

Illustration 5. Little girl is wearing a dress of pink organdy with attached panties. Dress is banded at the hem with a pink satin ribbon with picot trim and it has a ribbon belt with bow in front and tying in the back. The dress is further trimmed with a half vest in front with white picot trim that also edges the sleeves. There is a matching hat and pink leatherette pumps with white rayon socks. There is no tag or label.

Illustration 6. Naval officer wearing white duck trousers with navy blue flannel double-breasted jacket with gold braid at the sleeves. White cap has naval insignia and visor.

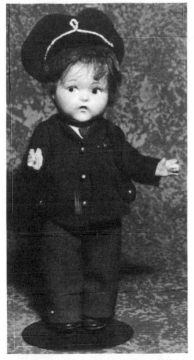

Illustration 7. Air Force officer wearing olive drab uniform with wings and gold buttons on jacket. Cap is brown and sports gold braid and stars. The trousers are attached to a white top and there is no clothing label.

college, the other children in high school and their support was a problem. However, she went ahead with courage and determination and moved her workshop from the family room of her home in Medford, Massachusetts, which she had converted into a small factory, to an old building in the city and slowly and steadily continued to expand. She believed that the most valuable commodity

in the business world was a good idea, in this case, her own dolls. She coined the slogan: **Fashion Leaders of Doll Society** and then later changed the name of her business to VOGUE DOLLS, INC.

The *Toddles* or composition *Ginnys* were offered in a variety of cute little girl clothes along with foreign costumes and makebelieve characters with new ones added every year. R & B dressed some of these dolls themselves, especially in the early years, but their workmanship varies somewhat from Vogue in that their clothing was buttoned on with white buttons. The early Vogue-constructed garments were tied on

Illustration 10. *Pirate.* This is a one-piece costume with sash and vest. Tan-colored cotton flannel pants have ragged edges and are attached to the white cotton bodice with ragged sleeves. Vest is blue felt with red trim and the sash is multicolored rayon ribbon tied at the waist side. Leatherette boots have the appearance of oil cloth and the sole of one is marked "priate." Hat is the same material as boots.

Illustration 8. *Alice in Wonderland* wears a blue cotton dress with white trim and there is a separate white cotton apron/pinafore over this. Dress is tagged "Vogue" in back; this is a white cotton label with "Vogue Dolls" written on a blue background.

Illustration 12. *Mistress Mary* is stamped on the bottom of her side-snap green leatherette shoes and she wears a long flower-print cotton dress with attached green pinafore with red and yellow trim. Her white cotton pantalettes are also attached to the dress and she has a matching hat and carries a rake for gardening.

Illustration 11. *Gypsy.* This doll is marked "R & B" and has the straight arm but is apparently dressed by Vogue. The panties and top are one-piece and over this she wears a pink and blue moire taffeta ribbon skirt with white organdy apron with applique trim. She has a yellow scarf tied on her head and golden earrings.

and also wool felt. Shoes were of various colored leatherette, slip-on pumps or fastened with snaps. There is considerable overlapping so it is hard to pinpoint the exact years. Also, there is a dearth of resource materials and there were no early catalogs to which to refer.

There seems to be two types of composition *Ginnys,* both very similar to each other. Early ones have the bent right elbow and are marked "VOGUE" on head and "DOLL CO." on the torso about half way down the back. Some of the markings on the head have become obscured with age. A slightly later version differs only in the arms which are both straight. Also, there is no mark on the head and the body impression is "VOGUE." Otherwise, the torso, legs and head are essentially the same although faces seem to differ sometimes due to the painting of the features; but invariably the eyes are blue and glancing to the right, eyelashes and brows are painted on in a certain fashion and the mouth is a cupid's bow. Some have only molded hair and others have mohair wigs added on top of the molded head. Some of the dolls are also impressed R & B, particularly later ones with the straight arm. I do not know the reason for this, but it is probably simply that Vogue bought up batches of dolls to dress regardless of their markings.

Illustration 9. Straight arm little girl wears a pale blue cotton party dress over an attached white slip of dotted swiss. The dress is a pinafore design tying in the back with a big bow and there is eyelet ruffle trim at hem and sleeves with a matching bonnet. Panties are separate and there are two hook and eye closings in back. The garment is also tagged with the blue and white Vogue label.

with string ties at the back of the garment; later ones had hooks and eyes. Many little dresses were made with attached panties; that is, the underpants and dress were all one piece. For the most part the early ones did not have attached cloth tags while later ones did. Many had small round paper labels designating them as VOGUE which were often lost or disintegrated when washed. At some point the shoes were marked on the sole as to the character the doll represented. Clothes were usually constructed of fine cotton materials

Ginny Doll Story
Part III

by JEANNE NISWONGER

Illustration 1. Mrs. Jennie Graves.

Illustration 2. Virginia Graves Carlson.

Illustration 3. *Toddles* and *Sunshine Babies.*

The *Ginny* doll was created by a woman who loved dolls, Mrs. Jennie Graves, who dressed dolls for fun and parlayed it into one of the largest firms in the country's 200 million dollar doll industry. Whether they are perched on a bed, slumbering in an attic trunk or cuddled in a little girl's arms, Mrs. Graves' contention was that dolls still held a large corner in any woman's heart. She had begun dressing dolls when about eight years old by gathering pieces of cloth left by the dressmaker who came to the house. After her marriage, Mrs. Graves whipped up eye-catching outfits for her children's dolls. Starting as a tiny business in 1922, the Vogue Doll

Shoppe was renamed the Vogue Doll Company by Mrs. Graves, the president of this million dollar business.

Mrs. Graves did not like the way dolls were dressed by manufacturers in the early days with their outfits tacked firmly on the dolls. Instead she used hooks and eyes on the little garments so that the dolls could be dressed and undressed just like real children. Starting in the basement of her home, the business soon grew and the garage was turned into a shipping room. Orders from department stores flowed in as word of her work spread. By the mid 1930s she had rented factory space in Medford, Massachusetts, and was employing

nearly 50 women. By 1950, the business occupied 15,000 square feet and her payroll quadrupled with 150 women sewing the clothes in their homes throughout New England and another 50 working in the factory.

The doll world has Mrs. Graves to thank for introducing wardrobe trunks with miniature outfits. However, it can never measure her service in recognizing that dolls should be as close to humans in looks and should receive as much attention as any human being when it comes to clothes.

The tiny costumes for the composition *Ginny* dolls, or *Toddles,* were designed by Mrs. Graves herself until the mid 1940s when her daughter, Virginia, who had worked part-time in the factory over the years, joined the company and became the designer for the next 25 years. A graduate of the Modern School of Design, Virginia Graves Carlson, dreamed up outfits with appropriate hairdos so smart that each doll seemed to have a personality all its own. Both mother and daughter believed that dolls should look like American children and should have up-to-the-minute fashions. Each year they would pore over fashion trends so that their tiny 'foster children' would be attired in the latest fasions.

The 8in (20.3cm) composition doll was produced by Vogue from the late 1930s until 1948, although it was probably sold in stores for sometime after that. Molded of sawdust or wood pulp combined with glue, the dolls lost favor following World War II in the doll world due to the fact that the composition deteriorated easily under certain weather conditions and it was also somewhat fragile with fingers and toes easily broken. As all were painted over, this was found to be less than satisfactory due to paint peeling and crazing.

World War II had brought about another source of material for doll production. The war, causing shortages in steel, had forced Americans to find a substitute and thus the modern day man-made plastic was produced. From then on, the doll manufacturers turned to plastic. Hence, this was the demise of the composition doll.

The composition *Ginny* or *Toddles* is highly collectible and beloved by doll collectors today. When she faded in the late 1940s, the

modern hard plastic doll now known as *Ginny* was born. At first unnamed, someone in the promotion department of the Vogue Company suggested that the doll be given a specific name. Everyone had their own idea, of course, wanting it named after their daughter, or a favorite female. Mrs. Graves soon put an end to the dissension and proclaimed that the doll would be named after her own daughter, *GINNY.*

ABOVE: **Illustration 4.** 7in (17.8cm) *Toddles - Cinderella Group.*

RIGHT: **Illustration 5.** 7in (17.8cm) *Toddles - Bridal Party.*

Illustration 6. *Toddles.*

Illustration 7. *Character and Nursery Rhyme* dolls.

Where Are The Widgets?

BY MARGARET GRONINGER

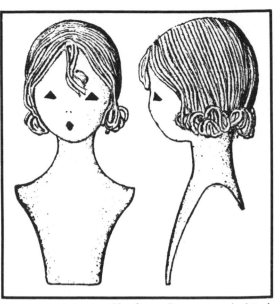

Illustration 1. Patent design, Serial No. 17,116. DOLL'S HEAD. Ray W. Dumont, New York, N.Y., assignor to Best & Co., Inc. . . . Filed March 20, 1926.

Very little that came out of the Art Deco era escaped that period's trademark: streamlined and stylized. The art dolls of the 1920s and 1930s were no exception.

Take the Widgets, for example.

What's a Widget? A unique cloth doll created by Miss Ray Dumont, a blue-jeaned, Amelia Earhart look-alike who was at one time under contract to the New York store, Best & Company, charged with the responsibility of supplying them with child mannequins for window displays. It would seem, in fact, that Dumont was probbably more famed for her mannequin work than for her dolls, as the latter venture probably only lasted three or four years. The mannequin work, carried on in Dumont's own studio, at least ranged into the mid-1930s.

Ray Dumont's mannequin creations should be examined with some care, since they appear closely related to her dolls, both in spirit and in form. Most of the Dumont display figures for Best were children (though one adult appeared in the July 1, 1926, issue of *Vogue*), and female (in a 1935 interview by the *Christian*

WIDGET

Illustration 3. Trademark patent, Serial No. 238,954. Ray W. Dumont, New York, N.Y. Filed October 21, 1926; claims use since August 20, 1926. Particular description of goods. — Dolls.

Science Monitor, Dumont admitted she much preferred doing little girls to little boys). All, regardless of age or sex, had a quality all their own. The molded faces possessed little pointed chins and only slight noses; mouths were tiny and eyes triangular; elbow and knee joints did not seem to exist on the better versions, as the forms bent only slightly there. As for the wigs, well, they were of a "beigey wool," often tightly curled, then plastered close to the head. The general appearance seemed somehow—French. And no wonder; Ray Dumont disliked the American-children-look that formed the inspiration for other mannequin makers in this country, so she selected as models the more slender, undimpled French types she had viewed on one Paris jaunt. Still, though each head was completely hand done and thus one of a kind, the designer cautioned that her mannequins were not portraits, but impressions. The finer mannequins she made of wood covered with suede or chamois as shown in the February 1, 1926, issue of *Vogue.* More roughly surfaced were some all wood children Dumont also turned out (for simpler clothes), examples of which can be seen in the June 8, 1929, *Vogue.* All looked like pieces of sculpture, perhaps by a Brancusi disciple. And all had the same basic face.

As did the dolls, which Dumont probably unleashed upon the New York scene around 1926. A design for a doll's head was patented that year, its designer listed as Ray W. Dumont, New York City, assignor to Best and Co., Inc., New York. Though the design did not mention the word Widget, the name did appear in a trademark also registered in 1926, and also taken out by Ray Dumont. Obviously the two went together!

Illustration 2. 1928 dolls, obviously Widgets; "smartly dressed in gay, crisp cotton costumes." About 18 in. (45.7cm) tall, and the middle one is sun tanned. Widgets are always found with black shoes.

Further proof of their alliance can be found in an illustrated description from the November 15, 1926, *Vogue,* which stated, "the 'Widgets' are engaging dolls with wonderfully lifelike personalities." The dolls were 26 in. (66cm) high; the girl boasted a blond worsted wig, the boy a wool bob. Both had mitten hands, slender bodies, long necks, triangular eyes that were probably painted, and appeared to sport rouged cheeks. The heads were almost identical to Dumont's patent design.

The Widgets stayed around for several more years. *The New Yorker* noted on December 3, 1927, Best's Widget dolls were still popular then, selling for $4.95.

The same publication gave Dumont's darlings more due the next year. In their December 1, 1928, issue, they reported about Best, "no special toy department, but one very special toy—the Widget Doll, deeply sunburned this year, and wearing pale woozy hair; boy dolls and girl dolls in darling costumes." Not only had tans been added, but the prices were raised—to $16.50.

Also in 1928, another magazine displayed dolls sold by Best that, though not identified as Widgets, surely were. The slim body structure and triangular eyes were there! However, the hair was looped rather than smooth, and the size smaller—down to 18 in. (45.7cm) tall. One was chicly suntanned, which would fit in with *The New Yorker* remark about the 1928 Widgets.

According to *The Fashion Dictionary* by Mary Pickens, chamoisette, the material used to make the Widgets, was a "trade name for closely woven cotton fabric, slightly napped by means of livery; used for gloves." And for dolls too, it appears. Worsted,

Illustration 5. 1929 all wood manniquins wearing clothes from Best; figures "from the Dumont studio." Different bodies, but faces like the Widgets.

which formed the hair on at least some of the Widgets, is defined by Webster's as "a smooth, hard-twisted thread or yarn made from long-stable wool."

That much is known. All the rest is mystery! For example, did the Widget popularity spawn an imitator, or did Ray Dumont work for concerns other than Best and Co.? The December, 1928, issue of *House Beautiful* showed a doll they called Patsy (no relation to the Effanbee lass) "with appealing face and white-wool hair," this "in Austrian peasant dress" and selling for $7.50 at Arden Gallery. Either a Widget or a close copy, the doll had the familiar boneless body

and triangular eyes, while the dress it wore closely resembled one shown on a 1926 Widget. But this 1928 doll was not sold through Best!

And that is not the only mystery. Why did the doll making venture cease? What happened to Miss Dumont? And was she the same Ray Dumont whose Alice in Wonderland paper dolls appeared in *McCalls* around 1915-1917?

Most of all, considering the dolls had wide national exposure for several years running, it seems odd that no examples have since come to the attention of the cloth doll collectors I know. Where are the Widgets?

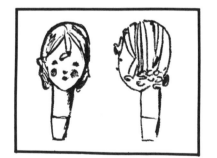

Illustration 4. Patent design, Serial No. 33,444. DISPLAY HEAD. Ray W. Dumont, assignor to Best & Co. Filed November 14, 1929. Dumont filed another patent design (FOR A MANNIKIN HEAD) in 1935; both are similar to the doll head design, the 1935 one less so than this one.

Illustration 6. 1926 child manniquin from Best; maker not identified, but obviously by Dumont. Note similarity to Widget doll.

TRUDY ...
A Composition Collectible

by PATRICIA N. SCHOONMAKER
© 1977 Hobby House Press, Inc.

Illustration 1. 18½in (47.0cm) *Big Sister Trudy,* three-faced doll turned to "Smily" expression; bits of blonde curly mohair was fastened inside cap; original name tag is tied to the right arm of the doll. *Photograph by John Schoonmaker.*

Illustration 2. *Big Sister Trudy* with head turned to Weepy expression, and modeling the originally designed dress material which identifies the doll in printed medallions of pink and blue. *Carlyss Keyes Collection. Photograph by John Schoonmaker.*

One of the last highly collectible composition dolls to be manufactured was *Trudy,* by the Three in One Doll Corporation, New York, New York. Louella Hart's *Directory of United States Trademarks* lists this doll as having been registered May 21, 1946; No. 495, 638. In August 13, 1946, the name *Trudy* is registered again under the lower number 422, 824. By August 20, 1946, the slogan "Sleepy, Weepy, Smily" was registered under No. 423, 088 with the note that this was republished by registrar. It seems great pains were taken to protect the doll's identity.

Trudy was issued in five versions, a perfect example of the costume - as well as the size, creating the identity of the doll. *Trudy* No. 1 was 14in (35.6cm) tall in pink and blue sleeping suit of a fleecy rayon material, but called wool in early publicity. *Trudy* No. 2 was described by the manufacturers as "a heart snatcher in fetching party print dress with gay bonnet

to match," 14in (35.6cm) tall. *Trudy* No. 3 was *Big Sister Trudy* with "sweet party pink frock with matching panties and bonnet." We can find no record of No. 4 which was evidently discontinued. However, *2nd Blue Book of Dolls and Values* by Jan Foulke lists a 16in (40.6cm) *Trudy* with composition arms and legs in dress and bonnet.

Trudy No. 5 was a 14in (35.6cm) example dressed in felt. The peaked hood is similar in pattern to that of the fleece sleeping suit, with felt overalls and long sleeved blouse. This version was said to be ready for a shopping spree or a workout in the sandbox! An added feature was a modern strap utility bag, an accessory likely to be lost over the years but would be simple to replace from observing the picture.

Trudy No. 1 was intended to sell for $5.79 and is most easily located while *Big Sister Trudy* cost $12.95 retail so was not, most likely, as

popular with parents. Yet this doll is the most deluxe collectible of The Three in One Doll Corporation. She is described as being 20in (50.8cm) tall but the one we examined measured 18½in (45.7cm) tall. Settling due to age could account for some discrepancy but manufacturer's measurements do not always coincide with the completed doll.

There was no marking on the actual doll but the two-sided oval tag hung from her wrist proclaiming "An Elsie Gilbert Creation" with "Patents Pending" at bottom. In center is "TRUDY" in large letters with "Trade Mark, Three in One Doll Corporation" below. The reverse side stated "Sleepy, Weepy, Smily" (correct spelling). The superior models with composition arms and legs were ingeniously marked by a specially designed material with "Sleepy Trudy," "Weepy Trudy," and "Smily Trudy" printed in circle emblems with tiny pink and blue flowers interspersed in the design on a white background.

Great Big Sister item had a double ribbon ruff on bonnet and collar. The body is of pink cotton material, cotton stuffed, with very chubby shaped toddler arms and legs. The quality of the composition is good. The coloring of the face was rather bright with eyes painted a vivid blue with lighter blue edge and large white highlight. The upper eyelid is outlined in the same light brown as

109

Illustration 3. Prototype advertising sent to prospective customers. Later dolls did not have the rickrack trim of jacket and artwork has been done on the eyelashes of doll that does not correspond to models found.

the seven upswept lashes and molded brows. The red upturned mouth adds an impish expression cheerful enough to brighten any day.

"Weepy" the crying face has good modeling detail with knit brows formed rather high on the forehead but the decorating artist has drawn them lower with two down-curving strokes to outline the tightly shut eyes. The wide-open, howling mouth is bright red with a pink lower lip. The serene "Sleepy" has brown brows, and outlined lower lids with five lashes curving downward. The mouth is heart shaped. The head appears to be a three-piece mold, well sanded but with very slight roughness under the paint.

The top turning knob is a molded extension of the head, covered with pink fleece material. The peaked hood is pink with a blue band around the face. This band has simply had a hole cut to allow the knob to pass through. The pink cotton body of the only example left in our collection has two-piece mitten hands with seams running down front center and back of arm. The chubby, shaped legs are seamed front and back as well. The fleece hood is not removable but

Illustration 5. Page from magazine *Toys and Novelties* of August 1947 which was repeated in September 1947.

THREE-IN-ONE DOLL CORPORATION
74-76 Laight Street, New York 13, N. Y.
BArclay 7-4116-7-8-9

September 30, 1947

Paradise Mansion of Dolls
214 West 62nd Street
Los Angeles, California

Gentlemen:

We are in receipt of your inquiry of September 27th and appreciate your
interest in our TRUDY Dolls. We are enclosing a descriptive flyer illustrating all four of our items. Our dolls are cellophane-wrapped, individually boxed, and packed in one, two and four dozen corrugated cartons.
Our price schedule is as follows:

	IN SIX DOZEN OR MORE LOTS	IN LESS THAN SIX DOZEN LOTS
TRUDY #1	$36.00 per dozen	$39.00 per dozen
TRUDY #2	42.00	45.00
TRUDY #3	54.00	57.00
TRUDY #5	36.00	39.00

Our prices are all F.O.B. New York and we are glad to advise that at the
present time we can accept orders for prompt delivery.

If there is any further information that you desire, please let us know.

Very truly yours,

THREE-IN-ONE DOLL CORPORATION

By
EDGAR WIHL, PRESIDENT

EW:SS
Enc.

Illustration 4. Actual company correspondence showing the wholesale prices of September 1947.

The Most Amazing Doll Creation in a Decade!

YOU MAKE HER *Smile*　YOU MAKE HER *Sleep*　YOU MAKE HER *Weep*

Illustration 6.

TRUDY No. 5

Illustration 8.

Question: — Why is TRUDY called the 3-IN-1 DOLL?　*Answer:* — Because she's actually 3 dolls in one — she smiles, she sleeps, she weeps — all with a single twist of the wrist.

TRUDY No. 1

Warm, cuddly lovable Trudy all dressed up in her smart, soft, pink and blue sleeping suit made of wool fleece. Every one of the three facial expressions endears her to her little owner. Fine quality throughout. Unbreakable composition head. 14" Tall. Packed in cellophane in individual gift boxes, 2 doz. to shipping carton. Shipping weight: 34 lbs.

TRUDY No. 2

Illustration 7.

Illustrations 6, 7 and 8. Four-sided advertising brochure that illustrates the various dolls described in the article.

permanently stitched to the neck of the doll body. Turning the top knob to activate the different cases causes a wooden dowel fastened solidly inside the head to revolve within a wooden collar upon which the head rests, which in turn is held in place by a wooden bead at the bottoms of the inner dowel. The entire mechanism is encased in a waxed paper cup to separate it from the cotton body stuffing. Our *Trudy* has smiled, slept, and wept enough for the wooden dowel end to have worn a hole completely through the paper cup bottom.

Among the related items to accompany the doll were an envelope

Queen of the Paper Doll World

TRUDY.

The amazing new ... Fast selling
CUT OUT DOLL SET

Here is Toyland's new "best seller" . . . the most sensational item for kids to hit the market in many a year. Yes . . .
here is a paper doll with *THREE DIFFERENT FACES* . . . a paper doll that

SLEEPS · SMILES · WEEPS

and owns enough clothes to dress and undress her completely a dozen times. There's a plastic scissors, too, that
won't cut anything but paper, which means that it's completely safe for any child to play with. America's leading
department stores and chains have already ordered and re-ordered in large quantity. So confident are we that
TRUDY will do a stand-out job wherever she is displayed
that we will ship as little as one dozen in order to "start
the ball rolling". Mail your order *NOW* and watch *TRUDY*
pile up profits for you!

Illustration 9. Original
advertising for *Trudy* paper
doll, August 1947. *Toys
and Novelties* magazine.

A FEW LEADING RETAILERS FEATURING THE TRUDY PAPER DOLL

BLOOMINGDALE'S
MACY'S
HEARNS
RICH'S
FOLEY BROS.
W. C. STRIPLING
BULLOCK'S
CARSON-PIRIE-SCOTT
JORDAN-MARSH
KRESGE
WOMRATH'S
and many others

THREE DOLLS IN ONE

THE ONLY MOVABLE PAPERDOLL WITH *Three* EXPRESSIONS

$7.20 PER DOZ. — FIXED RETAIL PRICE: 98¢
TERMS: 2% — 10 DAYS, NET 30 — **IMMEDIATE DELIVERY!**

A. T. R. PUBLISHING CO., INC. ·74 Laight St., New York 13, N. Y.

46

TOYS *and* NOVELTIES—August, 1947

with facsimile stamp postmarked
Baby-ville, U.S.A. from Elsie Gilbert.
The pink letter printed with blue
script read:

"Dear Little Friend,

*Up until this very momemt
Trudy has been my baby. Now she is
all yours!*

*Take very good care of her. She
needs a great deal of love and affection
to keep her happy. But should she
become a little pale, or should she
fall and hurt herself, ask your parents
to send her back to me and I shall
make her like new again for you.*

*I have a hospital called the Trudy
Hospital, where the finest nurses and
doll doctors live, who are there for the
express purpose of treating your
child. There will be no fee for hospital-
ization only a slight charge for the
medicine used to cure her.*

*I know you will have many hours
of great pleasure and happiness from
your child and I know too, that you
will love her as I do.*

*Good luck, little mother, Trudy
is all yours!"*

*Sincerely,
Elsie Gilbert*

A separate blue slip reads. "In
case Trudy's head should not turn
easily at the start, Hold her gently
by the back of the cap . . . and Trudy
will do her part." A large framed
print titled "Three Trudys" (originally
painted by Sig Arno) is occasionally
found for sale. A small reproduction
of the print by A.T.R. Publishing
Corporation was used at the top of
Three in One Doll Corporation
stationery.

The same publishers issued a
paper doll in 1947 they titled, "Queen
of the Paper Doll World." The actual
doll was illustrated in snowsuit upon
the cover of the paper doll box, with
see-through opening for the paper
doll version. She came with three
different faces, arms jointed at shoulders and elbows, as well as legs jointed
at hip and knee, making a unique and
different collector's item of the
period.

A Chronological History Of Dolls As Reported In Playthings Magazine

by EVELYN JANE COLEMAN

©1978 Hobby House Press, Inc.

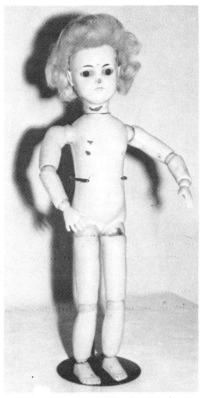

Illustration 1. 17½in (44.5cm) all steel doll. 1903, made by the Metal Doll Company. It has glass eyes. Interchangeable wigs are attached to the head by means of three snaps. The doll has open/closed mouth with teeth; spring joints at the neck, shoulders, elbows, wrists, hips, knees and ankles.

Illustration 2. Advertisement of E. I. Horsman in November 1903 showing the *Stella* rag doll.

Playthings surveyed the Toy World as seen through their magazine from 1903 to 1938. From this survey the following excerpts have been taken, which should be of interest to doll collectors. In these excerpts the reader will find references to many well-known doll firms as well as the names of firms which have long since gone into oblivion. (Any name that is also found in *The Collector's Encyclopedia of Dolls* is starred to enable the reader to obtain additional information.) In addition to the names of the firms the article refers to the personnel of these firms plus many of the important products. It is interesting to see whom they list and whom they fail to list. Horsman and Borgfeldt are frequently mentioned but the last time that Louis Amberg was listed by name was in 1911 when the company became Louis Amberg & Son. In *The Collector's Encyclopedia of Dolls*, there is practically the same amount of space given to each of these firms. The difference, however, between these firms was that Amberg was no longer associated with the Toy World in 1938, whereas the other two concerns were still prominent in the Toy World of 1938.

Since *Playthings* is an American publication, all of the firms listed in the Chronology are American and the dolls discussed had their origins in America, though a few like the *Bye-Lo* and the *Kewpie* were sometimes made in Germany, following the designs created in America.

Also there is strong evidence that *Playthings* only wished to write about favorable events (with the exceptions of the deaths of important figures in the Toy World) for there is a long discussion about gaining the right to continue to produce dolls during World War I. However, there is nothing about the doll industry of 1930 when the depression sank to its worst.

The use of the material necessitates some caution, for factual errors did creep into this 1938 chronological summary of *Playthings*. As an example, in 1906 it is stated, "Teddy Bears captured the market, deriving their name from Teddy Roosevelt's African hunting expedition." In 1906, Mr. Roosevelt was still President and the African expedition did not take place until 1909.

One month earlier (*Playthings*, August 1938), in an article on the

Illustration 3. 15in (40.6cm) *Babyland* rag doll; 1903 to 1920; made by E. I. Horsman Company. The doll has a lithographed face, original Dutch costume except for the pants which were copied from a 1905 picture of a corresponding doll. *Dorothy Annunziato Collection.*

death of Morris Michtom, the following is stated: "While hunting in Mississippi, Roosevelt refused to shoot a small bear because of its being young and cute, adopting it instead as a camp pet. A cartoonist, Clifford Berryman of the *Washington Post* . . . dramatized the incident in a drawing. The diminutive bear was dubbed 'Teddy' after the other character in the episode and the teddy-bear vogue followed naturally."

When using material written about the toy trade in their trade journals and by the toy trade in their own advertisements, problems sometimes develop. These problems, of course, include trying to interpret the correct meaning of the advertising statements which appear not only in the advertisements themselves but also in the text of the toy trade journals. The false claims often include the following statements: (1) The firm is the oldest doll manufacturing concern in America. (2) They are the first to have dolls with wardrobes. (3) They claimed that they had gotten one governmental protection such as a patent for a doll when actually they had gotten some other type of governmental protection such as a copyright. (4) They produced the largest number of dolls. (5) They made the best dolls and, of course, got out a new doll each year that was different and better than the doll which they had made the year before. (6) Also they claimed that the dolls had certain features such as unbreakable heads, which was sheer nonsense. In addition, another problem is trying to ascertain the founding date of concerns. For example, The Century Doll Company advertises in 1924, "15 years of doll manufacturing," which indicates that the firm commenced their manufacture of dolls in 1909. Then their advertisement in *Toy World,* February 1929, states, "Century Doll Co. Famous for Quality Dolls since 1912" and finally an article from *Playthings,* September 1928 refers to an obituary of Max Scheurer in 1933 and states that he founded the Century Doll Company in 1914. Thus there are three different dates for the founding of the Century Doll Company: 1909 recorded in 1924, 1912 recorded in 1929 and 1914 recorded in 1938. Lacking additional information to support or refute these statements, usually the most reliable information is the date taken from the earliest source, because there is less time for the records to be lost and for the distortion of the facts to have occurred. A similar situation arises with the Madame Alexander Company, for in the *Playthings* September 1938, article it states, "1926 . . . The Alexander Doll Co. was established during the early part of the year." This differs from the 1923 date which has recently been given by Madame Alexander herself as the founding date.

Keeping the above information in mind, here are excerpts from the September 1938, comprehensive article from *Playthings,* which gives a survey of the Toy and Doll World from the founding date of *Playthings,* 1903 up to the then present date of 1937.

A Chronological History, 1903-1938
from *Playthings,* September 1938

Playthings, 1903

"The first issue of *Playthings* was published in January, a tiny little book of sixteen pages and cover with seven advertisers . . . .

"Among the popular toys and games of the year were . . . Babyland* and Stella* rag dolls (Horsman*) . . . Steel jointed dolls (Metal Doll Co.*) were featured . . . Humpty Dumpty Circus* and Trinity Chimes were introduced by Schoenhut* . . . E. I. Horsman, Jr. was married in April.

"Deaths of the year included Geo. Borgfeldt,* founder of the business bearing his name at the age of 70; Henry Schwarz* famous toy man of Baltimore, 78 years old; . . ."

Playthings, 1904

"*Playthings* had now doubled in size, having 32 pages and cover . . . As the first toy paper in the world, it

The Celebrated
"BABYLAND"
TRADE MARK
RAG DOLLS
"Babyland" are the original high grade
RAG DOLLS

They are sold by the most prominent Toy Departments in the country.

They represent daintily dressed children, and can be dressed and undressed.

Made of the very best materials in thirty-four different styles.

From $2 to $8 per dozen.

SEND FOR CATALOGUE

Manufactured by

E. I. HORSMAN CO.
365-367 Broadway, New York

Illustration 4. Advertisement of E. I. Horsman in March 1908 showing *Babyland* rag dolls.

created great interest during its first year of publication.

"Cartoon characters appeared in toyland - Buster Brown* and Foxy Grandpa* . . . Bedelia was a rubber doll which cried when squeezed . . . Fairyland* rag dolls bearing the label of the National Consumers' League 'Made under clean and healthful conditions;' paper patterns for making dolls' clothes.

"*Playthings,* published the story of John Doll*, of John Wanamaker's,* Philadelphia.

"A group of men connected with Samstag & Hilder Bros.,* were remarkable for their long experience in toys, entering business as follows; E. U.

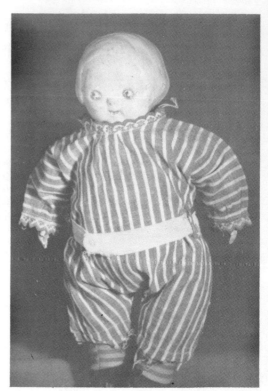

Illustration 5. 11½in (29.2cm); *Foxy Grandpa,* 1903 to 1907 designed by Carl Schultz as a character in a cartoon series which appeared in newspaper Sunday supplements. The doll is made of two pieces of printed cloth.

Steiner,* 1864; Phil. Koempel, 1867; Lewis Knerr, 1878; Dan. Frohman (not the theatrical man), 1882 and Sig Stoerger, 1886. Toy autos with three passengers and a driver were shown in 1904.

Playthings, 1905

"Geo. Borgfeldt & Co.* celebrated their 25th anniversary by the issuance of a handsome booklet . . .

"The Y-Do-I doll appeared on the market . . . This was a doll head with a short jacket but no body; the head and arms were operated by the fingers and amusement was created.

"Doll skates were introduced and snow skates were a novelty.

"Deaths of the year were John McLouglin who with his brother Edmund, founded McLoughlin Bros., in 1855; he was born on Nov. 29th 1827 . . ."

Playthings, 1906

"Teddy Bears captured the market, deriving their name from Teddy Roosevelt's African hunting expedition . . .

"Doll outfits took the popular fancy . . . Rag dolls with photographic faces were introduced . . . All metal folding furniture was shown.

"Louis Amberg, Brill & Co.,* became Amberg, Brill & Ullman . . . E. I. Horsman & C.,* went to 365 Broadway after a destructive fire at their former quarters, 354 Broadway . . ."

Playthings, 1907

"Many animals joined the toy zoo following the footsteps of the universally popular teddy bear.

Merry Widow Doll

"Mr. Jogger, the first of the tap dancing toys made its bow . . . Buster Brown's dog Tige appeared . . . Auto goggles for bears, and dolls followed the prevailing automobile fashions . . . There were electric-eye teddy bears and other animals . . . Teddy bear furniture was introduced.

"Geo. Borgfeldt & Co.,* announced that they were showing over three hundred lines of American made toys . . .

"Aetna Toy Animal Co., was organized by Benjamin Goldenberg* and Wm. Ehrenfeld . . .

"The deaths of the year included . . . Otto Dressel of the old established European firm of Cuno & Otto Dressel.*"
Playthings, 1908

"The vogue of the teddy bear and other animals continued practically unabated . . . Character dolls made in the likeness of actual children were announced . . . Cartoon characters were used in many toys, games and dolls. The Merry Widow* came to dolldom.

"Ta-Ka-Part Toys consisting of doll furniture, trunks and doll houses of sectional construction . . . The Colored National Baptist Association entered a plea endorsing negro dolls for negro children.

"The Billiken statuette swept the country as the God of Good Luck . . . Aetna Doll & Toy Co.,* announced the purchase of the Can't Break 'Em* doll line from the American Doll & Toy Mfg. Co.* . . . Straus, Haas & Co. was a new import house . . . H. B. Claflin Co. opened a doll, toy and book department."
Playthings, 1909

"Horsman* introduced the Billiken doll* with composition head and soft body; over 200,000 were sold within six months . . . *The Doll Book* by Laura B. Starr was published . . . Rolly Dolly toys (Schoenhut*), Blue Hill box kites (Horsman*) were introduced . . . Teddy's Adventures in Africa were added to the Humpty-Dumpty Circus* . . . Several lucky statuettes and dolls, including a caricature of Bill Taft, followed the footsteps of Billiken* . . . An interesting history of puppets and marionettes was published . . . North Pole dolls, animals and games followed the more or less simultaneous discovery of the North Pole by Peary (doll*) and Cook (doll*) . . . Aeroplanes and all sorts of flying toys were popular . . . Geo. Borgfeldt & Co.* moved into their new building at 16th St. and Irving Place, New York.

"The story of the famous (or infamous) dollar doll was told. Enormous quantities of these dolls

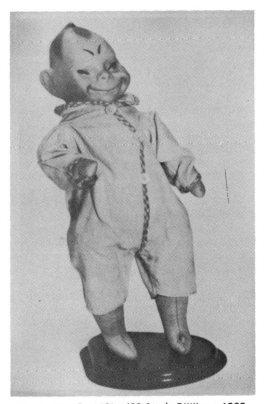

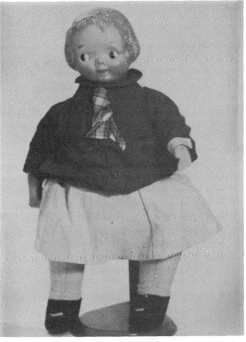

had been imported, competition becoming so great that a 60 centimeter (24 inches) doll with moving eyes and lashes and wig was being sold at 98¢, destroying profits ruthlessly . . .

"Deaths of the year: Marcell Kahle, President of Geo. Borgfeldt* & Co., at the age of 51; John R. Righter, of Selchow & Righter,* at the age of 70; . . . Margarete Steiff,* the German designer and manufacturer of stuffed animals age 72."

Playthings, 1910

"For the first time in the history of toys, sales in American made dolls, toys and games over the retail counter surpassed imports. Undoubtedly, the advent of the American unbreakable doll was an important feature in this achievement . . .

"The Baby Beautiful* doll was introduced by Hahn & Amberg* . . . Chantecler dolls and games appeared as a result of the popularity of Maude Adams in Rostand's play.

"Louis Wolf & Co.* moved to 221 Forth Ave., on the corner of 18th Street . . . The firm of Kahn & Mossbacher* was dissolved, M. L. Kahn continuing the manufacture of doll clothes and S. Mossbacher making playsuits . . . E. P. Claderhead planned a toy department for the new Gimbel Bros.* store in New York . . . Furs and fur sets for dolls and children were featured . . . Fashionable women started the fad of carrying dolls . . . J. B. Lewkowitz opened a new doll and toy department for Nathan Gutman & Co."

Playthings, 1911

"This year was marked by the rapid development of American made dolls. Horsman* introduced the Campbell Kids.* Schoenhut* brought out an all-wood doll, rubberless jointed. Ideal* dolls were featured. Many names and many characters appeared in dolldom . . . Louis Amberg & Son* was incorporated to succeed Hahn & Amberg* . . . Upholstered doll house furniture was featured . . .

"Fleischaker & Baum* introduced Muskat a lucky figure . . . Campbell Kids* appeared on the stage, a group of chorus girls being dressed in suitable costumes and masks.

"Walter A. de Montreville, Frederick Loeser & Co. Brooklyn, featured a French Wedding Fete as a doll display, all dolls sold from sample . . . Morris Michtom and A. Cohn dissolved partnership in the Ideal Novelty Co."*

Playthings, 1912

"The modern vogue of marionettes and ventriloquist dolls was foreshadowed by the production of a Punch & Judy Show provided with a blow pipe fitted with a reed to produce the ventriloquist effect.

"More and more American made unbreakable dolls were brought out. Fleischaker & Baum* introduced several new dolls - Dainty Baby (Baby Dainty*), Johnny Tu Face* and Miss Couqette* . . .

"Fred K. Braitling,* Bridgeport, Conn., moved into a new and larger factory . . . Ideal Novelty & Toy Co.* Brooklyn, enlarged their doll factory . . . The Ideal Novelty & Toy Co.* introduced the Rom-Tom walking animals.

"Deaths of the year: . . . Chas. F. Braitling,* manufacturer of dolls' shoes and wigs, age 72; . . ."

Playthings, 1913

"Nearly sixty per cent of all toys sold at retail were of American manufacture . . . A fully jointed domestic doll was introduced under the name of Yankee Doll.

"The Alabama Coon Jigger an American made mechanical toy was placed on the market by Ferdinand Strauss . . . Fred K. Braitling* showed his line in the Fifth Avenue Building . . .

"Many new types of character dolls were introduced, some of them with very fancy names . . . Schoenhut* introduced the Cavalry Horse, to be suspended from a boy's shoulders by straps . . . Rose O'Neil's* Kewpies* were shown by Geo. Borgfeldt & Co.* . . . Hansel* and Gretel* dolls were shown by Schoen & Sarkady.*

"Fleischaker & Baum* moved to 45 East 17th St., New York . . ."

A Chronological History of Dolls
As Reported in Playthings Magazine

by EVELYN JANE COLEMAN

© 1978 Hobby House Press, Inc.

Playthings, 1914

"The opening of the world war. During this year, imports of dolls and toys reached the highest figure in the history of the industry, being something over $9,000,000.00 (foreign value). American toys increased their lead over imports . . . Tinker Toys, made by the Toy Tinkers of Evanston, Ill., appeared on the market . . . Cartoon characters multiplied in dolls, games, toys and books. Movie characters appeared in dolldom . . . Colored wigs for dolls had a short lived spasm, just as they had with grown up ladies . . . The Eugenic Baby* was introduced (Perhaps as a prophecy) . . .

"Fleischaker & Baum* showed a Catholic Sister doll . . .

"Harry Landsdowne, of Strawbridge Clothier, Philadelphia, featured a Kewpie* Villa . . . Mason & Parker purchased the plant of R. Bliss Mfg. Co, Pawtucket, R.I., and moved it to Winchendon, Mass., making pianos, doll houses, etc . . . A Mama doll was featured by the Art Metal Works.*

"The Kant Krack Dolls* were the Delight of the Buyers Back in 1914."

Playthings, 1915

"E. I. Horsman Co.* and the Riemann, Seabrey Co.,* moved to the old Tiffany Building at Broadway & 15th St. . . . Paul Lindeman of L. S. Plaut & Co., Newark, N.J., held a doll dressing contest which attracted widespread attention . . . Charlie Chaplin dolls* were shown . . . Geo. Borgfeldt & Co.,* bought out the stock and assets of Bawo & Dotter* . . . A washable doll was shown under the name of Sanitary Baby* . . . Louis Wolf & Co,* added a domestic toy department . . .

"Ragtime Rastus, a figure dancing on a phonograph to the time of the record, appeared . . . Fleischaker & Baum* opened a salesroom on the street level of the Everett Bldg., New York . . .

"Deaths of the year: Albert Schoenhut* pioneer American toy manufacturer and founder of the A. Schoenhut Co.,* Philadelphia, age 63; Elisha G. Selchow of Selchow & Righter Co.* age 71; John P. Rider, President of the New York Rubber Co.,* age 80."

Playthings, 1916

"War drums in Europe rolled louder and louder in American ears, 'Made in the U.S.A.' was a popular slogan of the day as more and more playthings that were formerly imported were being expertly produced in this country. Dolls dressed as soldiers were big sellers. One group was called 'The Preparedness Kids.'*

"Among others prominent in the industry who died in 1916 were Emil Strobel, President of the Strobel & Wilken Co.* who had been associated with that firm for half a century; Edmund U. Steiner,* a veteran of 40 years' service in the trade, who had crossed the Atlantic Ocean 85 times."

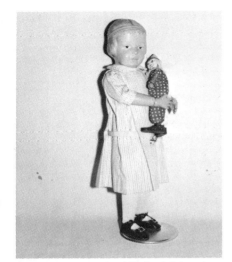

Illustration 10. 16in (40.6cm) Schoenhut all-wood girl; 1911; molded hair and molded blue ribbon around the head and tied in a small bow in back; decal mark on upper back. She is carrying a 7in (17.8cm) clown from the Schoenhut's Humpty Dumpty Circus. Clowns were included from the first 1903, in these circuses. *Alberta Darby Collection.*

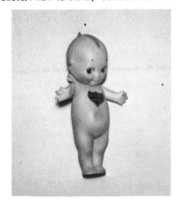

Illustration 11. 5in (12.7cm) all-bisque *Kewpie;* 1913; painted features and movable arms; paper sticker on front and back. *Edith Meggers Collection.*

Illustration 12. The "Kant Krack" slogan, 1910 to 1919, was used for the all Biskoline dolls made by Parsons-Jackson Company. This 10½in (26.7cm) doll which was advertised with the "Kant Krack" slogan, has painted and molded hair and eyes, bent-limb baby body with steel spring joints. There is a raised stork mark on the back of the head and on the upper back, which also has "Trade Mark// Parsons-Jacksons Co.//Cleveland, Ohio. *Mary Kahler Collection.*

Illustration 13. 14½in (36.9cm) *Charlie Chaplin* doll made by Louis Amberg & Sons, probably designed by Jeno Juszko; 1915. It has a molded composition head and hands, straw-filled body with pin and disk joints; original clothes including a black felt hat.

Playthings, 1917

"The United States entered the war . . . Reports came in from all over the country of members of the toy industry going off to war . . .

"Many dolls made their appearance dressed as soldiers, sailors, nurses, etc. and in the costumes of Allied countries . . . The Averill Mfg. Corp.,* introduced the Madame Hendren* line of baby dolls. They had previously made Madame Hendren* felt doll dressed character dolls . . . I. H. Davis and Fred W. Voetsch, formerly with Joseph Hanes* and Co., formed the firm of Davis & Voetsch* to act as manufacturers' selling agents and manufacturers of dolls and toys . . .

Playthings, 1918

" 'Christmas giving, which involves the purchase of gifts, should be discouraged,' said a statement of the Council of National Defense. The toy trade, in common with other industries, had been affected by restrictions and regulations arising from war conditions. Labor and fuel were very scarce, the transportation of merchandise was a difficult matter, but sacrifices were expected and wholeheartedly made. However, the recommendation of the Council of National Defense was a hard blow to an industry as closely tied up with Christmas sales as the toy trade. So vigorous steps were taken to have toys officially sanctioned as Christmas gifts.

"The Toy Manufacturers' Association had previously appointed a War Service Committee, with A. C. Gilbert as chairman . . . This Committee arranged a hearing before the Council of National Defense, which consisted of six members of the President's Cabinet. Mr. Gilbert made a most forceful presentation of what the American toy industry was doing, why it should be conserved in order

to hold its own after the war, and what American toys were doing to foster education and development of the nation's children . . . The Council thereafter issued a statement sanctioning toys as essential.

"An American made doll sold for $1.85. This was not due to the rising cost of living, however. The doll was sold at an auction for the benefit of the Red Cross . . . *Playthings* prepared a brilliantly colored 24" x 30" poster for store display, showing the contrast between a home with toys and one without playthings on Christmas, and under the pictures the wording, 'Are Toys Essential? Ask the Man Who Fights.'

"Among members of the toy trade who died this year were T. C. Schoenhut, Vice-President of the A. Schoenhut Co;* Geo. F. Riemann, Jr., President of the Riemann, Seabrey Co.,* who had been associated with the toy trade for 38 years; E. I. Horsman, Jr., only son of the pioneer toy and doll man, and actively identified with the E. I. Horsman Co.* since 1901, and Edward R. Ives, President and founder of the Ives, Mfg. Corp., who had been active in the toy business for 53 years."

Playthings, 1919

"The war over, this country was threatened with wholesale 'dumping' of German dolls, toys and other merchandise. *Playthings* conducted a vigorous campaign against such tactics in the toy trade . . .

"The novelty vogue of the year in the doll field was the 'beach doll.' These were fibre or wood composition figures of alluring girlies, many with veils, described in such lush terms as chic, charming, captivating, lovable, hugable, coquetish, adorable, dainty, vampish, chubby cherubs, demonically delightful, plutocratic peaches of peerless pulchritude, love pirates, beach flirts, star eyed sylphs of the sea and smiling sweeties of the silver sands."

Playthings, 1920

"The Milton Bradley Co., purchased the business of McLoughlin Bros., games and toy books, the books to be continued under the name of their original publisher.

"The early days of prohibition prompted three women passengers of the White Star liner *Cretic* to conceal a supply of brandy in the bodies of dolls which they carried as far as, but not past, customs officials . . ."

Playthings, 1921

"This year saw the advent of dolls that said Papa as well as Mama . . . The obstacle golf craze which was

Illustration 14. 12 in (30.5cm) *Liberty Boy;* 1917 to 1918; made by Ideal. It is completely made of molded composition including its clothes except for the felt hat.

Illustration 17. Mama Doll with flirting eyes, 1924-, has a composition head and limbs on a cloth body. It was made by Ideal Novelty & Toy Company. The eyes of this doll move from side to side and also open and close together or separately, thus causing the doll to wink. The eyes appear to be celluloid-over metal material. Original blue cotton dress and hat. *Dorothy Annunziato Collection.*

"SPLASH ME" DOLLS

Gene George's clever conceit. Flesh tinted bisque finished composition, painted features, tinted bathing suit and shoes.

Painted Hair—½ doz. in box.
F7944—5 in. asstd. kerchief caps.........Doz. **$2.25**
F7941—7 in. plaid taffeta kerchief caps...Doz. **$4.50**

Mohair Wig—Fashionable veil covered coiffure.
F7943—7 in. ½ doz. in box. Doz. **$9.00**

Illustration 15. Butler Brothers advertised in 1921 "Splash Me" Dolls, which show the starry eyes created by the long lashes. Both dolls shown here are wearing bathing suits and one has a veil.

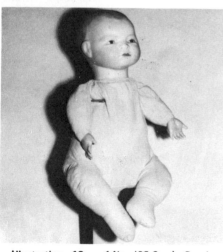

Illustration 16. 14in (35.6cm) *Bye-Lo Baby,* 1923, designed by Grace S. Putnam and distributed by George Borgfeldt and Company. Cloth body with celluloid hands made by the Rheinische Gummi und Celluloid Fabrik Co. Bisque head marked "1923 by//Grace S. Putnam//Germany."

to sweep the country several years later was foreshadowed in Schoenhut's* Indoor Golf, complete with sand traps . . .

"The American Doll Manufactures, Inc.* adopted a slogan, 'Avoid Childhood's Tragedy - a Broken Doll. Buy American Made Dolls.' Parades through the streets of many cities were organized, featuring banners bearing the slogan. E. I.

Horsman* led the New York parade . . .

"E. W. Seabrey . . . died this year. Ed Seabrey, President of the Riemann, Seabrey Co.,* started in the toy trade in 1892. He was only 46 when he died.

Playthings, 1922
"Flapper dolls* were very popular . . ."

Playthings, 1923
"The Bye-Lo Baby, Grace Storey's* creation, was introduced by Geo. Borgfeldt & Co.* . . . Jackie Coogan* visited every exhibit at the Toy Fair, gaining much newspaper publicity for toys . . ."

Playthings, 1924
"The Frank Gaby Ventriloquist Doll was introduced."

Playthings, 1925
"Several leading members of the toy trade died in 1925, including Henry F. Schwarz, son of F.A.O. Schwarz,* who had gone directly from school into his father's store and developed the business still further after the latter's death; Andrew K. Ackerman, President of the Strobel-Wilken Co.,* who had started to work for that firm 54 years before, when it was located in Cincinnati: . . .
"The Flirting Eye Doll introduced in 1925."

Playthings, 1926
"Dolls that apparently drank milk were introduced. Each doll had a glass nursing bottle filled with a milk-like liquid which was seemingly consumed when the nipple was placed in the doll's mouth. Later the bottle automatically refilled itself . . .

Illustration 18. *Shirley Temple* doll, 1934-, wearing her original green dress with the tag reading "Shirley Temple Doll Registered U.S. Pat. Off. Ideal Nov. & Toy Co." *Mary Dawson Collection.*

"The Alexander Doll Co.* was established during the early part of the year.

"Among the well-known toy people who died in 1926 were George Wilken, for fifty years Vice-President of the Strobel & Wilken Co.* Julius Chein, toy manufacturer; Benjamin Crandall, inventor, who died at the age of 103; Albert Bruckner,* doll maker since 1901; I. H. 'Ike' Davis, of Davis & Voetsch,* who had spent his entire business life in the toy industry."

Playthings, 1927
"Children's Day was established as the third Saturday in June. Endorsed by the Better Play for Children League, staunchly supported

Illustration 19. 15½in (38.1cm) *Snow White*, 1937/8-, copyright by Walt Disney Enterprise has an oil cloth face. *Dorothy Annunziato Collection.*

Illustration 20. Close-up of the bottom of the skirt on the *Snow White* shown in Illustration 19. *Dorothy Annunziato Collection.*

Illustration 21. 15in (38.1cm) Walt Disney's *Snow White;* all-composition doll made by Madame Alexander; 1938--.

by the American Doll Manufacturers and buyers, Children's Day provided a fine selling opportunity for stores in many parts of the country . . . Arranbee Doll Co,* moved to 894-900 Broadway, New York . . . M. L. Kahn* moved to 43-45 East 19th St., New York.

"E. I. Horsman,* for many years known as the dean of the toy trade died at the age of 83. He had a long and honorable career, starting in the toy business in 1865. After the death of his only son, to whom he was devotedly attached, Mr. Horsman* discontinued the sale of general toy lines and concentrated his entire energies on the manufacture and sale of dolls . . . A few weeks after Mr. Horsman's* death, Louis C. Witten-

berg, salesman for the Horsman* firm for 30 years, also passed away. Three days after this Benjamin Goldenberg* died. He was one of the country's pioneer doll and stuffed toy manufacturers. His firm, after making dolls for E. I. Horsman Co.,* for many years, was combined with the latter concern in 1919. Mr. Goldenberg* had been elected President of the firm upon the death of Mr. Horsman;* . . . Emile C. Loewe, maker of doll outfits for 30 years also died."

Illustration 23. Close-ups of both sides of the tag on *Sneezy. E. J. Carter Collection.*

Playthings, 1028

"Makers of mama voices in-auguarated an extensive advertising and publicity campaign to make the public aware of the difference between a real mama voice and a squeaker.

"Deaths came in 1928 to . . . I. A. Rommer, Secretary and Treasurer of the Ideal Novelty & Toy Co.,* since 1912, and inventor of many innovations in dolls and also in other industries . . ."

Playthings, 1929

" 'The Right Toy for the Right Age,' by Murza Mann Lauder, appeared in *Playthings,* and reprints were used by leading stores throughout the country for distribution to customers and sales people . . . E. Goldberger* opened a showroom in the Fifth Avenue Building . . . The American Character Doll Co.,* received over 37,000 inquiries from a color advertisement in *The American Weekly* in the middle of the year, and ran another advertisement in December . . . The Gund Mfg. Co.,* J. Swedlin, Inc. Successor, moved to 40-46 West 20th St., New York . . .

"Among those who died in 1929 were F. W. Trumpore of the Fleischaker & Baum* selling staff, and formerly a toy buyer for 40 years; Louis Levy, who had been with B. Illfelder & Co.* for almost half a century and a partner since 1907 . . .

Playthings, 1930 - Nothing relating to dolls.

Illustration 22. 9in (22.9cm) Walt Disney's *Sneezy,* 1928, one of the seven dwarfs made by Knickerbocker Toy Company, Inc., New York City, as part of their line of stuffed toys. The head, hands and feet are made of composition. *E. J. Carter Collection.*

Playthings, 1931

"F.A.O. Schwarz* after 22 years at Fifth Avenue and 32nd Street, moved to the new Squibb Building at Fifth Avenue and 58th St. This famous toy store was established in Geo. Borgfeldt & Co.* moved to 44-60 East 23rd St., New York . . . Jetur A. Penny retired after having been associated with the Strobel-Wilken Co,* for 32 years, being President of the firm for the last few years . . .

"Empress Eugenie hats, all the vogue this year, also appeared in dolldom . . ."

Playthings, 1932

"The Washington Bicentennial was celebrated this year, and many toys and store displays reflected the spirit of the occasion."

Playthings, 1933

"The firm of Georgene Novelties, Inc., was formed to make soft dolls and animals . . .

"Among those who passed away during 1933 were . . . John I. Anderson, President of the Selchow & Righter Co;* Andrew Foulds, founder of the firm of Foulds & Freure;* . . . Earl M. Watson, who conducted a toy business and doll hospital in Trenton, N. J., for nearly half a century; . . . Max Scheuer, one of the pioneers of the industry, who founded the Century Doll Co.,* in 1914 and continued to manufacture dolls until 1926."

Playthings, 1934

"The Dy-Dee Baby doll was introduced by Fleischaker & Baum* . . . Riemann, Seabrey Co.,* Inc. moved their showrooms to 1107 Broadway, New York, . . .

"The Shirley Temple doll was introduced by the Ideal Novelty & Toy Co.,* . . . Kay Kamen exclusive representative for Mickey Mouse and other Disney characters, opened a Chicago office in the Merchandise Mart . . .

"Death came in 1934 to Wm. M. Ferguson, head of the old established factory agency of the A. S. Ferguson Co.,* for over 40 years until he liquidated the business and retired in 1929; . . . J. L. Chapman, Sr., who was an executive of the E. I. Horsman Co.,* for more than 50 years and had retired ten years previous to his death; . . ."

Playthings, 1935

"The Dionne Quintuplets made their bow in doll form, being introduced by the Alexander Doll Co.* . . . Milton Bradley Co., McLoughlin Bros., Inc., Fleischaker & Baum,* The Geo. Franke Sons Co., and the American Character Doll Co., Inc.,* opened showrooms in the Fifth Avenue Building . . . The Colleen Moore Doll House, which had taken a corps of artisans nine years to build at a cost of about $500,000.00, was first shown to the public at Macy's, in New York. It was scheduled for a three year world tour with exhibitions featured all over the U.S. and abroad. An admission charge of ten cents was made to view this fairy castle, with all proceeds going to hospitals for crippled children, and it was expected that over $1,000,000.00 would be raised for this worthy purpose. . .

"Among toy members who died this year were Fred K. Braitling,* maker of doll shoes for 45 years and a charter member of the Toy Manufacturers' Association and Frank Klaproth prominent in the industry for many years and manager of the domestic toy department for Geo. Borgfeldt & Co.,* from 1906 until he retired in 1930."

Playthings, 1936

"The game of 4-5-6 Pick Up Sticks was introduced by O. Schoenhut, Inc.

"Among the members of the trade who died during the year were George Kolb, President of the Geo. Borgfeldt Corp.,* who began his business career with Geo. Borgfeldt & Co.* in 1883; and Harry C. Ives, toy train manufacturer for many years and at one time President of the Toy Manufacturers Associations."

Playthings, 1937

"Charlie McCarthy, that very close friend of Edgar Bergen, made his bow in the doll world under the sponsorship of Fleischaker & Baum* . . .

"Snow White and the Seven Dwarfs dolls and toys were placed on the market as the first full length feature picture by Walt Disney was ready for release.

"Death came in 1937 to Paul Averill,* who had been prominent in the toy industry for over 35 years; . . . to George Semler, for many years President of Geo. Borgfeldt & Co.,* who was connected with that firm from 1881 until a few years ago; . . . to Fred W. Voetsh (Davis C. Voetsh), active in the industry for more than 40 years; . . ."

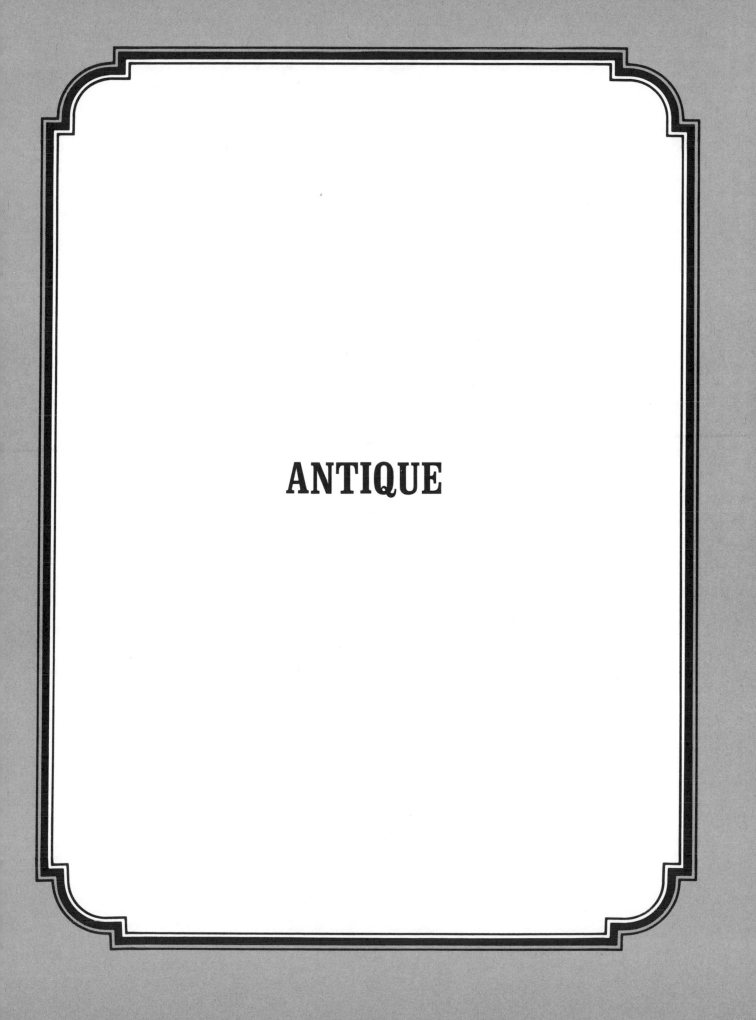

ANTIQUE

A Rare Find

BY MAGDA BYFIELD

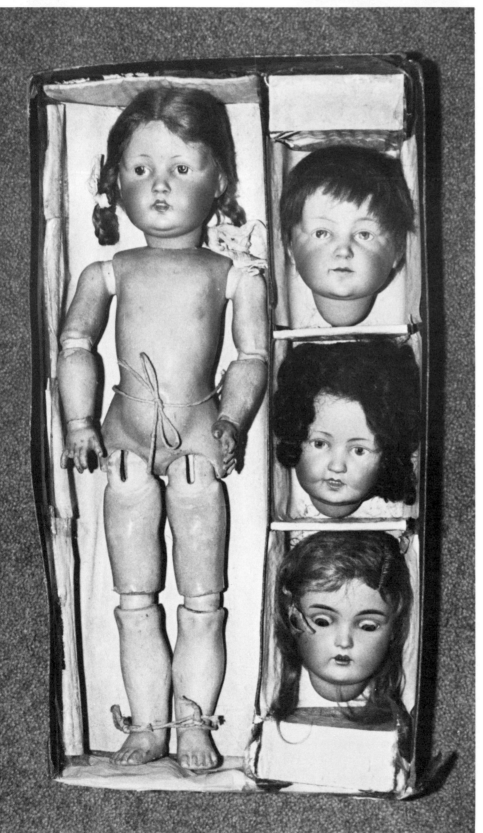

Illustration 1. Boxed set by Kestner containing complete doll and three extra heads. Box measures 9-1/2 x 18-1/2in. (24.1 x 47cm).

Doll collectors of three decades or so ago felt no need to "understand" dolls; they simply looked, and either felt something or not. If those collectors then found an emotive appeal, (which is still the prime force in the collecting of dolls today) that was the very best thing about it.

We now know that up to the early twentieth century doll makers did not feel the need to tell how they worked and very few records were made. Tantalizingly however, they marked, signed or code-numbered their models after about 1880 and from these meager and often perplexing scraps researchers have amassed and published information which thirty years back was non-existent.

There was nothing immediate about the knowledge that was gathered; the findings of one researcher opens doors for another, and the hunt for new facts can become quite obsessional. Without this quality—and the comradeship between students—further work would not be accomplished, and there is still much to uncover.

One collector once told me that her dolls were "a feast for her eyes," another, her "spiritual nourishment," and this must be true to some extent of us all, but most want to *know* more. I don't think people necessarily *feel* anything more through knowledge but they *appreciate* more, and this often results in the recording of rare specimens, and this in its turn provides new material for research.

The process of doll research is basically quite simple if one remains objective. It is to analyze what we see in the given doll before us and put down an equivalent in terms of writing. There is no trick involved—it is fundamentally a recipe for finding things out for oneself. But something exceptional usually has to trigger us off and in this instance that "something exceptional" was a boxed Kestner set of one doll and three additional heads. (*Illustration 1.*)

The theory has been put forward that this was a salesman's sample but there seems to be ample evidence that this is not the case. The box end label (*Illustration 2*) is printed in English and one therefore assumes it was destined for the British or American market. A sales sample had as yet no market and was designed as a kind of tangible catalog from which orders were taken. Such an item would seem unlikely to have required a label of this kind.

There is also evidence that the heads were intended to be interchangeable though not in the simple way that is found in some types of multi-head doll sets. A stout metal bar is situated beneath the neck socket opening in the torso over which the leg rubber is doubled and this is not found in standard Kestner bodies. All the heads have open crowns covered with closed pates plastered over, but inside each is a neck button and iron loop. The hook terminal that connects the loop to the leg rubber would make the interchanging of heads a comparatively simple maneuver—though not one that could have been undertaken by a child.

It seems more likely that this was an attempt to market a product that was at once a doll and a doll's hospital combined. In the event of the head mounted on the doll breaking, an immediate choice from three others was at hand and with nothing more than a buttonhook could be speedily placed in position with a neck guaranteed to fit the socket opening. This would have been of particular value to children living in remote areas out of reach of toy shops offering a repair service.

Illustration 2. Kestner label on side of box lid.

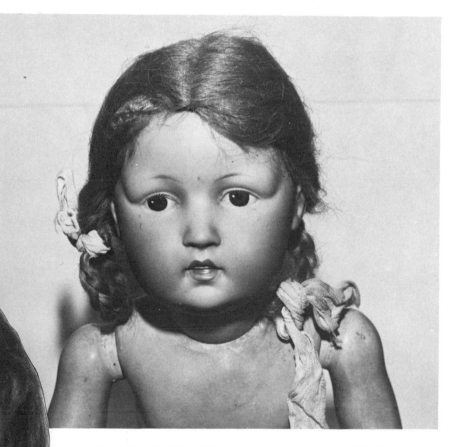

Illustration 3. (Above) Kestner doll-faced-doll incised 171. Open mouth with four upper teeth. Blue sleep eyes with upper and lower painted lashes. Heavy multi-stroke dark ochre eyebrows. Light brown mohair wig.

Illustration 4. (Left) Kestner character doll incised 180. Open/closed mouth with molded tongue and teeth. Dark brown painted eyes with pupils and white highlight dots. Black upper eyelines and red lid lines. Short black eyelashes painted above iris only. Thin arched light ochre multi-stroke eyebrows. Braided light brown mohair wig. Height of doll, 18in. (45.7cm).

It is interesting to note that all the sets that are so far known contain one doll-faced-doll and three character heads, though models vary. A collector from France reports having seen a specimen that contained among the additional heads a dog's head with socket neck, in place of one of the character faces. In *Illustration 1* the doll-faced-doll is model 171 (*Illustration 3*) and the three character heads are models 180, 186 and 187 (*Illustrations 4, 5* and *6*). None of the heads have any marks to indicate that they are Kestner products being incised only with mould numbers.

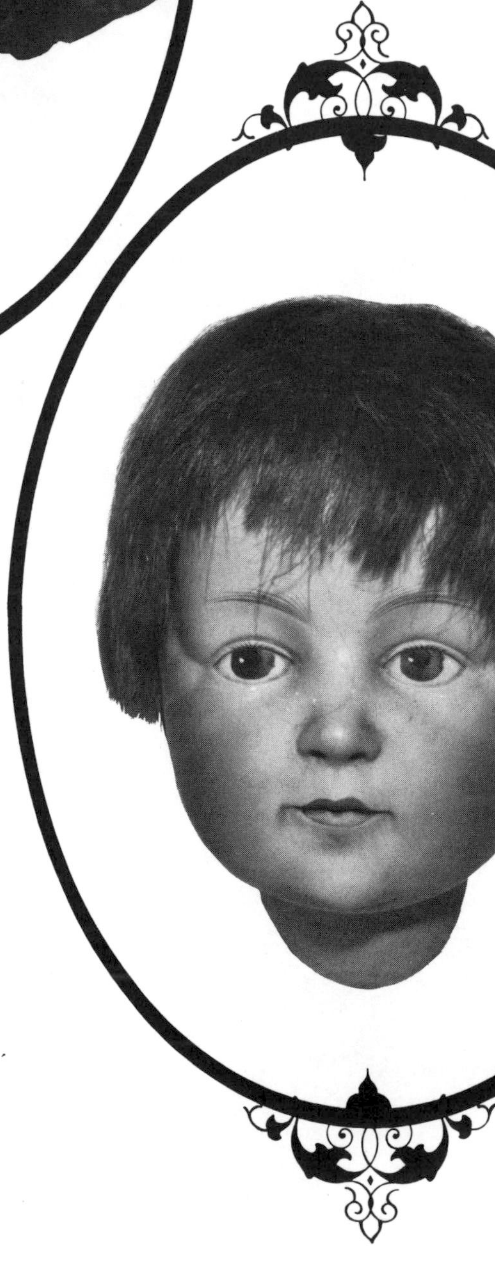

Illustration 5. (Above) Kestner character doll head incised 186. Open/closed smiling mouth with molded teeth. Blue painted eyes with pupils and white highlight dots. Black upper eyelines and red lid lines. Short black eyelashes painted above iris only. Multi-stroke dark ochre eyebrows. Dark brown mohair wig.

Illustration 6. (Right) Kestner character doll head incised 187. Closed mouth and painted hazel eyes with pupils and white highlight dots. Black upper eyelines and brown lower eyelines. Red lid lines. Short black eyelashes painted above iris only. Multi-stroke light ochre eyebrows. Light brown mohair wig in boyish style.

Christmas sleigh: 11in (27.9cm) C M Bergmann A M. Two German all-bisque *(Dolls from the MacDowell Doll Museum Collection)*.

A DOLLS' CHRISTMAS

A Photographic Essay
by Robert & Karin MacDowell

All dolls from the MacDowell Doll Museum collection.

"CHRISTMAS EVE" *Left: Marotte marked F. G. In sleigh: 11in (27.9cm) C M Bergamnn A M; 4in (10.2cm) all-bisque. Right: Papier-mache St. Nicholas. Background: Christmas tree with wax angels by Gladys MacDowell (NIADA).*

ABOVE: Doll house Christmas.

RIGHT: 15in (38.1cm) French Fashion marked F. G.

"FRENCH CHRISTMAS"   Large doll: 32in (81.3cm) Jumeau; Smaller doll: 15in (38.1cm) R D (Rabery & Delphieu). Background: Christmas tree with wax angels by Gladys MacDowell (NIADA).

"AMERICAN CHRISTMAS"   From left to right: 16in (40.6cm) David Copperfield by Madame Alexander; 17in (43.2cm) Darrow Rawhide, Connecticut; 19in (48.3cm) Schoenhut; 16½in (41.9cm) Babyland Rag, 1905, N.Y.; 11in (27.9cm) Topsy-Turvy by Brueckner, 1901. Front of Schoenhut: West Virginia stomper doll out of wood. Background: Same as above.

GERMAN CHRISTMAS From left to right: 17in (43.2cm) K Star R 116 A toddler; 25in (63.5cm) K Star R flirty eye; 19in (48.3cm) K Star R 121 toddler. Background: Christmas tree with wax angels by Gladys MacDowell (NIADA).

the door of hope reopened

BY PATRICIA SULLIVAN PLANTON

Everyone expects to fall in love at a doll show. Like many others, my affairs usually last only until I see the price tag on the doll. The 1978 Algoma Doll Show was the exception. I never expected my romance with a 12 in. (30.5 cm) oriental gentleman to last so long or to take me half way around the world, to his birthplace in Ning Po, China, or to discussing his heritage with Asian experts in the Library of Congress.

Many a doll collector has been accosted with the "buy me" look of a pouty Lenci or the "cuddle me" look of a bisque baby only a mother could love. We are all familiar with the slightly rowdy glances of the adorable Kewpies and no one walks away from a googlie. I should have known this was a different kind of doll because he said **nothing** to me — absolutely nothing! There is nothing worse than being given the "silent treatment." Yet his appearance and demeanor sparked the reference librarian in me into wondering: "Who are you?"

As the day wore on, I glanced at him from various angles as I walked about the show but still he revealed not a clue. You cannot appreciate the cliche "inscrutable oriental" until you have gazed into the serene countenance of a Door of Hope doll.

On the second day I broke down and bought him. The dealer could only tell me that he was made in a Chinese mission and his head and hands were carved of pear wood.

As librarian of our doll club and custodian of our treasure trove of books it was not difficult to identify him, but even the most prestigious of references referred to the well-known fact that the dolls were dressed by destitute women housed in a mission known as the Door of Hope. There was little else known and yet I knew there must be more. The dealer had mentioned "pear wood" and yet I could find nothing to verify this. So I began writing letters. My first was to Dorothy Coleman who encouraged me and clarified an item in her encyclopedia. Ning Po is not the name of the carver but rather the city where the carvers lived.

She in turn led me to Elsie Clark Krug, a remarkable lady, 90 years old, who wrote me: "relying on memory, which I cannot be sure is completely accurate, I will share with you what I recall about the Door of Hope." A newsletter she had written in 1958 added a wealth of information about the exquisite costumes which were exact replicas of those worn by the Chinese.

Still I wondered about the mission itself, who founded it and what happened to it. In addition to my letter writing campaign I was also in touch with my public library, through which I found a book entitled *A History of the Christian Missions in China* by Kenneth S. LaTourette. From this source I learned of the mission's foundress: "Miss Cornelia Bonnell, a graduate of Vassar, while teaching in a private school for foreign children, became impressed with the unhappy conditions of Chinese prostitutes. Accordingly, she resigned her position and became the first superintendent."

Having exhausted the facilities in my state, I was put in touch, via the teletype,

with a neighboring state library which sent me information from the *World Missionary Atlas*, an ancient volume which revealed that the annual income in those early days was $37,564 a year. I was to learn later that these monies came from the Shanghai Municipal Council, the Rotary Club and the American Women's Club as well as charitable groups throughout the world.

There was still one more stone left unturned — the Library of Congress. As a library science student we spoke that name with reverence. As I sent my letter off to Washington I silently prayed I would find some more answers, as so many of my letters sent to other likely sources were "returned to sender." Mr. Robert Dunn, Chinese Area specialist of the Asian Division answered my letter and sent materials taken from the *Encyclopedia Sinica*, parts of which are quoted here.

". . . A philanthropic work started in Shanghai in 1900 by a Committee of five missionary ladies, to rescue such of the many Chinese prostitutes in the Foreign Settlement as desired to leave a life of shame. The first Home was opened in a Chinese house in November, 1901, the first worker being Miss Cornelia L. Bonnell (died 1916).

"In 1904, a number of philanthropic Chinese offered to assist in the work, and the offer was accepted. They opened a Receiving Home, in the most notorious quarter of the settlement, and also secured by their influence the enactment of new municipal regulations favorable to public morality especially one limiting to 15 years the age at which girls might enter the brothels. One result of this was that a large number of kidnapped children were freed, and given into the

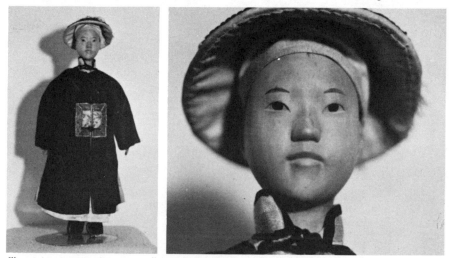

Illustration 1. 12 in. (30.5 cm) tall "inscrutable Oriental" Door of Hope doll, with carved wooden head and hands on a cloth body; painted features with long black queue. He is dressed in two silk kimonos. From *The Doll Book* by Laura B. Starr, we learn that the "inverted washbowl hat, tassle and feather" indicate his rank as a Manchu nobleman. "Like all people of his class, he wears an embroidered chest protector that indicates to the initiated his family or social status."

Illustration 2. Close-up of "inscrutable Oriental" Door of Hope doll. Note the pear grain wood of his face.

charge of the Mission, which in 1906 opened a Children's Home in the country at Kiangwan, near Shanghai. In the same year, an Industrial Home was opened, where the girls could be taught to work towards self support.

"In 1912 the Municipal Council pressed the Mission to undertake the care of the strayed, stolen and abandoned children found in the streets of Shanghai by the police, and guaranteed the necessary finances from time to time. The request was acceded to, and a Home for Waifs and Strays was begun.

"In January, 1917, the Mission reported 8 foreign lady workers, 36 Chinese assistants, and 420 women and girls in their care."

Mr. Dunn wisely suggested I write the Missionary Research Library in New York City for further information. So yet another letter went East beginning: Dear Sir, Could you please help me . . . .

From Mr. Seth Kasten, reference librarian of the Union Theological Seminary, I received the name of another gentleman who was interested in the subject and had done research. We exchanged letters on several occasions and he shared with me much of what he had learned of the dollmaking industry.

Many months have passed and my letter writing has ceased. Now people, having heard of my interest in the Door of Hope, write to me for information. My small Chinese friend no longer gives me the "silent treatment," for now he says: "You know who I am and what I am — now write my story."

My doll is one of a set of 24, although Mrs. Krug, in her newsletter, said others may have been made for special orders. The Kimport company imported the dolls all through the 1940's and if your doll club is fortunate enough to have the complete series of *Doll Talk* you will find many pictures and specific references to the individual dolls, many of which sold for as little as $2.50. The mission records, however, document that the society began making dolls in 1902.

Correspondence exchanged between this country and the mission foreshadows the end — prices were high

Illustration 5. 11 in. (27.9 cm) farmer and grandmother Door of Hope dolls. The farmer, on the left, is missing his original straw hat. His straw outer garment is used as a raincoat, and his rake is tucked into his belt. The grandmother, on the right, is dressed in a cotton kimono fastened with tiny 'frog' closings. *Rahr-West Museum*, Manitowoc, Wi.

Illustration 6. Close-up of farmer Door of Hope doll. Note his rake which is tucked into his belt. *Rahr-West Museum*, Manitowoc, Wi.

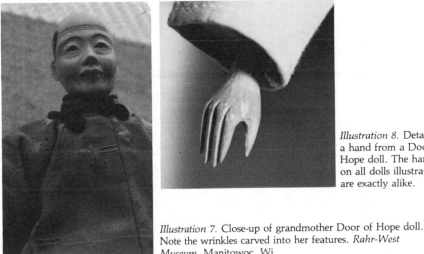

Illustration 8. Detail of a hand from a Door of Hope doll. The hands on all dolls illustrated are exactly alike.

Illustration 7. Close-up of grandmother Door of Hope doll. Note the wrinkles carved into her features. *Rahr-West Museum*, Manitowoc, Wi.

and silk was almost unprocurable. A letter received by Mr. Arthur McKin dated August 4, 1947, from 22 Robison Road (Chang Show Road), Shanghai, stated that the mission was still intact and "we were able to come back to it and carry on our work after several years of internment." Clara A. Nelson, who wrote the

letter, said they had "sent a few lots to the states and have had no (sic) difficulty in the shipment."

From a paper written by Mr. Ashley W. Wright entitled: *The Door of Hope Dolls: a History of their Origin*, we learn of the final chapter. "The Door of Hope Mission ceased to exist in Shanghai in 1950 when its property was turned over to the Communists and its foreign mission workers were asked to leave the country. The mission re-emerged in Taiwan. In 1977, the mission finally ceased to function entirely since the Taiwan government took over much of its work as its social welfare program expanded in scope."

And so the Door of Hope closed in 1977 only to be opened in 1979 by a small Chinese gentleman with help from interested friends all over America and a junior high school librarian who suspected that behind that subtle smile there was a story.

Illustration 3. "Young gentleman" Door of Hope doll, dressed in cotton three-quarter length tan jacket, blue trousers gathered and tied at the ankles and a white high-neck shirt fastened with a 'frog' at the neck. *Mrs. Emil Muuss Collection.*

Illustration 4. Close-up of "young gentleman" Door of Hope doll. *Mrs. Emil Muuss Collection.*

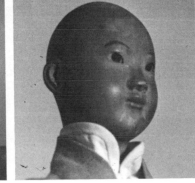

EFFanBEE's *Patsy Ann* with four *Patsyettes*. All of the dolls are wearing original costumes. For further details concerning these dolls see pages 42-45. *Photograph by John Axe.*

Jumeau, marked "DÉPOSÉ//E. 10 J." *Photograph by Howard Foulke.*

A Jumeau Family Album

A Photographic Essay by Howard Foulke

commentary by Jan Foulke

JUMEAU - - the magic word in antique dolls, the creator of the most lovely and life-like Bébés in the world. The doll creations of Maison Jumeau look like happy children with joyful faces. Sparkling laughing eyes, soft rosy-hued cheeks, lovely natural looking hair with loose tendrils to frame their faces - - all of these details contribute to the special appeal of a Jumeau doll. Chunky child bodies of posable composition and wood also add to the reality of the natural look. To doll fanciers the name Jumeau suggests a true work of art worthy of admiration and delightful to own.

The most rare and beautiful of Jumeaus, the elusive Long Face, probably one of the earliest Bébés of the family. Only the composition and wood body of the Long Face is marked with the blue stamp; her head has only a size number, but her look is unmistakable. Such softness of expression! This doll is usually found only in sizes larger than 24 in. (61cm). Jumeau won the gold medal at the Vienna Exhibition in 1873 and at the Paris Exhibition in 1878. Her blond mohair wig appears to be original. Her ears are separately applied. Marked: JUMEAU // MEDAILLE D'OR // PARIS. *Crandall Collection.*

LEFT: Since Emile Jumeau took over the firm around 1877, the dolls which carry his initials probably date just after that. This Bébé with the E.J. mark on her head has exceptionally gorgeous large deep brown eyes which provide a marvelous contrast to the pale bisque of her face. She is 21 in. (53.3cm) tall. *Richard Wright.*

ABOVE: This diminutive Tête Jumeau is an exquisite confection in her peach satin and ecru lace dress with chiffon bonnet. Her body with jointed wrists has the blue oval BÉBÉ JUMEAU sticker. She is 13 in. (33cm) tall. *H & J Foulke.*

LEFT: This 23 in. (58.4cm) E.J., also pictured in color on the cover has blond eyebrows which match her apparently original human hair wig styled in exceptionally long and narrow corkscrew curls. Her large luminous glass eyes, typical of Jumeau dolls, are handblown with a threaded iris covered with a drop of clear glass which gives them the brilliance of the natural eye. These are referred to as paperweight eyes because of the illusion of depth. Her body has the blue Jumeau stamp; her wrists are unjointed. Marked: DÉPOSÉ // E. 10 J. *H & J Foulke.*

ABOVE: Dolls with the red stamp Tête Jumeau mark on their heads represent a period in Jumeau production after the E.J. doll. Their faces usually have a somewhat higher color than those of the E.J.s. This 19 in. (48.3cm) doll has the red stamp on her head. She has the typical pert look associated with the Tête Jumeau dolls. Most of this is due to her large expressive eyes. Her body has the blue Jumeau stamp. Marked: DÉPOSÉ // TÊTE JUMEAU // BTE SGDG. *H & J Foulke.*

ABOVE: A rarely found Tête Jumeau with the lady body. This is not the kid body of the early Parisiennes, but a jointed composition and wood body with a molded bust, tiny waist and rounded hips. Her pink lips give a hint of a smile at the turned up corners, a feature typical of Jumeau dolls. She is 20 in. (50.8cm) tall. *Richard Wright.*

LEFT: Seldom found is this Jumeau family member with the incised marking on the head, also with red stroke marks. Her eyes, smaller than those of the later Jumeaus, are a beautiful blue which matches her blue leather marked E. Jumeau shoes. This blue has been carried out in her costuming, a newly made outfit of old blue and ivory satin. Her body has the blue Jumeau stamp; her wrists are straight. She is 15 in. (38.1cm) tall. Marked: DÉPOSÉ // JUMEAU. *H & J Foulke.*

LEFT: This 26 in. (66cm) Tête Jumeau has the same small eyes as the incised Jumeau doll, which is unusual for a doll with the Tête marking. *Richard Wright.*

BOTTOM LEFT: Another E.J., this one is 20 in. (50.8cm) tall. She has the heavier and darker eyebrows which are characteristic of the Jumeau dolls. Her clothes are replacements of an appropriate style. *Richard Wright.*

BOTTOM RIGHT: Another of the early Bébés is the so-called Portrait Jumeau. Like the Long Face, the head of the Portrait Jumeau is marked only with a size number, and her body has the same blue stamp. These early Jumeau bodies are rather chunky and solid; the wrists are not jointed; the fingers are fat. The eyes of this doll, which are longer and narrower than those of other types of Jumeau dolls, are very distinctive in color as well as shape. The iris is composed of a series of vivid light blue rods surrounded by a black background. She is 25 in. (63.5cm) tall. *Richard Wright.*

Dolls In Southern France
by DOROTHY S. COLEMAN

© 1978 Hobby House Press, Inc.

Illustrations 1 & 2. French-type composition doll. This particular one has an open mouth and teeth but many of them have closed mouths; period costume of the 18th century but doll is 19th century. This is an automata marked "A. Theroude, Paris." Height 16". *Coleman Collection.*

The average doll collector dreams about the wonderful French dolls one could find in France. All those marvelous A Ts, Brus, Jumeaus and so forth, must be seen everywhere in the land of their origin; but as is so often the case the dream and the reality are vastly different.

In April 1978 I had the privilege of exploring by car the South of France along the Mediterranean and including the Catalonean area of Spain which has been part of France at some periods in the past. This coastal area is one of the most beautiful and historic areas in the world. In addition, and of special interest to doll collectors, are the fine museums containing antique dolls.

How does one reach this Utopia? From the United States you can fly to Barcelona, Spain or to Nice in France. These international airports are virtually at the extremities of this area. The best way to see the country is by car, a small European car with gear shift is preferable, but you need an expert and intrepid driver.

This was Southern Gaul, home of many Romans and Visigoths. Medieval walled towns and castles abound. Some of the castles have become comfortable hostelries for the venturesome tourist, but automobiles can barely squeeze through the narrow medieval streets. Here the Pyrenees and the Alps meet the Mediterranean forming breathtakingly beautiful rides along the precipices bordering the sea.

These roads built into cliffs are called Corniches. The grades are very steep, the roads winding with hair-pin curves and guard rails are often non-existent or mere plastic posts that would be as much protection as a piece of paper. The driver must have steady nerves and gears are a necessity. If you are timid or a car is not feasible, most of the area can also be reached by train but certainly you will miss seeing many of the beauties and places of historic interest which the area offers.

Starting in the west of this coastal area, we first visit the Museo Romantico Provincial in Sitges. This is less than an hours ride from the Barcelona airport, along a Corniche of course. There a magnificent doll collection occupies almost an entire house and the wide variety of dolls are well displayed in beautiful surroundings. Practically all of the dolls are in original clothes. Some restoration may have been done to the clothes but it is difficult to detect. This is an outstanding early Spanish collection with many dolls that probably originated in France but there are very few French Bébés and no German character dolls that I can recall seeing. A large proportion of the dolls are French-type lady dolls in exquisite costumes of the second half of the 19th century. On the whole the dating of the dolls seemed farily accurate judging from the costumes. There are some fine automata, some early wooden dolls and a sizable number of the French-type composition dolls with kid bodies. Here and in Southern France these early composition dolls with wigs abound while we saw almost no early molded hair papier-

mâché dolls which tends to verify that the former were made in France and the latter in Germany.

At Sitges one is accompanied through the museum by an enthusiastic guard. He tends to hurry you past some of the most interesting dolls and you have to stop and admire his favorites which are often the least exciting to a doll collector. There are only a few postcards of the dolls available and no catalogs.

At this point I would like to warn any prospective visitor to this area that in Spain everything closes at one o'clock and does not open again until 4:00 or 4:30 p.m. or not at all. In France the mid-day closing is from 12:00 to 2:00 or 2:30 p.m. and places are generally open in the afternoon. Be sure to check the hours of opening for often museums are closed entirely one day a week. It takes considerable planning and luck with traffic, finding a parking place, and so forth, in order to arrive at museums in time to see them thoroughly before they close.

Proceeding eastward our next museum is the Rocomora Collection in Barcelona. This is a very fine costume collection in a mansion in downtown Barcelona opposite the Picasso Museum. Here the dolls are used to show costumes and all are nearly dressed in original clothes. They are French-type dolls and about equally divided between the bisque head lady and composition wigged types. The earlier costumes tend to be on the latter type. This is a much smaller collection of dolls than the one at Sitges but the marvelous people's costumes cannot help but fascinate any doll collector. Only two postcards show dolls and there are a few dolls shown in the catalog which, of course, is in Spanish.

Skirting around the Pyrenees on the Corniches of the Costa Bravure one enters France and soon comes into Provence. What doll collector has not heard of the Santons of Provence! What tourist is not overwhelmed by Santons in every shop window! These modern Santons are made of a cheap earthenware or vinyl for the most part. If you want to see genuine old Santons you may wish to visit the Musée du Vieux Marseille in the Maison Diamantee on the Rue de la Prison, Marseille. According to a publication of this Museum, Santons originated in Marseille towards the end of the 18th century. Jean-Louis Lagnel (1764 to 1824) is alleged to have been their creator. The Museum's collection of Santons dates from about 1830 to 1935.

One of the finest provincial museums is in Arles. Practically all

Illustrations 3 & 4. French-type lady doll, bisque head marked "F G 8", the F G is in a scroll, cloth body, holiday costume of a Boulogne fisherwoman. Height 26". *Virginia Dilliplane Collection.*

of the dolls in this museum are in original regional costumes. They show the great variety of the costumes of Provence. The costumes varied with the period, occupation, social strata, social occasion and so forth. A whole book could be written entirely on the costumes worn in this one region. The extensive display made one realize how ridiculous it is to refer to "the costume of Provence" as though there were only one. Most of the dolls in this Museum are French-type composition, but there are also a sizable number of wooden dolls with carved curls similar in appearance to the dolls formerly sold at the House of the Seven Gables in Salem, Massachusetts. After inquiring about these dolls and being informed that they were made in Beaucaire, a neighboring town on the Rhone River, we made a special trip to Beaucaire to see if we could learn more about them but were unsuccessful.

Probably the most famous doll museum in the South of France is the Musée National de Monaco in Monte Carlo. This Museum is in a spacious villa on the Avenue Princesse Grace. The entire villa is used for displaying the dolls collected by Madame de Galéa, all of which are on view, none being put away in storage. Madame de Galéa was born on or near the Island of Madagascar in the last century. When she was ten years old, about 1900, her family moved to Paris and she was only permitted to take one of her dolls with her. But when they reached Paris she was allowed to replace the dolls she had left behind and thus began her marvelous collection. She lived all her life in Paris and after her death in 1956 her grandson gave the collection to the Principality of Monaco.

The collection is particularly outstanding for its automata and French-type lady dolls. The guards operate the various automata at regular intervals during the day to the delight of the many visitors. Fortunately the museum has a talented craftsman who can keep the automata in running condition. However, this repairing of the delicate mechanisms necessitates the removal and frequently the destruction of the original costumes so that very few of the automata are in original clothes. The French-type lady dolls are more fortunate and some of these wear original costumes and even have additional clothes. The diversity of the faces on these French-type lady dolls is a revelation. Room after room is filled with them, yet no two faces appear to be the same. I have seen a great many of this type of doll in various collections and shows, but still there are a large number here that are quite different from any that I could recall seeing before. One

of these was dressed as a man and had a molded mustache.

We visited the Museum on three occasions and each time found some gem that had eluded our attention before. An early French molded cardboard doll placed inconspicuously at the back of a cabinet escaped our attention on our first visit. You need to return several times because there is too much to see on one visit and a person cannot adequately absorb all of it. A magnificent créche scene occupies the entire length of a large room. There are large dolls and small dolls. Practically all of the dolls were made before World War I and I do not recall seeing any German character dolls. One group of dolls acquired recently by Princess Grace consists of vinyl lady dolls dressed by famous Paris couturiers. The dolls are predominately French. French-type compositions, French-type bisques (mostly lady dolls) and French automata. There are numerous postcards, slides and even a booklet available on the dolls in this collection. But the automata are featured and the other dolls are somewhat neglected. It is truly worth the trip just to visit this Museum, but be sure to allow plenty of time to enjoy it and stop to see some of the other fine collections on the way.

The few antique dolls for sale in Southern France are more expensively priced than they are here in America. To our surprise most of the new dolls in shops are made of cloth, we saw more cloth dolls than vinyl ones. The cloth dolls come in all sizes and shapes, but they universally have heavy eye make-up, are relatively expensive and the artist-creator is usually publicized. We saw them in toy shops as well as novelty shops catering to tourists. Some of the cloth dolls had long limbs reminiscent of the Flapper dolls of the 1920s. We also saw some of these Flapper dolls with glazed china heads on the cloth bodies. Apparently Art-Deco is the rage in France and the price for these new china head dolls is $200 to $300.

We felt that the best French dolls to bring home were in the form of memories and postcards.

LEFT: *Snow White* from about 1939; 13in (33cm) composition; head is marked "PR. ELIZABETH//ALEXANDER;" dress is labeled "Snow White." RIGHT: *McGuffey Ana* from early 1940s; 16in (40.6cm) composition with dressed tagged "McGuffey Ana."

The doll in the full view is a 14in (35.6cm) *Toni* right out of her original box from about 1951. The head and body are the P-90 mold and are also marked: "IDEAL DOLL." The other doll is a 22½in (57.2cm) *Mary Hartline* from about 1953, the most unusual of all the Toni-type dolls. The head is a socket head and is only marked: "IDEAL DOLL." The body is marked: "IDEAL DOLL//P-94." The red majorette dress is a shiny rayon. For further details concerning these dolls see pages 74-78.

JOHN BUNNY

Illustration 1. Charcoal sketch of John Bunny.

From his waved and carefully parted hair, to his bulbous nose set off by deep laugh lines, his face bespoke character. In addition to being exhibited in such a lowly fashion, like an unclaimed horse in a stake race, he was marked **"FOR SALE."**

"How much!", I demanded of the unsuspecting owner. I was in my heroine garb, about to rescue this doll just as "Black Beauty" had been rescued from his cruel owners. I was going to restore him to his rightful place of dignity.

"That much!" I gasped. The heroic dialog was clearly at an end. My checkbook was badly depleated and, it appeared, this transaction would take some skillful negotating.

"Why are you selling him?" I began.

"Because he is so old and ugly," the dealer flatly replied.

"Some day we will all be old and ugly," I retorted in my best patrician voice. "Wrap him up! Carefully."

"John," I said, masking my own self doubts. "You are expensive, but you are worth it." In the months and years that followed, he has not only given me great personal satisfaction but has charmed many a ribbon from many a judge.

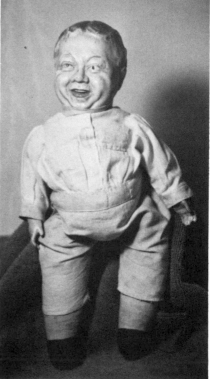

Illustration 2. 14 in. (35.6cm) high, cork stuffed muslin body with sawdust and an inner core of cotton. On the back of his head is deeply impressed: " © 34.//L.A. S. 1914." Doll has sandy brown hair, bright red lips and the black pupils in the eyes are surrounded by grey iris.

BY PATRICIA S. PLANTON

I do not talk to my dolls very often—only when I have something important to say. Last fall, when I opened up my October/November issue of **DOLL READER** and saw illustration 4 on page 17 I could not resist. John Bunny had won again! I did not meet this prestigeous gentleman at the National Convention. I met him as the winner of our club's "Ugly Doll Contest."

I had my doubts about the contest from the start because **none** of my dolls are ugly—unusual maybe, but not ugly. In fact, I could not believe that there would be enough dolls to have a contest.

All the dolls exhibited were bona fide children's play things. Some were crude and ugly, like the doll made from the family cow that died in the winter of 1929; some were strange and ugly, like the Indian doll made from a natural root whose arms and legs shot out at strange angles. There were weird dolls like the voodoo doll complete with its victim's hair. There were off beat dolls like "Gay Bob" and the "Flasher" and I had to admit in one way or another all the contestants were pretty ugly.

In the midst of all of these sat John Bunny, still in his original coveralls with its faded label which identified him as having been made by the Amberg Company in 1915.

142

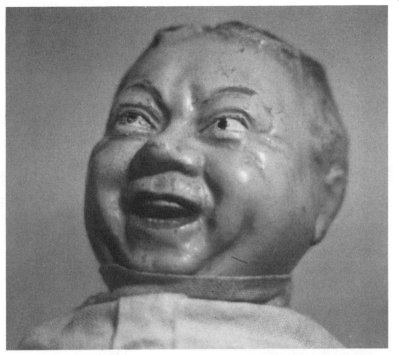

Illustration 3. Close-up of the head which is 3¾ in. (9.6cm) high. Note the five painted teeth on the bottom and the row of white teeth on the top.

Identifying the doll was easy. Johanna Anderton's *More Twentieth Century Dolls* has two pictures of him on page 1006. From this source I learned that John Bunny was a real person.

The real John Bunny was everybody's Santa Claus. When he died in 1915, a Dublin newspaper announced on its front page in large black print, "John Bunny is Dead, the best Known Man in the World." That may have been somewhat of an exaggeration as only those early theatre goers knew him as the comedy "star" that he was. He had left his established place as a stage actor to join the infant motion picture industry. He could foresee the future impact movies would have and he left a 25 year career in which he had performed in everything from minstrel shows to Shakespearean drama.

Of his contemporaries, he alone foresaw that the "flickers" were more than a novelty and would soon become a serious threat to the legimate stage.

In the summer of 1910 he made the rounds of the primitive studios in the New York area but found no one would hire him. His immense popularity on the stage had frightened off the producers. No one could afford him. Finally, he offered to work for nothing to prove that he could make the transition from stage to screen. Albert E. Smith and J. Stuart Blackton of the Vitagraph Company agreed to use him in one film and paid him the going wage of $5.00 a day.

When the producers saw the early rushes they were convinced that the portly John Bunny knew a great deal about acting. His 25 year apprenticeship had produced an experienced and successful stage comedian.

They were impressed by the expressive features of his face and the extravagant emotion they could convey. Equally impressive was the actor's size and build, for his short, barrel-like body weighed about 300 pounds. In 1912 he went on a diet and lost 40 pounds. The loss registered at the box office as well and he quickly regained his old form.

By 1913 his salary was $1,000 a week and he was mobbed by adoring fans wherever he went.

Much of his success came from making audiences cry one moment and laugh the next. In January of 1913 he made a return appearance in vaudeville but it proved to be too strenuous, for the immense body which housed this great talent was weakening. Overwhelmed by crowds, honorary banquets and formal welcoming celebrations plus an exhausting schedule of films, his health broke down. With the gradual development of heart and kidney complications and finally Bright's Disease he died on April 26, 1915.

The young boy from Brooklyn who ran away to become a roving player in obscure minstrel shows had made a lasting impression on the world of his time and on the motion picture industry which he regarded as a new art form. He saw it as more than a toy to amuse the ignorant masses, more than the pie throwing, slapstick humor of the burlesque stage. John Bunny foresaw colored as well as talking pictures and all of these things have come to pass.

If ever a posthumous "Oscar" were to be awarded, it should be to John Bunny, the portly prince, America's first popular film comedian.

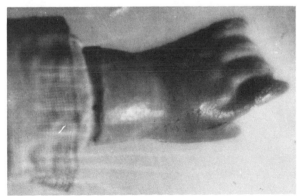

Illustration 4. "Gauntlet" hand made of composition and then painted.

Illustration 5. Moveable arms and legs are attached to the body with wires and metal buttons.

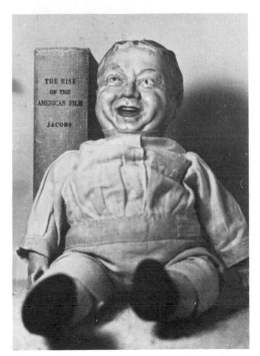

143

11in (27.9cm) composition *Kewpies* with jointed arms. Decal heart on chest reads: "KEWPIE//Des. & Copyright//by//Rose O'Neill. LEFT: Rarer black version has red instead of usual blue wings. *Helen Sieverling Collection.* RIGHT: White version. *Patricia Schoonmaker Collection.* For further details concerning these dolls see pages 85-88.

Child doll. Bisque head with pierced ears, glass stationary eyes, closed mouth. Marked on head "STEINER//FI^{AE} A 15." Body marked "Medaille d'Or Paris 1889." Maroon dress, beige lace hat. Height 19in (48.3cm).

Focusing On.....
A.M. Lady Dolls

by JAN FOULKE

Photographs by HOWARD FOULKE

© 1978 Hobby House Press, Inc.

Illustration 1. 13in (33.0cm) lady doll.

RIGHT: **Illustration 2.** 12in (30.5cm) lady doll

LEFT: **Illustration 3.** Close-up of the lady doll in *Illustration 2.*

The lady or so-called flapper dolls of the post World War I period are fairly difficult to find on today's doll market. Probably there are not as many available today because they were made for such a short period of time, when compared to the production period of child dolls. Several German companies including Cuno & Otto Dressel, Simon & Halbig and Armand Marseille made the lady dolls during this era. Both of the ladies pictured here are by Armand Marseille, mold 401.

Their bodies are of good quality composition with joints at shoulders, elbows, hips and knees. The torsos are flat-chested. The long, slender limbs have shaped unjointed wrists and ankles; the feet are shaped for high-heeled shoes. Their bisque heads have oval faces with high cheek coloring, thin brown eyebrows, gray sleep eyes with real lashes and bow-shaped

mouths with parted lips and four upper teeth.

The lady in Illustration 1 has brown mohair pulled back in a low bun, probably a replacement. She is wearing her original white lace-trimmed cotton undergarment with blue ribbons. She is the proud posessor of the wardrobe of original clothes. Her height is 13in (33.0cm).

The lady in Illustrations 2 and 3 is 12in (30.5cm) tall. She has her original blonde mohair wig in bobbed style. Her white silk stockings and white leather high-heeled shoes are original, but her dress, hat and parasol are borrowed from the other lady's wardrobe. The outer dress is made of yellow crepe with lace and aqua bead trim draped over an underdress of lace, also with bead trim. Her flower-trimmed hat and parasol match her dress.

The trousseau which belongs to the brown-haired doll shown in

Illustration 1 was apparently made by a professional dressmaker or seamstress, judging from the couturier styling and the finishing and the trimming details. No shortcuts were taken to hasten the job, and some of the detail sewing must have been very time-consuming. Her hats were also professionally made. We do not know whether this lady was purchased from the store with her wardrobe or whether she was purchased in chemise only and the dresses subsequently ordered. Whichever, it goes without saying that the trousseau would have been a costly item. The doll and clothes were found in the trunk with humped lid shown in Illustration 8. The trunk, however, predates the doll by at least 20 years, and we do not know whether it was always with her or if it was a later addition.

Now for a description of the trousseau. Only one dress is not

146

Illustration 4. Dresses and accessories from the trousseau belonging to the doll in *Illustration 1.*

Illustration 5. Dresses and accessories from the trousseau belonging to the doll in *Illustration 1.*

Illustration 6. Dresses and accessories from the trousseau belonging to the doll in *Illustration 1.*

Illustration 7. Dress and accessories from the trousseau belonging to the doll in *Illustration 1.*

Illustration 8. The trunk in which the doll in *Illustration 1* and her clothes were found.

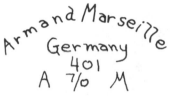

Illustration 9. Marking on dolls.

pictured since it was too fragile to remove from its plastic bag. It is a lovely red satin straight-line dress with sheer blue overdress with lace trim. It has a long blue sash, also tiny glass button.

In Illustration 4, the dress on the left is of white silk with lavender stripes. It has lavender piping for trim, also lace trim on neckline and sleeves. The dress has a matching belt. The middle dress is of dusty rose velvet with chiffon insets. Jet beads dangle from a high waist. There is chain-stitched trim, a lace underdress and a train with a large black bead butterfly. The dress on the right is of dusty rose silk, A-line style. It has black silk collar and cuffs, white lace detachable collar, black covered buttons and bogus buttonholes. The extra

back panel is pointed with button trim also. The hat is of natural straw with lavender ribbon and flowers.

In Illustration 5, the dress on the left is of rose wool with a brown silk blouse with lace inset. Brown buttons and braid trim are on the wrap-style skirt. The matching jacket/cape comes to a long point in the back. In the middle is a dress with a pink satin skirt and lace blouse and overskirt. There is a large pink satin bow at the waist in back and a smaller one further down the back. Flower trim is on the front belt. The hat is of natural straw with pink silk lining and covered with pink flowers. On the right is a bronze velvet straight dress with green beaded trim. The dress has a velvet inset with tassels and a light brown taffeta fringe overskirt. There is a pleated inset in the back of the dress. A green satin parasol and hat of tan velvet and natural straw with a feather complete the outfit.

In Illustration 6, the dress on the left is A-line and of black wool with velvet and lace trim. The net bodice was once lined with red silk. There is a matching jacket, and a hat of black plush with fuschia ribbon and jet bead trim. The middle dress is of aqua silk with pink crepe sleeves and neck trim.

There is an overlay of metallic lace with sequins and the train peaks in the back. The dress has a pink crepe bow with long ends and cut steel decoration and there is a matching parasol with flowers. The dress on the right is of gray silk with brown velvet ribbon trim and a lovely lace vest. There is a brown velvet belt. A hat of blue straw with blue velvet lining, ribbon and blue and white flowers can be worn with this dress.

In Illustration 7, the dress is of white cotton with ecru embroidery and openwork with scallops at waist and hem. The hat is of natural straw with a plaid multi-color ribbon band and a red feather. Other articles from her turnk are clockwise: red shoes and clutch bag, white leather high heels, white silk stockings, mirror, embroidered handkerchief, comb and scissors which work.

Both of these dolls are from the collection of Mike White, and we appreciate her kindness in being willing to share them with others.

China head, cloth body, bisque arms, original commercial clothes, ca. 1860s. Doll is almost in mint condition. Upper left shows mirror reflection of gold snood and tassels. Height of shoulder head: 2½in (6.4cm). Height of doll: 12½in (31.8cm). *Coleman Collection.*

Decorated China Heads

by Frances Walker

China dolls were a popular collector's item in the 1930s and 1940s. They later lost their popularity and have largely been ignored by collectors of the 1960s and 1970s. One reason for this was expressed by a young collector friend of mine who remarked that china dolls all look alike. The purpose of this essay is to show a few dolls that are different and cannot be confused. None of these heads are marked or dated by their maker; all have a special, well-defined and painted feature that is an identifying mark.

Right:
6-1/2in. (16.5cm); Long narrow face, long neck, well-modeled shoulders showing collarbone. Her only mark is an incised 11 on the center back of the shoulder. She has 3 sew holes, front and back. The black hair is combed smoothly from a center part over the ears, then drawn up into braids encircling the back of the head. Centered in the circle of braids in the back is a molded comb painted to represent tortoise shell. She is highly-colored, having almost a real flesh color. Her eyes are blue-gray. A fine black line outlines the top of her eyes; a red dot is in the corner. She is looking up. There is a slash of white through the pupil going to the right which highlights the eyes. The nostrils have dots of red and the lips are well-painted. The head is not dated but she is a well-executed doll.

Left:
4-3/4in. (12.1cm) China head which is clearly modeled with a long neck and a rather broad face. The black hair has a widow's peak with center part; the sides are rolled back from the face with fine brush marks. The ears are partially exposed. In back of her ear there is a curl which extends to the shoulder. The rest of the hair is gathered in a gold snood which is low on her neck. The snood is elaborate with a gold bow on the top and a tassel on each side back of the long curl. Her cheeks are rosy and the nostrils are defined by red. The eyes are blue; the top of the eye is defined with a fine black line and a red line. Her black eyebrows are feathered.

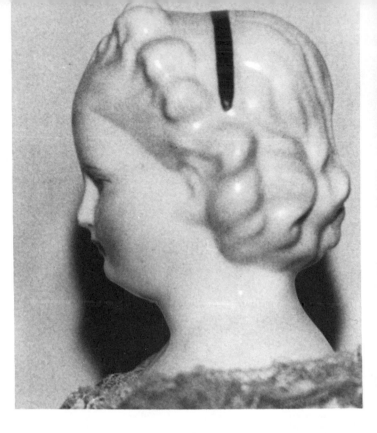

Above left:
The 4in. (10.2cm) head has a short neck, double chin and exposed ears. The black hair is drawn back from the face with fine brush marks. In the back the hair is smooth to the top of the ears, then it is arranged in nine vertical curls which extend to her shoulders. The curls are held in place by a gold-colored round comb so well-painted that the teeth show. She has blue eyes with a white dot highlight. There is a red line over the eye. Her complexion is white with red cheeks, her mouth is nicely painted and she has pierced ears. She is 15-1/2in. (39.4cm) tall and has an old cloth body with china parts.

Above right:
This doll has a blonde china head. The hair is brushed back from the face into a circle of tousled curls. The back hair is held by a black band over the top of her head. Below the band the hair falls to the neck in casually arranged curls. She has deep blue eyes and nicely painted features with exposed ears. The doll is 15in. (38.1cm) tall with a cloth body that has kid arms.

Left:
This 4-1/4in. (10.8cm) head has black hair waved from a center part into a gold luster snood on the back of the head. The snood is held by a white doubled ruffled band with a gold edge. On the top of her head the ruffle forms a bow. In front of the bow is a bunch of blue grapes with green leaves. The doll has blue eyes with a red line over them, rosy cheeks, exposed ears and a white complexion. She is 14in. (35.6cm) tall on a cloth body with china parts.

Right:
This is a 2-3/4in. (7cm) bonnet head. Her hair is combed smoothly down from a center part in eight curls low on her shoulders. Most of the head is covered by a white bonnet. The bonnet is made with a ruffle around the face which meets under the chin. The trim is a deep rose line and appears to look like a ribbon which extends completely around the bonnet, in back of the ruffle. The doll has blue eyes with a red line over them and has nicely painted features on a round, young girl's face. She is 11-1/2in. (29.2cm) tall on her cloth body with china parts.

Left:
This 3in. (7.6cm) head has blonde hair with center part, deep waves, short braid over the ears and hair to the shoulders below the ears. She wears a black snood over the back of her hair. The snood is held onto the front by a blue fluted ribbon which gives the appearance of a crown at the top of her head. The bottom of the snood is held by two bands, one below the other, of blue fluted ribbon going well down onto her shoulders. She has blue eyes with red lines over them, light brown eyebrows, rosy cheeks, a small red mouth and red dots in her nostrils. The doll stands 11-1/2in. (29.2cm) tall. She has a cloth body with old china arms and legs with flat ankle boots.

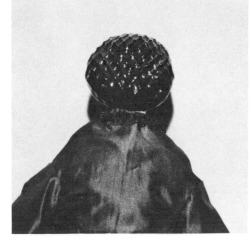

This 3-3/4in. (9.5cm) head has black hair waved from a center part into a gold snood. The hair puffs out at the sides. Over each ear there is a large gold tassel. She has small blue painted eyes, accented by a red line, a small rosebud mouth, pink cheeks and a white complexion. The doll is 13in. (33cm) tall on a cloth body with leather arms and cloth feet with red kid shoes.

This 3-1/2in. (8.9cm) china head has black hair brushed back from the face in a high roll that extends from ear to ear and then goes into a large knot. There are fine brush marks about her face. Above each ear is a nosegay of three hollyhocks, two blue, one red, surrounded by green leaves. Across the knot there is a large blue bow with ends extending to the shoulder. This doll has small blue eyes, exposed ears and a white complexion. Her shoulder plate is deep and her neck is long. She is 12in. (30.5cm) tall on a cloth body with china parts.

This brown-haired head measures 2-1/2in. (6.4cm). The hair goes straight back from the face with very fine brush marks. There is no part but there are rolls on the side. The back is drawn up into a large twisted knot. Behind each ear is a group of green leaves with a purple morning glory on the right. A four-petaled, rose colored flower with a yellow center and a bud is on the left. This doll has a creamy complexion, finely painted features, a long neck and exposed ears. She is 11in. (27.9cm) tall on a stiff white kid body.

This 2in. (5.1cm) head has black hair, a center part and waves ending in curls which extend to the neck behind each ear. The back is arranged in an extended bun. The decoration is a band that stands up like a tiara, extending from ear to ear. The front of the band is gold colored; the back is rose colored. She has exposed ears and very well-painted features. She is on a cloth body with old china parts. The doll is 7in. (17.8cm) tall.

Jumeau all original except for wig, dressed in pink cotton satin, probably from late 1880s. Teddy Bears, possibly old Steiff.

Martha Thompson
~American Doll Artist~

by MARGARET WHITTON

Illustration 1. Martha Darwin Thompson, age 20.

Photographs by HARRY BICKELHAUPT

Martha Darwin Thompson is considered to be one of the finest American doll artists of the 20th century. Her death in 1964 deprived doll collectors all over the world of the opportunity to know a truly fine, generous individual, who was completely dedicated to her art work.

Many collectors today have never had the opportunity to own or see her beautiful doll creations and the purpose of this article is to share with them, through photographs, her works of art.

Martha Thompson was born in Huntsville, Alabama, the eldest of the three children of James Lanier Darwin and Martha Lee Patton. Her father was a surgeon and physician and her mother an artist and accomplished pianist. During her early years, she attended both private and public schools in Huntsville, Alabama, and attended the Howard Seminary in West Bridgewater, Massachusetts, The Museum of Fine Arts, The Newschool of Design and The Massachusetts School of Art. She inherited her mother's love and appreciation of music and was herself an accomplished violinist. However, her first and ingrained interest was art. At the age of three she sat by her mother's side watching her as she painted her miniatures on ivory in watercolor, sometimes attempting to draw and paint the same object. Martha won many awards throughout her childhood years for her drawings and as a child loved to write and illustrate stories. One of her early efforts was a small notebook of stories, profusely illustrated, called "The Book of Odds and Ends." This was written at the age of six. As she became older, this writing and illustrating continued and she wrote fantasy stories illustrated with finely cut silhouettes. Her interest in the art medium covered watercolor, pen and ink, pastels of children and modeling in clay which finally led her into creating dolls.

After a long period of trial and error, Martha settled upon a fine porcelain to be used in the making of her dolls. All of the steps required to make a doll were done by Martha

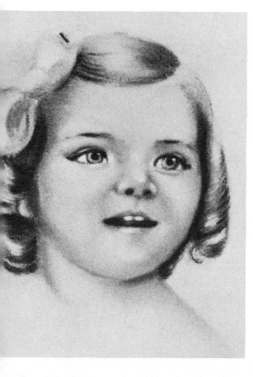

herself. The designing, sculpturing, painting and firing of the heads were all accomplished by her.

The British Royal Family held a certain fascination for Martha and she created dolls in the likeness of Queen Elizabeth, Princess Margaret Rose, Prince Charles and Princess Anne. Prince Philip was sculptured by Martha's son, Murray, as were many subsequent male dolls. The list of famous people she made is large and varied. Prince Ranier, Grace Kelly, Dwight and Mamie Eisenhower and Henry VIII and his wives are but a few in this group.

The creation of groups of 19th century dolls, designed from steel engravings in fashion magazines, are truly works of art. The delicate, fine bonnets and special wigs molded for these porcelain heads are beyond description. To own one of these dolls is an inspiration.

Illustration 2. A pastel drawn by Mrs. Robert R. Cook, sister of Martha, from a photograph of Martha at the age of three.

Martha Thompson was also a collector of antique dolls. She loved the attractive French ladies but her real love was the Heubach character child. Always willing to share her interest in dolls, she wrote articles about the Heubach's dollhouse dolls and Schoenhut dolls for the *Toy Trader* magazine. Many of her friends talk about the times they sat around her dining room table watching her work on her dolls, or talking about some discovery she had made about dolls of years gone by. She was always willing to share any knowledge she had with collectors who had a real love for dolls.

Martha Thompson was a charter member of the National Institute of American Doll Artists and a member of the Doll Study Club of Boston.

In closing I would like to mention my good friend Margaret Finch of New Rochelle, New York. She has costumed many of my Martha Thompson dolls in a manner beyond description. Her dedication to researching the costume, the proper fabric and the excellent workmanship is superb. She is also a member of the National Institute of American Doll Artist and I am proud to have in my possession the beautiful Martha Thompson dolls and the equally lovely costumes created for them by Margaret Finch.

ACKNOWLEDGEMENTS

I am grateful for the cooperation of Mrs. Robert R. Cook, sister of Martha Thompson, for making the photographs of Martha available for this article and the information about Martha's early life. I would also like to thank Mrs. Mae Connors, who was a close friend of Martha's, for her assistance.

ABOVE: Illustration 3. Martha Thompson and her son, Murray.

RIGHT: Illustration 4. The home where Martha Thompson grew up in Huntsville, Alabama.

La Duchess De Longueville. Doll made by Martha Thompson and costumed by Margaret Finch.

Martha Thompson Dolls

A Photographic Essay

by Margaret Whitton

photographs by Harry Bickelhaupt

Illustration 1. A rare small size Queen Elizabeth of England. Costumed by Margaret Finch in the robes of the Order of the Garter.

RIGHT: Illustration 2. A pair of dollhouse dolls. The gentleman was costumed by Martha's sister, Mary, and the lady by Jeannette Finan.

BELOW LEFT: Illustration 3. Anne of Cleves, fourth wife of Henry VIII. This doll was created after a portrait by Holbein and costumed by Margaret Finch.

BELOW RIGHT: Illustration 4. Anne Boleyn, second wife of Henry VIII. The likeness was taken from a Holbein crayon drawing and was costumed by Margaret Finch.

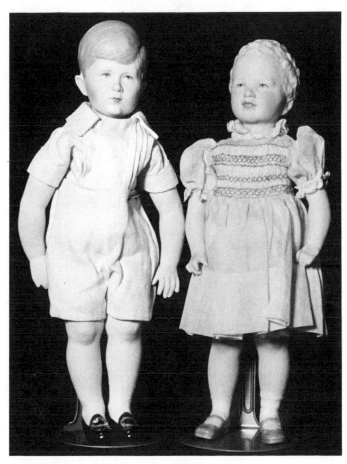

ABOVE LEFT: Illustration 5. Princess Anne of England at a later age wearing the ever popular hand-smocked dress. *The Margaret Woodbury Strong Museum Collection.*

ABOVE RIGHT: Illustration 6. Peddlers with molded hats. Five different types of peddlers were made. Costumed by Margaret Whitton. *The Margaret Woodbury Strong Museum Collection.*

RIGHT: Illustration 7. Prince Charles of England at the age of five. *Frances Walker Collection.* Princess Anne with her hand-smocked dress. *The Margaret Woodbury Strong Museum Collection.*

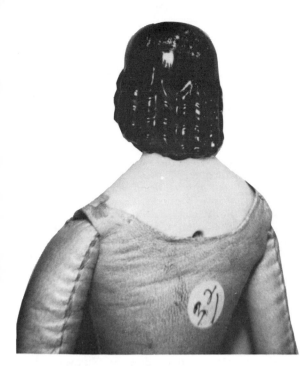

Illustration 1a

Illustrations 1a & 1b. Pink china head with long curls on a pink kid non-gusseted body.

Illustration 1b.

China Dolls

BY DOROTHY & EVELYN JANE COLEMAN

According to the new U.F.D.C. *Glossary*: China dolls are made of glazed porcelain. This means that they have a shiny surface and are translucent but not transparent. However when the china is thick it is almost impossible to see light through it. China dolls include: all-china dolls, dolls with china heads and limbs and dolls with only the head made of china. Often the china head was bought separately and the body was made of cloth at home. The china head dolls on commercially-made cloth bodies were often referred to in the trade as "Nankeen Dolls." Some of the mid-19th century china dolls were on wooden bodies or on kid bodies.

Most of the china dolls were made in the German States of Europe although china dolls were made in other countries as well, especially in France, Denmark, Japan and even in the United States. Ruth Gibbs made china dolls in America in the 1940s and 1950s. But the billions of German china dolls were made chiefly in the second half of the 19th century.

Glazed porcelain began to be used for dolls around 1840. There have been claims for china dolls before 1840, but so far none of these claims have been validated. Collectors often try to date their china dolls from the period of the molded hair style. The type of hairdo usually indicates when the mold was first made and, if the style was successful, the mold could have been used for decades. For example the wavy-hair low-brow type of china dolls were made from about

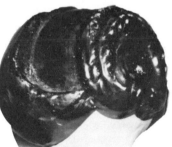

Illustration 2a

Illustrations 2a & 2b. Cream-colored china head with molded eyelids and a braided knot in back. The knot is high on the head denoting an early style.

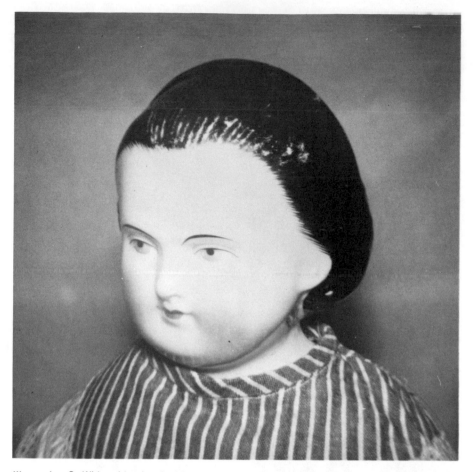

Illustration 3. White china head with brush marks, a comb across the top and snood in back.

These dolls have age, beauty, rarity and durability in their favor. Although a good china may cost as much as $1,000 or more, they are still relatively inexpensive when compared with some of the newer and less rare bisque bébés and character dolls.

Braids, knots, snoods, shoulder length curls and hair ornaments such as beads, flowers, combs, etc. are found on the rarer hairdos. Generally the more of these unusual features, the rarer the hairdo. The line over the eye was a common decoration and does not necessarily indicate a fine grade of china doll nor an early one. Some of the features indicating a fine, early china head are: a line drawn wholly or partially around the iris of the eye; a molded eyeball and eyelid, as well as a white eyeball on pink or cream-colored heads; or an ellipse in the nostril rather than a simple dot also shows a quality doll. When the lips are painted so that they appear slightly parted with a thin white area between the lips, it usually indicates a quality product. Brush marks show extra work in painting the head and the detail in the molding indicates whether the pouring mold was new or not. It does not necessarily indicate the newness of the master mold which would be a clue to the date of the doll. Pierced ears are a

1880 at least up until World War II. Thus the hair style indicates when the mold first came into use but not the date of a particular doll. The most precise method of dating china dolls, as always, is from their original clothes. Unfortunately due to their age and the fact that early collectors who specialized in china dolls had little regard for the original clothes, a few china dolls have retained their original clothes.

Collections of dolls that were made in the 1930s and 1940s usually have a large proportion of china dolls. Bisque child dolls in that period were too recent to be considered prime collectible dolls and most collectors concentrated on the earlier china dolls. Many of these early collections are now coming on the market but the rare-hairdo chinas are quickly purchased by knowledgeable collectors. Most newer collectors are not familiar with china dolls, other than the common types and because they lack knowledge, they do not appreciate the rarer china dolls. An elaborate hairdo china is probably far rarer than the ATs, A. Marques, etc. Very fine dealers, such as Grace Dyar, often have a selection of rare-hairdo china dolls.

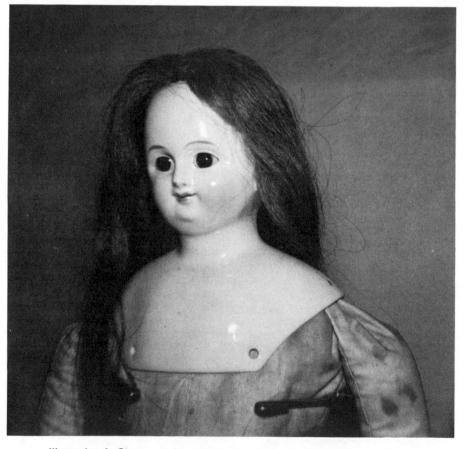

Illustration 4. Glass-eyed china head with wig; the china is cream-colored.

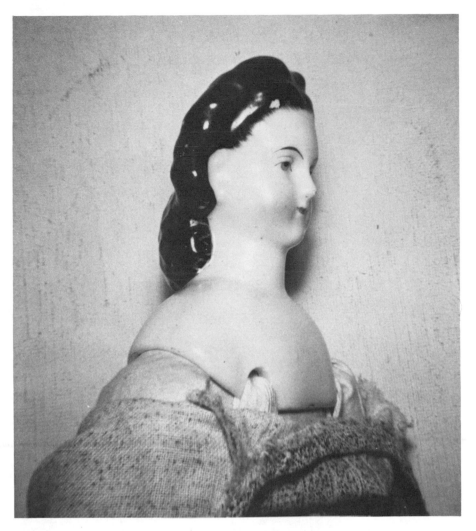

Illustration 5. White china head with gilded snood and hair ornament, brush marks and molded earrings.

special feature found on a few china dolls made chiefly in the 1870s and 1880s. The pink china heads are rare and usually earlier than the white ones.

Collectors often dress their china dolls as ladies unless they have the very short hairdos in which case they are dressed as males. Thus they fail to recognize the fact that dolls with extremely short hair can be babies as well as boys and men. China heads with long necks and faces represent ladies, but ones with short necks and round faces generally represent children. The majority of the china heads have short necks and round faces. The earlier ones with curls can represent either little boys or little girls but it should be remembered that boys wore dresses until they were fairly large in the 19th century.

Although the early collectors redressed their china dolls, frequently they kept the old clothes and currently at auctions these old garments are appearing in sizable numbers. Prices

Illustration 6. Black band across the top of the cafe-au-lait colored hair on a china head with curls on the shoulders.

for separate clothes have risen markedly recently, but if a collector can find a suitable contemporary costume, the doll is enhanced tremendously. If the garment is of the correct period and size, it will usually fit the doll very well. The material of the doll is also a necessary consideration. A wax doll's outfit will be too wide for a china doll. But the shapes of the bodies of most china dolls were made so that they could fit the prevailing fashion.

Early china heads almost never have a recognizable maker's mark. A few exceptions include those made by K.P.M., Royal Copenhagen and Jacob Petit. The collector should be wary of dolls with the Meissen crossed swords, the Nymphenburg cross-hatched mark and the Berlin "W" as these marks were all imitated by a doll factory in Wallendorf, Thuringia. The Rudolstadt factory also in Thuringia used the crown over a "N" that is almost identical to one of the Capo di Monte marks.

Some collectors are fearful of being sold reproduction china dolls. Actually it is far easier to reproduce a bisque head than it is a glazed china head and there are many more reproduction bisque dolls on the market today than china ones. The very high price of the bisque dolls add incentive to this practice. Most of the early china heads were pressed rather than poured. The slip was rolled out like dough and pressed into the mold leaving some rough edges inside the head and an unevenness that can usually be detected along the edge of the shoulders. Poured slip which is presently used is smooth and even throughout. The poured slip was used to some ex-

Illustrations 7a & 7b. Pink china head with the K in a bell mark of Kling on the back of the shoulder plate.

163

Illustration 7b.

Kenechi
by THELMA BATEMAN

11in (27.9cm)
Japanese-Oriental toddler.

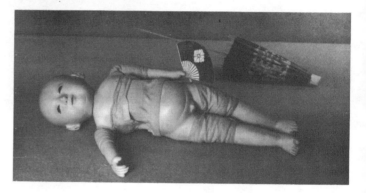

tent in the 19th century, especially in the last quarter. A pressed china head is nearly always early but a poured one may or may not be late. The slip today seldom has any kiln dirt or impurities whereas black specks are often found in the 19th century china heads. Most early china heads have wear marks on the hair in appropriate places, while the reproduction heads are pristine.

If you weary of looking at doll-faced bisque dolls, get an early china doll. Its beauty will grow on you. The china doll can be several generations older than the popular bisque dolls. The variation in mold types is probably greater than that afforded with bisque dolls, because of the many different molded hairdos. This is a feature that nearly all china dolls have while most bisque dolls have simply a wig. Interest in fancy-hairdo china dolls is growing but few appear on the market. Because of their relative rarity and lack of current popularity the prices for elaborate-hairdo china dolls are still moderate. Therefore last but not least, at present a rare china doll costs far less than a less rare bisque doll.

Editor's Note: The china dolls pictured here are in approximate chronological order, and from the Coleman Collection.

We *know* you are in your own private patio - that is not the point. If you do not get under that parasol soon, you will be sunburned in all the wrong places!

"Kenechi," the little boy who has everything, and is Japanese-made is also a "breather" with holes in his nostrils. His almond-shaped glass eyes are black and pupilless and there is a curved groove for a chin line. The head, with lovely flesh color and delicately colored cheeks, fits loosely down over the neck and turns slightly to left or right, but not clear around. The deep chest and back are in one piece and extend under the arms. The same type of Japanese composition found in the head also makes the lower part of the torso, the lower arms and hands as well as the lower limbs and feet. The hands and feet are beautifully modeled; notice the deep groove on soles of feet and the separate big toe. Upper extremities are made of stuffed heavy unbleached cotton.

"Kenechi" has his gray long sleeved kimona on and a happy smile (closed mouth) on his little face so perhaps there is no sunburn after all. His threadbare kimona is padded with cotton around the neck and down the front and trimmed with orange and white Japanese print lined with thin orange silk. He also wears a thick padded belt of matching orange-figured silk which makes into an obi in back.

Further proof of no sunburn - he is not squawking but he could as his squeaker still works.

"Kenechi" now belongs to Kathryn Sigrud of Granada Hills, California.

"The Many Faces Of Belton"

A PHOTOGRAPHIC ESSAY

by
Cherry Bou

Research is still underway to see if something more definitive can be discovered about the so-called Belton-type dolls. Thus far nothing at all has been uncovered that associates this type of doll in any way with M. Belton, a French doll maker who was associated with Jumeau in the mid-1800s. I have yet to discover why this particular doll maker was associated with this particular doll and who first made this apparently unwarranted association between the two. There is no proof that these dolls are solely of French origin and all we can say with any assurance at this time about such dolls is that "Belton-type" refers (by custom) to a method of stringing certain bisque heads. The glossary committee of U.F.D.C. has agreed to continue using the term as a descriptive one and defines Belton-type heads as "bisque heads made with one, two or three small holes in the pate, but otherwise uncut."

The difficulty in researching these dolls is complicated by the fact that only a very few have been found on marked bodies. The heads themselves are seldom marked with anything more revealing than a mold or size number. A great many of them have no marks on either head or body. The quality of the bisque heads and of the body materials vary greatly from very fine to extremely crude. To further add to the reseacher's frustration, very few of these dolls are found with original attire, which might help to identify their age or origin.

Some similarities among these dolls, besides the holes in the pates, are that they almost always have closed mouth, ears which are pierced into the head rather than through the ear lobe and that many of them are found on rather crude composition bodies with elongated, stick-like legs, pronounced stomachs and buttocks. There are, of course, exceptions as you shall see.

Appealing 11in. (27.9cm) doll of fine quality with head marked 120//2. Mulatto coloring, black lamb's wool wig. Dressed in original red and white striped cotton chemise. *Dorothy Wernsdorfer Collection.*

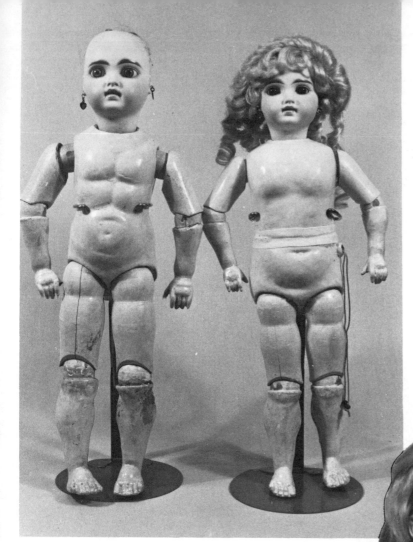

Right:
Doll marked 137//3, 12-1/2in. (31.8cm) tall. The head has only one hole and the body has one-piece arms and legs. *June Jeffcott Collection.*

Above:
Two examples of same mold number, #117. The doll on the left is 16in. (40.6cm) and head is marked 117//8. The doll on the right is 15in. (38.1 cm) and is marked 117//6. *Strong Museum Collection.*

13-1/2in. (34.3cm) Doll with wood and composition body; head with three holes is marked 137//6. *Cherry Bou Collection.*

20in. (50.8cm) Doll with typical composition body. Head is marked 100//9//X. *Coleman Collection.*

Right:
11-1/2in. (29.2cm) Indian doll w[ith] mold mark #244; three holes in pa[te?] one-piece arms and legs with heel[ed] shoes. *Strong Museum Collection.*

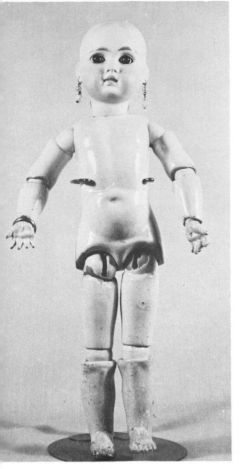

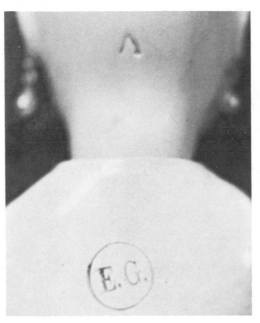

Above and right:
14in. (35.6cm) Doll with unintelligible head mark; featured in Brenda South's *Heirloom Dolls.* Marked E.G. body. *Esther Menthe Collection.*

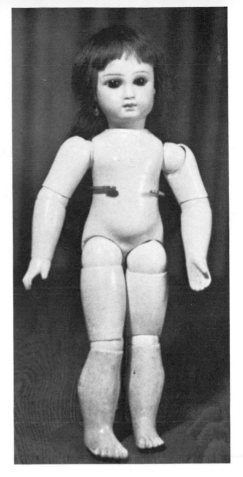

5-1/2in. (39.4cm) Doll with head marked 183//6; saucer dome has three holes. *Ollie Leavister Collection.*

An example of a doll marked only with size numbers, this 12 in. (30.5cm) doll is rare in that it is one of the very few which has been found in its all-original outfit. She is marked with only #4 on her head which has two holes in its rounded dome. The head fits over a pegged neck. *Leona Peterson Collection.*

The dolls in the photographs above and below are examples of the rare Belton-types of fine bisque heads which are found on wooden-jointed bodies also of very high quality, often with carved hands. Some of these bodies have been marked E.G.

Below:
20in. (50.8cm) Doll, head marked with #10; fine-quality wood body marked E.G. *Strong Museum Collection.*

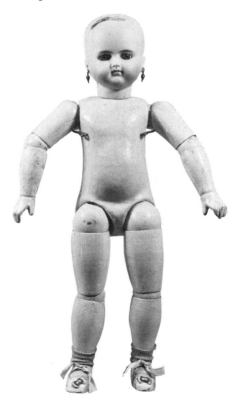

Shown here are examples of dolls marked only with size numbers

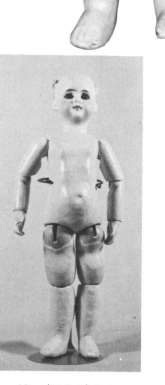

Left:
12in. (30.5cm) Doll; wooden body is incised #3 at top of back and on bottom of feet. Head is marked only with #1. *Pat Stall Collection.*

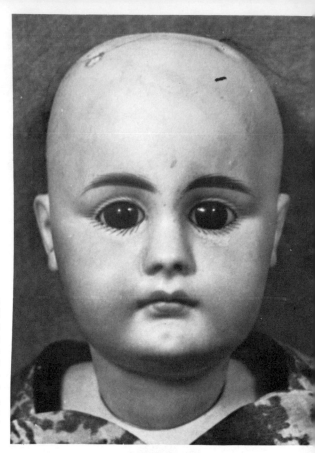

Right:
This is an example of one of the few Belton-type dolls that has been found with a known maker's mark. This 18in. (45.7cm) doll has the Simon and Halbig mark S9H//949 on the back of the head. The saucer dome has three holes; there is a slight indentation around the crown of the head which is probably a cutting line. This model, 949, is more often seen with an open crown. *Ollie Leavister Collection.*

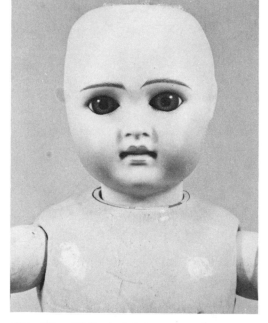

This 20in. (50.8cm) doll is marked #12 on the head. She has two holes in her saucer-like dome. *Strong Museum Collection.*

Right:
Several dolls have been reported with the letter B marked on the head. Here is a 10in. (25.4cm) one on a crude body with heeled painted boots. The head with three holes is marked 2//0 over B. It is wishful thinking to wonder if the B really stands for Belton! *Coleman Collection.*

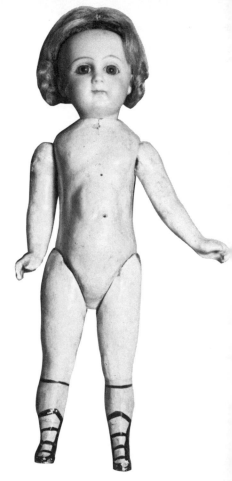

12in. (30.5cm) Doll; rounded dome with two holes over the ears. Head is marked AM//1, showing that Armand Marseille also used this method of stringing doll heads to bodies. *Ollie Leavister Collection.*

Fanciful "French" Fashions in Miniature

BY SYBILL McFADDEN

Illustrations 1 & 2. This adolescent Fashion in her three-quarter length dress may have been redressed, as the outfit somehow lacks the elan of Paris. She was purchased in this red paisley wool fitted dress trimmed with black velvet, and the straw bonnet was tied under her chin. She wears brown high-button shoes and her petticoat is showing ever so slightly beneath her skirt.

The stylish world of Lanvin, Cardin, Saint Laurent and Dior were not to be heard from for more than a hundred years in the distant future when these tiny fashion models, or "Poupées Modèles," as they were sometimes called, began crossing oceans and foreign boundaries in the 1860s and 1870s to carry the latest word of the lavish and costly modes of Paris to the eagerly awaiting feminine world.

Here we present seven miniature representatives of that French world of fashion whose sizes range from only 10½in. (26.7cm) to 12in. (30.5cm). They are, in most respects, exactly like their larger sisters, except perhaps for

the fact that they turn up less frequently and are a bit harder to find.

The seven illustrated here are all on shapely stitched kid bodies, some with kid leather cording over the stitching. The kid arms are gusseted at the elbows, ending in hands with tiny individually-wired fingers. The "teen" or adolescent Fashion is an exception. Her hands are mitt-like with stitched fingers.

Contrary to most larger French Fashions, they do not have gussets at the knees; their hard, straight, kid legs descend from a protruding derriere. There is a reason for this. The large overstuffed kid "rear" provided a kind of natural built-in bustle to hold the

train of the gown in an unbroken, nicely descending line to the floor. (See illustration #11) This construction is found especially on the miniature Fashions, so as to require less underclothing which gave a bunched look to the small figure. It is not to say that the large Fashions are not sometimes made in the same manner, but it is less common with them. They are more often seen gusseted at the knee.

Practically nothing can be found about the miniature French Fashion as such. All is thus conjecture. Were they merely smaller versions of their more opulent sisters, or did they have some specific purpose?

History tells us that in the 1860s Germany sent their lovely Parian heads to America -- (in especially large numbers at Christmastime) -- to candy and jewelry stores. There ladies bought the heads, sometimes with accompanying arms and legs, and fashioned bodies for them. They then dressed them in gowns of fine silks, satins and laces, and these lady dolls graced their boudoir tables, or a corner of the Victorian parlor. So we know that as early as Civil War days, ladies in America were collecting dolls. We know, too, that the larger size French Fashions were intended for ladies. Could the miniatures then, have been designed to instruct their small daughters in the art of sewing a fine seam?

But, you will say, the miniatures arrived, just as did the larger dolls, already dressed in the latest Paris gowns designed by the great couturiers of the day. True, but does that necessarily preclude each doll's elegant French creation from serving as a model and inspiration for the small would-be seamstress? More than one outfit was needed for a lady of fashion -- even a miniature one!

But even supposing this conjecture to be true, one fact remains an enigma which almost rules it out. The author has found every body on all the miniatures she has seen to be in pristine condition, appearing never to have been played with by children. The hand-stuffed kid bodies are white, shiny and new-looking after more than a century-and-a-quarter, which might indicate that if the dolls came dressed, they remained so. The hands, while on the whole in good condition, show somewhat more wear.

Illustration 3. Appearing properly shocked, these fashionable French ladies, perhaps promenading on the Champs Elysees, are thoroughly enjoying the latest Parisian scandal! [All three dolls are 12in. (30.5cm)]

Illustration 4. The center lady, listening attentively, so as not to miss a word of it all, is marked "F.G." on her shoulder. She wears a black velvet jacket, brown pin-striped taffeta skirt, black fur chapeau trimmed with a black feather, and in this close-up photo, carries a French hat box.

Illustration 5. The first lady gossiper has unusually large blue paperweight glass eyes, explained perhaps by the fact that she is a marked Jumeau. She wears a grey faille gown embroidered with tiny silk dots, and trimmed in lavender. A pale lavender plume of aigrette feathers crowns her chapeau.

Illustration 6. The third lady, seeming almost to be shaking her head in disbelief, is marked "F.G." in a scroll on her shoulder. She wears white satin decorated with black cording, tiny black buttons and an apron overskirt trimmed with dozens of tiny black tassels. A black net veil secures her matching hat. In this close-up photo her exceptionally large and lovely blown glass eyes can be seen better, and she has uncovered her lavish original brown mohair wig. It is styled with two tiny French braids across the top of the head, "squiggle" curls at the temples and shoulder ringlets.

Many experts do believe that the Poupée Modèle was not only intended as a servant of fashion but a play doll as well, and common sense would have us believe that when the primary purpose was fulfilled, or the styles changed, the girl children of the family inherited these French Fashions, transposing them into play dolls. If so, however, it has to follow that the dolls were treated with great respect, perhaps never even undressed!

Remarkable on these tiny 12in. (30.5cm) and under dolls are the fine quality bisque heads on kid-lined shoulder plates. Miniature blown glass eyes bulge slightly in the same manner as the large size Fashions. And the close-up illustrations of each attest that none of their distinctive and individual expressions are lost, even though the heads are often as small as 1½in. (3.8cm) to 2in. (5.1cm) high!

The three dolls at the tea table wear their original gowns. The trio of "gossipers" have been redressed, we are sure, though two were purchased dressed as shown and one was without clothes.

Illustration 7. Friends, no doubt, of long standing these Parisiennes are about to refresh themselves from a hand-painted Limoge tea set.

Illustration 8. The guest on the left is the smallest French Fashion we have come across being just 10½in. (26.7cm) tall. She is marked "F.G." and boasts her original Paris gown with a sweeping train. True, it is disintegrating somewhat from having been worn constantly for 120 years - poor dear! It is red silk with bands and cording of light tan. Her lovely blond original mohair wig is worn in an up-do with a chignon at back. Her tiny tan chapeau was designed so as not to hide her enchanting small face with black-rimmed blown glass eyes of blue, perfectly feathered eyebrows, heart shaped pursed mouth, pierced ears and red drop earrings.

Illustration 9. The guest on the right has lavender-blue eyes, and her original mohair wig is in tiny ringlets. She is 11½in. (29.2cm) tall, and is a bit heavier of figure than the others...too many petit fours? Her original wool gown, perhaps dictated by the color of her eyes, is lavender with a low-cut lace-edged bodice and a beige apron overskirt topping the floor length lavender skirt. She is unmarked, but when placed side by side with a kicking, crying Steiner Bébé in the author's collection, the similarity is astounding. The paleness and quality of the bisque, the painting, the blown glass eyes, the original ringletted mohair wigs, and feathering of the brows on both dolls is identical. Can she be an unmarked Steiner Fashion?

Illustrations 10 & 11. In the center, the hostess in white is 12in. (30.5cm) tall and wears a lovely lawn dress befrilled with lace and white satin ribbons, and culminating in a graceful train. In this close-up photo you will see that she has a most unusual face with large grey-blue blown glass eyes and pouting mouth. Her brown wig is upswept with one tiny French braid encircling the head and chignon on top. She is unmarked.

And so with many questions unanswered, we conclude our presentation of seven miniature French Fashions. We hope you have enjoyed them -- or as they, themselves might say, "Amusez-vous bien!"

Dolls of the Grand Duchess of Russia

BY DOROTHY S. COLEMAN

The whereabouts in 1928 of the dolls and toys belonging to the murdered children of the Russian Czar Nicholas II is reported in *Playthings.* Earlier reports indicated that the Czar's daughters had fabulous dolls. One doll and its trousseau required a special emissary to conduct it from Paris to Russia.

The playroom of the Czarevitch in the summer palace at Tsarskoe Selo near Leningrad is described as "one of the most elaborate playrooms of all time." After the Revolution the palace was turned into a museum and the playroom was left just as it had been when the Czarevitch played there.

The dolls that belonged to the little Russian Grand Duchesses were assembled in the Museum at Tharkoies Selo. Fifty more dolls were added to this museum collection in 1928 which suggests that many more had been there previously. Each doll was carefully labeled with the name of the Grand Duchess to which it originally belonged. One of the proposed tests of the true identity of the claimant purporting to be the Grand Duchess Anastasia was whether she could pick out her own dolls among the group. Unfortunately it is not known if the test was ever made and if it was made, how successful it turned out to be. It seems likely that a Grand Duchess or even a pretended Grand Duchess might hesitate to return to Russia while it was in the hands of the murderers of her family.

Hopefully these dolls are still in this museum as inquiries at the Hermitage, the famous Russian Museum, have failed to uncover any sizable collection of dolls there.

There are a considerable number of dolls in the Museum of Toys in Zagorsk which is the toy capital of the U.S.S.R. Zagorsk, located near Moscow, was primarily a center of folk art dolls and toy making. There are a few bisque-head dolls in the museum but most of the dolls are made of wood, clay or papier-mâché and appear to be of local origin. None of the dolls are identified as having belonged to the little Grand Duchesses, but the all pervading Communist propaganda found in the writings about the Zagorsk Museum would probably ignore any references to the Grand Duchesses.

*Source: *Russian Toys*, Progress Publishers, Moscow, Russia.

The Dolls Of Jules Steiner
A Comparative Study

BY JAN FOULKE
PHOTOGRAPHS BY HOW FOULKE

M_y love affair with the French Steiner dolls began in 1974, for that was the year I met "Mamselle." Standing as she was on the counter of my favorite doll shop, all 28" (71.1cm) of her in red velvet, she was certainly stunning, but her appeal, to me, went further: it was the special something which develops between a collector and a doll that kept drawing me back to her over the other hundred dolls on display. As I circled the shop, always coming back to sigh over her, I told myself that this feeling was ridiculous. I didn't collect bisque dolls. Not only that, I couldn't buy one with such an enormous price tag! Subsequently, I left the shop with a box of assorted smaller dolls, "Mamselle" still standing on the counter.

Sometimes the old adage "out of sight, out of mind" absolutely refuses to work—and visions of that doll spun round my head. Finally after several days I could stand the torment no longer: I must own that doll. My husband was tired of hearing about her: "Go ahead and buy her," he said. I called the shop owner in a state of euphoria, only to come crashing down to reality when she told me the doll had already been sold! I was devastated, but at least the torment was over.

However, that is not the end of my story about "Mamselle" because four months later on Christmas morning, there was "Mamselle" standing next to my tree. I hugged and hugged her, laughing and crying both at the same time that such a marvelous treasure was really mine. My husband was the one who had bought the doll, and I never suspected.

Société Steiner was founded by Jules Nicholas Steiner in 1855 in Paris, France. After 1891, he was no longer in charge and the direction of the company passed to a succession of other heads until 1908. Apparently Société Steiner did not join the S.F.B.J. conglomerate of doll makers formed in 1888 which included Jumeau, Bru and others.

Judging from the number of patents registered to them, the Steiner firm apparently worked hard to improve their dolls and to try new innovations. They had patents for eye movement, walking, talking and other

Illustration 1

mechanisms for dolls as well as for improved processes for making heads and limbs. Several times the firm won medals for their dolls at the Paris Exhibition, the most exciting in 1889 when they were awarded the gold medal (Medaille D'or).

Steiner dolls usually have beautiful smooth bisque, almost creamy, with delicately tinted cheeks. Their eyes are alert, but not oversized like those of the Jumeaus; their lips are full, but tinting is pale so they do not show up as well in photographs as those of other French dolls. Dolls from the early 1880s often have round faces; those of the 1890s are more rectangular. Société Steiner created a wide range of dolls—too many styles and types for one small article, so we are choosing a sampling to include here and will discuss their characteristics.

Illustrations 1—3
Jan Foulke Collection
"Bourgoin" Steiner.
Marks on head (incised);

S^{TE} A O

Red writing:

J. Steiner B^te S.G.D.g J. Bourgain S^N_F

Marks on body: Partial black stamped mark with a decipherable J.

This type of Steiner is usually dated about 1880. Her wide forehead and full cheeks give her face a round appearance. Her chin is not well defined, but does have a faint dimple. Her eyebrows are a delicate blonde with minute brush strokes. Her blown glass eyes each have a vivid blue iris with a black rim and many tiny dark spokes in them. Often this type of doll has wire eyes (explained later in de-

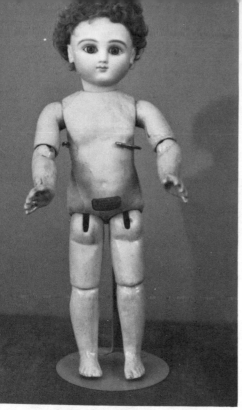

Illustration 2

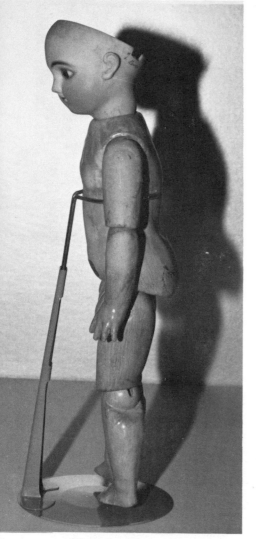

Illustration 3

tail), but although her head is cut for the lever, she never had moving eyes and was apparently a less expensive model. Painted lashes are a series of lightly-made black strokes and eye sockets are outlined in black. Her pierced ears are rather plain and simply modeled. Her mouth is typically Steiner with light tinting; two pronounced peaks on the upper lip and a turned up corner. The original pate is of dark brown cardboard. Her curly kidskin wig is a replacement of the proper style as her original hair had been eaten off its skin wig cap.

Her original body is in excellent condition. At the knee and elbow joints, the typical purple undercoating which Steiner used can be seen. Fingertips and toes still retain traces of the red-lined nails. As is typical of French doll bodies in general, there is little anatomical detail: upper limbs are straight, as are the knee joints; toes are only faintly modeled. There are no separate ball joints; wrists are straight and fingers are stubby; stomach is flat; derrière protrudes only slightly, gently rounded. She is 14" (35.6cm) tall.

Illustrations 4 and 5
Jan Foulke Collection
Baby Steiner.
Marks on head (incised):

S^{TE} C 4/0

Red stamp located at sides of crown opening at left:
J. STEINER B.S.G.D.G.
At right: illegible, but could be a repetition of the left side as on the doll in *Illustration 7.*
Marks on body: None.

This Steiner baby is a scant 7" (17.8cm) long with size 4/0 head. Her face is of the type associated with the "Bourgoin" mark. She has the same pate, slight nose, upper lip, ear and eye shape as the doll shown in *Illustrations 1 3.* Her brows are light and feathered also, but her gray lashes are longer and heavier in proportion to her size, and the eye sockets are not black-lined. Her eyelids have a rose tint. She has the 1880s patented wire-eye mechanism. The lever protruding behind her ear opens and closes her dark blue gray eyes. Notice how the head is cut to accommodate the lever. She probably had a lamb's wool curly wig which has been lost.

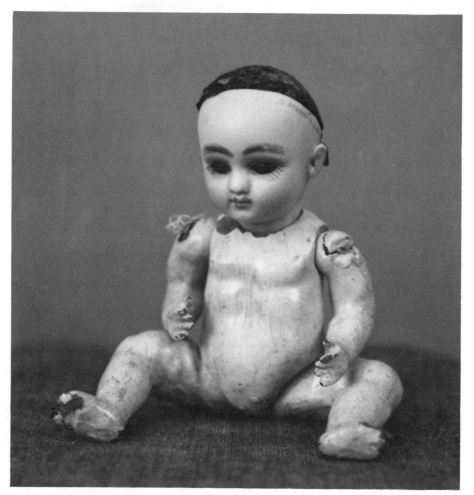

Illustration 4

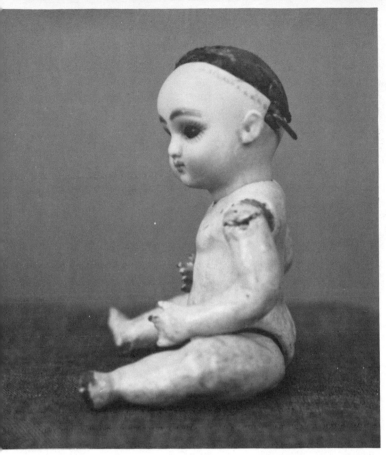

Illustration 7

Illustraton 5

Illustration 7
Mike White Collection
Marks on head (incised):

S^{TE} C 4

Red stamp at each side of crown opening:

J. STEINER B.S.G.D.G.

Eyes (incised on back of eyeball):
STEINER
4
S.G.D.G.
Marks on body: None

Her papier-mâché body, which shows some detail in molding of arms and legs, appears to be a forerunner of the bent-limb babies so popular after 1909, and certainly indicates her to be a rare Steiner type. Not shown in the illustrations is what appears to be her original clothes—a child's guimpe and dress of the late 1880s.

Illustration 6
Crandall Collection
Hardly the prettiest of Steiners in her stripped down condition, yet very interesting is this mechanical doll. In her torso is a mechanism which moves her legs, arms and head while she cries "Mama." This is operated by the key which protrudes from her side. Her head of a pale, almost parian finish with rosy cheeks is round with a wide short neck, completely closed dome and open mouth with two rows of tiny teeth. Her small eyes are pale blue, a paperweight type with blue lining at the eye sockets. Her eyebrows are long and tiny, arching slightly. Her pierced ears have little detail.

Her torso is cloth-covered cardboard; arms and lower legs are composition. There is no mark on the heads of these dolls, but the mechanism carries the Steiner mark. This doll is 16" (40.7cm) tall, but this type was also available in other sizes. She is hard to date precisely and could possibly be as early as the 1870s as she has charac-

istics associated with the early Steiners. Also some of these types of bodies have been found with wax-over-papier-mâché heads.

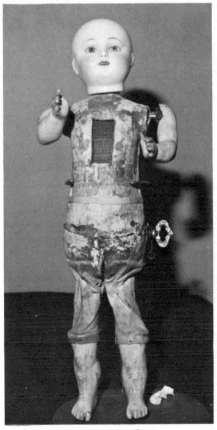

Illustration 6

This 22-1/2" (57.1cm) Steiner has a longer, lower face than that of the "Bourgoin" or the baby, as well as a higher forehead. She has the interesting wire mechanism to operate her blue eyes which do not have the depth of permanent paperweight eyes because they are set into what appears to be a bisque eyeball which is not as fragile as the glass eyeball of the German weighted eyes. Also the eyes must be flatter to allow room for opening and closing which is not possible with bulging eyes. She has her original purple cardboard pate, typical of many Steiner dolls. Also there is a little more detail in her ears, which are also pierced. Her eyebrows are soft. Her mouth is typical with two peaks on upper lip and turned up corners.

Her body is unmarked but has Steiner characteristics including the short, fat fingers. She is later than the "Bourgoin" since she has jointed wrists, probably dating from the late 1880s. Her long, blonde, human hair wig appears to be original.

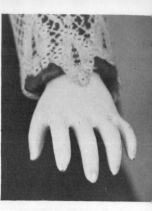

Illustration 9

Illustration 10

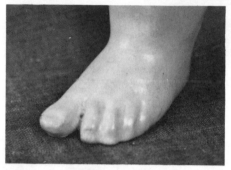

Illustration 11

Illustration 8

Illustrations 8–13
Jan Foulke Collection
Marks on head (incised):

A-19
PARIS

(Red stamp):

"LE PARISIEN"

Marks on body (purple stamp on hip):

BÉBÉ "LE PARISIEN"
MEDAILLE D'OR
PARIS

Finally, here is "Mamselle," easier than the others to date because her trademark, "Le Parisien" was registered in 1892. She is typical of the Steiners with the rectangular face, with just a hint of a chin. Her eyes are dark blue paperweight with good depth as she does not have the wire type. Her eyebrows are darker brown and more pronounced than those on earlier Steiners; eye sockets are wider, not as almond-shaped as earlier ones. Her neck is longer. Her mouth has the same soft color and shape. Her nose is longer with a more defined shape. One of the most interesting changes is in the intricate modeling of her ears which contain a large, deep canal as well as more intricate folds. Another unusual aspect is her original cork pate as most Steiners have cardboard ones.

Her body is similar to that of the

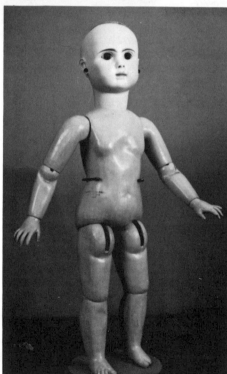

Illustration 12

"Bourgoin" and a comparison shows three major differences: fingers are longer and thinner; wrists are jointed; and the big toe is separated.

She is wearing her original clothes, a deep red velvet dress in Kate Greenaway style. Her shoes are marked Steiner. Her hair and hat are replacements.

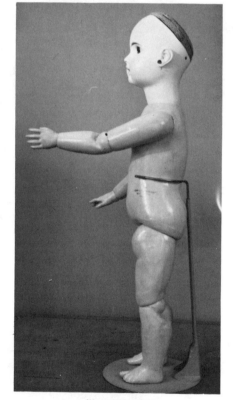

Illustration 13

EXPLANATION OF SOME TERMS USED
IN STEINER MARKS

S^{TE} —probably society or company

$B^{TÉ}$ —patent registered

$S.g.D.g.$ —without guarantee of the government

J. Bourgoin—unknown but perhaps an associate as here it is preceded by a J. Elsewhere it isn't.

J. Steiner—head of Société Steiner, 1855-1891.

Thelma-Marie

by THELMA BATEMAN

Illustration 1. Thelma-Marie in her ivory challis pink flowered dress.

Both photographs and the following text are courtesy of Thelma Bateman. They are reprinted from *Delightful Dolls: Antique and Otherwise* ©1966. $12.50

This Bébé Jumeau has two large doll trunks crammed with lovely old French clothes, most of them handmade, plus dozens of accessories. Check the complete list at the end of this vignette.

Thelma-Marie has a beautiful bisque head, secured to her fully-jointed papier mâché body by a hook fastened into a block of wood in her chest. Her enormous full blown glass eyes are dark brown and stationary. Her original human hair wig (cork cap) is golden-blonde, still beautiful and luxuriant. The modeling of her features is lovely; her ears are pierced and applied; she has dots in her nostrils and inner eye corners, and her mouth is closed. There is a deep dimple in her chin and one under her nose. Stamped in red on the back of the neck is "Déposé Tête Jumeau Bté S.G.D.G.-11-." Although jointed at the wrists, her hands and fingers are quite large and thick. Stamped in blue ink on her back is "JUMEAU-MÉDAILLE d'OR-PARIS."

Because of the style of her clothes and accessories, a voice box, plus the wrist joints, she should date around 1885.

The voice box is in her left side. Pull one of the two strings, each with a black glass bead, and Thelma says "Mama." Pull the other string and she says "Papa." There really is a difference in the sound of these words. "Papa" is shorter and snappier. Chummy, n'est-ce-pas?

Contents of Thelma-Marie's Trunks
2 pr. high-button leather shoes
3 pr. slippers - - one marked "Jumeau"
12 pr. sox - - short silk, lace, cotton, long wool
7 purses - - all kinds
2 pr. leather gloves (they fit, too)
3 fans
5 hankies
2 silk ribbon garters
6 tiny hat pins
1 washcloth - - fringed
2 sheets
2 pillow slips
2 toys

11 assorted bonnets and hats - - chic!
1 maroon sateen ruffled parasol
1 pegnoir - - cotton border-print - - adorable!
3 nighties - - white cotton
1 flannel underskirt
2 pantywaists
1 winter undershirt
6 panties - - plain and fancy
4 cotton underskirts - - much lace and embroidery
1 cotton print play dress
2 white cotton dresses - - lace and embroidery
2 silk sachet bags
1 ivory challis dress, pink flowered (See Illustration 1.)
1 soft robin's egg blue fine wool dress - - tailored
1 ivory silk dress: full gathered yoke clear around, gathered wrists, very full skirt and yards of narrow old ivory ribbon in bows with long loops
2 short ivory flannel jackets
1 green wool sweater
1 ivory, tan and blue plaid short jacket with silk bound peplums
1 light blue and ivory striped flannel coat: heavy ecru lace collar and cuffs, ribbon belt tied in front, 2 ribbon pompons on the back
1 bright robin's egg blue wool cape: velvet yoke
1 exquisite velvet bonnet to match, trimmed with daintiest silk lace, wide silk dotted ribbon and shower of tiny pink French buds and roses - - luscious!
1 ermine tippet and muff
1 larger muff and matching lap robe of lamb's wool
1 beautiful hand-crocheted wool afghan with long knotted fringe: made in the muted tones matching the rest of her wardrobe, alternating blue and beige 4in (10.2cm) strips, each strip cross-

stitched with sprays of bright flowers. Overall size 21in (53.3cm) by 36in (91.4cm). Comfy!

1 old china commode set: bowl, pitcher, soap dish and soap, toothbrush dish, chamber and waste bucket

1 all-bisque doll, barely 1¼in (3.2cm) high, jointed at shoulder and hips; painted hair and eyes; dressed in blue silk

1 blue silk and net lined toilet article basket (like one pictured in 1869 *Godey's Lady's Book*) fitted with 2 hairbrushes, 1 comb, clothes brush, mirror with handle (all of bone), powder box with wee wool puff, and tiniest button hook

1 silver curling iron in silver case

Jewelry including coral necklace and earrings, tiny rosary, and wee round locket with 2 tiny pictures inside

Darling old French sewing box with 2 thimbles, tiniest needles, eyeglasses that fit, wee scissors, penknife, and beeswax with a 1in (2.5cm) china doll sticking out

Various quaint boxes and baskets to hold all the goodies

2 old wooden doll trunks - - very large, with trays (one covered) and rounded tops. These were made in this country. French trunks not shipped here with doll. Too bad!

Illustration 2. Thelma-Marie surrounded by her bonnets and hats.

Dolls: Bicentennial Treasures

by DOROTHY S. COLEMAN

In this bicentennial year we are especially aware and appreciative of our heritage. We make pilgrimages to historic sites. We revere historic documents from Magna Carta down through the ages. Our television is filled with scenes and people depicting historical episodes that are part fact and part fiction. History, whether written or oral, has a way of being distorted according to the views and opinions of the historian. Time has changed buildings and landscapes. Theatrical plays and especially the costumes in them are designed to please modern audiences rather than to portray accurately the way our ancestors really looked and dressed.

Perhaps for most people this pseudo-portrayal of our ancestors is satisfactory. But why should we be satisfied with half truths when something better and more accurate is available, namely dolls in original clothes. Here we have facts, a true representation of what our ancestors wore and how their clothes were worn. Probably one of the most rewarding things from our new book, *The Collector's Book of Dolls' Clothes,* is the many letters and tributes we have received from costume historians. Our labor of seven years in studying dolls in original clothes is amply rewarded if it can open the doors of learning to those seriously interested in our past.

With most treasures, and our dolls in original clothes are certainly historical treasures, there comes responsibility. All too often collectors have enjoyed playing with their dolls by ripping off the old clothes and making new ones thus destroying forever the historical value of the doll. Too many dealers, both here and abroad have changed heads, limbs and torsos so that not only are the clothes not original to the doll but the parts are not native to one another. This unfortunate process has been considerably augmented by the fact that a much higher duty was charged on a whole doll than on a group of parts. There are many stories of visits to suppliers in Paris where rooms were littered with parts of dolls being readied for shipment to America. We cannot blame American dealers, especially if they are not thorough students of dolls, if they cannot always put the jigsaw puzzle of the dolls' parts together correctly. This is another reason why a doll that is obviously in original clothes is so important because it usually gives assurance that the doll as well as the clothes are of one origin.

In this bicentennial year [1976] doll museums have sprung up all over the country. This appreciation and publicizing of antique dolls is most commendable. The good museums show practically only dolls in original clothes and are both enjoyable and educational to noncollectors as well as collectors. A recent survey by the *American Collector* showed doll collecting ranking second only to household items which included glass, china and many other things and ranking far ahead of coins and stamps. The collecting of dolls is an ever increasing hobby both numerically and in understanding of its historical importance.

Doll collecting is pleasing to our appreciation of beauty but its greatest importance is its historical representation. Recently the well-publicized dolls, Lord and Lady Clapham, were declared to be national treasures in Britain. Our own collections may not have dolls as old or rare as Lord and Lady Clapham but our dolls in original clothes are historical treasures nevertheless and should be especially appreciated in this bicentennial year.

Leather Mystery Dolls

BY FRANCES WALKER

Do doll mysteries intrigue you? Do you ever buy a doll because you want to learn about it? To be fascinated by doll mysteries is rather like the mountain climber who said he climbed mountains because they were there. The mystery dolls are always "there." We know that the identities of makers of unmarked chinas, parians, etc. are always going to be mysteries because there is just no way of finding out more about them. All avenues to knowledge seem to be closed forever. There are some more recent dolls about which we have a better chance of finding information. It is hidden somewhere, so we probe and sometimes we are rewarded.

About 15 years ago I saw a small 5 in. (12.7cm) leather doll that I found very appealing. She was in a private collection but I was allowed to examine her. She was all leather; her head and body seemed to be molded and painted. Her arms and legs were attached at the shoulders and hips. The limbs were not jointed, but were bent as is common with baby dolls. (See *Illustration 1*.)

Her clothes appeared original; they were the style of the 1920s. Her sleeveless dress was of white cotton, made with a yoke to which the skirt was gathered. She had darling kid shoes and a bonnet to match her dress. Her back was stamped "Made in France." (See *Illustration 2*.)

After that initial introduction to the leather baby (as I thought of her), I met another, also in a pri-

Illustration 1. From the *Margaret Whitton Collection.*

Illustration 2. Same doll as shown in *Illustration 1.*

vate collection. This one was a boy with dark hair, while the one in *Illustration 1 & 2* was blond, but there was no denying the great similarity in expression, construction and materials. He was dressed in a hand-knit suit.

Several years later I was able to buy one of these dolls (a little blond girl), then later, a blond boy in a knit suit came into my possession. None of these dolls are marked, nor are they identical, but they all look alike the way handmade duplicates in any craft look alike. Yet they have an individuality of their own. The girls had dresses of similar style and the boys had knit suits. (See *Illustration 3.*)

Illustration 3. From the *Frances Walker Collection.*

In the last two years I have either seen or heard of approximately another 40 of these dolls. They all have the same characteristics, but are all slightly different. The biggest difference is that a few have straight legs rather than bent baby legs. These straight leg dolls are 6-1/2 in. (16.5cm) tall. (See *Illustration 4.*)

The torso of the leather doll is seamed on each side and down the center back. It has a small protuberance at the top over which the head fits. The arms are shapely and bent with two handsewn seams. The hands are cut in one with the arms; they have separate thumb with fingers

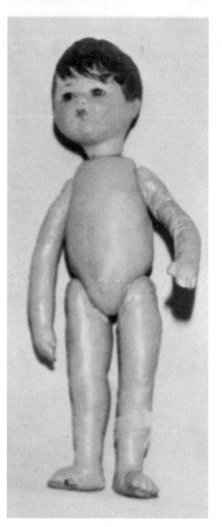

Illustration 4. From the *Frances Walker Collection.*

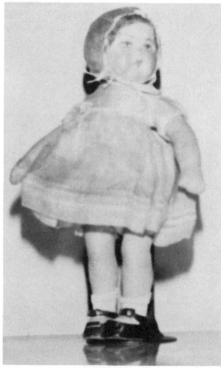

Illustration 5. From the *Joan Rock Collection.*

indicated by stitches.

The feet are cut separately with a seam down the back of the heel and along the sole of the foot. The toes are indicated with stitches. The foot is then fastened to the leg at the ankle. The majority of dolls that I have seen have bent legs made with two seams. Some have straight legs and appear to be an older child. The foot is made and attached the same whether the leg is bent or straight. Some straight-leg dolls are dressed girls; others as boys—just as the bent leg babies are. (See *Illustration 5.*)

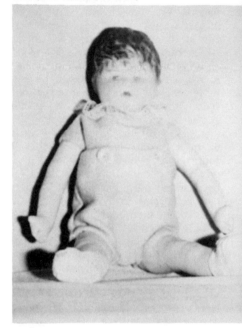

Illustration 6. From the *Sara Kocher Collection.*

The doll is put together with elastic strung through to the outside of the arms at the shoulders and through the legs at the hips. Some of the dolls have small patches of leather which cover the knots. I imagine they all were made this way originally.

The heads I've left to describe last, not because they are the least important, but rather the most important, because here is where the greatest variety exists, and they are the hardest to describe. In those I've handled, the size varies as well as the appearance.

The only joining of the leather is up the back of the head. The edges of the leather are then drawn together and overlapped on the top of the head. This is cleverly done for it appears to be part of the hair. (See *Illustration 6.*)

The faces are well modeled with fat cheeks, deep set eyes, cupid bow mouths and well defined ears. The noses are small with clearly marked nostrils. Some noses are more pug than others. (See *Illustration 7.*)

I have a theory that the heads started out as a flat piece of leather into which the features were tooled, as leather has been tooled for generations. After the features were worked into the leather, the wet leather was worked and stretched from the underside to form the chubby cheeks and little round chin. Then while the leather was still damp it was shaped over a head form and glued into place. The excess was pulled to the top of the head and tooled into hair.

One of the dolls I have seen (not pictured) has a slight crack in the back of the head where the leather has pulled apart. The interior is not stuffing, but a hard substance (perhaps plaster). The edges have come unglued, and it is obvious it was never sewn. There are no stitch marks in the leather. The leather is very thin, but even so I feel the features could not have been so deep, small and fine if pressed in a mold.

The complexions of the dolls vary from very light blond to a real suntan brunette. The eyes vary from very pale blue to a deeper blue and brown. They all have pupils and are painted with highlights. All the features are well painted— red dots in the nostrils, red lips, even the ears are touched with red. The eyelashes and eyebrows are done in appropriate colors according to the eye and hair color.

The hair is deeply modeled in a wispy manner, with locks coming forward on the forehead. It does not cover the ears, but comes down on the back of the neck.

Now comes the mystery. Where were these dolls made and by whom? I have seen one stamped on the body "Made in France," but only one. I've looked hard for another marked doll. Recently, a doll appeared with a tag sewed in her clothing, "Made in France," but the body was unmarked. I was told by one collector that the family she got her dolls from said they were bought in Italy.(See *Illustration 8.*) If they were sold abroad and brought to the States by a private party, the law requiring goods be marked with the country of origin would not apply. The stories that have come with some of these dolls indicate that they were the property of well-to-do families who traveled and could have purchased them in Europe. In several instances, several have come from one family.

In a 1918 report in *Les Arts Francois, Les Jouets* by Leo Claritie there is a picture of two doll heads of leather made by Mme. Lazarski. One of these doll heads has features similar to the leather dolls I have been studying. The one in the pictures has a wig. None I have seen have a wig. The picture may have been of a sample doll and it was decided to make them with painted hair. Who knows?

Les Arts Francois listed Mme. Lazarski, 83 Faubourg-Saint- Honore, as being in charge of a Polish work-shop making dolls. She had a second listing at 17 rue. Bussonade. There she headed a workshop of artists creating dolls.

The Colemans *The Collector's Encyclopedia of Dolls* lists Mme. Lazarski, World War I-1925, as a maker of luxury dolls in cloth, kid and wax and character felt dolls.

Upon examining these dolls I am convinced they could not have been mass produced in a factory. I felt they could easily have been produced as a home industry. We know that doll making frequently was done in the home, then assembled in a factory. Since I've seen the Mme. Lazarski picture and read about her workshop of doll artists, I wonder if my little friends came into being in a work-shop of Polish refugee artists in France. If that is their origin, it would explain their similarities and their differences. Maybe some day we will learn their exact origin, and in the meantime I will keep on studying and loving each one I see. I hope that one will hold the key to the secret.

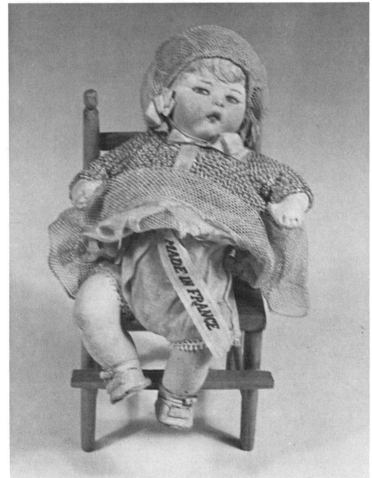

Illustration 8. From the *Frances Walker Collection.*

Illustration 1. 16-1/2in. (41.9 cm) French bébé marked: "H" with bisque socket head. She has fixed eyes, closed mouth and pierced ears. Her wig is mohair. She has a composition ball-jointed body. Manufacturer unknown.

Beautiful Faces

BY MAGDA BYFIELD

During the last quarter of the 19th and first quarter of the 20th centuries there were produced some of the loveliest doll faces of all time. Until the mid-19th century doll makers had produced mainly adult female dolls of static convention. Some time after the turning point in this long-standing tradition came striking representations of babies, girls, adolescents and ladies with distinctive features. By 1880 the doll maker was offering successive stages in the portrayal of youth which not only extended the scope of doll making but entirely reshaped it. This change of vision largely came about when "biscuit" porcelain gained the day in the late 1860s and a technical perfection was achieved in the representation of complexions very like flawless skin. The possibilities for interpretation in this fabulous substance we now call *bisque* was continuously explored for the following half century varying from period to period and from country to country. The glory of late-19th century doll making belongs to France and that of the early-20th century to Germany as the dolls illustrated here demonstrate.

These dolls had an enthralling life-likeness overlaid with a gem-like purity. Their faces were, of course, idealizations and what we see is not the whole truth about a face, but it is the face the doll maker wished to present to his patrons and to posterity.

He was largely concerned with producing images of perfection, and had of necessity to disregard a total degree of honesty. Particularly in the 19th century, beautiful dolls were produced *not* looking like the girls for whose nurseries they were destined but as adults would have liked them to look, and this in itself is only an apparent contradiction because it is highly informative about the aesthetic sensibility of the day.

When we look on some of these outstandingly lovely doll faces we have no assurance that we are looking at faithful portraits but we do know that we are seeing *la belle idéal* of the time. Dolls constitute a separate branch of portraiture unlike any other but this is not to say that the faces are less well observed. Doll makers strove to reconcile a fashionable interpretation with natural appearances. Nature was rearranged, simplified and idealized; Fashion has always imposed its personal vision on reality.

Although an immense change of attitude took place and largely replaced the popularity of the beautiful immutable dolls of the 19th century with the coming of the tempestuous *Character Dolls* early in the 20th century, this by no means marked the close of an epoch of beautiful dolls and undisguised romanticism. Though they were overtaken by those life-

Illustration 2. 25-1/2in. (64.8cm) French bébé marked: "F.R." Bisque socket head has fixed eyes, closed mouth and pierced ears. Her wig is mohair; she has a composition ball-jointed body. Made by Falck & Roussel.

Illustration 3. 18in. (45.7cm) French bébé marked on head and shoulders: "Bru Jne 8" with bisque swivel head and bisque shoulder plate and forearms. She has kid leather articulated body with kid covered wooden upper limbs. Lower legs are of enameled carved wood. Head has fixed eyes, closed mouth and pierced ears. The wig is human hair.

communicating, forceful "Characters" some undeniably beautiful dolls were produced in the new genre. They can perhaps be said to be lacking in the proud inscrutability of their 19th century sisters but they are fully the equal, artistically, of the earlier dolls. Indeed the later beauties can be described as unashamedly bourgeois but they are pert with their own kind of elegance. Gone may be the aristocratic reserve and detachment but in their place we see a realism that is humble and intimate.

Any selection must be conditioned by personal taste and I hope I have illustrated this article suitably with a choice of three beautiful French dolls from the last quarter of the 19th century and three lovely German dolls from the first quarter of the 20th century.

The design of dolls may follow the strangest and most tortuous of paths but human nature and nursery requirements remain fundamentally the same. The motives which over past generations have prompted the creation of so many lovely and fascinating dolls will remain. There will always be doll makers with the aim of setting down for us and posterity a record of the ideal of their time.

Illustration 4. 17in. (43.2cm) Character doll marked: "Simon & Halbig//1448//S & H." Bisque socket head has sleep eyes, closed mouth and pierced ears. Wig is of human hair. She has a composition ball-jointed body.

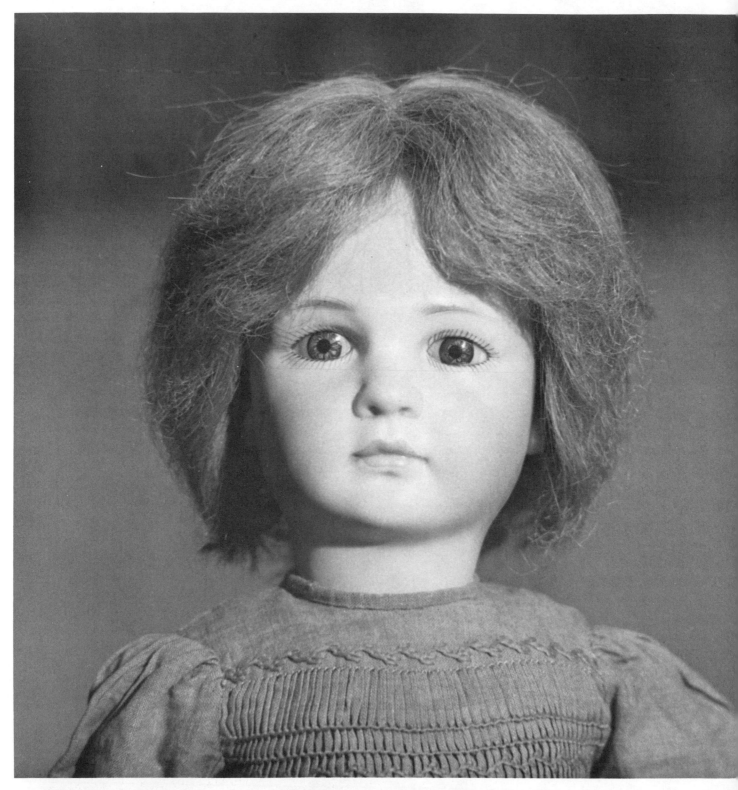

Illustration 5. (Above) 22in. (55.9cm) Character doll marked: "K & R"//Simon & Halbig//117A." Bisque socket head has closed mouth, sleep eyes and mohair wig. She has a composition ball-jointed body.

Illustration 6. (Right) 11-1/4in. (36cm) Character lady doll marked: "Armand Marseille // Germany // 401 // A 5/0 M." Bisque socket head has closed mouth and sleep eyes. She has a slender adult-type composition ball-jointed body.

Gebruder Heubach Dolls

by JAN FOULKE

photographs by HOWARD FOULKE

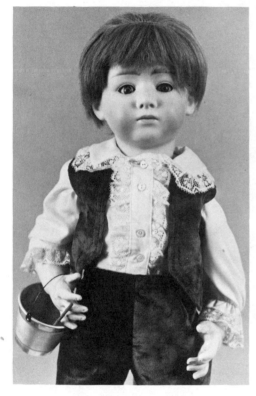

Illustration 1. One of the most beautiful Heubach pouties is this 26 in. (66.0cm) boy, a really large doll for a Heubach since most tend to be smaller. He has a particularly appealing expression with his very full cheeks, protruding ears and eyes larger than those of the pair in Illustration 5 His eyebrows are especially lovely as they are composed of tiny brush strokes which give them a soft natural look. His mold number is 7246. *Ruth Noden Collection.*

In the annals of the German bisque character dolls, there is no company whose work I admire more than that of Gebruder Heubach. The variety of dolls which this company produced is staggering. While other companies who produced character dolls seemed to stick to a small number of models in what was, after all, an experimental field at first, Heubach seems to have plunged in with enormous force. It seems safe to say that they specialized in the making of character dolls and were one of the first companies to produce them in significant numbers. Their doll line included very few of the dolly-faced

girls which were the standard and dominant line of other German doll makers, this at a time when the market for character dolls was really untried and very limited. It seems that the character dolls were not an instant success, and it took several years for the line to become established. Even then, the dolly-faced dolls continued to be the most popular and to dominate the stores and mail order catalogs.

In 1910 and 1911, the editorial pages of *Playthings* contained quite a few discussions about the character dolls, mostly promoting them as an addition to the dolly-faced doll, not as a replacement for her. The February 1910 *Playthings* editorial calls the character doll "a wonderful representation of a human being". . . especially appealing "to lovers of the natural and artistic." In January 1911 a *Playthings* article discusses the character doll:

In general, the cast of countenance is shown in cheerful moods, and the expressions show a degree of youthful intelligence which will certainly please the buyers of these lines of goods. They are lifelike in every detail from the unformed head of the tiny baby boy to the faintly formed double chin, the dimple, the strongly outlined bones in the forehead and the round, red, chubby face of the older youngster; these dolls are typical of the ages they are to represent.

Not only are Gebruder Heubach dolls noted for the variety of faces, moods and personalities presented, they run the whole gamut of emotions from smiling, bubbling and happy to pouting and even temper tantrums. The mood of the child as revealed by the facial expression has been caught exactly by the artist with the feeling and respect which would be shown a real person. No company's dolls appear to be more lifelike than those by Gebruder Heubach. The artists paid exact attention to detail, which after all seems to be the most important point in producing lifelike doll faces. It is the shape of the mouth, the size of the eyes, the protruding

Illustration 2. One of the sweetest googlies, this little 7 in. (17.8cm) girl has small round brown sleep eyes which look to the side. Her cheeks are very full, and she has just the tiniest mouth. She has both upper and lower painted lashes. Her orange dress and hat are original. She has the fat papier-mâché body typical of the googly dolls. She is incised with the Heubach square mark as well as her name "Elisabeth" stamped in green. *Richard Wright Collection.*

ears, the molded hair with crown, curls and bows, as well as the delicate painting and tinting -- all of these small things which add up to one big successful creation. The artists at the Heubach factory did these things extremely well.

For some time I have been interested in studying and attempting to catalog the work of the Gebruder Heubach factory. In this volume #3 of my Focusing On series is presented the beginning of my work on this subject. I stress that this is only a beginning because the output of this factory is enormously large and I have come to the conclusion that to catalog it all may indeed be the work of a lifetime.

Included in my book *Focusing On . . . Gebruder Heubach Dolls* are a chart of marks and a discussion of the art of the Heubach brothers, as well as a presentation of smiling character dolls, pouties, googlies, mechanical dolls, dolls with traditional faces, Christmas novelties, special character dolls, all-bisque dolls, piano and position babies, action figures, child figurines and the beginning of a catalog of Heubach mold numbers.

Illustration 3. This is one of the very popular Heubach dolls with a laughing face. These must have been very good sellers as they turn up quite often in several varieties. This one is thinner through the lower face and has no double chin as some of the others do, so it makes him an older child. His dimples are very pronounced. Fourteen inches (35.6cm) tall, he is on an excellent composition jointed body. His clothes are old. Unfortunately, he has no mold number, only the incised sunburst mark. *Richard Wright Collection.*

Illustration 4. This appealing little 7 in. (17.8cm) boy is incised with the Heubach square mark and the mold number 8589. His hair is painted with just a tiny bit of molding in the curls on his forehead and above his ears. His eyes are large and very carefully molded and painted with heavy lashes across the top, a typical Heubach characteristic. His mouth is small, yet well defined. He is also on a fat papier-mâché body. *H&J Foulke.*

Illustration 5. This darling pair of Heubach pouties have glass eyes and closed mouths. The little girl is just 10 in. (25.4cm) tall, an example of mold number 6969. Her big brother is 11½ in. (29.2cm) tall, an example of mold number 6970. Both are on good quality jointed composition bodies, and have been costumed by their owner. *Gail Hiatt Collection.*

ABOVE: Illustration 6. One of the most rare of the Heubach characters with glass eyes is this grinning boy incised with a Heubach square mark and 8316. He is 17 in. (43.2cm) tall on an all-wood jointed body. The fact that one of his eyes has been set in at an off-angle certainly contributes to his mischievous look. Most spectacular, however, is his broad mouth with a row of seven enameled teeth. His dark eyes and hair give good contrast to the lovely flesh coloring of his face. Obviously, he is an older child than many of the Heubachs, as his nose is sharper, he has no double chin and his lower face is thinner. *Richard Wright Collection.*

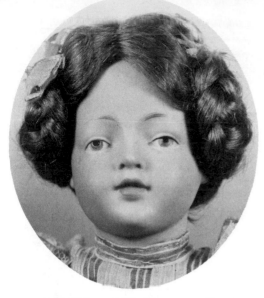

A KESTNER PORTFOLIO

PART 1

BY ROBERT & KARIN MacDOWELL

*taken from *Collector's Encyclopedia of Dolls*, page 355.

ABOVE: 11" Kestner. Head incised 178. Closed mouth, intaglio brown eyes, original mohair wig, composition body with straight wrists.

ABOVE: 19" Kestner, head incised XII. Closed mouth, brown sleep eyes, rare body of kid and composition. Wig not original.

LEFT: 13" JDK 260 (incised back of head). Open mouth, 4 upper teeth, brown sleep eyes with lashes, composition body with very long lower legs. Doll is entirely original.

LEFT: 16" Kestner, head incised 7. Closed mouth, blue sleep eyes, original blond mohair wig, composition body with straight wrists.

BELOW: 21" Kestner, head incised 14. Closed mouth, brown sleep eyes, composition body with straight wrists. Original blond mohair wig.

BELOW: 20" long Kestner 226. Open/closed mouth, 2 upper teeth, blue sleep eyes, bent limb 5 piece body. Wig not original.

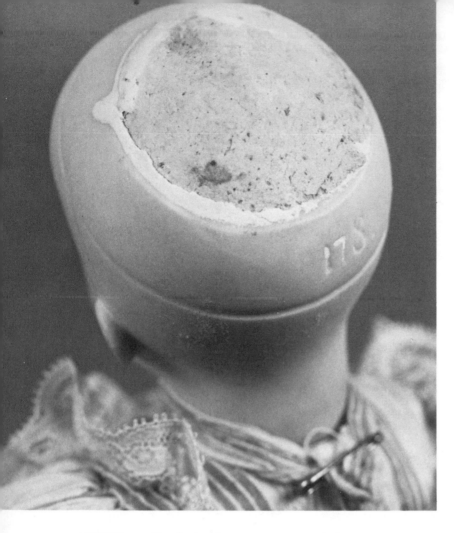

ABOVE: 16" Kestner shoulderhead. Back of shoulder incised 698 Germany N. 7. Closed mouth, cobalt blue sleep eyes, original blond mohair wig, kid body with lower bisque arms. The bisque on the shoulderhead is very pale.

ABOVE: Typical plaster pate used by Kestner.

RIGHT: 21" Kestner "Gibson" girl. Bisque shoulderhead. Back of shoulder incised P made in Germany. Blue sleep eyes, closed mouth, single stroke eyebrows, original blond mohair wig. Kid body, lower bisque arms.

A KESTNER PORTFOLIO
(PART 2)
BY ROBERT & KARIN MacDOWELL
Photographs by the Authors

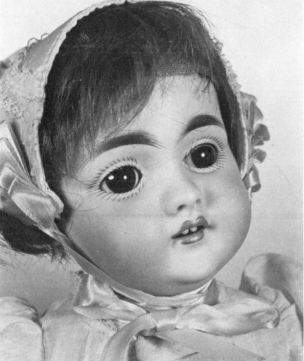

ABOVE LEFT: Illustration 10. 15" Kestner. Head incised made in Germany F 10. Open mouth, 2 upper teeth, brown sleep eyes, original human hair wig, composition toddler body with straight wrists.

LEFT: Illustration 11. 23" Kestner 152. Open mouth, sleep brown eyes, original human hair wig, fully jointed composition body. Compare with Nr. 14 which has the same mold number!

ABOVE RIGHT: Illustration 12. 33" Kestner 171. Open mouth, sleep blue eyes, human hair wig, fully jointed composition body.

Illustration 13. 17" long Kestner. Head incised Century Doll Co. Kestner Germany. Closed mouth, blue sleep eyes, molded hair, cloth body with composition arms.

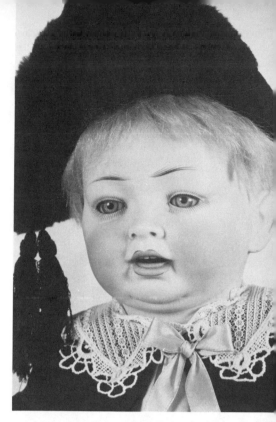

Illustration 14. 18" Kestner 152. Open mouth teeth, molded tongue, very light blue/grey eye original blond mohair wig. Bent limb 5 piece body

Illustration 15. 17" Kestner 167. Open mouth, sleep brown eyes, original human hair wig, jointed composition body.

Illustration 16. 9" all bisque Kestner. Swivel neck with kid lining. Movable arms and legs. Molded on shoes and sox. Head incised 4. Open mouth, 2 molded in upper square teeth, tongue. Sleep brown eyes. Wig believed not original.

Seldom Seen *Schoenhuts*

by SYBILL McFADDEN

Dolls are made of Magic. Toys transport us to the World of Make-believe and Let's Pretend.

Let's pretend, then, that it is the year 1911 in Philadelphia. You and the writer are about to take a tour of the Schoenhut factory. Albert Schoenhut himself, the great toy-maker and inventor of toys, is going to personally show us around.

Author: Touring your beautiful factory today is a great treat, Mr. Schoenhut. You say it covers five acres of floor space! I believe I have heard that your toy business did not begin with such a large and elegant building.

Mr. Schoenhut: Not at all. The Schoenhut family has been making toys for 150 years. In the 18th cen-

Illustration 1. 14in (35.6cm) molded-hair character boy, Catalog #14/205 - - 1911. *R. Zimmerman Collection.*

Illustration 2. 14in (35.6cm) Character Face Schoenhut Doll with label "Jan. 17, 1911" plays a Schoenhut upright piano with 12 "ivory" keys and 8 black. The front panel is lithographed with the name, and two angels on either side of 10 nymphs or muses dancing in flowing gowns. The little piano is 8½in (21.6cm) tall, by 10in (25.4cm) wide by 6¼in (15.9cm) deep.

tury in Wurtemburg, Germany, the family worked in a tiny cottage room, making one, or perhaps two or three different articles. Now in this 20th century in America, my six sons and I employ many, many workers in this modern concrete factory building equipped with large, light, airy rooms. Our automatic machinery makes hundreds of different toys everyday!

Author: It is indeed wonderful! I see we are now in the section where the toy pianos are made. I understand your little piano marked a new era in toymaking. It was your first toy, was it not?

Mr. Schoenhut: Oh, yes! I invented this toy piano using steel plates that are accurately tuned so that a child's ear for music is improved. This is the first piano with true tone. Formerly, the few toy pianos made in Germany had glass plates glued on strings. Music? There was none! Also the tone of my little pianos is permanent - - they never get out of tune! The keys on all keyboards are

Illustration 3. LEFT: The baby grand piano, mahoghany finish, with 19 keys. RIGHT: Child's size upright piano with 15 ivory-type keys and 10 black. Instruction book came with every piano.

the same width as those on a real piano so that a child unconsciously learns to spread the fingers.

Deep in the heart of every child is a passion for *real* life, for *true* stories. I realized this and made a toy piano on which real tunes could be played. The pianos have been good sellers from the beginning. These pianos are gladdening the hearts of millions of children all over the world. We export them and our other toys to Germany, Great Britain, continental Europe, Australia and South America.

Author: How exciting! Oh, here we are in the shooting gallery. What a lot of different games for small hunters! This "Big Game Hunter Set" fascinates me. I see it can be used indoors or outdoors. The Indian pops up when the bear is hit! I believe it has several variations, doesn't it - - a lion, a buffalo?

Mr. Schoenhut: Yes, the guns shoot balls or corks. They are as much fun for the father as for the boys, and satisfy the innate desire to shoot without the dangers. We also make toy shooting galleries which hang on the wall for target practice.

Author: Now we are coming into the doll section. This interests our group the most, as nearly all of us are doll collectors. What do you call this amusing round doll which bobs around and looks like a nursery rhyme character?

Mr. Schoenhut: That is our "Rolly Dolly." It is intended mainly for babies. It is becoming more popular every year. No foreign-made toys of this sort have ever approached these. The iron weight placed inside, on the bottom, to balance the Rolly Dolly is fastened by our patented

arrangement, so that it can never fall out of place. In other words, the principle upon which the Rolly Dolly is built is retained until the toy is worn out. This is a vitally important point, because the source of pleasure from these Rolly Dollies is their return to an upright position when upset. Our Rolly Dolly toys are all painted with oil colors which do not come off in a child's mouth.

Illustration 4. 7in (17.8cm) Rolly Dolly with painted yellow hair, white collar, and orange suit with black tie and stripes. Head is loosely jointed to bob when dolly is rolled. The Rolly Dolly is of heavy papier-mâché.

Author: What a fun place this is! I hear that your most important and ambitious invention is your new wooden doll which you have just introduced this year.

Mr. Schoenhut: Yes! We call it the "Schoenhut All-Wood Perfection Art Doll." It has cost us thousands of dollars to bring these dolls to their present point of perfection. All of the faces are beautiful child faces. A famous sculptor made the models for the heads. They are made on special machines invented for the purpose. The oil colors can be washed without injury. The Schoenhut All-Wood Perfection Art Doll grows old gracefully. It never loses an arm or a leg, nor does that fatal catastrophe - - a broken head - - ever occur. The doll is patented with steel spring hinges and swiveled joints. Look at this molded-hair boy. All these dolls can be posed in such a lifelike posture; you will agree they look most lifelike.

Illustration 5. "Big Game Hunter" 12in (30.5cm) long 11in (27.9cm) high. Indian pops up when bulls-eye is hit. *R. Zimmerman Collection.*

They *are* alive to the delicate fancy of the child. It is a real playmate, posed to run or jump, stand up or sit down, everything except laugh and cry or speak and sing.

We also make the clothes for these dolls. Not "doll dresses and suits" but facsimilies of real children's clothes, so that our dolls look like up-to-date little girls and boys. See the molded hair boy in his striped sailor suit with a star on his dickey and his trousers in the latest "knicker" fashion for boys? The styles and workmanship would do credit to any child's modiste!

Author: They are indeed lifelike, charming and well-dressed dolls! In addition, they are so well-made that it looks as if they will last through the years, and someday, perhaps they will be collector's items! Here is an unusual doll. What is this one called?

Mr. Schoenhut: This is our "Jolly Jigger." We introduced it last year in 1910. These dancers are operated by your own hand - much more interesting than if they were operated mechanically by clockwork. The smallest child can set them in motion, and when accompanied by any kind of music, the effect is simply overwhelming, and the merriment beyond description!

Author: There is no end to your ideas for amusing children. I know you have made dolls of the comic characters of Max and Moritz out of the funny papers. And two years ago in 1909 you introduced "The Farm Set."

thank you for this personal tour. It has been a wonderful experience.

Mr. Schoenhut: Come again, all of you!

****

(Note: The author's remarks are her own. Mr. Schoenhut's comments are adapted from the old Schoenhut Catalog entitled "Forty Years of Toy Making 1872-1912")

****

Illustration 6. 11½in (29.2cm) Dutch boy, "Jolly Jigger." Papier-mâché head and limbs. Doll dances when shaken. Patented December 27, 1910. *R. Zimmerman Collection.*

Illustration 7. 14in (35.6cm) and 12½in (31.8cm) Schoenhut boy and girl with blonde mohair wigs and the early "pouty-type" faces. Boy wears original button, clothes and stand. Girl's clothes have Paris labels in them - interesting in that this doll was probably exported to France from Philadelphia, dressed in Paris in the dark blue velvet outfit, and somehow returned to her native land where she was purchased in the 1930s.

Mr. Schoenhut: Yes, it is quite popular with both boys and girls. You Ladies seem to like the milkmaid or farmer's wife. She usually carries a wooden milk pail. She, as you can see, wears a blue dress with an oil-cloth collar. We brought out The Farm Set in two sizes. In addition to the milkmaid there is the farmer in a straw hat with his wheelbarrow and rake, a pig, a cow, a duck, and a feeding trough for the animals.

Author: Dear me! I see our time is almost up, and we have not even visited your famous circus area!

Mr. Schoenhut: This is true. But the circus is a whole department in itself. So you will have to come back another time just to see and talk about it.

Author: We will look forward to another visit, Mr. Schoenhut. We

Illustration 8. 8½in (21.6cm) "Maggie" and 7in (17.8cm) "Jiggs" from the comic strip, "Bringing Up Father," by George McManus, one of the earliest comic strips which ran until World War II. *R. Zimmerman Collection.*

195

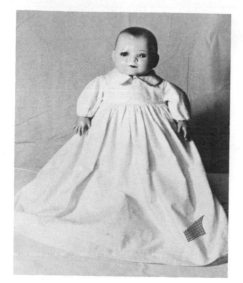

Illustration 9. 15½in (39.4cm) "Bye-Lo." Wooden head, celluloid hands with the turtle mark. Baby body similar to that used on Grace Storey Putnam Bye-Lo. Was declared an infringement on her patent and taken off the market. *R. Zimmerman Collection.*

THE YEARS AHEAD

Albert Schoenhut was 62 years old when this imaginary trip was made through his factory. The following year, in February 1912, he died. His six sons carried on the business for many years until in 1934 the A. Schoenhut Company closed its doors and filed for bankruptcy. In the intervening years the sons had introduced the doll athletes dressed as football and baseball players, the bent limb baby and the toddler with the same head as the baby, the walking dolls, and the sleeping doll. Theirs also were Maggie and Jiggs from the comic strip "Bringing Up Father" by George McManus in 1924, the doll houses and furniture, and a train station to go with their wooden trains. Theirs was the wooden baby doll which was declared an infringement on the Grace S. Putnam Bye-Lo Patent and had to be removed the market, today, a rare Schoenhut collectible. However, their accomplishments never quite equalled in charm or popularity the success of their father and founder, Albert Schoenhut.

The last dolls produced by any of the sons was the "Pinn Doll Family" by Otto Schoenhut, who had permission to market it in 1935 from its designers, Myers and Landquist. As you know, these dolls are not in the character of the earlier Schoenhut dolls, and were never very popular, but are nonetheless historically interesting.

****

Illustration 10. Doll from the "Pinn Doll Family" marketed by Otto Schoenhut Co. in 1935. Designed by Emily T. Myers and her adviser, Olga Landquist. *R. Zimmerman Collection.*

Schoenhut Gift Leads To International Career

BY ALICE DeRIENZO

Margaret Whitton spends part of her time these days working on her upcoming book on the Jumeau doll.

Margaret Whitton received a gift of a 1911 Schoenhut doll many years ago, took an interest in dolls and in doll collecting and today is an international authority on dolls and the Curator of the doll collection at the Margaret Woodbury Strong Museum in Rochester, New York.

How does a single gift lead to a career as curator of one of America's leading doll collections?

Mrs. Whitton became interested in dolls when she was a young housewife in New Rochelle, New York. "My two children were little and I was more or less confined to the house. I wasn't the type to spend the whole day cleaning," she said with a smile, "so I got a job, through a friend, sewing doll costumes for the B. Altman Company in New York."

When Mrs. Whitton's friend gave her the Schoenhut doll she did some research on the doll and the Philadelphia company that manufactured it. Her interest in dolls grew until eventually she started her own doll mail order business. She bought groups of dolls, kept the ones that interested her and advertised and sold the rest through the mail. Margaret Woodbury Strong was one of the many people who bought dolls from Mrs. Whitton.

Mrs. Strong died in 1969, leaving a legacy of over 300,000 separate objects, among them 27,000 dolls, for the start of what she called a "museum of fascination."

Mrs. Whitton was the first person to start running "picture sheets" of her dolls with the ads, now a common practice in trade journals. Her expanding knowledge also led to numerous articles and publications on the history of dolls. Before joining the museum staff in 1974, she wrote a book in conjunction with Francis Walker on the history of uncut cloth dolls entitled *Playthings By the Yard.* In 1978, with a committee from the United Federation of Doll Collectors, Mrs. Whitton helped compile *A Glossary of American Dolls.* Next year, her book on the history of the French Jumeau doll will be published by Dover Publications.

At the museum Mrs. Whitton and her assistant are busy cataloguing the dolls, grouping them for exhibit and "cleaning them up" for the museum opening in 1982. "A great many collectors feel that dolls should not have their faces cleaned because it detracts from their original condition," Mrs. Whitton said with concern. "I don't agree with that, because original condition does not mean dolls with dirty faces."

A great many people people have enjoyed the behind-the-scenes efforts of Mrs. Whitton and her care of the museum's dolls. This year she selected the dolls from the museum's that adorned the White House Christmas tree. (Her husband, Curator of the museum's toy collection, selected the toys.) The end result produced one of the most beautiful trees in presidential history.

Mrs. Whitton has also worked with the U.S. Information Agency in arranging the 1977 "World of Dolls" exhibit in Kuala Lumpur, Malaysia, which attracted three-quarters of a million visitors. The reception was equally as enthusiastic in France last year when some of the Strong Museum dolls and toys were part of the "American Toys, 1925-1975" exhibit at the Louvre's Musee des Arts Decoratifs. After a tour of four French cities, the dolls returned to the United States and are now on loan to the Smithsonian Institution's Traveling Exhibit program.

Mrs. Whitton was arranging exhibits long before coming to the Strong Museum. In 1967 she was contacted by the U.S. Information Agency to provide dolls from her own collection and others as part of the "Creative America" exhibit for the Canadian Exposition in Montreal.

Exhibits are only one aspect of Mrs. Whitton's work with dolls. Her knowledge of them prompted film producers to contact her when they needed two dolls for the oscar-winning movie, *The Miracle Worker*. "It was very difficult to find two identical dolls from the time of Helen Keller's childhood," Mrs. Whitton said. "Besides that, they had to have eyes that closed. One doll was sort of an understudy for the other in case something happened to one." After Mrs. Whitton found the dolls and costumed them, she became concerned that they might possibly be damaged. "There was one scene where Patty Duke, in a rage, had to throw her doll at her teacher, Anne Bancroft," Mrs. Whitton recalled. "I searched all over for a doll with a similar looking face and finally found one with a vinyl head. That's the one they used for the throwing scene. They reserved the other two dolls for close-ups."

Mrs. Whitton's warm friendliness and enthusiasm for her work is evident when she speaks about the dolls in the collection. "I think it's so amusing when manufacturer's come out with a doll that does something 'new'—like talking," she laughed. "There was a 'talking' doll or phonograph doll as early as 1880." She hastens to add that though an idea for a doll may not be new, there is always something new to be learned about them.

One of her discoveries since working at the Strong Museum was in a box from the Columbian Exposition of 1893. It bore the label of the Libbey Glass Company and contained an elegant doll dressed in a spun glass costume. "I wasn't sure if the doll and the box went together, or whether the doll had just been stored in it, so I wrote to the Libbey Company," she said. She was excited to learn from them that the doll had been sold in the box at the Exposition. Libbey had made the first spun glass gown for a well-known actress and had also costumed the dolls in spun glass as part of that display.

The excitement sparkled in Mrs. Whitton's eyes when she talked about another very rare doll in the Strong collection. The doll has three wax masks which are separate from the head. The masks represent infacy, youth and old age and can be attached to the face. Mrs. Whitton said that to her knowledge this particular doll has hever been pictured, and is very unique.

Studying the history and production of dolls is one aspect of Mrs. Whitton's job as Curator. She and her husband have also initiated two other important programs at the museum. A large collection of manufacturer's toy and doll catalogues has been added to the museum's library. Also, the Whittons have done considerable research to obtain patent records on dolls and toys. They have now compiled over 3,000 such patents. "I feel that catalogues from the time period, which show how dolls were advertised, are an important part of the collection. As for the patents, anyone who has ever tried to get a record from the Washington office without a patent number will appreciate how invaluable our library will be," Mrs. Whitton said.

Knowledge of dolls has also led Mrs. Whitton to her role role as chairman in the yearly judging of dolls for the United Federation of Doll Collectors, which has over 12,000 members. Those dolls are not museum dolls, but are owned by individuals, and are judged on condition, rarity and other attributes.

Mrs. Whitton loves her work and certainly deserves her title as an authority on dolls, but she is careful about the label of "expert." "Dolls are a fascinating part of any culture, and in studying them there's always something new to be learned. Even the so-called experts don't have all the answers," she said with a slight smile, "you're always discovering something."

This photo of Patty Duke holding the dolls used in the movie *The Miracle Worker* was given to Margaret Whitton by the producers of the film. The doll on the left is bisque; the one on the right is vinyl. They were costumed and provided for the movie by Mrs. Whitton.

SOME DOLLS FROM THE
MARGARET WOODBURY STRONG MUSEUM

Above: Papier-Mâché Ladies. These are four papier-mâché head dolls with leather bodies, wooden arms and legs and original clothes. The heads show unusual hairstyles from the late 1830s and early-1840s and they were all made in Germany.

Upper left: Character-Face Doll. This is a 19in. (48.3cm) bisque shoulder head gentleman with black curly wig, brown glass eyes and a molded moustache and teeth. The modeling on the face is exceptional with deep, sculptured wrinkles on the forehead and a double chin. No markings are on the doll as to manufactuer but it is probably German. Ca. 1900.

Left: Wax-Pate Fashion Doll. This is a 22in. (55.9cm) bisque head fashion with a swivel neck and blue glass eyes. She has a typical fashion-type kid body. An indentation was made in the scalp, wax poured into it, and the hair was inserted into the wax until a wig was formed. This process was patented by Josef Kubelka of Vienna in 1884 and then patented in the United States in 1889.

199

LENCI DOLLS

by DOROTHY S. COLEMAN

Illustration 1.   23in (58.4cm) Dschang-Go. Magda Byfield Collection.

shown to have been made in the Lenci factory. This is especially true of the early Lenci dolls. On the other hand about half of the dolls called "Lenci" and sold at antique shows and auction were only Lenci-types and not real Lenci dolls. A few collectors and dealers such as Jan Foulke have studied Lencis and would rate higher than my 50 percent in accuracy. However, we all need a great deal of study to differentiate between Lencis and Lenci-type dolls.

This new book, *Lenci Dolls, Fabulous Figures of Felt,* for the first time except for a small entry in our *The Collector's Encyclopedia of Dolls,* gives the number code series and original names of Lenci dolls. Most collectors know what a K★R 100 looks like, but how many collectors know what a Lenci 300 looks like. Despite the fact that they have probably seen as many Lenci 300s as K★R 100s. The Lenci code is carried further and a 300/1 Lenci doll wears a different outfit from the 300/2 doll. For example all 300/12 Lenci dolls will wear the same type of outfit and carry the same accessory, namely a rake.

Lenci dolls are numbered from 101 to 2000 as well as many of them having individual names: *Mimi, Fukuruko, Kufi, Mozart, Madame Bovary* and so forth. The identification of your particular Lenci doll may take a little study but this new book has not only a comprehensive index

but also a table matching the heights with the series numbers. The known height of your doll thus limits the number of possible series numbers that need to be studied and the index provides the pages where these series numbers are discussed. If your doll has a mark or tag, another table helps you to date and identify your doll.

This new book will enable you to recognize whether your doll wears its original clothes and has its original accessory, if any. If the accessory is missing, you will know what to seek in order to replace it.

The number of items other than dolls made by Lenci will astound most collectors. These include hats, purses, tea cosies and so forth. A large collection of non-doll Lenci products could be made from the information in this book.

The identification of an unmarked doll is very difficult and in most cases impossible. With a Lenci doll there are many clues, especially when the original clothes are on the doll as so often happens. As is true with practically all dolls, identification cannot be made by looks of the doll alone. Lenci-types often resemble Lencis. However, when an unmarked doll matches exactly in appearance and clothes a doll shown in a Lenci Catalog, *Playthings* or a marked Lenci doll, it is almost certainly a twin of that particular doll and can be identified with reasonable certainty. Collectors will need to study this book but should find it fascinating to follow the many clues to a satisfactory solution.

Not only will this book help you to better recognize Lenci dolls but also to have greater appreciation of those that you have and to date them.

Most collectors consider the Lenci dolls can be recognized fairly easily. I did indeed until I started to study them in depth for a book on these beautiful Art Deco dolls. Then I discovered how wrong I and other collectors had been.

This book is based on numerous contemporary advertisements and articles in *Playthings* as well as three Lenci Catalogs and several other catalogs of the pre-World War II period. In addition to this source material a large number of marked Lenci dolls and Lenci-type (not Lenci) dolls were studied.

My appreciation of the artistry of the Lenci dolls grew as the study progressed. Also I realized how little was known about Lenci dolls heretofore. Many of the dolls that I had not recognized previously as Lencis were

Illustration 2.   13in (33.0cm) Lenci. *Photograph by Cherry Bou.*

Illustration 3. A pair of Lencis. *Margaret Woodbury Strong Museum. Photograph by Bettyanne Twigg.*

Illustrations 4 and 5. 14in (35.6cm) Lencis. *Margaret Woodbury Strong Museum.*

Originally Lenci dolls cost more than French Bébés except Jumeaus which were priced about the same as the Lencis. Today bisque-head character dolls and portrait dolls command astronomical prices while Lencis are relatively inexpensive, despite the fact that they are outstanding both as character dolls and as portrait dolls.

Antique dolls are becoming rare and expensive. Many collectors are turning to post-World War I dolls which remain within their financial reach. Of all the dolls made between World War I and World War II, known as the Art Deco period, few can compete with the artistic charm of the Lenci dolls. In addition to their worth as an art object, they are exquisitely made, especially the ones in the 1920s and early 1930s.

Lenci Dolls, Fabulous Figures of Felt provides the information needed to identify and to appreciate these desirable dolls more effectively than has been possible hitherto. The more we know about our dolls, the greater is our pleasure in them. The learning is a part of that pleasure. In this new book you will find a great deal to learn about Lenci dolls.

QUOTATIONS FROM PLAYTHINGS MAGAZINE RELATING TO LENCI DOLLS

Compiled by
DOROTHY S. COLEMAN
© 1977 Hobby House Press, Inc.

Playthings, June 1929, pages 175 to 177. "The Italian Toy Industry" by the National Export Institute.

"In 1919 the first factory was opened in Turin devoted exclusively to the manufacture of stuff dolls painted in striking color schemes. The output of this factory soon attained such a high degree of perfection that it was able to hold its own even on such a fastidious market as that of Leipsic [sic]." This, no doubt, refers to the Scavini factory making Lenci dolls.

"It is only since the war that a Turin factory made a daring break with tradition and placed on the market a novel type of doll, made entirely of stuff, but one which could fully satisfy and develop the childs' innate love of beauty.

"The first experiments in production and the early efforts to popularize these dolls with the public were anything but easy; soon, however, such progress was made with the techniques of the work and the quality of the output improved so rapidly that it succeeded in winning the favor of the public both in Italy and abroad.

"At the present time some 800 workers are permanently engaged in making these stuff dolls and everything points to a brilliant future for these delightful toys, which are popular not only with children but with grown-ups. The dolls are dressed in all kinds of costumes, illustrating those of the several regions of Italy, as well as in fashionable modern sporting dress, and in historical or theatrical costumes. The workshops also turn out most attractive puppets, among which figure prominently the traditional 'máschera'* the several parts of Italy, formerly so characteristic a feature of the carnivals and pageants for which the Peninsula was famous.

"This great variety of dolls are all manufactured on the same fundamental lines; they are hollow, made of felt, shaped and sewn by machinery. They are then painted, and receive from highly skilled and specialized artists the finishing touches which confer on them the individuality which is their distinguishing charm. The dolls are then handed over to other workers who dress them from top to toe in clothes which are models of refined taste and elegant simplicity. Here again felt is the only material used, care being taken that the costumes be complete down to the most minute details and true to the period or type to which they belong."

Like most promotional articles some of the statements are not entirely accurate. It is known from the Lenci catalogs that not all of the clothes on the dolls were made of felt as stated above. It is also doubtful whether all Lenci dolls at this time, 1929, had the hollow felt bodies. Many of them did have this type of body but the sizes smaller than 17½in (44.5cm) have all been found with stuffed bodies. Nevertheless a contemporary account such as the one given in *Playthings* provides fascinating information.

Playthings, October 1929, page 103.

"Kirsh & Reale, Inc., sole American agents for the Italian-made Lenci Dolls, report that at least four or five times as many Lenci Dolls will be sold in the United States this year as ever before. The Mssrs. Kirsh & Reale, say that buyers throughout the country appreciate the fact that stock is carried in New York City and that they can stock the Lenci line without the fuss and trouble which would be occasioned if they had to import it themselves direct from Italy. The recently introduced Lenci display mannikins are said to be making a great hit. Made with characteristic Lenci fidelity and beauty, they are striking models of real children, and are proving exceptionally popular with large stores everywhere."

Playthings, October 1938, page 62. "Dolls That Are Not Toys" by Elinor Henry Brown.

"Lenci dolls from Italy are toys dolls that collectors love as much as children do. For twenty years Madam Lenci has been making international costume dolls and life like children with complete wardrobes."

*Máshera means mask in Italian.

LENCI PORCELAINS

by DOROTHY S. COLEMAN

In our book *Lenci Dolls* mention is made of the porcelain products of Madame Lenci, especially her Madonnas. Recently several articles pertaining to the porcelain Lenci products have come to light.

The prestigious periodical *The Studio* around Christmas time in 1929 had an article on "Modern Italian Ceramics, Some Examples from the 'Lenci' Studios." This article states, "We find the genius called 'Lenci' after having made a name for itself in designing and fashioning, among other things, those amusing felt dolls which are to be seen in nearly every toy-shop in the world, turning its attention to ceramic figures . . .

"We have seen a few examples from a very large collection which has just been produced by this famous workshop. Entirely different in material and character, they possess the qualities of decoration in form and colour and a certain lightness in humour which give them the flavour of 'Lenci' creations . . .

"Broadly speaking, these ceramics are the result of team work. A team of sculptors, painters and craftsmen, under the presiding genius of 'Lenci' are taking a pleasure in their work and working for the good of the show. This spirit unconsciously perhaps, seems to work its way through its products . . . Here, thanks to the skill of 'Lenci' we have that certain liveliness which is both amusing and attractive.

"The National Museum of New York has acquired some of the first pieces but, at the time of going to press (1929), we understand that 'Lenci' ceramics have not yet been put on the market but arrangements are being made for an exhibition of them in the late Autumn in London."

The products shown in this article are a Madonna nursing her baby and figural bookends designed by Vacchetti. The greatest number of items are attributed to a designer named Sturani. These include a covered vase with a female figure for a handle, a covered dish with a bird for the handle, two flower holders in the shape of women's heads, one of these is weeping. There are also two Sturani figures - one of an intoxicated youth clutching a lamp-post and the other of a soldier throwing a ball or a bomb. Madame Lenci designed a boy riding on the back of a snail that resembles one of the felt figures shown in the 1930 doll catalog. Another artist named Quaglino, designed a boy holding bouquets in each hand and seated on a stylized elephant. Two other porcelain figures are not identified as to designer. These are a nude woman frightened by a tiny snake and a maiden holding a fish beside a lily pond.

Dorothy Midgett of Richmond discovered an article in the September 1931 issue of *Arts and Decoration* titled "Rare Modern Porcelain by Lenci of Italy Famous for Subtle Animal Portraiture." The animals include a mother deer nuzzling her baby, otters teasing a fish, a sea gull with drooping wings and a lioness or tiger with a semi-nude woman.

Dorothy Midgett is also responsible for finding a December 1936 article in *Arts and Decoration* on Lenci Madonnas entitled "Little Mary, Queen of Heaven." The same nursing Madonna designed by Vacchetti for Lenci is shown in this article as appeared seven years earlier in *The Studio*. This was called the "Madonna delle Mamme," the Madonna of all mothers. This Madonna is described as follows, "[Its] gentle and soothing beauty adorns a niche in the Maternity Hospital in Florence, inspiring mortal mothers to keep their children instead of committing them to charity. [The] quaint little Mother, the 'Madonna of the Snows' who is the patroness of Alpini, a crack Italian regiment, . . . wears the same picturesque and colorful cape and stubby wooden shoes that are worn by the peasant mothers and sisters of the Alpini. [The] still and gentle 'Madonna of the Resignation' . . . wears a cape with a Byzantine design of birds and elks, and a nun-like white coif. She is very young and meek and has a definitely archaic air. [There are] three variations of the 'Madonna of the Laplands,' with her exotic Mongolian slant eyes. She carries her Child like a true Lap woman, hugged close against her for warmth. The 'Madonna delle Figlie di Maria' (Madonna of the Daughters of Mary), . . . is the young Virgin, and wears a blue and white wimple of severe design to indicate her purity. She has a look of endearing innocence and her delicate hands are folded in naive humility.

"The . . . gracious 'Madonna of the Dove,' a plaque done in bas-relief, shows the Della Robbia influence. She wears a gaily figured gown, and the Child has an expression of cherubic glee."

Two Lenci Madonna-type figurines, allegedly from the Chicago World's Fair of 1933, have black "Lenci" signatures under the glaze. One of the Madonnas is dressed as a barefoot peasant with a paisley shawl around her shoulders, a scarf on her head and a white rabbit in her hand. Perhaps one day the name "Lenci" will mean to collectors exquisite porcelain figures as well as beautiful felt dolls.

Tiny Dolls

by CLARA HALLARD FAWCETT

©1976 Hobby House Press, Inc.

Editor's Note: This article is reprinted from the November 1943, *Hobbies Magazine*.

MINIATURES of anything, whether by the hand of man or the hand of God, are always fascinating to the thoughtful person - - the dwarf in the circus, the miniature garden, the toy theatre or house, the kettle made from a penny, the peach-pit basket, etc. ad infinitum; so it is with the tiny doll.

This love of the miniature is with us from childhood. There was once a little girl named Clara Hallard, whose love for the wee doll was even greater than her attachment to the big one, which she could dress and bathe and tuck into bed, and hug and scold as the mood fitted, for around the miniature she built a whole world. An orange crate served as a two-story house; a pint-sized basket as a carriage; a wheelbarrow turned on its side so

that the wheel revolved, made a satisfactory merry-go-round; a pan of water, a lake for bathing; branches of the huckleberry, in season, were transformed into a whole "apple orchard," for the fruit was penny-doll size; and the golden rod in bud, a "pear orchard." In winter, when outdoor play was not feasible, a cardboard box fitted with cardboard desks and benches, became a school room. The fairy tale "Thumbelina" and others dearly loved were dramatized around the tiny doll.

Clara, who came to this country from England, will never forget her first penny doll. It was purchased with her first American penny. Near the school which she entered at the age of five, was a small shop presided over by a dear lady who beamed upon the upturned face of one so small that she had to stand on tip-toe to see the contents of the counter.

"My name's Clara," said the child. "What's your name?" Surprise of surprises! "My name's Clara, too," came the answer. "What can I do for you?" The words so astonished Clara - - to think that a grown-up

could have a name without a "handle" - - that for awhile she just stared open-mouthed.

With the utmost patience the storekeeper waited while the penny dolls, all of them in sight, were thoroughly scruntinized. There was a thimble-sized blonde with a fascinating pigtail but the face was ugly, and Clara could not endure anything ugly, so it was turned down, not without a look of longing at the pigtail. Another, a "frozen Charlotte" (pillar doll to some), would never do, because it could not sit down or wiggle its arms - - it was frozen stiff, arms to side, leg to leg; too bad, because it had a pretty face. But there was quite an array of "proper" tinies, bisque or unglazed china with movable arms and legs, which could be clothed easily and made to sit. All these had to be examined with minute care; the feautres must not only be centered, but the coloring good. Even in those days, Clara was a connoisseur.

At last the penny purchase was made. The patient shopkeeper bid goodby to her young customer, and then and there a life friendship began,

Illustration 1. "Tinies" from the collection of Mrs. Raymond P. Baker of Columbus, Ohio. Reading from left to right, upper row, the two china-headed dolls are of the middle 19th century period. The two papier-mâché-headed dolls on the right about 1830. Lower dolls are late bisque. Largest 6½in tall; smallest 2½in.

Illustration 2. China-headed miniatures with saw-dust-stuffed cloth bodies. Smallest is 2¾in tall. *Courtesy Mrs. W. A. Waples.*

and a collection of tinies started. A search for accessories resulted in metal furniture - - two chairs and a "settee," - - shining like silver and of handsome scroll work design with *red plush* upholstery at a cost of 25 cents, a stupendous sum. It took a long time to save that much, but such magnificence was worth sacrifice. An eager purchase was a baby carriage of the same material and design and with the cutest of sunshades (lined with pink cambric) dangling above the seat. For the modest sum of 10 cents it was purchased for the "baby," which, owing to its half-inch size, had to be a "frozen Charlotte." Perhaps the phrase "modest sum of 10 cents" does not apply here, for it took Clara two weeks to save that amount, two weeks of firm resistance against the temptation to buy candy. More pennies must be saved for "adults" to accompany the "child" dolls; a "woman" one-third taller than the "children," with a knot on the back of her head, and a gentleman with tiny whiskers. "Knots" and "whiskers" came high. A Family of distinction needed a horse to draw the pint-sized split wood berry basket vehicle. The shopkeeper who was Clara's namesake and her favorite, had a beautiful horse, just the right size (Clara was a "stickler" for proportion), but it cost too much. However, a 15-cent tiger ("make believe it is a horse" said Sister) finally drew the "carriage."

It was a fateful day when Mother said, "You are too old to play with dolls," and big brother said, "My goodness, whoever heard of a great big girl like you playing with dolls?" Sister, not much older, had long since given up the childish pastime. Regretfully, the whole collection was handed over to little Ida next door, who accepted them with concealed joy.

Time passed, Clara was married, and an absorbing new "live" doll, a daughter, came to bless the household; "the prettiest baby in the nursery" said a hospital nurse which of course was true, for isn't every mother's baby "the prettiest baby in the nursery?" As the child grew, she in

turn, came to love doll-play fully as much as had her mother in the old days, and again drama centered around the tiny doll. One day, as the five-year-old was seated in the middle of the floor, Mother Clara, tiptoeing through the room, heard these words: "A rustle of silk announced the coming of the princess."

Now that child is grown and has a collection of miniatures carved with her own hands, as well as others of every conceivable variety.

It would be interesting to know how many women dramatists received inspiration in childhood from doll play. We know of at least one who carried the love of tiny dolls into adult life. We quote from Mrs. Frances Hodgson Burnett:

"I invariably stop and look into toy shop windows wheresoever I come across them - - whether in Paris, where they are too deliciously beautiful for words; in London; in little English, German or Italian towns or villages, anywhere and also everywhere. I plant myself unashamedly before them, and disregard all else.

"The day before the Jacobean cabinet* revealed its true character to me, I was walking though a village and saw a small shop whose window presented objects before which I paused transfixed. There were a small Japanese tea table, and six small chairs made of bamboo. On the table was a tiny Japanese tea set of green ware, the teapot with a wicker handle. And around the tea sat a small Japanese family, composed of a mamma, a papa, and three unextinguishably beautiful Japanese babies, all in dazzling kimonos and with shaved heads except the mamma, who wore fans in her hair. It is impossible to resist and pass them by. (This was the Japanese family of old, of course, not the Japanese of today.)

" 'I will go in and buy them,' I said in that sneakingly specious

manner in which we always make plausible excuses for our weakness. 'I can give them to some child.' "

"The unadorned truth was I did not want to give them to 'some child.' I wanted them for myself because they were so human and so delicious and tiny and quaint and that part of my being whose childhood belonged to the period when perfection in doll-land had not been achieved, had never yet been satisfied."

Mrs. Burnett purchased not only this doll family, but other small dolls and their paraphernalia, and then came the problem of where to put them. Quoting again:

"Perhaps the Jacobean cabinet had been slightly bored that afternoon and truly wanted something to do. It looked at me as I glanced toward it. 'Give them to me. I'll take care of them' it said.

"It was the very place for them. The lower part of it, when its doors were opened, revealed two substantial shelves. I opened the doors and kneeled down. I took out one delightful thing after another and set them in order, arranging a little scene."

When Mrs. Burnett left England for America, the "toy cupboard," as she called the cabinet, was brought along, but since she had given away its contents, it had to be repopulated, and the "rooms" refurnished. She says: "I have built houses and furnished them; I have made gardens in various countries and revelled in them; I have written quite a number of things; but I do not think that anything I have done has been more amusing and satisfactory to me than the Toy Cupboard."

Mrs. Burnett's enthusiasm for little dolls is expressed in her story, "Racketty Packetty House."

One of the best examples of famous collections of small dolls is the great Queen Victoria, whose dolls are described in the book *Queen Victoria's Dolls* by Frances H. Low (reprinted from the *Strand Magazine,* 1892).

Tiny dolls have been made for centuries, and a search for the old

*Mrs. Burnett purchased a fine Jacobean cabinet in Kent, England, and it was in this cabinet that she kept her dolls.

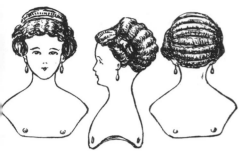

ones will bring to light many delightful surprises. As in the larger dolls, hairdress, material and general shape of the head and limbs are indications of period. The fancy hairdo of the big, expensive dolls was reproduced in miniature. In her collection of small ones, Clara has a six-inch perfect doll with the most elaborate hairdress. The head, one and one-half inches tall, is shown in sketch No. 1. Notice the earrings.

Among the rare little ones in the same collection is the five-inch fully jointed wooden "peg" doll of the early Victorian era. This had a knot on the back of its head and curls at either side of the face - - (sketch No. 2).

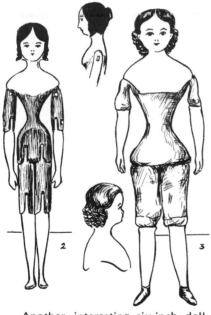

Another interesting six-inch doll in the same collection (see sketch No. 3) is the one with corkscrew ringlets. Her black hair, straight in front, is brought down on either side of the face from a center part, and looped up over the ears. She has a pink lustre complexion, and her features and coloring are perfect. A Washington, D.C., collector reports that a doll of this type has been in her family since the 1780's.

The two dolls represented in sketches Nos. 4 and 5 (3½ inches tall) are, respectively, china and Parian-headed, with cloth body, dating about 1850 to '60. Coloring and

features of both are perfect. The "boy" is unusual. His brown hair, slightly glossed, shows fine brush marks at the temple.

Number 6 is one of the rare tinies with ringlets falling over the shoulder. A back-comb holds the curls in place. She has china head, arms and legs, and a sawdust filled, cloth body, and dates from about the Fifties.

Number 7 is a still rarer china-head, a lady of "parts." A tiny china bow decorates the braided knot at the back of her head. Her face, neck and shoulders are of pink luster, a lovely contrast to her blue eyes, and she knows she is a beauty!

Number 8 is a china "frozen Charlotte," dating from the "covered waggon" era. A black band en-

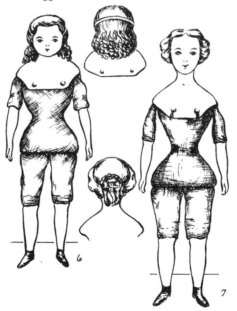

circles her blond head. The hair, combed straight back from the face, falls in slightly curled fashion at the back. Another doll of this type in the same collection has well defined shaded blond ringlets. The latter is of finest Parian, with gold lustre shoes, a real aristocrat.

Number 9 is a "Gay Nineties" white Bisque bonnet doll. The blue and red trimming on her flaring

bonnet contrasts nicely with her light brown bangs. Her arms are attached to the body with wire, the legs, stationary.

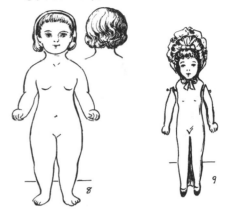

While the Clara Fawcett collection includes dolls as small as half an inch (made on a stick pin) and others only slightly larger made of wood, china, celluloid and iron, the most prized tiny antiques in the collection are Nos. 10, 11 and 12. Number 10, nine-eighths inches tall, is the most perfectly jointed precious metal doll one could imagine. It is jointed at shoulders, hips, elbows and knees. The parts shaded are of gold, the rest, white with black hair and shoes. She brings back fond memories of the Rue Vignon in Paris, where many happy hours were spent, and of a little antique shop near the hotel.

Numbers 11 and 12 were handed down from the childhood days of great "Aunt Lida," who, were she alive, would be close to a hundred years old. The great niece of the original owner played with them as a child. She wove many fantastic stories around the one-and-one-fourth-inch mite with swinging arms and legs, and handknit dress represented in No. 11. Number 12, a "frozen Charlotte," looks a trifle weary, but completely resigned, - - who wouldn't after nearly a hundred years of child-play?

The china and bisque-headed dolls of Mrs. W. A. Waples of Louisville, Ky., and Mrs. Raymond P. Baker of Columbus, Ohio, shown in the photographs, are good examples of the attractiveness of the tiny doll. Now, as in the years long gone by, the miniature doll is dear to the heart of womankind.

Fortune-Teller or "Fate Lady" Dolls

BY MARGARET WHITTON

Photographs by Barbara Jendrick

Illustration 1. A china shoulder head, mounted on a wooden articulated body with china forearms and lower legs. Her costume is cloth with an underskirt of cutout paper pieces. One section has been opened to show the hand written fortune. Note the hole in the right hand that has perhaps been created to hold a wand.

Illustration 2. A sketch showing the "Fate Lady" that appears in the children's book, *The Girl's Own Toy Maker,* by E. Landells.

Dolls from the collection of the Margaret Woodbury Strong Museum, Rochester, New York

There is a close relationship seen between the traveling pedlars and the fortune-tellers of the early 19th century. The fortune-teller, or "Fate Lady," traveled the countryside in the company of pedlars who sold their wares from town to town. Their popularity was tremendous and for a small fee, people from all walks of life could have their future predicted.

Inevitably, the idea of creating fortune-telling dolls came about. These creations were primarily needlework projects and made use of dolls of all materials such as wood, wax, cloth, leather, bisque, china, papier-mâché and so on. A popular type of doll that was often used for the "Fate Lady," was the china shoulder head

with an articulated wooden body, china forearms with a hole molded in the right hand and china lower legs. The hole found in the china hand could well have been made to hold the wand that pointed to the different fortunes as the doll turned on the circle.

In 1833 and 1838, a girl's activity book called *The Girl's Own Book,* was published in England. This book was written by a Mrs. Childs. Included in the book are instructions for making a fortune-teller or "Fate Lady" doll. The instructions are as follows: "This is a toy made of about a quarter of a yard of pasteboard, cut round and covered with white paper.

The flat surface is ruled for mottos, and all the lines meet in the center. The writer should be careful to draw a line of red or black ink between each, to make them distinct. Exactly in the center of the circle, a wire is inserted; and on that is fastened a neatly dressed jointed doll, of the smallest size. In one hand she holds a small straw wand, with which she points to the poetry beneath her. The wire is made steady by fastening it in the center of a common wafer-box, covered and bound to correspond to the rest of the toy. The doll is just high enough above the pasteboard to turn round freely. When you wish your fortune told, twirl her round rapidly, and when she stops, read what her wand points to".

This same doll, with instructions for making it, appeared in several editions of an English book titled, *The Girl's Own Toy Maker,* by E. Landells. This was somewhat similar to the earlier book, *The Girl's Own Book.* Several editions of the Landells book were also published in the United States by E. P. Dutton & Co of New York. This second version of the construction of a fortune-teller varies in some measure from the original instruction pages and the illustration shows a different type of doll. Both books contain excerpts from a lengthy poem, "Lines to a Fate Lady," by Mrs. Ann Maria Wells. The poem provides some of the mottos or fortunes to be written on the circular pasteboard base of the doll. Mrs. Wells composed both happy and sad mottos in this poem, such as:

"Emma an heiress shall come out,
And shine at ball, and play, and rout;
While Timid George, who has a dread
To go unguarded up to bed,
Is doomed - a fate for him how sad!
To march afar, a soldier lad.
A band of warriors, brave as he,
Would form a droll light-infant-ry."
"But here's Louisa - she must try
The lady's skill in destiny.
Listen! A modest, gentle maid;
No foolish airs her mind degrade;
Possess'd of talents, virtue, grace,
Her Poorest charm's her pretty face."

Another type of fortune-teller doll is pictured, complete with instructions for making it, in a German children's book called, *Herzblattchen's Zeitvertreib,* that emphasized "activities for little boys and girls, the education and development of life and surroundings." The published date is not given for this book but judging from the illustrations showing the fashions worn by women and children in the book, it appears to be from the 1880s. A full page, color illustration, shows a full length doll with a bodice and overskirt of fabric. The lower skirt is made of cut-out paper pieces that have fortunes or poems written on them. The pattern for the fortune paper pieces is shown alongside the doll. The instructions, translated from German, read as follows: "The cut-out is for a doll about 12cm high - dressed in a tightfitting petticoat. Take 130 different colored cut-out papers like the one shown in the illustration. Write on each piece a nursery rhyme, poem or puzzle. Turn the bottom of the paper up (like shown in the drawing) to line A-B. Fold the paper in half on line C-D. Take a large needle and push four holes through as shown, use thick or double yarn and pull through the top holes first, adding,

Illustration 3. An illustration for a fortune-teller doll, described, complete with a pattern and instructions, in the German children's book, *Herzblattchen's Zeitvertreib.*

Illustration 4. A commercially made fortune-teller or "Fate Lady." No manufacturer is known but it is marked "Patent Pending in U.S. and Abroad." The upper part of the doll is a flat piece of wood covered with lithographed paper. Her paper skirt has the fortunes printed on it and the entire doll is mounted on a turning cardboard circle with the months of the year and the signs of the Zodiac.

according to color scheme, each cut-out. Repeat with the lower holes. Use the above yarn and gather and tie on the waist of the doll. Keep the lower yarn loose so it will look like a hoop skirt."

A supplement to *The Young Ladies Journal,* for 1884, printed a doll and instructions for making her. This was called "The Shaksperian [sic] Oracle." Any type of doll may be used but in this case they suggest using a china head and costuming her in the Elizabethan style. A long wand in her hand points to an oracle which is printed on a circular stand. One side is for the ladies, the other for the

gentlemen. Mention is also made of the fact that the magazine will supply "The Shaksperian [sic] Oracle," made up (the circular base) by parcel post for five cents.

Very few of these fortune-teller dolls are found intact or in good condition. The paper skirt dries out and becomes brittle with the constant opening and closing of the folded paper. Fortunately, the instructions for creating these dolls have been preserved for us in these early activity books for girls, enabling the doll collector or young girls to possibly create a fortune-teller or "Fate Lady" for herself.

Illustration 5. (Above) A bisque fashion doll with a shoulder head and a kid body. This is an example of what can be used to create a fortune-teller. The upper part of the costume and her traditional high, tapered hat, is made of cloth. The paper skirt has hundreds of brief fortunes bound together at the waist to form a skirt.

Illustration 6. (Left) Another very popular type of doll used for making a fortune-teller is the peg-wooden with a "Tuck Comb." One of the paper cutouts is shown in open position revealing a hand written fortune.

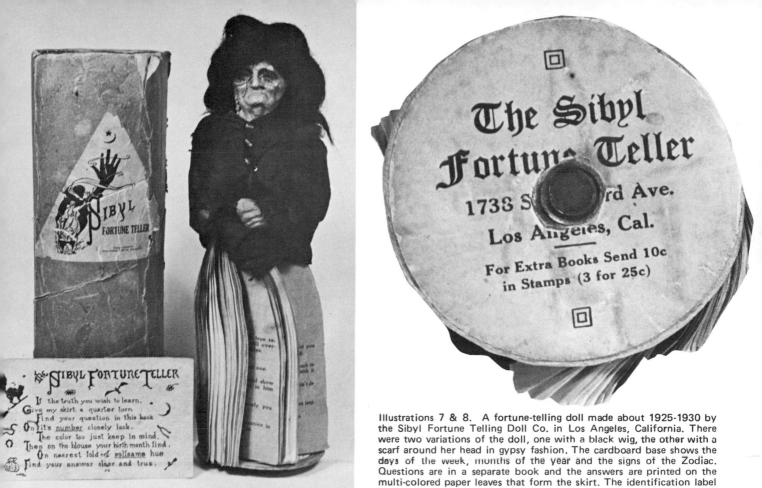

Illustrations 7 & 8. A fortune-telling doll made about 1925-1930 by the Sibyl Fortune Telling Doll Co. in Los Angeles, California. There were two variations of the doll, one with a black wig, the other with a scarf around her head in gypsy fashion. The cardboard base shows the days of the week, months of the year and the signs of the Zodiac. Questions are in a separate book and the answers are printed on the multi-colored paper leaves that form the skirt. The identification label on a cardboard base is shown at right.

Learning From
Antique Doll Bodies

BY FRIEDA MARION
Photographs by Richard Merrill

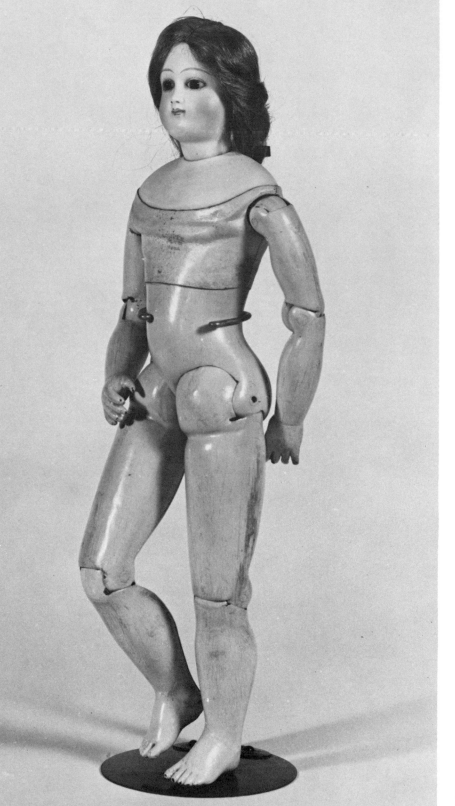

A rare French doll with original body of laminated fabric, from the collection of the late Estelle Winthrop. From *Doll Collectors Manual 1967;* permission of the Doll Collectors of America, Inc.

Although the head of an antique doll is undoubtedly the most important part, the proper body is essential if a collector is to own a worthwhile item. This is *not* to say that heads alone are not valuable—they certainly are— but there is a difference between a fine old head, which is just that, or a complete antique doll. Collectors naturally tend to seek the latter.

Unfortunately, many new collectors only notice the head when buying a doll, and since the body may be well covered with clothes, investigation may be delayed until the doll is paid for and taken home. Sometimes this results in dismay when the body is found to be an obvious replacement, especially if it is poorly made or totally unsuitable to the head. In such as case, the collector is faced with the unpleasant realization that she has actually paid for a doll's head and has very little else of value.

The more advanced collectors are usually familiar with all parts of old dolls and can make an educated guess concerning the suitability of the body for the head. Some manufacturers, such as Heubach, made charming bisque character doll heads which they mounted on cheap, cardboard bodies which were stapled down the middle, and these are original and correct although the novice collector might easily imagine that the body had been replaced. However, J.D. Kestner made both fine-quality heads and bodies, usually marked. Sometimes a body stamped or labeled with the J.D.K. trademark is found with a rather inferior unmarked bisque head and here we may assume that the original head was broken and replaced with an inexpensive one of another manufacture.

Many replacements were done while the doll was still a plaything. Fond parents were likely to buy a new china or bisque head for their child's favorite doll if the original one was damaged, and we have only to turn to catalogs of the early part of the century to see that these heads were sold retail as well as wholesale.

Old catalogs are a good source of primary research to show us just how dolls were assembled when they first came on the market. Fortunately, a number of old catalogs have been reprinted and are available to the interested collector, and are especially valuable to the novice who is not familiar with the construction of dolls made before her own playdays.

The Colemans, in *The Collector's Encyclopedia of Dolls*, have been able to give us pictures from catalogs showing German and Swiss porcelain doll heads dating between 1845-1860 (see page 119). Since these heads were often sold retail and put on homemade bodies which were perhaps replaced more than once over the years, it is not easy to say what is an "authentic" body on a very old china-head doll. In this same book, the Colemans also show us an old catalog page dated around 1845-60, (page 133), picturing dolls constructed with turned wooden, peg-jointed bodies having china heads and limbs, and it is from such sources that we learn exactly how these early dolls were made.

Although dolls are usually designated by the material of the heads (i.e. china, bisque, wax, papier-mâché), the term *wooden doll* generally refers to one with the body made of wood. In the *Handbook of Collectible Dolls* by Merrill & Perkins, the section devoted to wood (Volume 3, pages 223-240-H) mainly refers to dolls with wooden bodies, many having wooden heads also but some with heads of molded plaster or composition. The "Door of Hope" dolls, made in China at the Door of Hope Mission during the early 20th century, are considered to be wooden dolls as their heads and limbs are of hand-carved wood although the bodies are of cloth. But a rare doll with china head and limbs on a pegged-wooden body, such as those shown on page 133 in *The Collector's Encyclopedia of Dolls*, is found on page 108-C in *Handbook of Collectible Dolls* (Volume 4) with the chinas! Obviously, the beginning collector must do considerable studying to become familiar with the nuances suggested by categorizing particular dolls in relation to their head and body types.

Perhaps the most inclusive article on wooden dolls was printed in the *1964 Doll Collectors Manual*, researched and authored by Ruth E. and R.C. Mathes. Unfortunately this book is now out of print although it occasionally turn up at doll auctions or estate sales. However, the *1967 Doll Collectors Manual*, which is still available, features detailed information on

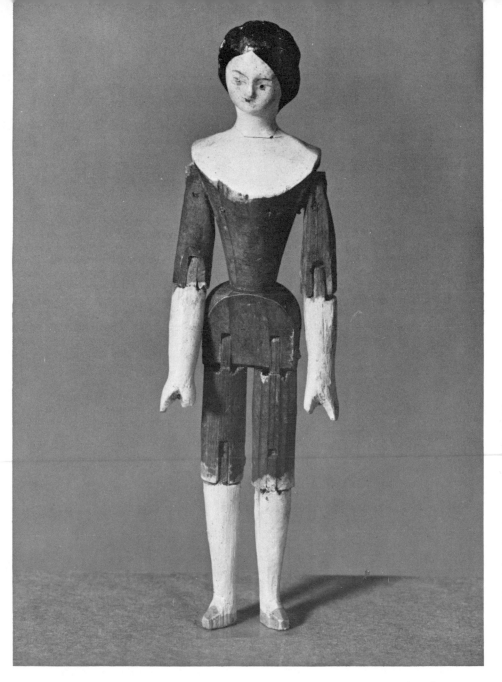

A 5in. (12.7cm) peg-jointed wooden doll with gesso covered head, skillfully repaired. *Collection of the author.*

other interesting doll body types. "The Enigma Doll," by Jo Elizabeth Gerken, is an authoritative compilation of information on fascinating dolls made with mid-sections of alternating portions of cloth (or equally pliable material) and wood, composition or something quite firm. The *1967 Doll Collectors Manual* also contains a feature by Madeline Merrill on the rare, laminated-cloth dolls. Both this article and Jo Elizabeth Gerken's are accompanied by clear, detailed photographs. Such books with articles devoting attention to details of doll bodies are very helpful to the collector and form the basis of a good reference library.

Since many old catalogs have been reprinted, it is possible to acquire information without undue expense, even though few collectors can expect to find genuine catalogs of the mid-1800s such as the ones found in *The Collector's Encyclopedia of Dolls*. A more recent catalog in my own collection, a 1928-29 mid-winter Montgomery Ward & Company issue, displays German bisque-head, ball-jointed dolls still for sale at that late date, which explains why doll collectors in the early 1940s dismissed such dolls as not worth adding to an antique collection. Collectors who can remember playing with these dolls, or whose older sisters owned them, may cherish the German bisques but can hardly

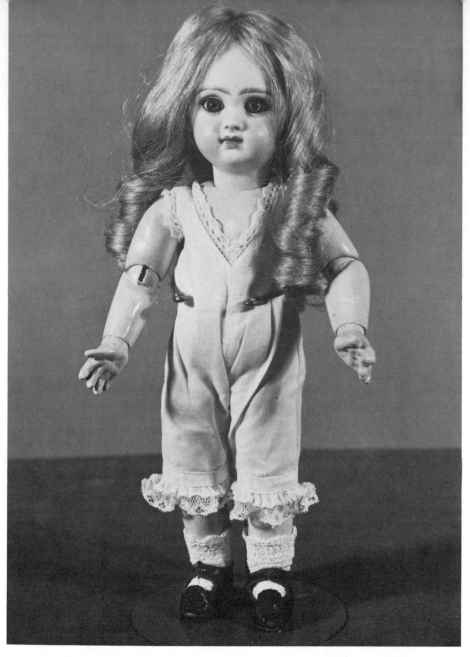

Not all French dolls were made with unjointed wrists. This 12in. (30.5cm) charmer is marked in red on the head—
"DEPOSE
TETE JUMEAU
Bre S.G.D.G.
3"
with several hand-painted lines, and an incised "3". Stamped in blue on the original body—
"JUMEAU
MEDAILLE D'OR
PARIS"
Collection of the author.

bring themselves to consider them antiques.

Bodies are made up of a number of parts. My Montgomery Ward catalog mentioned above advertises a 16-1/2in. (41.9cm) doll with a bisque head and "kidiline" body, described as a fine-grade white, imitation kid which is waterproof. The arms are composition. The picture clearly shows the disk-type joints used at shoulder, elbow, hip and knee, fairly common on dolls of this period. Early familiarity makes it easy for older collectors to recognize such bodies which are sometimes inappropriately paired with older heads.

French ball-jointed doll bodies are different than the more common German types, and we would prefer to find a good-quality French head on its original French-made body if possible. Some of these are marked, but even if the torso is unmistakeably correct, the

hands may have been changed. Hands are distinctive and in the case of a high-quality doll they may be of special value. Consider the graceful bisque hands on a kid-bodied Bru!

French dolls were often made with the lower arm in one piece and these so-called unjointed wrists are very desirable. A few years ago a dealer offered a lovely little Jumeau whose unjointed wrists were almost certainly the small-sized forearms of a German model. Such dolls are shown in *Armand Marseille Dolls* by Patricia R. Smith, page 38, or *Open Mouth Dolls*, by La Vaughn C. Johnston, page 56. In *Handbook of Collectible Dolls*, page 5, the two French doll bodies are shown with the comment that the "one-piece hand and forearm [is] typical of French dolls although this rigid wrist *may* be found on some German dolls."

Since hands made by French man-

ufacturers were somewhat larger and shaped differently than those made in Germany, a French doll with German hands, even of the "gauntlet" type with unbroken wrists, does not look right to the knowledgeable collector, and the value is reduced.

Replacement parts are sometimes unavoidable. Most advanced collectors are willing to accept this if the part is either an old one of the proper period, or a new one that has been handcrafted in a careful reproduction of the old. Dolls were playthings, not ornaments, and it is natural that they should suffer some wear during the long years that they were played with and lovingly abused. However, it is still important, both for today and the future, that the many parts of dolls be assembled to tell the true story of their times and origin, for in this way dolls can not only delight us but make an invaluable contribution to history.

DOLL ARTIST

The English Costume Dolls Of Ann Parker

BY SHIRLEY BUCHHOLZ
Photographs Courtesy of Ann Parker

Illustration 1. Doll Artist Ann Parker

Twenty seasoned doll collectors toured Britain. Shepherded by the grande dame of the doll world, Dorothy Coleman, they were savoring the banquet of dolls, dolls' houses and toys presented for their pleasure by museums and private British collectors. Dessert came in a most unusual place—a gift shop at the Roman Baths. For it was there they were introduced to the handcrafted Costume Dolls of Ann Parker. True, her dolls had been discovered earlier by American collectors, but never by a group of this size. The staff of the shop was overwhelmed, for the usual number of dolls sold was perhaps one a week, but that day the total supply of 42 dolls was depleted in an hour, with immediate orders placed for 65 more!

What was it about Ann Parker's dolls that excited these experienced collectors? It was the same thing that the Standards Committee of the National Institute of American Doll Artists found in 1977, when they voted her an Associate Member of NIADA. It was the intrinsic artistry displayed in her "people-figures." In only four years Ann's dolls had gained international attention. In fact, most of them are purchased by foreign collectors.

"I am not a doll collector," she says, "although I fondly remember some Lenci or Chad Valley dolls I had as a child. I just make dolls." Indeed she does! When, as a teen-ager in Wales during World War II she made some costume dolls for a Red Cross bazaar, little did she dream that one day her dolls would be sought avidly by doll collectors in both hemispheres. Those few dolls from the bazaar with their carved cork heads and features painted with watercolors have no doubt disappeared, but they were the "beginning."

Ann Parker Costume Dolls were born in the winter of 1972-1973 when she was looking for something to do while her husband and daughter were on a ski holiday. She decided to make a doll for tourists. It was not a case of a rank amateur trying her hand at an unknown field, but a trained artist working in another medium. As a young girl, Ann had attended art school in Bristol and in London. She had then gone on to work as a commercial fashion artist, illustrator of

Illustration 2. The Picadilly Flower Girl.

children's books and "educational comics" and a portrait painter. Many of the skills necessary for designing the doll she had in mind were already highly developed, but she had never carved before. Her only training in sculpture was one term at art school. "I really hated it," she says. "All that mucking about in wet clay!"

A trip to a craft store provided plasticene which she made into a sausage-like figure which she then cast in plaster of Paris. Ann carved this and added to it until she had the desired effect. Finding that plaster of Paris was too difficult to work with, she searched for a tougher plaster. It took her about six months of experimentation in her kitchen to learn to do the figures well.

Ann had hoped to find a plastics factory to produce the undressed dolls, but was unable to locate one that would maintain her high standards. So, with her usual spirit of determination, she bought some plastic

resin and began to cast them herself.

The demand for her dolls was more than she could handle alone, and a small cottage industry developed in Bognar Regis. A doll does not "just happen." The combined skills of the artist and her helpers go into each one. Ann Parker's standards are high, as are the wages she pays the women who work for her, so the resulting dolls are of exceptional quality. All the figures are made by hand and she estimates there are at least forty hours of work on each finished doll.

Since costume design was one of her prime interests, Ann decided to concentrate on a regional costume for her first doll. And so, the "Picadilly Flower Girl" (*Illustration 2*) with her red hair came into being. She was first offered to the public in a gift shop in Bath in April 1973. Upon deciding whom each doll will represent, Ann scours the museums and libraries for paintings and photographs. She generally uses five or six portraits if possible, and chooses the best for the head. Costumes, in most cases, are done from portraits as well, and as close a likeness to the original as she can make it, considering that proper fabrics and trims are difficult to find.

The master figure, a different one for each character, is carved from plaster. She says she does this in the drawing room on a tray while seated in a nice, comfortable chair since it takes quite a long time. George Washington (*Illustration 9*) took about three months. She then makes rubber molds in the kitchen and casts the figure, keeping the first few to use as models for the designing of the costume. The molds and materials for casting are then given to the three ladies Ann has trained to make and assemble the bodies. They take them home and re-

Illustration 3. Princess Charlotte, 1796-1817. Only child of George IV. Wife of Leopold who became King of Belgium. Had she lived, she would have been Queen of England.

Illustration 4. Polly with her Kettle.

pregnancy. She seems to assist in making babies!"

There are 29 different dolls to choose from. A few are the same doll dressed in different costumes, such as the "Picadilly Flower Girl," "Nell Gwyn" and the "18th Century Flower Seller." And then there are the wonderful portrait dolls—Fanny Burney and Charlotte Brontë, both done from paintings in the National Portrait Gallery.

Royalty is depicted in such readily recognizable figures as Henry VIII (*Illustration 5*), resplendent in fur and jewel-trimmed brocade with a short sword hanging at his side, and looking as if he had just stepped out of Holbein's portrait. A great favorite is Queen Victoria (*Illustration 6*) in her later years as the Widow of Windsor.

turn the finished product to her each week. She then does the necessary fine carving to finish the heads and paints the faces.

The dolls next are sent to the three women who were taught to do the hair styles Ann designs for each character. Most are done of mohair, but George Washington's wig is of the crepe hair used for false beards in the theater. The artist makes these wigs herself because they are so difficult. She can do only two in a day and this accounts for the fact that this particular doll is considerably more expensive that the others.

The hair finished, they are then parceled-out to the "dressers," women she has taught to make the elaborate costumes she designs. Each lady dresses specific dolls. Ann's mother who is 83 does Jane Austen and Princess Charlotte who was the only child of George IV. Charlotte (*Illustration 3*) is splendid in her silver regency gown and long, white, silk gloves—a truly beautiful doll. Ann says she is extremely careful about giving "Polly" (*Illustration 4*) of "put the kettle on" fame to just anyone for, as she tells it, "Several of the ladies who worked on her have since given up because of

Illustration 6. (Above) Queen Victoria.

Illustration 5. (Left) King Henry VIII sports a real beard, not a painted one.

215

Illustration 7. Admiral Lord Nelson, 1758-1805. The most beloved of English heros. He destroyed Napoleon's fleet at Trafalgar. He never wore an eye patch. His blind eye was the result of a detached retina.

Elizabeth I with the characteristic hollows in her face, beloved by her subjects and known to them as Gloriana, is richly dressed in brocade with gold trim. Ann Boleyn, wife of Henry and mother of Elizabeth, who, Ann Parker says, came alive with her laughing eyes as she worked on her, must have been quite stylish. Her fur-trimmed gown, copied from an original painting, was a style that became popular about ten years later. Queen Anne, regal in her purple velvet, is a handsome woman, not pretty. A striking likeness.

Other historical personalities represented are Lord Nelson (*Illustration 7*) who, according to Ann, was a most difficult doll to do since all his portraits are completely different. She finally used a photograph of his death mask at the Victory Museum in Portsmouth and says she was surprised at how well he turned out. The Duke of Wellington was done from paintings by Lawrence and Winterhalter. He is quite dashing in his white trousers and red coat trimmed with gold braid. A favorite everywhere is Beatrix Potter holding a furry Peter Rabbit. Her gentle, wistful expression tells much about this remarkable woman who was so ahead of her time.

Bridging the Atlantic is Lady Randolph Churchill (*Illustration 8*), the lovely American Jenny Jerome and mother of Sir Winston. She is a marvel of miniature couture. Her lush purple gown of silk and satin, draped and pleated to perfection, is copied from one Jenny wore in a portrait with her two sons. The aristocratic tilt of her head, the perfect little hat of flowers

Illustration 9. George and Martha Washington.

Illustration 8. Lady Randolph Churchill.

and the tiny muff carried in her left hand all blend into a feeling of elegance. And from our side of the ocean are the Washingtons, George and Martha (*Illustration 9*). These are the only numbered editions. Their likenesses are quite astounding. The artist worked from portraits and from the death mask taken by Houdin of our first President. He stands almost a head taller than his plump little wife, serious and well-tailored in the outfit we tend to think of as "Colonial." They appear as we usually think of them—rather elderly.

Ann Parker dolls are about 12in. (30.4cm) tall. Their heads and bodies are of one-piece construction with wired arms. Each has its own stand of finished wood and wire designed to hold the figure in a distinctive position. On the front of the stand is a gold label with the name of the doll printed in black letters. All of the dolls have 1x2in. (2.5-5cm) wrist tags.

One side is red printed in gold and reads:

ENGLISH COSTUME DOLLS
©
Ann Parker
hand made in England

On the reverse side is black printing on white with the name of the doll, the dates of the person's life and a bit of their biography.

Students of history will greet old friends when they see Ann Parker's Costume Dolls. Others just may be tempted to "dust off the books" to read and learn more about these fascinating people who come to life in her hands.

SHEILA WALLACE
artist in wax

BY CAROL-LYNN ROSSEL WAUGH

Wax portraiture is a neglected art. When it was in its heyday, names like Madame Tussaud, with her famous size figures, and the Montanaris, known for the wax dolls they introduced at the Crystal Palace Exposition, stood out in the field. Today we can add the name of Sheila Wallace to the list.

This young Pennsylvania woman creates modern wax dolls that are works of art and labors of love. Historic portraiture her specialty, and she breathes life into long-dead names and faces that come from the pages of history books. To Sheila Wallace history is neither dead nor dull; it is people and personalities and with fascination. And she seeks, in her work, to bring these individuals once more to life, to give them concrete form. "The characters (in history books) are real people — they're real to me. History has become personalized," she explained in an interview. This en-

thusiasm is evident in her work, for her creations have vitality and personality.

Long years of European training as a portrait artist form the basis of her skills. After completion of the General Certificate of Education exams in art at both the ordinary and advanced levels in Devon, England, she studied painting, drawing, sculpture and fine arts at the Heatherly School of Fine Art, completing her art education with a concentration on sculpture and anatomy at the City and Guilds Art School in London. She also studied with the craftsmen of Madame Tussaud's waxworks. This intensive training forms a broad basis from which she can draw in her dollmaking.

Although Ms. Wallace has been interested in costume dolls for quite some time — she had the idea to do a costume doll of Marie Antoinette when she was only thirteen years old — dollmaking was not foremost in her mind during schooling. The Pennsylvania artist trained to be a sculptor. "I did not go to school to learn to make dolls," she explains. "I do not think there are any such schools. I sort of invented techniques on my own."

It was while she was working as a secretary in London, doing commissions in her spare time, that dollmaking worked its way into the sculptor's life. She began making plaster of Paris dolls, but soon her father convinced her to work in wax. After much research into traditional methods of wax sculpture, she hit upon a formula which is based on one used by European wax modelers of the 17th century. The old methods, however, have been adapted and improved.

These modern dolls have heads, hands and sometimes lower limbs modeled from bleached beeswax. They are solid wax, unlike the old dolls which were either hollow, having been cast from molds, or dipped wax, over papiermache. Because of this the heads are impervious to freezing, whereas the old ones were not. And the sculpted dolls are

The Empress Eugenie of France (1826-1920). Married Napoleon III and reigned from 1853 to 1871.

surprisingly durable. Since the melting point of beeswax is 125°, they can be kept easily in the average home.

The balance of the doll is of other materials. Ms. Wallace constructs a wire armature for the figure, to allow it flexibility in posing. Over this she builds a cloth body filled with polyester fiber. Most often lower limbs are constructed of composition, with footgear fitted to the foot, not molded on.

When the body is complete, the hair on the head, eyebrows and the hands (of male dolls) is individually implanted, by needle, into the wax. The faces are then painted with either oils or watercolors, in accordance with the styles of cosmetology prevalent at the time the individual lived. Ms. Wallace is particular about accuracy on this matter and researches each time period and its styles thoroughly before commencing a project. In fact, before each doll is begun, she spends a great deal of time ascertaining the correct physiognomy, costuming and life-

18th century gentleman with interchangeable wigs.

Pierrette-style fashion model inspired by a fashion plate, circa 1914.

style of the person to be depicted. Whenever possible, she prefers to work from death masks or contemporary portraits of the individual. Most dolls are historical figures, ''not just because I am superstitious of making dolls of living people, but because I prefer to work on subjects with more general appeal, and I love historical costume.''

Costuming is meticulous and time consuming, but a favorite aspect of the process for the artist. It presents many challenges, the most demanding being those involving scale and materials. ''Scale is so important to costuming,'' the artist noted. ''You can learn about costumes from seeing the originals in museums, and you get a feel of the period.'' But modern fabrics are difficult to use in designing period costumes. ''Today everything is made for durability and is washable. People do not wear damasks or brocades anymore.'' Cloth made from all natural fibers is more and more difficult to find, and fabrics that will fall properly and give the correct impression of the full-scaled antique ones are nearly impossible to come by. Modern synthetics make washing easy and pressing effortless, but these qualities are an enormous obstacle to the doll artist who is striving to create an 18th century person with accurate and permanent folds in his costume.

Concepts about clothing have drastically changed since the time of Marie Antoinette, one of Ms. Wallace's favorite subjects. Many of the garments of that time could neither be washed nor cleaned, and clothes definitely ''made

The actress Lillie Langtry in a traveling costume.

Queen Elizabeth I (1533-1603) of England.

the man,'' describing his station in life for all to see. The Pennsylvania artist prefers to only depict those people whose clothing has something to say. She notes that for the nobility, costumes were worn as symbols of class or position, not necessarily for warmth and convenience. And some of these clothes were certainly elegant.

''Most of my clothing is hand sewn in order to be authentic,'' stated the dollmaker. ''I do, sometimes, use the sewing machine, but only where appropriate — in other words, on costumes dating from a time when the sewing machine was in

general use. I do all the work myself, from the doll, through the costuming, even to the stands. I'm very independent!''

Completed dolls are 18 in. (45.7 cm) to 21 in. (53.3 cm) in height and are one-of-a-kind collector's items. Each doll takes roughly one month to six weeks to finish and Ms. Wallace spends a rigorous ten hours each day at her work. She is not certain exactly how many dolls she has completed: ''I don't really know how many dolls I made, counting cast waxes and limited editions, but the one-of-a-kinds must be roughly 50 by now.''

Wallace dolls are in demand by discriminating collectors and museums on both sides of the Atlantic, including a museum in Florida and the Victoria and Albert Museum (Bethnal Green), London, England. They retail for between $400 and $500 each, and, according to Patricia R. Smith's *Modern Collector's Dolls Identification and Value Guide,* they are worth between $200 and $300 more than they sell for.

Their creator is a member of O.D.A.C.A. (Original Doll Artist Council of America) and the Costume Society of America. For some time, she has been associated with Kimport Dolls of Missouri, which helps her find markets for her dolls. Other outlets are through other shops, representatives, galleries and advertising.

For Sheila Wallace a love of history and portraiture has combined to create a consuming career. She seems destined to be included one day in the history books of dollmaking. For already she has been termed, by those in the know, ''a contemporary Madame Tussaud.''

Detail showing the face of Marie Antoinette and her youngest child.

Mostly Mini - The Dolls Of MARGO GREGORY

BY SHIRLEY BUCHHOLZ

Illustration 1. 7 in. (17.8cm) all bisque boy "Steve" dressed like the Heubach football player. Molded black ribbed stockings, brown shoes. Painted features and a skin wig. Jointed at hips, shoulders and head. Dog is commercially made. Incised on back with Margo Gregory's signature. *Photograph by John Axe.*

positioned realistically. About a dozen of the dolls are one-of-a-kind, sculpted directly in the porcelain before firing while the rest are made from her original molds.

All of the dolls wear carefully researched costumes that have been copied from old prints or other pictorial sources. Especially entrancing are the ladies promenading with their mustached or bearded husbands. Some have toddlers in tow while others push prams with minute jointed bisque infants attired in lacy baby dresses.

The "street dolls" may have either molded hair or mohair wigs, and some even have molded hats. The two baseball teams are eye-catchers in their 1900s uniforms and molded caps. Their little wooden bats were carved by one of Margo's greatest boosters, her husband, Greg.

Margo Gregory was a fine choice to make the little people of Marthasville for she specializes in miniature. Most of her dolls are 1½ in. (3.8cm) to 9 in. (22.9cm) tall, but she has made a few in the 12 in. (30.5cm) — 14 in. (35.6cm) range.

When Patsy Powers decided to display her Bliss houses in the Toy Museum of Atlanta, she felt that a diorama of "Marthasville, July 4, 1900" would be appropriate since that was what Atlanta had once been named. The large problem facing her would be to find the "people" to live there. To locate that many antique dolls of the proper size, sex and age could take years of diligent searching and she did not have years; the museum was already under construction.

Then she thought of the little 6 in. (15.2cm) French Fashion-type doll she had recently purchased from a transplanted Yankee doll artist, Margo Gregory. Patsy approached her with the idea of designing and making the inhabitants of "Marthasville." Margo agreed and thus embarked on the most challenging project of her doll-making career, nearly 100 tiny people in perfect scale for the colorful lithographed Bliss houses that line the streets of the display.

The heads and limbs of the "street dolls" as Margo calls them, are of porcelain and the bodies are of padded wire armature which can be

Her smallest, which is displayed in a shadow box, is a completely jointed 1¾ in. (4.5cm) child of porcelain with painted features and a mohair wig. With it is an exquisite little wardrobe consisting of two straw hats, two dresses, drawers, chemise, petticoat, cape and bonnet, all of which fit perfectly.

The charming all bisque children are usually jointed at the neck, hips and shoulders and have molded shoes and stockings, but for one 7½ in. (19.1cm) toddler she designed a body with nine joints. Some of the dolls have molded hair, but most have wigs of either mohair or sheepskin. The latter is becoming almost a trademark for her creations since she favors it for one-of-a-kind dolls. Margo dyes the skin to the color she desires, makes the wig, trims it and then curls it with a hot needle.

Illustration 2. 7 in. (17.8cm) all bisque, one-of-a-kind portrait girl. Features sculptured directly into the porcelain without the use of a mold. Jointed at neck, shoulders and hips; blue painted eyes with white high-light dots; feathered eyebrows, pierced ears, sheepskin wig, above knee black stockings with red-brown high heel shoes. Girl freely holds three little bisque dolls - each one different and each one with a sheepskin wig. Dollies left to right: 1¾ in. (4.5cm) all bisque, jointed at shoulders and hips; 2 in. (5.1cm) all bisque, jointed baby with bent limbs; 2 in. (5.1cm) bisque head baby with flange neck, painted sleep eyes. All dolls are dressed in white organdy and lace. *Photograph by Constantine Gregory.*

Illustration 3. Lady doll, 5¾ in. (14.7cm) tall with painted eyes and mohair wig. Strolls 2 in. (5.1cm) all bisque baby. *"Marthasville" Toy Museum of Atlanta. Photograph by Constantine Gregory.*

Illustration 5. 1¾ in. (4.5cm) all bisque jointed doll with her nine piece miniature wardrobe.

The small all-bisques have molded, painted eyes with the exception of the perky little googlies in their sophisticated sun-suits. They, the fashion ladies and the larger dolls have glass eyes.

Fashion ladies have porcelain heads and limbs on cloth bodies, as do the few larger sized dolls. Their outfits are made of new but completely appropriate fabrics which have been "aged" to look antique. They are fully dressed from the "skin" out.

Costuming is an area in which Margo excels. The clothes are delicately made with fine detail and an abundance of handwork. Some, such as her "Bunny Children" are whimsical, but for the most part, they are authentic.

In addition to her dolls, Mrs. Gregory uses the heads she designs for making copies of old candy containers that look right at home in an antique Christmas display. The bases are cardboard or molded forms covered with cotton batting that may

be white or colored. Glitter adds that Christmas sparkle so loved by Victorians.

Her collection of antique dolls was the inspiration in 1968 for Margo to make a doll of her own. Lack of formal art training has not deterred her, for she has the eye and hand of a highly skilled artist. Like others before her, she tried wood carving and sculpting in papier-mâché. Finding these unsatisfactory, she took courses in ceramics and china painting and gained experience making reproductions.

Illustration 4. 6 in. (15.2cm) tall baseball players with swivel heads, molded baseball caps. *"Marthasville," Toy Museum of Atlanta. Photograph by Constantine Gregory.*

Illustration 6. 7 in. (17.8cm) Bunny Children. All bisque, jointed at shoulders and hips. Blue painted eyes that glance to the side, feathered eyebrows, mohair wigs. Bunny outfits made of cotton batting. *Photograph by Constantine Gregory.*

When she discovered porcelain, Margo found the medium that appealed to her artistically. After a great deal of experimentation, she has perfected her methods of obtaining a bisque with color and texture much like that of the old dolls.

Production of her dolls is quite limited since so many are one-of-a-kind and even those for which she uses her molds are in short supply. Her newest ladies with applied bonnets of lace dipped in slip are already spoken for by the Toy Museum of Atlanta where these 6 in. (15.2cm) ladies will be displayed in an 1850s store. Collectors of artist dolls are fortunate indeed when they are able to add one of Margo Gregory's to their collections. Her dolls are incised on the back with her signature.

Illustration 8. 16 in. (15.2cm) tall priest with swivel head, painted eyes, molded mutton chops; mohair wig styled in back on head to give the appearance of being partially bald. Wears wire spectacles. *"Marthasville," Toy Museum of Atlanta. Photograph by Constantine Gregory.*

Illustration 7. 5 in. (12.7cm) all bisque googlies, jointed at shoulders and hips. Blue glass eyes; mohair "bab" wigs. Dolls wear blue organdy sun suits trimmed with lace. *Photograph by Constantine Gregory.*

Illustration 10. 5¾ in. (14.7cm) tall baby nurse, bisque shoulder head with molded hair. She holds a 2 in. (5.1cm) bisque baby in bunting. Standing at her side is 3½ in. (8.9cm) bisque boy. *"Marthasville," Toy Museum of Atlanta. Photograph by Constantine Gregory.*

Illustration 9. 7 in. - 8 in. (17.8cm - 20.3cm) candy containers with bisque heads and mohair wig. Head on right made to look like the 'laughing Heubach.' *Photograph by Constantine Gregory.*

Cecilia Rothman
San Francisco Doll Artist

BY SHIRLEY BUCHHOLZ
Photographs courtesy of Maury Rothman

NIADA artist Cecilia Rothman now works almost exclusively in porcelain to achieve her marvelous portrait dolls. As with most of our doll artists, she had worked for years in many media. It was her admiration for the beauty she found in other artists' porcelain dolls that moved her to try her hand at it in the early 1970s.

She says, "I do love it. It is a temperamental medium to work with, many disappointments and distractions with it, but well worth the trouble it may involve."

A native Californian, Cecilia Rothman has spent most of her life in San Francisco, her birthplace. Although the boarding school she attended stressed art education, she has had little other formal training. But she had, however, a heritage of art. Her father, a man who had seven degrees, was a doctor, an artist and musician. Her mother was a talented woman who encouraged Cecilia in her artistic endeavors.

While in school as a teen-ager, she was confined to bed for a time with rheumatic fever. To occupy herself during the enforced leisure, she sculpted and painted. Her mother brought her art books to read, and she says, "It was there my art education began. I really had the masters as my teachers."

For as far back as she can remember she has loved dolls and worked with them. Her first in her teen years were mostly of carved sugar pine and balsa wood. It was during this period she made her 9-1/2in. (24.2cm)

Illustration 1

"Mephistopheles" (*Illustration 1*) that took First Award/Best of Class at the

IDMA (International Doll Makers Association) Convention in 1974. There have been three porcelain copies made of this all-wood doll. In her last years of school she worked extensively with marionettes, not only making them, but also writing the scripts.

During her adult life, she has worked in many different artistic areas purely for the enjoyment of it. She sculpted, volunteered as a painting instructor at a school for the blind and designed jewelry for two firms in San Francisco. But she always went back to dolls.

From conception through completion, the dolls of Cecilia Rothman are done by her alone. She enjoys the research into the character of the person she hopes to portray in porcelain, and it is quite evident in her portrait of "John Muir in Yosemite" (*Illustration 2*) that she has captured the spirit of one of our nation's early conservationists. There is an aura of tender

Illustration 2

ness and compassion about this figure with his little water ouzel perched on his arm that never fails to move the observer. Indeed, it is the opinion of many collectors who have seen him that he is one of the finest of the so-called "Artist Dolls" or, as NIADA prefers them to be called, "People Figures."

Cecilia first exhibited her dolls at the 1974 Convention of IDMA in Reno. She took ten dolls and went home with twelve ribbons and the International Gold Cup. The latter along with two ribbons was awarded to her "Princess Lovelia" (*Illustration 3*). This doll was done from the same mold as the portrait of Cecilia's daughter.

Illustration 3

Her very first portrait doll was "Voltaire" (*Illustration 4*). She made him of papier-mâché because she had been told that it was not possible to achieve good detail with that medium and she had to try it to see if she could. She chose Voltaire because she considered him a colorful person. The results were successful. The artist was only 17 or 18 years old at the time! He also took a First Award in 1974.

A tiny lute of French inlay was the inspiration for "Nadine" (*Illustration 5*), an 18th century lute player that is only 6in. (15.2cm) tall. There are four porcelain copies of the original which was made of sculpy. "Nadine" took Second Award at IDMA's Convention in 1975. First Award went to "Rosetta-Gypsy Princess" (*Illustration 6*). The original of this popular doll is dressed in fine old silk materials, but the copies are dressed in similar modern fabrics. All accessories, including the tambourine, for this 12in. (30.5cm) porcelain doll were made by the artist.

Illustration 5

Illustration 6

Illustration 4

Illustration 8

Illustration 7

Illustration 9

like texture.

The doll as an art form has always existed. It is the artist's interpretation of life as he sees it in his own time. Cecilia Rothman's dolls tell a story. Her more recent works have been of people who espoused causes. John Muir, who with Teddy Roosevelt's (*Illustration 7*) help, fought to save Yosemite and the wilderness; Evangeline Booth (*Illustration 8*), the original Salvation Army Lassie; Sojourner Truth (*Illustration 9*), the unlettered black women who spent much of her incredible life span (1797-1883) fighting for her people; Miss Jane Pittman, another renowned black women; and most recently the Paiute "Princess" Sarah Winnemucca who in the 1880s pleaded with the populace, with the government and even with President Hayes for her people's rights (a lost cause). Sarah's costume, carefully researched and made by the artist, has over 4,000 tiny beads sewn on it. This is surely an indication that she does not spare herself in the creation of her art.

Rothman dolls and paintings have only been signed since about 1970. They were first signed on the back:

Cecilia © (date)

Since 1976 when she was invited to become a member of the National Institute of American Doll Artists or NIADA, an organization of considerable prestige, they have been signed:

Her dolls measure from 2in. to 27in. (5.1 to 68.6cm). They are made in a variety of materials and from combinations such as all-wood, all-porcelain, papier-mâché head with wood or cloth and wire armature body, porcelain or sculpy with cloth and wire armature, etc.

Cecilia Rothman's People Figures are not the kind of doll one buys at the nearest toy store. They are treasures painstakingly done by an artist to be cherished by the lucky person who owns one or more. Her production is very limited and the products are expensive. But they are well worth the wait and the money!

It was the encouragement of her husband Maury and her friends in the San Francisco Doll Club that brought Cecilia back into the world of doll making. We are indebted to them for that. Mr. Rothman says, "Some of the most beautiful people in our lives today are doll people." There are thousands who would agree with him. For me, one of those beautiful people is Cecilia.

Cecilia Rothman has carved many wooden dolls that are completely jointed. They range in size from the 10in. (25.4cm) "George and Martha Washington" to little elves of about 6in. (15.2cm). Naturally, all the woodens are one-of-a-kind, but so are many of the porcelains. For porcelains, she pours slip into a basic head mold of appropriate size and then carves the features directly in the porcelain.

Some of her dolls are capable of standing free, but she gives all of them stands unless they are seated as is "John Muir of Yosemite" (*Illustration 2*). For him, she made a mold and cast a ceramic boulder which she painted with acrylics to give it the proper rock-

Illustration 1a

Illustrations 1a & 1b. All-bisque "Happifats" have brown hair and eyes. The girl wears a pink dress with blue sash and shoes; boy wears green jacket and shoes, beige pants. *Taken from The Collector's Encyclopedia of Dolls.*

Information about the designers of dolls is somewhat scarce. Yet there would not be any dolls without the designers. They were some of the most important people in the creation of dolls. Therefore it was quite a thrill when an article written by Kate Jordan was discovered in the April 1914 issue of *Toys and Novelties*. Kate Jordan designed several dolls, probably the best known being the Happifats, those rotund little dolls generally found in all-bisque. Kate Jordan writes as someone with very definite ideas and a likeable personality. We are indeed privileged to become acquainted with her through the following article.

The lengthy title is "Kate Jordan on the Doll, Well Known Designer Writes Entertaining Tale in Which She Tells of Doll Designing and Declares Dolls Are Not Toys." This controversial title certainly piques our curiosity and we hasten to read the article written in the first person by Kate Jordan herself:

"Do we, I wonder, fully realize the importance of the doll? Do we take the doll as seriously as we should? By we, I mean grown-ups, for certainly none of the adorable one to ten-year-old mothers of my acquaintance has ever shown the slightest tendency to levity in this regard.

"There is a great deal of talk these days about returning to the primitive in playthings so that the child's imagination may have scope to develop. Perhaps the wiseacres are right if they really mean playthings, toys and such. But to class dolls as playthings—what an indignity! Let them learn to make the distinction, let them wake up to the truth that it is not development of the imagination but of the divinely im-

Illustration 1b

planted maternal instinct that is the doll's chief business.

"This being realized, what a wonderful, what a responsible task is that of the designer of dolls. How, you ask, did I find the courage to enter such a high calling? Or to get down to plain facts, how did I happen to take up doll designing? Perhaps I had best evade responsibility by answering that I didn't. It took me up, almost.

"Ten years ago when an art student—a very intermittent art student, much of my time being spent earning expenses—a certain job fell into my hands. It did not seem especially alluring in itself, being the making of prosaic little pen and ink drawings in a large importing house. So it began, and for years all the spring months were spent on little sketches of china, toys and dolls.

"Of course, the dolls interested me most, and let me say that ten years ago they were not one-fourth so inter-

esting as now. If the past decade has been one of marvelous growth and development, particularly along feminine lines, my Lady Doll has kept up nobly in the movement.

"There is nothing so far to compare with the European bisque, which we cannot imitate. Yet bisque is both heavy and brittle. Our American unbreakables are heavy, too heavy for babies' dolls and also very uncertain as to reproduction of the model. One American firm is doing creditable work in wood [Schoenhut], but how unsympathetic it is to the touch! How lacking in the precious quality of cuddlesomeness! A doll of any hard substance is such a long, long way from the ideal. A more or less yielding body is an essential to the perfect doll all designers are striving toward.

"I would almost say that we need strive no further, that perfection has been attained in Frau Kate Kruse's adorable 'toy babies,' but that their necessarily high price puts them out of general reach. And I am for the democratic spirit in dolldom as elsewhere.

"Here occurs to me a question that I have often asked myself in view of the fact that certain extremely homely character babies have had a surprising success. Is the homeliness an aid to the child's illusion of reality, or is it only the far swing of the pendulum away from Florabella of the infinitesimal mouth and preposterous eyes?

"For a while I doubted the child's preference; I thought the choice was probably of the buyers themselves pleased with novelty and that the doll mothers accepted the ugly babies and loved them just as real mothers do, but now it does not seem so certain to me that this is the case. Yet there surely is no reason why moderate homeliness should lessen the human quality. It is risky in doll designing, as in other art— yes, art, for that is what it has come to be—to make prettiness the first consideration. Insipidity is apt to result, or cold, classic regularity. But in my work I shall try to avoid either extreme, in the belief that character may exist with some degree of attractiveness."

Since both Borgfeldt and Amberg produced Happifats, it seems likely that the "large importing house" for which Kate Jordan worked was probably Borgfeldt. If this is true, the bisque dolls made from her designs were handled by Borgfeldt while Amberg may have used her designs in the production of some of their composition dolls.

An Artist in Felt...

Original Felt Dolls

R. John Wright

by SHIRLEY BUCHHOLZ

Illustration 1. 18 in. (45.7cm) gray-bearded *Seth* wears pants of felt and a shirt of cotton with handsewn button-holes. He carries a miniature copy of an old oak pitch-fork. With him is a small 8 in. (20.3cm) elf showing the Steiff influence. Uncompleted dolls in read show body construction. All dolls are signed on the left foot.

Every work of art says something about its creator, and nowhere is this more evident than in the world of dolls and their artists. In many cases the physical resemblance of a doll to the person who designed it is startling, but in all cases the doll reflects something of the artist's personality. Magge Head's dolls always seem to have a twinkle in their eyes, Lita Wilson's have her quiet beauty and those of Wee Paulson are mischievously impish.

NIADA artist R. John Wright's dolls are gentle. They are little men and women of felt who must live in some enchanted land, for they have an elfin look about them. Their eyes are bright and their smiles are sweet. Most of the men have beards or moustaches and many of the women wear kerchiefs and aprons. With their little handmade accessories they seem an industrious group indeed.

The dolls designed and made by John Wright are the product of a small cottage industry in New England. When the demand became more than he and his wife, Susan, could handle, he employed some local people to help with the sewing. Those hired had to first pass a test to meet his high standards of workmanship. The miniature accessories, oak tools, brooms and baskets, are all commissioned to be made by craftsmen who regularly produce full-sized versions of these things. Much of the work is still being done in their home by the young couple. They do all the molding of the felt, painting of the features and styling of the hair, which is of natural fibers. Of course, all of the designs for the dolls and their costumes are executed by Mr. Wright.

One always wonders what inspired an artist to make his first doll. When the question was put to John Wright he replied, "I lost my job in the hardware store." An intriguing answer!

Back in 1970 when he was about 23, John Wright and his cat left Michigan in his little car, planning to travel to California. However, he decided that the car would not make it that far and headed instead for New England. He knew no one in the East, but being an artistic and creative person, soon became friends with some of the people involved with New Hampshire's League of Craftsmen. Although the craft renaissance was just beginning across the country, New Hampshire already had a well-established craftsman organization that had built up since the depression.

These were wonderful and exciting people to the young artist. They took him and his cat in and showed him how; although it would be quite a time before he was a self-supporting artisan, it was a very possible and desirable alternative if he were willing to work and sacrifice and settle for a somewhat more modest standard of living. It also helped to have talent!

One of the artists, Gail Duggan, was earning her living making porcelain dolls and at this point, Wright had an idea that some day he too might make dolls. For the next few years his time was spent picking fruit, working on a farm, in a bakery and unloading grain for a feed store. While these efforts provided him with money to maintain himself, he knew they were preventing him from using the talents he had and from building something for himself. So, in 1976 when he was abruptly laid off from his job clerking in a hardware store, the opportunity presented itself. It was now or never. He made a doll. John Wright tells it this way:

"I must say it was one of the harder things I have ever had to do and also one of the most exhilarating. In one afternoon I made the first step in what I knew to be a long and exciting journey. This doll, by the way, was largely inspired by Steiff. I had a lot of Steiff animals as a child and a lot of

Illustration 2. Susan Wright sews a wig to a doll's head. Handmade baskets used as accessories hang in the background.

European toys. Recently I had seen some pictures of early Steiff dolls which fascinated me.

"I had bought Susan a little Singer featherweight sewing machine for Christmas the past year and I got it out. On it I sewed a crude head and body, but when it came time to sew the arms, the thread ran out and I didn't know what I was going to do because I was pretty excited about this and I wanted to finish it, but I had no idea how to thread the darn machine! So, I sewed the rest by hand. I put button eyes on it and I stuffed it with some sheep's wool that Susan had around for spinning. It did not have any legs. It seems now like a small thing to get so excited over, but not only had I never made a doll before, I had never sewn anything before and I was impressed by how easy it seemed to come. I kept thinking about how the second one could be even while I was making the first one. How it could be a little better. Perhaps I could do something different. It all seemed to hold so much potential.

"I wrapped the doll hurriedly in a blanket and I went out to meet Susan who had no idea I was doing this. She greeted it with an equal amount of unfounded enthusiasm. We both knew something big was happening. The very next day I went to Dartmouth College in Hanover because I remembered a large selection of doll books in the library and one picture in particular of some cloth hillbilly dolls by a Grace Lathrop. (It wasn't until much later that I found out more about this talented NIADA artist.)

"I was greatly inspired by these early cloth dolls that she made and I made a similar type doll with jointed arms, sewn knees, button eyes and wool hair made from an old piece of yellow flannel. He looked like he must have lived under a rock, but he was a complete doll. He had legs and I learned a little more about the sewing machine although I still didn't know it went in reverse.

"When I went to buy cloth to make a third doll I wasn't sure whether I was going to use cloth or felt. I did have an idea that the latter would be cuddly and nice for a doll so when the store had only felt in what would be a skin color, I bought it instead of calico or cotton. I guess that's how I started using felt for all my dolls.

"This time I made a doll out of flesh colored felt and gave him an ill-fitting shirt and pants and suspenders. In the next few days I made six variations of this first man. Curiously enough, they were all men at first.

"Neither Susan nor I could stop looking at those dolls! We were so proud and excited. We looked at them over our breakfast, we looked at them over lunch. We thought they were great. Susan was supportive of me at this time in more ways than one! I took these six dolls down to the local craft store here in Brattleboro and was very flattered when they took them on the spot. You could imagine how excited I was when on the way home a friend drove by and shouted that he had seen the dolls at the shop and while he was there one had been sold to an out-of-state customer. This was before I had even got home! To have sold meant a lot to me. A reorder was soon in the mailbox and I was on my way. All this happened within a few days of having been a clerk at a store."

The next six months was a learning period for the young artist. He looked for ways to improve his dolls structurally and for more efficient methods of production. It was time-consuming to trace all the patterns on the felt, so he printed them on. He later discovered that with a hydraulic press and custom dyes he could do even better. During this period he made and sold over 100 of these early creations.

Finding ways to improve upon the design of the dolls proved to be an around-the-clock project for John and Susan Wright. They consulted all the books they could find, wrote hundreds of letters and talked with anyone they could who might be of some help with the problems they encountered. The toy industry is notoriously secretive and many of the processes and techniques have gone to the grave with their originators. Most of what Wright learned, he did on his own.

John discovered that in England teddy bears were still being made with rotating joints and since this was what he wanted for his dolls, he sent for some to study. He found that he could make these joints himself and was able to use them in a way that was efficient and effective, two of the most important requirements for the manufacture of his dolls.

It was not until Jean Schramm of the Enchanted Dollhouse in Manchester, Vermont, showed him her collection of Lencis that John Wright realized that felt could be molded. But how?

It was a challenge met with hard work, the use of the kitchen oven and waffle iron and anything else that looked promising. He even took dolls to the hospital to be x-rayed! Wright felt that everything he put into the search at this time was an investment in the future. He said that he and Susan knew at the time that this was going to be going on for many, many years.

He had the right to be optimistic. He had taken some of his first molded felt dolls to a large wholesale buyer and within just a few hours was

Illustration 3. R. John Wright in the workroom with some of his creations.

Illustration 4. 18 in. (45.7cm) *Guido* and *Elsa*. The dolls are constructed to stand well alone.

booked up for a full year, quite an overwhelming response to an artist who had only made his first doll a brief two years before.

The faces of Wright dolls are first sculpted in clay from which plaster and then metal molds are made. These are coated with teflon for easy release. The old makers had to use oiled paper. In the pressing process, the felt is not only bonded to buckram, it is treated with a special clear sizing for added strength and to make a smoother surface upon which to paint the features.

The sewn bodies are stuffed with kapok and cotton and the wigs are stitched directly onto the doll's scalp. Upon completion the dolls are signed, dated, numbered and dressed. Besides the cardboard tag on the wrist there is a signature "Wright" on the bottom of the left foot. Then

the dolls, properly costumed and with their accessories are shipped to several exclusive shops, one as far as Hawaii, and to mail order customers.

His own words tell a lot about this young man and the dolls he makes. Listen.

"I believe that part of the success of my dolls was a certain longing in people for a doll or toy made with a lot of personal care and ingenuity like they used to make things. Most of my sales are not to doll collectors, but rather to ordinary people who perhaps, since they were children themselves, have not seen a doll they wanted to own. This awakening in people is beautiful to behold and produced a great deal of enjoyment to me and Susan. I see it as a bonus.

"The first reason I make dolls is to satisfy my own longing for some-

thing like this in the world, thereby making my vision a reality. To me it is a challenge to make such a doll well, that is, a doll that emits a certain message and is flawless technically. But it is even more of a challenge to make it efficiently and in sufficient quantity to get an income and to supply the demand.

"I have no desire to sell designs to some other company so that they can produce them wrongly. Most companies would not be very interested in making a doll this way. They would probably want to make it out of vinyl. There is something about the old ways that really appeals to me and I think it says something for the appeal of the doll.

"I knew early on that only I could produce them this way. I really admire the old companies, Steiff, Kathe Kruse and Lenci who produced a playworthy product artistically and in quantity. This is no easy task and I still have much to learn to reach this goal. But it is true that every doll that I make is more artistic and more sturdy than the last one. Whether they are ever played with or not, it is very important that the dolls retain a certain toy quality as opposed to a figurine or purely representational aspect. Movability plays a big part in this toy quality. And also sturdiness. Although I admire the ornamental and more adult qualities in some of the artist dolls, toys are my first love and I want the dolls to really be like toys."

John Wright says he thinks that everyone has an obsession and his is dolls. We collectors would tend to nod our heads in agreement and thank that unknowing gentleman in the hardware store who started this talented young artist on his way to success.

R. John Wright dolls are extremely well constructed of felt. Their heads swivel and their arms and legs move realistically and well. The fingers are beautifully stitched and stuffed to give the appearance of separate digits. Toes are delineated by stitching. The wigs and facial hair of the men are well made and very appropriate. The clothing is of excellent quality that fits well and is fastidiously constructed. It is also completely removable, being fastened with small gripper-type closures and, would you believe, hand-sewn buttonholes? The shoes, boots and the like are made with the same care that goes into the perfectly scaled model tools. These dolls can stand proudly beside any of their antecedents.

John Wright was elected to NIADA (National Institute of American Doll Artists) in September 1979.

The Marcy Street Doll Company

by Carol-Lynn Waugh

Illustration 1. This hand-carved sign depicting Molly the doll hangs over the doorway of the Marcy Street Doll Company in Portsmouth, New Hampshire.

Illustration 2. "Karen" is 15in. (38.1cm).

Near the waterfront, Marcy Street snakes its way through Portsmouth, New Hampshire's historic "Strawbery Banke" district. It attracts thousands of admirers each year who come to enjoy the 18th century atmosphere and browse through the many quaint shops. Hand-carved signs abound, and among the nicest of these is the one that hangs over the Marcy Street Doll Company. Reminiscent of the figureheads that once adorned the clipper ships in the adjacent harbor, it depicts Molly, one of the unique creations of Debby Anderson and Ann Stevens. I have a special affection for that sign, for, you see, I own Molly.

But my story is not so much about Molly as it is about her creators, Debby and Ann, the two talented cousins who specialize in marvelous one-of-a-kind felt dolls.

Debby Anderson, a pert blond, is the sculptor of the team. A tomboy in her youth, dolls held little interest for her until she received her cousin's gift, Catherine Christopher's *Doll Making and Collecting* some eight years ago. Reading this book made Debby realize that dollmaking would allow her to combine her talents as seamstress and oil painter, so she began to experiment in modifying commercial patterns. Admiring friends created such a fuss over the resulting dolls that Debby quickly decided to move into original designs.

By trial and error, over the years, she developed a technique for making jointed, pressed-faced dolls of felt. Each is completely hand-done and ranges in height from 11in. to 18in. (27.9cm to 45.7cm). First, faces are molded over doll heads which Debby sculpted of self-hardening clay. Then the faces are painted. This is a most critical procedure, for it is here that the doll gets its personality. The heavy felt is difficult to paint upon; it smudges and dirties easily, and there is the additional frustration of expressions which do not seem to work. But if everything goes well, the doll is fitted with a wig of French human hair. A character is decided upon, and Ann begins her work of designing the clothes.

Ann Stevens, an efficient brunette, has always liked dolls but, unlike Debby, her interest is in costume design. She has been making doll clothes for years. As Debby puts it: "When we look at a group of dolls, I look at their faces; Ann sees their clothes. Together we get a good idea of the doll as a whole."

Ann's greatest interest is classic children's clothing, but occasionally she modifies contemporary full-sized garment styles to fit a doll's personality. Dresses, slacks, sweaters, hats and shoes all show signs of the delightful creativeness which began when, as a child, Ann invented wardrobes for the paper dolls her mother made.

Indeed, paper dolls still remain an important interest today. For, by herself, Ann has developed a line of paper dolls which are poster-size interpretations of classic fairy tale characters such as Red Riding Hood, Snow White and Goldilocks and the Three Bears. These are full-color reproductions of her watercolor paintings.

Both facets of a felt doll's construction progress simultaneously and the team averages about one completion a week. Perhaps the only reason the Marcy Street Doll Company is not more famous is that it has only finished 90 dolls since its inception in April, 1978. Debby and Ann seem to think of their creations as real personalities, as well they might. All are delightful, but with each doll the artists' styles evolve a bit so that the current dolls are more sophisticated than earlier ones like Molly. For example, a recent innovation enables the heads to swivel back and forth.

A family album contains a photograph of each doll and even without consulting their records both women can rattle off the location and well-being of most of their creations.

At first these engaging toddlers and children remind the observer of Lenci dolls, but on closer inspection, one finds little similarity between them other than that of materials. Lencis, although designed by a woman artist, were mass-produced, Italian, and, with some exceptions, rather similar in expression. Marcy Street dolls are unique, with different names and personalities and very American. They possess an extremely appealing aesthetic quality. When seen in person, it is quite clear each is a work of art. And in years to come, it is also quite clear that Debby and Ann's dolls will be highly valued by discriminating doll collectors.

Illustration 4. "Molly", an early Marcy Street Doll.

Illustration 3. "Heidi" is 14in. (35.6cm).

Illustration 6. "Daniel" is 17 in. (43.2cm).

Illustration 5. "Heidi & Fritz" are 14in. (35.6cm).

Baby Bridget.

The Elizabeth Barter Cloth Doll

BY ELIZABETH BARTER
Member of NIADA

The methods and materials that are used in making the Elizabeth Barter doll are varied, drawing from techniques that are associated with both cloth and modeled dolls. The method comes primarily from a cloth-doll making tradition, in that the fabric provides a base upon which more refined modeling, carving and sculpting techniques are used. The completed faces have a texture and appearance that are not unlike bisque in some respects. They have detailed three-dimensional features and a smooth matte finish. When bisque dolls are made, the artist begins by sculpting a clay head from which a mold will be manufactured. Such molds will be used to produce a series of similar heads. The faces of the Barter Dolls are individually sculpted, but no mold is made from the final product. Each doll is completely unique.

Due to the large time commitment that is involved in attaining the desired combination of facial expression, body construction and costuming, the process of making these dolls becomes a very personalized effort.

Although it may not be possible to describe the efforts that are involved in creating dolls of this type, it is possible to outline the procedures and materials involved.

The entire doll is made from muslin that is tinted flesh color. The head is cut from three pattern pieces: two side pieces and a center piece. After these three pieces are sewn together, the head is firmly stuffed with polyester fiber. The manner in which the head is stuffed will determine the general shape of the face and head. If a model or a photograph is being used, this is the time to refer to it, as the accurate reproduction of the shape of the head and face can be a strong factor in achieving a good resemblance. When the shape of the head is satisfac-

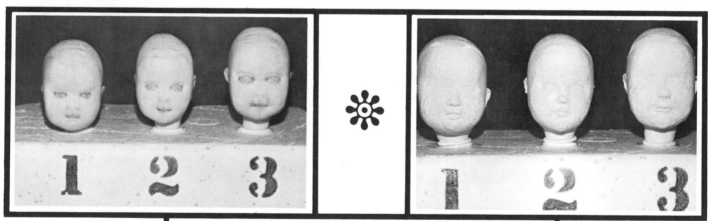

Heads are stuffed, features sketched in.

Features are built up with modeling material.

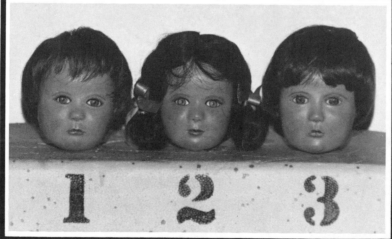

Faces are finished, hair attached.

tory, the face is sectioned off and the features are sketched in with pencil.

The placement of the features on the face will show the approximate age of the child that the doll represents. For a young child, the features are placed on the lower half of the face. The distance between the eyes should be the same as the width of the eye itself. The nose, mouth and chin should be approximately the same width. The ears are placed at the upper end of the jaw with the top of the ear in line with the eyebrow and the bottom of the ear in line with the tip of the nose.

The face and neck are then sealed with gesso to assure proper adhesion of the acrylic modeling material.

With a painting knife, and using the modeling material, the individual features are built up. The forehead and cheeks are rounded out and the eyes, nose, mouth and chin are modeled.

A great deal of time must then be spent shaping and sanding the facial features. When the resemblance is good, and the face is perfectly smooth, it is ready to be painted.

Baby has short neck, bent arms and legs, closed hands.

Slender bodies, moveable arms and legs.

Several coats of flesh colored paint are applied to the surface of the face and neck. The eyes, eyebrows and eye-lashes, cheeks and mouth are painted, and a coat of matte finish is applied to seal the face. The eyes and mouth are finished in gloss.

Applying just the right hair style is important. This may be done in three ways. The hair may be rooted directly into the head, a properly styled wig may be applied or a combination of the two may be used.

The body of the doll is constructed from four pattern pieces that are sewn together and firmly stuffed with polyester. The arms and legs are moveable and are attached by an elastic cord that runs through the body. The head is attached by neck rings and may be turned to any position.

Doll number 1, Baby Bridget, is 15 in. (38.1cm) long. She has dark blond hair and grey-blue eyes. The baby has a short neck, bent arms and legs and closed hands which are typical characteristics of a baby.

She is wearing white knit underwear and stockings and white kid slippers. Her petticoat is peach, trimmed with tucks and lace. Her cream colored dress has a hand-tucked bodice and long puffed sleeves. The skirt is trimmed with tucks, lace and ribbon. The bonnet matches the dress and is lined in peach. It is trimmed with a lace ruffle and peach colored ribbon. She is also wearing a hand-embroidered bib which ties at the back.

Doll number 2, Nora, is 16 in. (40.6cm) tall. She has bright blue eyes and dark brown hair. Her hair is braided and looped over her ears with pink ribbons. She is wearing white underwear and petticoat, both trimmed with tucks and lace. Her stockings are pink cotton and her brown leather shoes have ankle lacings. The dress has a white organdy bodice with double puffed sleeves. The skirt is

Remi and Nora.

raspberry colored linen with brown linen trim and an attached sheer apron. She is also wearing a brown velvet vest that is hand-embroidered.

Doll number 3, Remi, is 17 in. (43.2cm) tall. He has green eyes and strawberry blond hair. He is wearing tan ribbed underwear, green and white striped stockings and green leather shoes. His pants are tan wool felt with a green leather waist band that buttons onto a green checked vest. His jacket is rust velvet with beige lining. His hat is tan wool trimmed with a green leather band and green and tan feathers. He is carrying a brown and tan woven basket.

Many of the Barter dolls are interpretations of old photographs of children. The dolls and costumes, including leather shoes, hats, toys and other accessories, are original and made by the artist. Due to the small, sometimes minute scale of the clothing and accessories, much hand work is involved in their creation. The clothing is often embellished with hand embroidery and trimmed with antique lace. Antique trim and accessories are always sought and provide attractive and authentic additions to the costuming. The dolls are signed, dated and have the NIADA label on their backs.

The characteristic which most obviously distinguishes Barter dolls from others is the uniqueness in design and construction of the facial expression. The process described here allows the doll maker an unusual degree of flexibility in the rendering of facial features which cannot be achieved through other methods of cloth doll construction. The resulting product has a strongly defined three-dimensional face which is perhaps responsible for the individuality and the popularity of these dolls.

The Becketts New Doll Artists

by JEANNE NISWONGER

ABOVE: Illustration 1. June Beckett holding *Toodles*. From left: *Joey, Jill,* "Bob's Boy," *Debbie* and *Pouty Patty.* Above are teddy bears and *Bitsie.*

LEFT: Illustration 2. June Beckett carving doll from wood block.

"Two heads are better than one" so the old saying goes and this certainly is true in the doll world of June and Bob Beckett, who together are creating some very unique and distinctive hand-carved wooden dolls that will be of special interest to discriminating collectors. While many husbands often encourage their doll artist wife in the creating of original dolls, Bob actually is co-partner with June in producing BECKETT ORIGINALS. These dolls are made of white or sugar pine or other types of wood as available and the features are painted with oil-based colors and finished with a lacquer spray. Some dolls have wigs and others have sculpted or painted-on styles which tend to give the dolls their own individual personality. All designs are originals with the Becketts, not only the doll itself but clothes and body patterns. Every doll is signed and dated by the artists and each outfit is tagged with the BECKETT ORIGINAL label. Most are limited editions and numbered. Sometimes only 20 dolls are made in the series.

How did the couple get started on this interesting hobby turned business? Well, June has been a long time lover of dolls and started collecting a number of years ago when a friend gave her some antique dolls. Then, over the years, she added to her collection which eventually included some very old wooden dolls. Always interested in making dolls, June first made rag dolls, but she found that she could not get the exact expressions she wanted on the faces of the cloth dolls. Bob has always been handy at woodworking and it was while building a garage at their home that June picked up a

Illustration 3. 12in (30.5cm) *Pouty Patty* and 12in (30.5cm) *Happy Hal.*

Illustration 4. "Bob's Boys" and playthings.

Illustration 5. From left: *Timothy* (holding a teddy bear), *Gregory, Bitsie, Debbie, Toodles, Joey* and *Jill.*

small block of wood that had fallen from Bob's lathe and got the idea of carving a small doll. After experimentation in carving her first wooden doll, June came up with one that pleased her and began carving more.

Bob always cut out the 'blanks' for her. These roughed-out forms have only the location of ears and nose marked. Using razor sharp tools, she chips away and slices out little wedges to make the doll's ears stand out. The wood allows her to get the precise expression she wants on each doll's face. Little button noses and fat cheeks are characteristic of the Beckett creations.

The Becketts' workshop is located on their lovely ranch home outside of Paso Robles, which is located about half way between San Francisco and Los Angeles, California. The couple has raised a family, have one grandchild now and a high school aged daughter still at home. They have an interest in photography and often take pictures of children that later may form the basis of the face of a new doll.

Such is the case of *Pouty Baby,* the doll that appears to be about to burst into tears. She is 12in (30.5cm) tall, has a dynel baby wig on her carved head, cloth bent-leg baby body with porcelain hands. She wears a short baby dress and matching panties, long stockings and felt shoes. A twin to her that June is working on now is *Happy Hal* who will be the exact opposite. *Hal* has a grin, dimples, a baby wig and cloth body with wooden hands and sports a pair of overalls and pin dotted shirt with felt shoes.

One of June's favorite dolls is a Kewpie type called *Toodles* which is just 6in (15.2cm) tall and dressed in pajamas and holding a tiny teddy bear which June also makes. This is probably her best known doll and she has made over 250 heads for this model. She has improved each one as she went along and declares that she has no formal artistic background or training for this work; she just loves doing it!

Besides providing the basic block forms for the dolls, Bob also tries his hand at carving and has come up with his own original creations appropriately called BOB'S BOYS. His special dolls are 12in (30.5cm) brothers named *Gregory* and *Timothy. Gregory* has a typical little boy grin, painted-on hair, cloth body and limbs and is attired in overall and shirt with hand-made felt shoes. *Timothy* is very similar but has carved hair. Together June and Bob make 8in (20.3cm) *Jill* and *Joey,* a little girl and her brother. Bob makes the bodies and legs and June does the arms and heads. These were the very first dolls they produced and were inspired by the Vogue 8in (20.3cm) doll, *Ginny.* Their arms are peg jointed at the shoulder, the hips and neck are not jointed. They have fat little fannies and tummies. *Jill* has a short cotton dress with matching panties, shoes and socks and *Joey*'s outfit matches and

consists of a jumpsuit.

Still another doll is 12in (30.5cm) *Debbie,* a precious toddler with a cherubic baby face, dynel wig, brown eyes and a polyester-filled cloth body and limbs. She is attired in a two-piece topper and pants outfit and has felt shoes. Then, there is another baby doll, tiny 6in (15.2cm) *Bitsie.* Her carved baby head has colored-on curls and she has a soft stuffed body and legs. She wears a long baby dress and bonnet, socks and diapers. While the original had blue eyes, the Becketts now offer her in six different variations such as Indian, Oriental, black, asleep and awake. It is interesting to note that for the darker skinned dolls, the couple uses redwood.

June's teddy bears are very popular among collectors. They are completely handmade of felt and are jointed at the hips and shoulders and come firmly stuffed. There is a tiny 2in (5.1cm) on and also 3in (7.6cm) and 5in (12.7cm) sizes. There is even a choice of colors such as brown, pink, yellow, gold, white, blue and red.

Susanna Oroyan, "Daumier of Dolls"

BY CAROL-LYNN ROSSEL WAUGH

The dolls Susanna Oroyan creates are like a ham sandwich on rye in a world of Wonder Bread. They are not for everyone, but they have a distinctive pungency and tang which is very appealing to those who can appreciate it. However, they are an acquired taste.

For those who expect a doll to be docile and pretty and merely stare back at the viewer with a vacuous smile, Oroyan dolls have no charm. These small-scale people have vitality and spunk and carry a message which is at times sardonic and outrageous. Each doll delivers a silent commentary on some aspect of the human condition. The ODACA artist explains: "I'm trying to express human beings: their earthiness, vanity, bravado, pride, innocence, vulgarity. I make PEOPLE--real or ideal."

A modern-day Daumier of dolls, the Oregon native strives to capture and embody the foibles and fantasies of mankind in her work. Her subjects range from the mundane--a frumpy housewife in tattered housecoat and curlers, aptly titled, "The Lady of the House" (most of her dolls are titled), to the sublime--elegant Shakespearean characters or idealized princesses astride unicorns. Their very diversity is amazing. Fashion ladies, hippies, elves, Santas, Dickensian characters, frumps, tarts, knights in armor and fairies all come to life under the artist's talented fingers.

The talented doll designer, who has made dolls since the age of nine, is self-taught and has experimented with many media during her doll making career. Currently she employs polyform (a type of low-fire synthetic clay) and fabric. She likes the different effects that each medium affords. "I can do different things with them. I can be "loose" working with fabric--ultra creative--and graphic sculpting."

This flexibility of medium enables the doll maker to give extraordinary personalities to her brainchildren. Her polyform characters often have exaggerated features and poses which convey the essence of their personas, in the time honored tradition of theatrical puppets such as Punch and Judy, but with a modern, more deft, subtle, and, at times, ironic touch.

Cloth in the hands of Susanna Oroyan is an apt vehicle for her wry sense of humor. Exaggeration and wit are the strong suit of her satires in fabric, which range in size from less than one foot (30.5cm) tall to over life-size. Size and scale are at times intentionally distorted, as they are in political cartoons, to shock the viewer into looking at her work, at what it has to say to him/her.

Both types of dolls have the same basic body construction, a padded wire armature. This enables them to be positioned by Susanna in attitudes relevant to the character being depicted. The pose of the doll is very important, and Mrs. Oroyan designs each doll as a whole to be an aesthetic object, like a piece of sculpture, to be viewed in one way only. In the same way, clothing in sewn directly to the body, for it is intrinsic to the interpretation of the personality being created. Oroyan dolls are not play dolls to be undressed.

Each of the Oregon artist's dolls shows well her personal creative approach to doll making. Fabrics, wire, clay, cloth and "found objects" are combined sculpturally with such insight and cleverness that the final result seems inevitable, belying the long painstaking hours of research, planning and execution that underlie it.

Titania

Miss Piggy

Santa

236

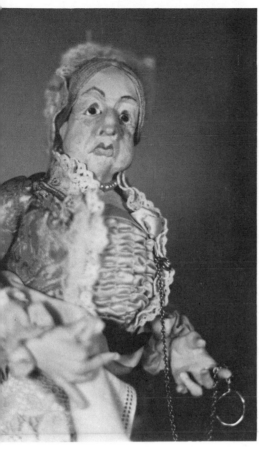

These dolls have won numerous blue ribbons and awards at national doll conventions in the last six years. Always controversial and outstanding, they have more than once caused judges to blush or to argue against their very acceptability for entry into competitive judging. When asked if this intensity of feeling on the part of the doll establishment bothered her, the artist replied: "I really don't care what the public or doll collectors think. The important things are that a) I like what I did and b) the person who buys it likes **IT** and not the "idea of a collectible worth money." Fortunately, my stuff is enough strange that when someone buys one I know he really likes the doll **ITSELF**, for what **IT** is as an expression of an idea."

All Oroyan Originals are necessarily one-of-a-kind, and each has a vivacity and presence rare in the world of dolls. They are designed to interact with the space around them. They demand liebenstraum--living space--and refuse to be lined up on a shelf with their tamer kindred. Unique and controversial, they are impudent enough to elicit emotions from spectators--far from accepted doll behaviour. People either love them or hate them, and to the petite doll artist, that is fine. She knows that not everyone goes through life on a diet of Wonder Bread.

Aunt Sophia

H. Mellowfellow, purveyor of Hip Hats and Cool Caps with his creator Susanna Oroyan.

Diamonds and Dolls

by MARGARET WHITTON
Curator of Dolls,
Margaret Woodbury Strong Museum
Photographs by BARBARA JENDRICK

Illustration 1. Portrait doll of Princess Elizabeth (now Queen) of England in her wedding gown by Dorothy Heizer.

Illustration 2. Close-up of the *Princess Elizabeth* doll by Dorothy Heizer.

Bride dolls through many generations have been very popular with both little girls and big girls alike.

In the doll collection at the Margaret Woodbury Strong Museum, there is a portrait doll, made in 1948 of Queen Elizabeth of England in the gown she wore for her wedding to Prince Phillip on November 20, 1947. The doll and costume were designed and created by the late Dorothy Heizer of Chatham, New Jersey. With meticulous care Mrs. Heizer achieved a remarkable likeness of Elizabeth. She created a miniature of the original bridal gown of white satin and a long mouseline train, both embroidered in a beaded design copied painstakingly from photographs of the original gown. The design was made up of approximately 45,000 tiny seed pearls, rhinestones and pearl-colored beads. A tulle veil with jeweled crown and a bouquet of three varieties of orchids completed the ensemble.

The doll was sold by Mrs. Heizer to the late Mary E. Lewis, first president of the United Federation of Doll Clubs. Mrs. Lewis built up a large collection of bride dolls which she took with her on speaking engagements, lecturing on doll collecting, bridal traditions and costumes. Many of the dolls had real jewelry created for them but the finest of all was the diamond engagement ring made for this *Princess Elizabeth* doll in 1951.

This ring is one of the well-known Artcarved diamond rings and was made by them at Mrs. Lewis's request. A letter from the company to Mrs. Lewis reads as follows:

Illustration 4. Close-up of the detail work on the dress worn by the *Princess Elizabeth* doll.

Artcarved
diamond and wedding rings
J.R. WOOD & SONS, Inc.
216 EAST 45th STREET, NEW YORK 17, N.Y.
W. WATERS SCHWAB, *President*

February 28, 1951
of our 101st year

Mrs. Mary E. Lewis,
798 Ocean Parkway
Brooklyn, 30, N.Y.

"Dear Mrs. Lewis:
I hope you like the engagement ring we created for your Princess Elizabeth doll.
Am sure you will be interested to learn that this ring is the smallest engagement ring we have ever made in our one hundred and one years of ring making, and I am confident that it is the smallest ring ever made by any one.
We are very happy to have had the opportunity to make this ring for you."
Cordially yours,
W. Waters Schwab

To complete the story, the Strong Museum has had the ring appraised and authenticated by Mr. William Scheer of the E. J. Scheer Inc. jewelers of Rochester, New York. It is a 14K yellow gold, six-prong engagement ring containing one full-cut diamond weighing approximately .11 carats.

The *Princess Elizabeth* doll was purchased by Mrs. Strong after the death of Mary Lewis and holds a prominent spot in the museum's large collection of some 25,000 dolls.

Illustration 3. Close-up of the diamond ring specially made for the *Princess Elizabeth* doll.

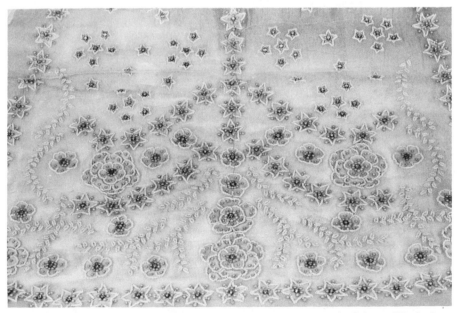

Illustration 5. Close-up of the detail work on the dress worn by the *Princess Elizabeth* doll.

Rose Sullo & Her "People Figures"

BY DEE RABEY

Hobo King

President Nixon Meeting Chairman Mao, 1972.

The Prospector

When was the last time you recall seeing a man with an organ grinder and monkey, complete with hurdy-gurdy music for everyone's entertainment?

The past comes alive with the artistic talent of Rose Sullo who recreates bygone memories. Her "people figures," "works of art," "portraits in miniature" or dolls (whichever you prefer to call them) are certainly creations depicting the historical past. These "people figures" represent life in the streets of New York from a few years ago: musicians, the butcher, the gardener, blacksmith and immigrants from Italy, Ireland and Germany. Rose gives the "people figures" a breath of life when she creates and makes-one-of-a-kind dolls.

While attending the famous art and engineering institute, Cooper Union in New York City, Rose created her first dolls.

Rose searches through magazines, newspapers and books selecting photographs that show fine details of face, arms and legs for her 12 in. (30.5cm) portrait dolls. Occasionally members of her family lend a helping hand in the research or in photographing the completed figure.

Self-hardening clay is used for her "people figures." The clay must be kept wet as she sculpts the head, hands and legs, molding the shoes onto the feet. Some figures have glass eyes and

they must be inserted while the clay is wet and the eyelids are sculpted around them. Any accessories befitting the character of the figure are wired to the hands with very fine copper wire.

When Rose first began using self-hardening clay, after the sculpting and waiting for the model to dry, she would find cracks in the figure. This created a real problem until she realized that it happened because the clay was drying too fast. The figure shrunk but the armature didn't - hence the cracks. The clay must be systematically exposed to the air to avoid cracks. Rose regulates the drying process with plastic bags, allowing the model to dry slowly; thus she has control of the drying from the inside to the outside.

As soon as the clay parts are thoroughly dried, they must be sanded and smoothed. Rose uses oil paints for the features which take about a week to dry. The wire armature figure is then wrapped with cotton knit strips to create the desired shape, attached to a wooden base and dressed.

Rose dresses the dolls making sure any prints and stripes are to the scale of the figure. Garments for the upper half of the figure are hand sewn and slipped on. However, any garments for the lower half are fitted and hand sewn onto the armature with meticulous care due to the immovable base. She knits sweaters and scarfs using mending yarn to keep the accessories in proper perspective and complete the ensemble.

Each doll takes about one month from the starting point of clay sculpting to the fitting of the clothes. Rose marks her figures with her name and the year incised on the back of the head.

In 1972 Rose created "people figures" of the "Journey for Peace" commemorating President Richard Nixon's visit with Chairman Mao of the Republic of China. The figures were presented to President Nixon and Rose received a personal letter of acknowledgement of the gift.

Rose exhibits dolls to aid charitable organizations, lectures and presents slide programs for social and civic groups. During one of her exhibits, she was displaying her "Mudgutter Band" consisting of a tuba, cornet and trombone player inspired by sidewalk concerts given by musicians Rose had witnessed as a little girl in New York. The tuba player was a short, fat man with blown out cheeks playing his tuba. Suddenly his duplicate appeared in front of the table, laughing excitedly. He called to his wife and daughter, "Come here, come here, see your papa!" in a slightly German accent. He had been a tuba player and played in just such a street band. It was as if Rose had used him for the model - she could hardly believe her eyes.

Singing Waiters

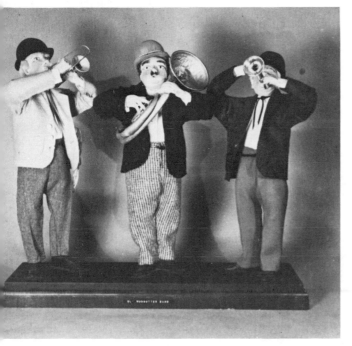

Mudgutter Band

Rose Sullo became a member of the National Institute of American Doll Artists (NIADA) in 1970.

An artist uses skill and imagination to create an object of beauty which demonstrates taste and ingenuity. Sculptress Rose Sullo has shown the world her "people figures" reflecting her special love of people as she sculpts and paints each. You would be wise to watch for future creations by Rose which will be a special reminiscence of bygone days.

"Faith Wick"

by HELEN BULLARD

Violently alive, people-oriented, Faith Wick turns out a volume of work which is staggering. Sixteen different designs for one producer; 130 designs for another; 12 for a third; a whole growing flock of designs for the fourth and a mere four for a leading doll manufacturer.

How does she keep up with all of this? How does she sit at her table at an exhibition and model a new face while she talks to a stream of visitors? Who knows?

Illustration 1. Clown.

Besides boundless energy and a husband who does the hard work of keeping tract of the business, there is her receptive public. Surely that is a pallid understatement – her public has to be wildly enthusiastic or she would be snowed under with unsold pretties, and she is not.

When she needed a higher degree to qualify for a teaching job she wanted, her husband Mel agreed to move the whole family to Minneapolis, Minnesota, to an empty house to which they brought almost no equipment. The baby slept in his carriage, the second child in the bathtub, and the other two in sleeping bags. The parents, also. They continued to live with a minimum of equipment and Faith got her Masters Degree.

As soon as her new job was going smoothly, Faith and Mel bought a run-down Theme Park nearby which featured large cement figures and animals in parlous condition. So Faith turned to sculpturing replacements, unaware that she was readying herself for creating dolls.

They have sold the Theme Park and now live in an 18-room house with three pianos.

Born in Minnesota's Iron Mining Range to a doctor and a nurse, Faith saw many workers from foreign countries and read many books of fantasy and romance. At present she spends much of her time looking after her various producers and traveling about the country making appearances in stores and merchandise markets. She also teaches private classes in sculpture around the country.

Her catalog of manufactured designs at the moment is as follows:

1977. Dolls manufactured in porcelain by Doll-lain Company, Melar, Illinois. Still being made. FATHER CHRISTMAS and 16 other characters; made in limited editions, some, 100 copies; others, 300 copies. $300-1,500. Marked: " ©1977//Faith Wick". CHRISTMAS GROUP: Limited Editions of 100 each. *Father Christmas,* 20in (50.8cm); *Eve,* 12in (30.5cm); *Advent,* 10in (25.4cm); *Epiphany,* 7in (17.8cm). "THE FANCIES" Using variations of one face. Limit: 300 copies of each; all 14in (35.6cm) tall. The figures are: clown, baseball player (black), newsboy, frontier girl, skier and sailor. Also grandpa and grandma in swing, 18in (45.7cm); and Pierrot clown, 20in (50.8cm) (100 only).

1978. Dolls reproduced in a Grand Rapids, Minnesota, cottage industry. Porcelain; usually limited to editions of 100; sold through representatives in major merchandise markets and

Illustration 2. 16in (40.6cm) *Anchors Aweigh* and *Party Time,* Faith Wick dolls for Effanbee.

242

Illustration 3. 15in (38.1cm) *Maid of 1776,* a Wicket Original. *Photograph by Lorena Dureau.*

Illustration 4. 19in (48.3cm) *Young Gerald Ford,* a Wicket Original. *Photograph by Lorena Dureau.*

fine stores. Marked: " ©1978// Faith Wick". ONE HUNDRED THIRTY DIFFERENT CHARACTERS: historical, storybook, and the like. UNSEEN PEOPLE: witches, fairies, goblins, gnomes, elves, brownies; 16-32in (40.6-81.3cm). $500-800 each. CLOWNS: Pierrot, mimes, traditional; 11-25in (27.9-63.5cm). $300-600 each. CHILDREN: Many races; character faces; 12-25in (30.5-63.5cm). $400-600 each. LITERARY FIGURES: Dickens, Biblical, nursery rhyme, fairy tale; 15-25in (38.1-63.5cm). $400-800 each. HISTORICAL FIGURES: American and English; 15-25in (38.1-63.5cm). $400-800 each. PORTRAITS: Stars of stage and screen, musicians, authors, and so on; 18-25in (45.7-63.5cm). $500-1,000 each. CHRISTMAS: Santa, elves, and so on; 9-30in (22.9-76.2cm). $150-750 each. MINIATURES of a variety of subjects. 1in (2.5cm) to 12in (30.5cm). $100-300 each. These dolls are handled by a national sales organization: Davis-Grabowski of Miami.

Meet and talk with FAITH WICK

Wicket Dolls Grand Rapids, Mn.

Illustration 5. Faith Wick and some of her creations.

243

Illustration 6. 16in (40.6cm) Gnina, a Wicket Original. *Photograph by Lorena Dureau.*

1979. SMALL CHRISTMAS TREE ORNAMENTS of people and animal figures; 5in (12.7cm). Twelve different subjects. Porcelain. Made by Silvestri Art Company of Chicago under a royalty agreement. Fabrication in the Orient. Unlimited quantities; no markings.

1980. DOLLS, JEWELRY, FIGURINES, TABLE TOP. Porcelain. Made by Schmid, Boston, under a royalty agreement. Fabrication in Europe. Limited editions. Incised markings or hang tags.

In July 1980, Faith Wick sold one of each of her designs plus several NIADA dolls from her collection for $100,000.

Jeseco Character Dolls

BY JOHN AXE

Illustration 1. Michael and Sadie O'Neill.

Michael O'Neill of Blackpool, England is an artist in the truest sense. Better than that, he is a true doll artist. The limited edition character dolls created by Mr. O'Neill are original works of art. They are not copies or reproductions of old dolls nor are they borrowed from the design of other doll makers. Michael O'Neill's dolls are the product of innovative creativity and artistic genius. He is the only male wax doll maker in the United Kingdom.

Blackpool is a city of about 154,000 persons and is in Lancashire on the Irish Sea of northern England's west coast. Blackpool owes its growth to the Lancashire industrial area and its long sandy beach. It is the most popular seaside resort in all of England and each year its more than 5,000 hotels and inns receive more than 8 million visitors, catering to a demand that developed in the late 1700s. Mr. O'Neill lives and works here in a detached ex-vicarage, or the parsonage that was once the home of the ministers who served the nearby Methodist Church.

The collector's dolls created by Michael O'Neill are fashioned from a medium that attained its highest form in doll making in England—poured wax. Poured wax figures and dolls date back to Ancient Times. The Egyptians used wax representations of their gods in funeral rites; the Greeks made wax dolls for children's playthings; the Romans preserved wax masks of the image of departed loved ones and even painted portraits using wax as a print medium. During the Middle Ages wax figures were made of saints, monarchs and prominent personages. In Renaissance times modeling in wax assumed even greater importance. Sculptors and artists, such as Michaelangelo, used wax models as preliminary sketches for their statues. Wax continued to be used as a medium for statues and portrait figures, especially in Church decoration, over the years. Wax was used for the modeling of the figures which were later translated to pottery, as in the relief design on Jasper Ware and Wedgwood. In recent times exhibitions of wax works have been displayed throughout the world. The most famous of these wax exhibitions was founded by Madame Marie Tussaud in London in 1842.

Madame Tussaud, born in France in 1761, learned the art of creating life-size wax portraits in Paris from her uncle. During the French Revolution of 1789 she was imprisoned as a Royalist because she had been an art tutor at the French Court. During the Reign of Terror she was assigned the gruesome task of making masks from severed heads—many of them from persons who had been her close friends —that were fresh from the guillotine. The exhibition that was established in London after Madame Tussaud emigrated to England contained then, as it does now, contemporary and historical characters, featuring both the famous and the infamous.

Michael O'Neill learned the refinements of the exacting and demanding art of modeling wax figures in a wax works that was established in Blackpool by Louis Tussaud, the grandnephew of Madame Marie Tussaud.

Illustration 2. Jeseco Character Dolls. Nursery Rhyme Series. Each doll is 28in. (71.1cm) high. From left to right: Old King Cole (gray hair); Old Woman Who Lived in a Shoe; Old Mother Hubbard; Old King Cole (brown hair); Jill and Jack.

When Mr. O'Neill heard of the opening of a position for an artist-modeler he applied along with 39 other artists. The other aspirants were equipped with various diplomas and degrees and had received formal art training. Michael was self-taught and his background was only a love for creating clay models of animals and people, a hobby since childhood. Each candidate for the position was required to submit a life-size head of a recognizable individual. Michael selected as his subject the American actor Lee Majors in his role as television's "Bionic Man." Michael got the job and his wax figure of Lee "became a *Major* attraction" at the Blackpool wax works.

The likeness of Lee Majors that was created by Mr. O'Neill was even transported to a distant hospital in England when it was learned that a seriously ill little boy was a great fan of the television series. When the child opened his eyes and saw the "Bionic Man" at his bedside, the wax model was credited with speeding his recovery.

As a person who was always interested in people and in creating three-dimensional renditions of the human form, it was natural that Michael O'Neill was attracted to dolls. They became an ideal vehicle for his theories of creating works of art.

It was in England that the art of making wax dolls attained its highest point and its greatest popularity. Like the realism of the Tussaud wax figures, dolls cast from wax have a very lifelike appearance that can not be rendered in any other medium. The coloring that comes through the wax has the same effect as the coloring that is seen in the human complexion, which shows through several translucent layers of the epidermis. Wax dolls, by having the proper complexion color mixed into the liquid wax, have the illusion of human skin.

Wax dolls were common in the ancient world but it was at the Great Exhibition of 1851 in London that they

Illustration 5. Old Mother Hubbard. 28in. (71.1cm) high. This version has gray hair that is individually inserted, as is the hair of all the Jeseco dolls. Note the variation in the costume and the handmade suede shoes with real eyelets for the laces.

Illustrations 3&4. Old King Cole wearing his crown and showing his bald head. 28in. (71.1cm) Tall.

attained great prominence for collectors. The exhibit featured the wax dolls of Madame Augusta Montanari and her son Richard Napoleon Montanari. The Montanari dolls had the hair, eyebrows and eyelashes individually inserted into the wax and the modeling was more realistic than any earlier English wax dolls. Montanari dolls were not "types" or crude representations of human beings. They

looked like real people. The Pierotti family also made wax dolls in England and won awards for their work at the International Exhibition of Wax Models in 1862 in England. The hair, rather than being individually inserted, was set into the wax in slits. The bodies were made of white calico, into which the wax head, shoulders, arms and legs were fitted. Montanari and Pierotti dolls were rather expensive even when they were new and, like the products of all wax doll artists, could not be turned out in volume quantities.

The wax dolls of Michael O'Neill are influenced by the Montanari method of hair insertion and by the Pierotti method of multi-layer wax casting, which gives a more natural re-

Illustrations 6&7. "Fonzie." 34in. (86.4cm) high. The individually inserted hair shows in the enlargement.

sult as it permits the translucent coloring effect seen in the human countenance. But the doll creations of Michael O'Neill completely originate with the work of the artist and with his vision of what he wants to express.

Michael O'Neill, inspite of his ancestral Irish name, is English and his work is an English product. The top floor of the vicarage where he lives in Blackpool has been converted into his studio. Because of his great enthusiasm for his wax doll creations, Michael has resigned his position at the Tussaud wax works to concentrate his talent on his art. The dolls begin as clay models made from natural clay dug from the earth at Devon, England. The faces are taken from real people and the modeling of the features shows his complete knowledge of anatomy and bone structure. In his Nursery Rhyme Series (*Illustration 2*) The Old Mother Hubbard was an old lady he met in a park in Blackpool (*Illustration 5*). Jill, of Jack and Jill, was an English girl who sat for him as he modeled her likeness in clay. Famous characters like "Fonzie" (*Illustrations 6&7*) and "Elvis" (*Illustrations 7&8*) take weeks to perfect in clay, as they must pass a rigid test: strangers are invited into the studio to

inspect the model and not knowing who they are viewing, they must recognize the likeness immediately. If they do not, adjustments have to be made in the features. The next stage in creating a doll is to make a plaster mold of the wet clay model into which the boiling wax can be poured. When the wax has set it can withstand both hot and cold temperature extremes, as the formula contains both beeswax and hardening agents. Next the eye sockets are burned out from the inside of the head, a very delicate operation, and hand-blown glass eyes are positioned in place. One of Mr. O'Neill's most carefully guarded secrets is his method of inserting individual hairs into the scalp so that the dolls have a natural hairline and crown and that when the process is completed the hair can be washed, combed, set and styled. Real human hair is used in this operation and the insertion of the individual strands may require up to two days time to insure that the technique has been properly followed. Mr. O'Neill permits no one to observe the process of hair insertion, and no mistakes can be made as it is being done since they can not be corrected.

Each doll created by Michael O'Neill is handmade from conception

to completion and each is an individual work of art. Even if several figures are cast from a single mold each is considered an "original" in art forms. For example, each rendition of Rodin's famous statue "The Thinker," which is in several different art museums, is considered to be an original because each came from the original mold created by the artist himself. (Ceramics and bisque reproductions do not fall into this category.) Each of Michael O'Neill's dolls is signed and each one carries a signed certificate of authenticity. The dolls are half life-size, larger than the dolls of most other doll artists, and are based on real persons, yet they are truly dolls—not just scaled-down images of people. The dolls are Michael's concept of how *he* sees the individual who is the inspiration for the doll, rather than the doll being only a photographic reproduction. The dolls of Michael O'Neill are original works of art rather than copies of other designs or renderings; however they are created using traditional methods that have been employed by wax modelers for centuries, and in many cases the techniques are virtually extinct.

Mr. O'Neill says that "wax is the medium which appeals to me most. It is one of the oldest known artistic mediums and one of the most natural. All sorts of materials have been used throughout the ages to represent the human face but none can give the life-like appearance of wax. My wax dolls are images, facsimilies if you like, of living people—be it an old woman in a park who could be no other than Old Mother Hubbard or 'Fonzie' or 'Elvis' themselves. My dolls are not antique reproductions because there are no antiques like them, so the collector may be certain that I have not copied a Montanari head by taking a mold of it. (That would be very simple, but cheating.) Nor are my dolls modern because I employ only traditional techniques. My dolls are really ME!"

Michael's wife Sadie is a qualified art and craft teacher and a true artist also. She helps in mixing the proper wax coloring for complexion tones and painstakingly researches the costumes which she designs and creates. All designs and materials are authentic, although modern fabrics are used. Old Mother Hubbard wears a hand-knitted shawl, "Fonzie" is dressed in a real leather jacket and "Elvis" wears real shoes. The sewing work and pattern design for clothing and bodies is also done by Sadie's mother. The bodies are strong muslin packed tightly with a mixture of polyester and cotton which makes the dolls hold their shape, yet they are supple enough to sit naturally.

Michael O'Neill's dolls are offered under the name JESECO CHARACTER DOLLS. The name comes from the first two letters of the names of his sons Jevon, Sean and Conal. The dolls have been exhibited in Europe and in the United States and are in private collections throughout the world.

The JESECO dolls are real dolls and they are real art. The Nursery Rhyme Series shows the artist's love for all people—the old and the young; those who have the beauty of youth and those who have the beauty of age. The Celebrity Series presents another group of individuals in doll form who have been admired and loved by young and old alike. The attention to detail in both the modeling of the dolls and in the authentic costumes demonstrates Michael and Sadie O'Neill's enthusiasm for their work. Their own personalities are implanted in the dolls, all of which evoke happy memories and are the expression of their view of life. One can be certain that they enjoy creating their dolls.

At present Michael O'Neill is researching and designing the Shirley Temple who was so popular and beloved as a child film star. I am privileged to have met the O'Neills and to have examined their work. We can only wonder what new creations will spring from Devon clay and English imagination!

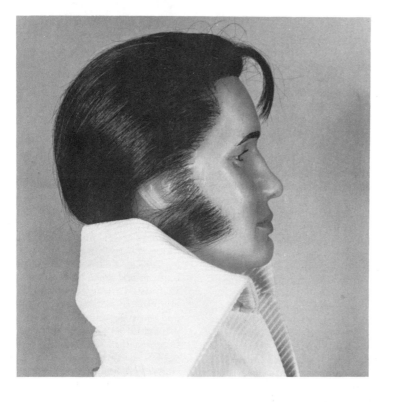

Illustrations 8&9. "Elvis." 36in. (91.4cm) high. The modeling of the features of Elvis Presley shows a combination of characteristics from his early, more youthful years, until the later stages of his career when he began to look more mature.

INDEX